AME ENGAGE™

Welcome to the fully integrated and interactive online learning hub for
Key Accounting Principles, Volume One, Fourth Edition.

Online & Interactive

AME Learning's integrated and interactive online learning hub, AME Engage™, contextualizes the study of accounting in a practical, hands-on online learning environment. Designed to personalize the learning experience and engage students *before* class, our multi-sensory online tutorials guide students through the key accounting concepts for each chapter. These tutorials help students to *learn by doing,* using a variety of effective learning tools ranging from gaming to interactive problem solving.

In order to encourage students to truly understand the concepts rather than simply rely on memorization, AME Engage™ features randomized algorithmic homework questions, allowing students to practice the same concept repeatedly at their own leisure. The "Take me to the text" online homework feature links each question to the relevant examples in the digital textbook, immediately providing students the help they need at any time and from anywhere. Instructors have full control over all resources in AME Engage™, and can therefore effectively tailor their online environment according to their own teaching style.

Unique PIN Code

If you purchased this book brand-new, the PIN Card (image to the right) is attached to the front cover. Open this to get your unique **PIN Code**, then follow the instructions to log in to AME Engage™.

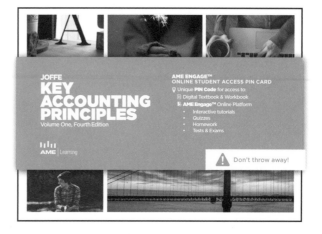

Don't have a PIN Card?

If you **did not** purchase this book brand-new, you will need to purchase your unique PIN Code at www.amelearning.com/store or contact your campus bookstore.

Instructor looking for access?

Please contact your AME Learning representative.

AME ENGAGE™

Welcome to the fully integrated and interactive online learning hub for
Key Accounting Principles, Volume One, Fourth Edition.

The AME Learning™ Cycle

The AME Learning™ Cycle is an integrated learning method that puts a unique focus on pre-class **interactive tutorials**. These tutorials are seamlessly integrated with all other components of the program, and will allow students to not only better prepare for in-class work, but they will also help students to engage with difficult concepts while effectively leading to successful knowledge retention.

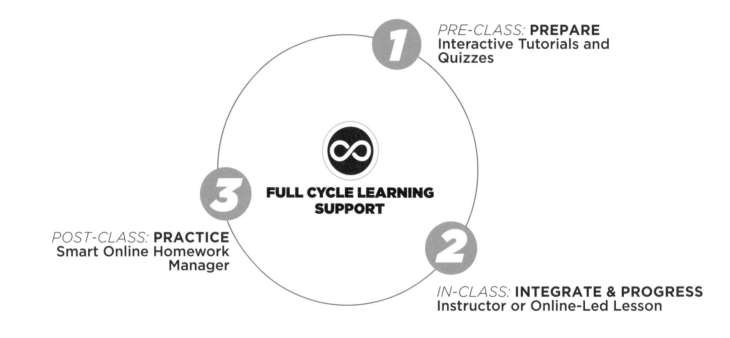

1 PRE-CLASS: **PREPARE**
Interactive Tutorials and Quizzes

FULL CYCLE LEARNING SUPPORT

3 POST-CLASS: **PRACTICE**
Smart Online Homework Manager

2 IN-CLASS: **INTEGRATE & PROGRESS**
Instructor or Online-Led Lesson

AME Engage: Features

Interactive Online Tutorials
Perform real-world accounting transactions with our innovative Accounting Map™.

Online Homework Manager
Algorithmic homework questions, assignments, projects, cases, tests and quizzes.

Resource Library
Focus-in on key lesson objectives with Microsoft Excel™ worksheet templates and our vast PowerPoint™ library.

Digital Textbook
Practical explanations and examples seamlessly integrated with workbok and online tutorials.

Digital Workbook
Hundreds of questions and cases perfectly integrated with textbook lessons and interactive tutorials.

KEY ACCOUNTING PRINCIPLES

Volume One, Fourth Edition

Lead Author
Neville Joffe

Contributors and Reviewers

Bharat Aggarwal, BBA, MBA, CMA
Sheridan College

Jason Armstrong, CPA, CGA
Fanshawe College

Maria Belanger, CPA, CA
Algonquin College

Ben Carnovale, BBA, MASc
Confederation College

Annette deWeerd, CMA, CGA, MBA
Northern Alberta Institute of Technology

Dave Hummel, CPA, CA
Conestoga College

Laurette Korman, MBA, CMA
Kwantlen Polytechnic University

Chris Leduc, CPA, CA
Cambrian College

Kayla Levesque, CPA, CA
Cambrian College

Sarah Magdalinski, CA, MPACC, BCOMM
Northern Alberta Institute of Technology

Rachel McCorriston, CPA, CMA, MBA
Fanshawe College

Penny Parker, MBA, CPA, CGA
Fanshawe College

Susan Rogers, CPA, CMA
Sheridan College

Ruby So, B. Comm, CA, CGA
Northern Alberta Institute of Technology

AME | Learning

Textbook ISBN: 978-1-926751-27-6
Workbook ISBN: 978-1-926751-28-3

Key Accounting Principles, Volume 1, Fourth Edition
Author: Neville Joffe
Publisher: AME Learning Inc.
Content Contributors and Developmental Editors:
        Kobboon Chotruangprasert/Graeme Gomes/Kyle Kroetsch
Production Editors: Joshua Peters/Melody Yousefian
Copy Editor: Nicola Balfour
Indexer: Elizabeth Walker
Typesetter: Paragon Prepress Inc.
Vice President and Publishing Manager: Linda Zhang
Cover Design: Sasha Moroz/Bram Wigzell
Online Course Design & Production: AME Multimedia Team

1 2 3 MCRL 17 16 15

This book is written to provide accurate information on the covered topics. It is not meant to take the place of professional advice.

For more information contact:

AME Learning Inc.
410-1220 Sheppard Avenue East
Toronto, ON, Canada M2K 2S5
Phone: 416.479.0200
Toll-free: 1.888.401.3881
E-mail: info@amelearning.com
Visit our website at: www.amelearning.com

About the Author

Neville Joffe created the AME Learning System after spending more than 25 years leading and transforming teams in the manufacturing and distribution industries. His innovative style of management is characterized by a unique philosophy: bottom-line business success is dependent on the financial literacy of an organization's employees.

The truth of this philosophy first revealed itself when he helped to transition his 400 person company to sustainable profitability after a period of loss and decline. For the company and its employees, this newly acquired business acumen had opened a world of opportunity and prosperity.

This experience highlighted the importance of a financially literate employee base. From here, Neville sold his stake in the company and focused on fully developing and patenting the AME Accounting Map™ – a learning framework that borrowed from the ideas of Game Theory to create a multisensory toolkit for true learning, interaction and engagement. Neville took his system around the world, training internationally with corporate clients, government institutions and non-profit organizations.

After years of successfully training clients around the world, Neville set his eyes on the sector responsible for producing the employees that inevitably ended up in his training sessions: Education. Understanding that our colleges and universities were the front lines of training for the corporate world, Neville adapted his system to suit the needs of higher learning institutions. Since then, he has worked with practicing accounting professionals and educators to develop seven textbooks that accompany the AME Learning System for use in higher education institutions around the globe.

The AME Approach to Learning Accounting

AME utilizes a unique method to simplify accounting concepts, using step-by-step logic to ensure that the subject is extremely easy to understand. Accounting concepts are communicated using straightforward language and AME Accounting Maps™ that make potentially complex transactions simpler and easier to follow.

The AME Accounting Map™ is used throughout the textbook to show the impact of transactions on the financial statements. It is a visual representation of the balance sheet and income statement. The Accounting Map™ is also used in our interactive tutorials. Increases and decreases in values of specific items are clearly shown on the Map without needing to resort to technical accounting terminology.

The Accounting Map™

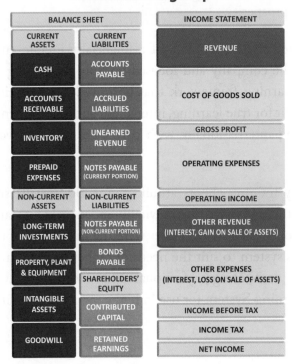

This textbook is part of a larger and blended program that is being used to teach the course. As an instructor it is recommended to follow these steps to ensure your students get the most out of the program.

1. Encourage students to use the interactive online tutorials before attending each class.

2. Use the PowerPoint™ presentations to provide visuals to assist with teaching the material.

3. Online quizzes are available to test student's comprehension of the material. Quizzes can be used either before or after class.

4. Online post-class homework questions are available to test student's ability to complete accounting problems. These should be used after class.

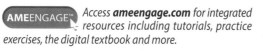 *Access **ameengage.com** for integrated resources including tutorials, practice exercises, the digital textbook and more.*

Every chapter has reminders for students to check their online course for additional resources to help explain the accounting topics.

The learning outcomes in each chapter are prepared using Bloom's taxonomy. In the textbook, each blue heading in the chapters is linked to at least one learning outcome. The learning outcomes are also linked to all the questions in the workbook.

Chapter 4
THE ACCOUNTING CYCLE: JOURNALS AND LEDGERS

LEARNING OUTCOMES

❶ Distinguish between debits and credits

❷ Describe the accounting cycle

❸ Explain how to analyze a transaction

❹ Record transactions in the general journal

❺ Post journal entries to the general ledger

❻ Prepare a trial balance

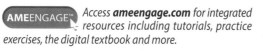 *Access **ameengage.com** for integrated resources including tutorials, practice exercises, the digital textbook and more.*

Transition to Debits and Credits

We have been using the terms increase and decrease to record transactions in T-accounts, but formal accounting requires the use of debits and credits. In the debit and credit system (unlike increases and decreases), a **debit** is always recorded on the left-hand side of an account and a **credit** is always recorded on the right-hand side. DR represents debits and CR represents credits.

Debit DR	Credit CR

Remember that debit and credit do not always mean increase or decrease. A credit means an entry on the right side of the account, and it may cause the account to increase or decrease, depending on the type of ac-

WORTH REPEATING

In accounting, there are always at least two parts to a transaction. For each transaction, the total value of debits equals

At the end of the chapter is a summary, highlighting key points for each learning outcome.

AMEENGAGE Access **ameengage.com** for integrated resources including tutorials, practice exercises, the digital textbook and more.

In Summary

Distinguish between debits and credits

⟳ Debits are recorded on the left side of an account and credits are recorded on the right side. For the accounting equation to be correct, the total value of the debits must equal the total value of the credits. This will ensure that the accounting equation stays in balance.

⟳ Assets, expenses, and owner's drawings increase with debits and decrease with credits. Liabilities, revenues, and owner's capital increase with credits and decrease with debits.

Describe the accounting cycle

⟳ The accounting cycle consists of the steps required to prepare financial statements. The cycle repeats every period.

Explain how to analyze a transaction

⟳ Analysis of transactions begins with source documents which indicate a transaction has occurred. The analysis helps to determine which accounts are affected, whether they are increasing or decreasing, and whether they are debited or credited.

Each chapter has a Review Exercise covering the major topics of the chapter. The Review Exercises are prepared so students can complete them and then compare their answers to the solutions. Solutions to the Review Exercises are in Appendix I of the textbook.

———————————— **Review Exercise** ————————————

Catherine Gordon is running her own proprietary business called CG Accounting. CG Accounting provides bookkeeping services to small and mid-sized companies. The company prepares financial statements on a monthly basis and had the following closing balances at the end of May 2016.

CG Accounting Balance Sheet As at May 31, 2016			
Assets		**Liabilities**	
Cash	$4,200	Accounts Payable	$2,300
Accounts Receivable	3,100	Unearned Revenue	600
Equipment	6,000	Bank Loan	4,000
		Total Liabilities	6,900
		Owner's Equity	
		Gordon, Capital	6,400
Total Assets	$13,300	**Total Liabilities & Owner's Equity**	$13,300

CG Accounting uses a variety of accounts and account numbers in its accounting records.

Account Description	Account #	Account Description	Account #
ASSETS		**REVENUE**	
Cash	101	Service Revenue	400
Accounts Receivable	105		
Prepaid Insurance	110	**EXPENSES**	
Equipment	120	Advertising Expense	500
Accumulated Depreciation	125	Bad Debt Expense	505
		Depreciation Expense	510
LIABILITIES		Insurance Expense	515
Accounts Payable	200	Interest Expense	520
Interest Payable	205	Maintenance Expense	525
Unearned Revenue	210	Office Supplies Expense	530

In addition to the Review Exercise solutions in the appendix, you will also find a handy chart to illustrate some key differences between ASPE and IFRS organized by chapter and topic.

Appendix III

ASPE VS IFRS

Chapter	Topic	Accounting Standards for Private Enterprises (ASPE)	International Financial Reporting Standards (IFRS)
	When to use	• Private organization (sole proprietorship, partnership, private corporations) • No plans to become public in the near future • ASPE also used by most competitors	• Public corporation or owned by a public company • Private organization intending to become public in the near future • IFRS already adopted by most competitors • Private enterprises adopting IFRS by choice for other reasons, such as, in anticipation of a bank's requirement for IFRS-based financial statements in loan application

The workbook is comprised of assessment and application questions.

• Assessment questions (AS) are designed to test theory and comprehension of topics.
• Application questions (AP) are split into Group A and Group B problems. These questions test the ability to perform the accounting functions, such as creating journal entries and financial statements.

Chapter 4

THE ACCOUNTING CYCLE: JOURNALS AND LEDGERS

LEARNING OUTCOMES

❶ Distinguish between debits and credits

❷ Describe the accounting cycle

❸ Explain how to analyze a transaction

❹ Record transactions in the general journal

❺ Post journal entries to the general ledger

❻ Prepare a trial balance

AMEENGAGE *Access **ameengage.com** for integrated resources including tutorials, practice exercises, the digital textbook and more.*

Assessment Questions

AS-1 (❶)

What does

A debit is

Application Questions Group A

AP-1A (❶ ❸)

Esteem Fitness provides fitness services for its customers. During June 2016, Esteem Fitness had the following transactions.

Application Questions Group B

AP-1B (❶ ❸)

Have-a-Bash is owned by Shelly Fisher and provides party planning services. During April 2016, Have-a-Bash had the following transactions.

Some additional segments

This textbook was designed to make your learning experience productive and engaging. To that end, we have added some segments to each chapter that highlight learning objectives.

A CLOSER LOOK

The *A Closer Look* segments are meant to closely examine a part of the chapter to broaden your understanding of an underlying concept. They may also include an example that applies the concepts being learned, in a way that is easy to understand and follow.

WORTH REPEATING

The *Worth Repeating* segments are meant to remind students of concepts in accounting already learned, and to highlight current concepts being taught that are "worth repeating."

IN THE REAL WORLD

The *In The Real World* segments are meant to provide applied examples of elements being learned. They are meant to put some of the concepts being learned in context and to drive home the point that eventually, accounting has to be done outside the classroom. We hope that these segments give you a sense of what "the real world" can be like for the accountant or business professional.

ASPE vs IFRS

The *ASPE vs IFRS* segments are meant to discuss differences in the treatment of the topic being covered in the chapter based on the two different *sets* of accounting standards. Not all topics will have a difference between the two.

Brief Table of Contents

Detailed Table of Contents

Chapter 5: The Accounting Cycle: Adjustments

Chapter 6: The Accounting Cycle: Statements and Closing Entries

Chapter 7: Inventory: Merchandising Transactions

Chapter 8: Inventory Valuation

Chapter 9: Accounting Information Systems

Chapter 10: Cash Controls

Chapter 11: Payroll

Chapter 12: Using Accounting Information

Chapter 1

FINANCIAL STATEMENTS: PERSONAL ACCOUNTING

AMEENGAGE *Access **ameengage.com** for integrated resources including tutorials, practice exercises, the digital textbook and more.*

LEARNING OUTCOMES

❶ Describe the purpose of accounting

❷ Describe the balance sheet and the income statement

❸ Define an accounting period

❹ Explain how the accounting equation works

❺ Explain accrual-based accounting

❻ Explain how to account for debt and assets

❼ Explain how to account for prepaid expenses

❽ Distinguish between capital and revenue

❾ Demonstrate how double entries are recorded in T-accounts

The Purpose of Accounting

Accounting is a system to identify, measure and communicate all the financial activities of an individual or a business. Personal accounting tracks how much an individual is worth. Whether you choose a simple or luxurious lifestyle, you need money to sustain your personal life. Most people want to save enough money to allow them to retire comfortably. The better you can manage your finances and bring in more money than you spend, the more you will be worth.

It is important to maintain records of the activities that increase or decrease your net worth (i.e. how much you earn, how much you invest and how much you spend). The key concepts that drive your personal economic life are very similar to those used in business. In fact, learning basic accounting is a crucial life skill for everyone.

Most people associate accounting with calculators, computers and long lists of numbers. That may be true to some degree when you are a practicing bookkeeper or accountant; however, understanding accounting involves not only numbers but also a logical way of thinking.

Here is an example of the logic behind one of the concepts you will learn in this course: the concept of net worth. Which scenario in Figure 1.1 would you prefer?

Scenario 1

Assets (what we own)

Cash	$3,000
Contents of Home	6,000
Automobile	15,000
House	80,000
Total Assets	**$104,000**

Scenario 2

Assets (what we own)

Cash	$5,000
Contents of Home	8,000
Automobile	20,000
House	100,000
Total Assets	**$133,000**

FIGURE 1.1

Scenario 2 appears to be preferable. However, some crucial information is missing.

In examining the scenarios in Figure 1.2, which one would you now prefer? You must not only look at how much you **own** (assets) but also consider how much you **owe** (liabilities).

Scenario 1

Assets (what we own)

Cash	$3,000
Contents of Home	6,000
Automobile	15,000
House	80,000
Total Assets	**$104,000**

Liabilities (what we owe)

Bank Loan	$0
Credit Card Account	2,000
Mortgage	60,000
Automobile Loan	5,000
Student Loan	5,000
Total Liabilities	**$72,000**
Net Worth*	**$32,000**

Scenario 2

Assets (what we own)

Cash	$5,000
Contents of Home	8,000
Automobile	20,000
House	100,000
Total Assets	**$133,000**

Liabilities (what we owe)

Bank Loan	$8,000
Credit Card Account	4,000
Mortgage	80,000
Automobile Loan	5,000
Student Loan	10,000
Total Liabilities	**$107,000**
Net Worth*	**$26,000**

FIGURE 1.2

*Net worth = things you own – things you owe

Even though you may own more in Scenario 2, you also owe a lot more. The end result is that Scenario 2 is worth less than Scenario 1.

The Balance Sheet

The **balance sheet** is a permanent document that is used to record what you own (assets), what you owe (liabilities) and what you are worth (net worth) on a specific date. To expand a little on assets, an **asset** is something you own that will benefit you now and in the future. This would include items such as the cash you have, the house and car you own, the furniture and electronics you have in your home, and investments you have made. Cash is listed first since it is the asset that you use most often.

On the other hand, **liabilities** are what you owe, your obligations. Usually, these obligations mean you owe cash to someone else. One example of a liability would be unpaid accounts. Unpaid accounts include amounts owing on credit cards, and bills for items like utilities or cell phones that you have not yet paid. Other longer term liabilities include items such as bank loans and mortgages. Unpaid Accounts is listed first since this is the debt you have to pay first.

Net worth is what is left if you cash out (i.e. successfully sell all your assets and get the value equivalent to the recorded amount) and pay everything you owe, your liabilities. Tracking the amount you are worth is a fundamental component of accounting in both your personal life and your business life.

Assets = all that you OWN

Liabilities = all that you OWE

Value of Assets = $75,000

Value of Liabilities = $50,000
Net Worth = $25,000

The balance sheet provides a snapshot of your financial position. The difference between the value of what you own and what you owe represents your net worth. The date of the balance sheet is presented as "As at ..." because it represents a snapshot of your finances at a particular point in time. For example, a balance sheet prepared on December 31, 2016 would have the date "As at December 31, 2016."

In Figure 1.3, note that you have only $7,000 in cash. At this point, if you needed to pay everything that you owe ($105,500), you would need to sell some of your assets (i.e. convert the value of your assets into cash, also known as *liquidating* your assets). Although you may think that you

Personal Balance Sheet As at December 31, 2016			
Assets		**Liabilities**	
Cash	$7,000	Unpaid Accounts	$500
Contents of Home	5,000	Mortgage	100,000
Automobile	10,000	Bank Loan	5,000
House	120,000	**Total Liabilities**	**105,500**
		Net Worth	**36,500**
Total Assets	**$142,000**	**Total Liabilities + Net Worth**	**$142,000**

FIGURE 1.3

are worth only the $7,000 you have in the bank as cash, your true value (or net worth) is $36,500.

Note that net worth is equal to assets minus liabilities. We will discuss this relationship later in the chapter.

In Figure 1.4, despite the fact that your cash balance is lower, your net worth is higher.

In Figure 1.5, you have a negative bank balance, meaning that you have a bank overdraft. However, your net worth is significantly higher than in Figures 1.3 and 1.4.

Note that in accounting, negative numbers are expressed in parentheses. For example, –$2,000 is shown as ($2,000).

In Figure 1.6, you have a large amount of cash, a valuable home and an expensive car. However, your net worth is lower than the previous three scenarios. This is because you borrowed a large amount from the bank for your house and car.

The net worth reflected in Figure 1.5 (with the negative cash balance) is actually greater than that in the other figures.

Personal Balance Sheet As at December 31, 2016			
Assets		**Liabilities**	
Cash	$1,000	Unpaid Accounts	$5,000
Investments	18,000	Mortgage	100,000
Contents of Home	4,500		
Automobile	10,000	**Total Liabilities**	**105,000**
House	120,000	**Net Worth**	**48,500**
Total Assets	**$153,500**	**Total Liabilities + Net Worth**	**$153,500**

FIGURE 1.4

Personal Balance Sheet As at December 31, 2016			
Assets		**Liabilities**	
Cash	($2,000)	Unpaid Accounts	$10,000
Investments	30,000	Mortgage	80,000
Contents of Home	5,000	Bank Loan	7,000
Automobile	10,000	Car Loan	6,000
House	180,000	**Total Liabilities**	**103,000**
		Net Worth	**120,000**
Total Assets	**$223,000**	**Total Liabilities + Net Worth**	**$223,000**

FIGURE 1.5

Personal Balance Sheet As at December 31, 2016			
Assets		**Liabilities**	
Cash	$50,000	Unpaid Accounts	$15,000
Investments	8,000	Mortgage	220,000
Contents of Home	12,000	Bank Loan	60,000
Automobile	50,000	Car Loan	40,000
House	250,000	**Total Liabilities**	**335,000**
		Net Worth	**35,000**
Total Assets	**$370,000**	**Total Liabilities + Net Worth**	**$370,000**

FIGURE 1.6

The Income Statement

The **income statement** is primarily used as a temporary record to record transactions relating to revenue and expenses. **Revenue** is an increase to net worth caused by providing goods or services in exchange for an asset, usually cash. In your personal life, revenue is usually earned by working and earning a salary. **Expenses** are costs and a decrease to net worth caused by day-to-day activities. These costs are incurred and will be paid later or use up an asset, usually cash. In your personal life, expenses can include items such as rent or food.

The purpose of the income statement is to determine the change in net worth over a specific period of time. The date of the income statement is presented as "For the Period Ended …" since the statement covers a period of time. For example, an income statement prepared on December 31, 2016 covering a year would have the date "For the Year Ended December 31, 2016."

If you did not want to use a formal income statement, you could merely record every transaction in the net worth section on the balance sheet. Since revenue increases net worth and expenses decrease net worth, you could record every revenue and expense amount directly into net worth on the balance sheet. However, this method would not keep track of the details of the type of revenue or expense you had.

Instead, you could note revenue and expenses on a separate document (the income statement).

Personal Income Statement For the Year Ended December 31, 2016		
Revenue		$36,000
Expenses		
Food Expense	$12,000	
Insurance Expense	1,000	
Maintenance Expense	800	
Rent Expense	15,000	
Utilities Expense	700	
Total Expenses		29,500
Surplus (Deficit)		**$6,500**

FIGURE 1.7

Figure 1.7 illustrates a sample personal income statement. This shows that $36,000 was earned during the year and expenses amounted to $29,500. The difference between revenue and expenses is a surplus of $6,500, which will be added to the person's net worth. If expenses are more than revenue, then a deficit is recorded and this deficit would be subtracted from the person's net worth.

A CLOSER LOOK

Imagine playing a sport without a scorecard. It would be difficult to play the game effectively without knowing the score while the game is played. Your economic life is no different. It is crucial to monitor how your day-to-day activities impact your net worth on a monthly basis to allow sufficient time to change spending behaviours to fit within your income. Remember that there is a difference between cash and your net worth.

Accounting Periods

You can keep changing net worth continuously; however, for accounting purposes, it is more convenient to record changes to net worth in separate periods. You can use any period you choose as an accounting period. An **accounting period** is the time frame in which the financial statements are prepared and can be one year, six months or one month, as shown in Figure 1.8.

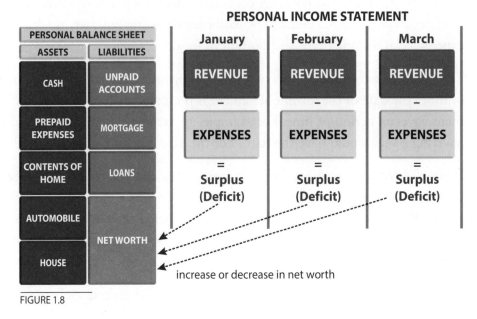

FIGURE 1.8

If you use a month as your accounting period, you can look back at previous months (periods) and estimate what your expenses and income will be in the coming months. You can also estimate the surplus or deficit you will generate each month. If you are saving for a major purchase such as a car, a new computer or an expensive entertainment system, you will be able to determine when you will have enough money to buy the desired item or at least provide a down payment.

Some advantages of using monthly accounting periods for your personal financial statements include
- tracking regular monthly living expenses (e.g. rent, cell phone)
- frequently assessing realistic expectations
- controlling errors effectively

The Accounting Equation

The accounting equation is shown in Figure 1.9.

Assets	Liabilities	
$100	– $70	
	= 30	**Net Worth**

If assets minus liabilities = net worth, then mathematically...

Assets	Liabilities	
$100	$70	
	+ 30	**Net Worth**
$100	**$100**	

assets must equal liabilities plus net worth

FIGURE 1.9

While Newton's Third Law applies to science, the same concept can be applied to the logic of the accounting equation: "For every action there is an equal and opposite reaction"—that is, transaction and financial consequence. In accounting terms, a double entry of the same value is always made for every transaction. This means that each transaction has at least two entries. The logic of the double entry is based on the **accounting equation**

Assets = Liabilities + Net Worth

Imagine the accounting equation as a scale with each side in balance; the left side of the scale would include assets and the right side would include liabilities and net worth.

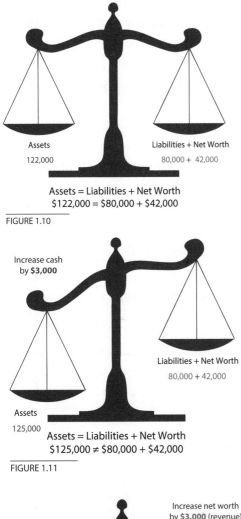

The scale must always be in balance, as shown in Figure 1.10.

Assets
122,000

Liabilities + Net Worth
80,000 + 42,000

Assets = Liabilities + Net Worth
$122,000 = $80,000 + $42,000

FIGURE 1.10

Increase cash by **$3,000**

Liabilities + Net Worth
80,000 + 42,000

Assets
125,000

If you received $3,000 cash, it would increase your assets. Recording only the increase in cash will cause the scale to go out of balance, as shown in Figure 1.11.

Assets = Liabilities + Net Worth
$125,000 ≠ $80,000 + $42,000

FIGURE 1.11

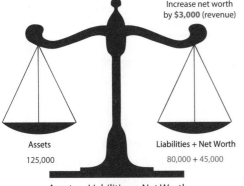

Increase net worth by **$3,000** (revenue)

To get the scale back into balance, you must ask yourself why you received the cash. If you received the cash because you earned it at your job, then the $3,000 must also increase net worth. This will be recorded as revenue and bring the scale back into balance, as shown in Figure 1.12.

Assets
125,000

Liabilities + Net Worth
80,000 + 45,000

Assets = Liabilities + Net Worth
$125,000 = $80,000 + $45,000

FIGURE 1.12

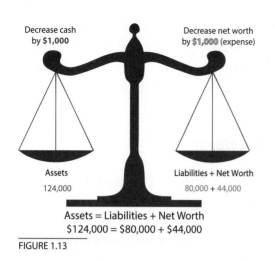

Decrease cash
by $1,000

Decrease net worth
by $1,000 (expense)

Assets

124,000

Liabilities + Net Worth

80,000 + 44,000

Assets = Liabilities + Net Worth
$124,000 = $80,000 + $44,000

FIGURE 1.13

Soon after, if you made a cash payment of $1,000, your assets would decrease in value. The scale would only stay in balance if you record the $1,000 somewhere else. Ask yourself, "Why did I make a $1,000 payment?" If you made the payment for rent for the month, then the $1,000 must also decrease net worth. This will be recorded as an expense and leave the scale in balance, as shown in Figure 1.13.

Using the logic from the discussion above, we can see that without a logical opposite entry, the balance sheet will not balance. Figure 1.14 shows how the transactions are analyzed using an accounting equation. The only way to keep it in balance is to impact at least two accounts. The first two transactions were discussed above in terms of balancing the scale. The Explanation column in Figure 1.14 is used to provide more details on why net worth changes.

---

1. Deposit $500 in wages

Assets	= Liabilities	+ Net Worth		Assets	= Liabilities	+ Net Worth	Explanation
1,000	700	300		1,000	700	300	
+ 500				+ 500		+ 500	Receive wages
1,500	1,000			1,500	1,500		
1,500 ≠ 1,000 (not logical) ✗				1,500 = 1,500 (logical) ✓			

---

2. Pay cash expenses of $100

Assets	= Liabilities	+ Net Worth		Assets	= Liabilities	+ Net Worth	Explanation
1,000	700	300		1,000	700	300	
+500		+ 500		+500		+ 500	Receive wages
-100				-100		- 100	Pay expense with cash
1,400	1,500			1,400	1,400		
1,400 ≠ 1,500 (not logical) ✗				1,400 = 1,400 (logical) ✓			

---

3. Pay entertainment expenses of $200 with credit card

Assets	= Liabilities	+ Net Worth		Assets	= Liabilities	+ Net Worth	Explanation
1,000	700	300		1,000	700	300	
+500		+ 500		+500		+ 500	Receive wages
-100		- 100		-100		- 100	Pay expense with cash
	+200				+200	- 200	Pay expense with credit card
1,400	1,600			1,400	1,400		
1,400 ≠ 1,600 (not logical) ✗				1,400 = 1,400 (logical) ✓			

FIGURE 1.14

In the third transaction from Figure 1.14, $200 of expenses were paid with a credit card. The additional $200 owed on the card represents an additional liability so we increase liabilities by $200. Because the charge was for an expense, we must also decrease net worth by $200 so that the accounting equation remains balanced.

Introduction to T-Accounts

To help record transactions, and to help keep the accounting equation balanced, we will use T-accounts. The **T-account** gets its name from the way it looks, just like a capital T. An **account** allows us to track detailed information about the values of individual items such as cash and unpaid accounts. Every item will have its own T-account. Increases and decreases to each account are recorded here: increases on one side and decreases on the other. The category of the account (asset, liability, net worth, revenue or expense) will determine which side of the T-account is the increase and which side is the decrease.

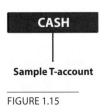

Sample T-account

FIGURE 1.15

As you complete one accounting period and start the next, the ending balance of the assets, liabilities and net worth will carry forward and become the opening balances of the new period. Normally these opening balances will show up on the increase side of the appropriate T-account.

Figure 1.16 shows how the T-accounts behave in each category. The following diagram can be used to help memorize which side is an increase and which side is a decrease for T-accounts.

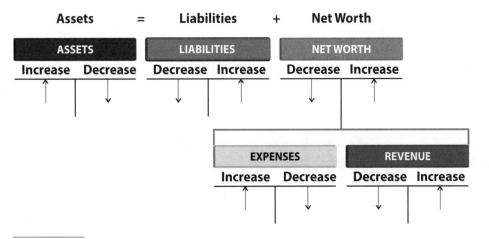

FIGURE 1.16

All assets, such as cash, use the left side of the T-account for increases and the right side for decreases. You can remember this by referring to the accounting equation. Assets are on the left of the accounting equation and assets use the left side of the T-account for increases.

All liabilities, such as unpaid accounts, use the right side of the T-account for increases and the left side for decreases. Again, refer to the accounting equation. Liabilities are on the right side of the accounting equation and liabilities use the right side of the T-account for increases.

Net worth also uses the right side of the T-account for increases and the left side for decreases since it is also on the right side of the accounting equation.

Revenue increases net worth and expenses decrease net worth. The more revenue earned, the more should be added to net worth. Therefore the revenue T-account increases on the right side and decreases on the left side. The more expenses incurred, the more should be subtracted from net worth. Therefore the expense T-accounts increase on the left side and decrease on the right side.

The balance of a T-account at the end of the period is simply the difference between all the increases and decreases. Figure 1.17 shows an example of the cash account. Since cash is an asset, the left side of the T-account is for increases and the right side is for decreases. Cash has an opening balance of $1,000, which is shown at the top of the increase side of the T-account. After all transactions have been recorded, we total both sides of the T-account, which is shown in red in the figure. The increase side will include the opening balance in addition to the transactions. The difference between the increase and decrease sides is $4,400, which is

INCREASE		DECREASE
+	**CASH**	**-**
Opening Balance	**$1,000**	
	1. 2,000	2. 1,500
	4. 4,000	3. 1,000
	5. 500	6. 600
Subtotal	7,500	3,100
Closing Balance	**$4,400**	

FIGURE 1.17

the closing balance of cash. The difference is placed on the side which had the larger subtotal, which is the increase side in this example.

Accrual-Based Accounting

A typical reason for personal financial failure (and small business failure) is not understanding accruals. People tend to think intuitively that an increase in cash represents an increase in wealth, and vice versa. The notion of the accrual is recognizing how much you are worth at a point in time.

Accrual-based accounting means that revenue (an increase to net worth) and expenses (a decrease to net worth) are recorded in the period in which they occur, regardless of when cash payment is received or paid.

So far we have assumed that every expense is paid when it is incurred. In reality, many expenses are not paid until a later date. The examples in Figures 1.18 and 1.19 illustrate how expenses are recorded as they occur.

Assume that you have $1,000 of cash and net worth of $1,000. If you pay for a $300 expense with cash, your cash and your net worth will decrease by $300 (see Figure 1.18).

If instead you receive a phone bill for $300 to be paid next month, there would be no change in cash in the current month. However, the phone debt (or unpaid accounts) would increase by $300 and net worth would decrease by $300 (see Figure 1.19). In other words, you would recognize the expense which decreases net worth.

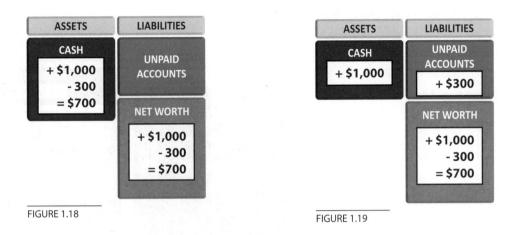

FIGURE 1.18

FIGURE 1.19

In general, keep in mind that the word "expense" relates to a decrease to net worth, which does not necessarily relate to cash.

Cash Flow vs. Accruals

There are two key points to understand.

❶ **Cash flow** relates to cash flowing into and out of the bank account, which is not necessarily directly connected to net worth.

❷ **Accruals** relate to net worth, which does not necessarily connect to cash flow.

Both points are important and distinct.

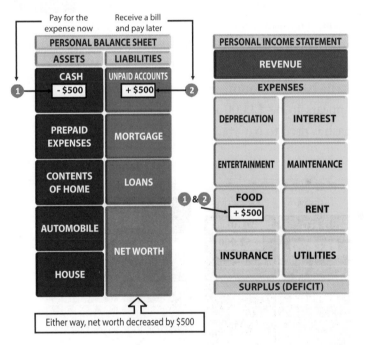

FIGURE 1.20

Cash-Based vs. Accrual-Based Accounting

If a cash-based method of accounting is used, then revenue and expenses are recorded only when the cash is received or paid.

As illustrated in Figure 1.21, at the end of January you deposit $3,000 salary earned that month and you pay expenses of $2,000 using cash from the bank. The difference between revenue and expenses results in an increase in net worth of $1,000, which happens to be the same as the increase in cash.

Suppose that you deposit salary of $3,000 in January, but choose to charge all $2,000 worth of expenses to your credit card, which is to be paid in February. When you use **cash-based accounting,** your net worth appears to be $3,000 in January, since no cash is used to pay your expenses.

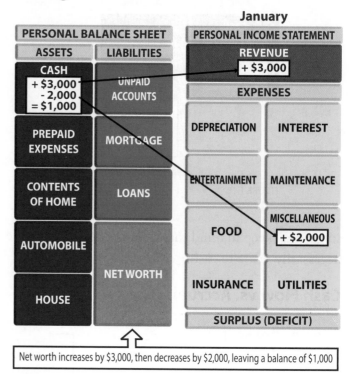

FIGURE 1.21

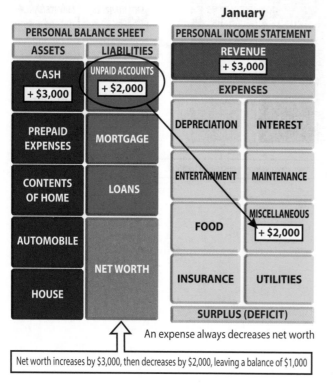

FIGURE 1.22

If you are using accrual-based accounting, you need to recognize the expense in January, the month in which it was actually incurred.

In Figure 1.22, the income statement for the month of January shows that you have matched the revenue of $3,000 (an increase in net worth) to the expenses in January of $2,000 (a decrease in net worth), resulting in an overall increase in net worth of $1,000. Cash remains at $3,000 because you have not spent any of it yet.

The accrual system of accounting recognizes the change in net worth even though payment is not necessarily received or paid.

Four transactions that occurred in January are presented below. Their impact on the balance sheet and income statement are shown in Figure 1.23. Keep in mind that the accounting equation must always stay in balance.

1. Earn and deposit $5,000 in salary. Cash increases by $5,000 which increases the total assets in the accounting equation. Why did cash increase? Because you deposited your salary. Net worth increases, which is shown as revenue on the income statement.

2. Pay $1,000 in cash for food expenses. Cash decreases by $1,000 which decreases the total assets in the accounting equation. Why did cash decrease? Because you bought some food. Thus, net worth decreases, which is shown as food expense on the income statement.

3. Record a $500 credit card bill for gasoline expenses (due in one month). Cash is not affected; however, you have a debt which must be paid next month. Debt increases which increases the total liabilities in the accounting equation. Why did your debt increase? Because you will have to pay for the gasoline at some point in the future. Net worth decreases, which is shown as gasoline expense on the income statement.

4. Record a $1,500 credit card bill for entertainment expenses. Debt increases which increases the liabilities in the accounting equation. Why did your debt increase? Because you will have to pay for the entertainment at some point in the future. Net worth decreases, which is shown as entertainment expense on the income statement.

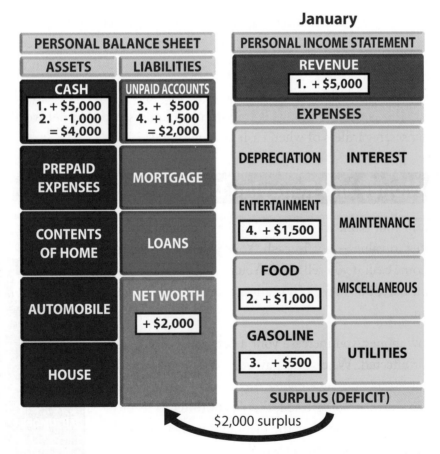

Remember: Everything that is shown on the income statement will impact net worth

FIGURE 1.23

We can also illustrate these transactions with the accounting equation to ensure that assets equal liabilities plus net worth. This is shown in Figure 1.24.

Assets	=	Liabilities	+	Net Worth	Explanation
+ 5,000				+ 5,000	*Received salary*
- 1,000				- 1,000	*Paid food expense with cash*
		+ 500		- 500	*Billed for gas expense*
		+ 1,500		- 1,500	*Billed for entertainment expense*
4,000		**2,000**		**2,000**	

4,000 = 4,000

FIGURE 1.24

The accounting equation is balanced

$$\text{Assets} \quad = \quad \text{Liabilities} \quad + \quad \text{Net Worth}$$
$$\$4,000 \quad = \quad \$2,000 \quad + \quad \$2,000$$

As the examples in Figure 1.23 and 1.24 illustrate, you need to match your expenses for the month with what you earn for the month. According to the concept of accruals, the credit card expenses would be recognized in January when they were incurred, not in February when they are paid.

It is easy to mistakenly think that since cash increased by $4,000 that net worth also increased by the same amount. This is not the case. It is important to understand that net worth is affected by revenue and expenses, regardless of when cash changes hands.

Borrowing Money and Repaying Debt

Other than cash in your bank account, every other financial aspect of your life relates to values—not to cash. Your assets have value, but will only become cash if you sell them. Your liabilities represent an obligation you have, but they do not affect your cash until you actually pay them.

When you borrow money, you increase your assets and your debts. Net worth is not affected. When you pay your debts (principal), you decrease your assets and your debts. Again, net worth is not affected. Since net worth is not affected, there is nothing to record on the income statement. Remember, the income statement is used to track the reasons for a change to net worth.

For example, assume you borrow money from a friend and then repay the money.

1. Borrow $100 from a friend: you have more cash, but your net worth does not change.

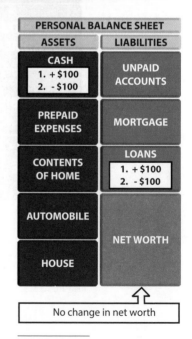

FIGURE 1.25

2. Repay your friend: you have less cash, but your net worth still does not change.

The T-account entries are shown in Figure 1.26.

FIGURE 1.26

Only assets and liabilities are affected, so there is no entry on the income statement. There is no change to net worth.

Figure 1.27 demonstrates that not all the cash you spend would necessarily be used to pay expenses. For example, you arrange for a loan of $15,000 and your loan repayments are $500 each month. There are three transactions to consider.

Transaction 1

Receiving the loan will increase cash and increase the loans liability. There is no impact to net worth.

Transaction 2

Pay the interest portion of $400. Net worth has decreased and an expense should be recognized.

Transaction 3

Pay the principal of $100, thereby reducing the amount owing to the loan company. Your net worth does not change and there is no need to record this transaction on the income statement.

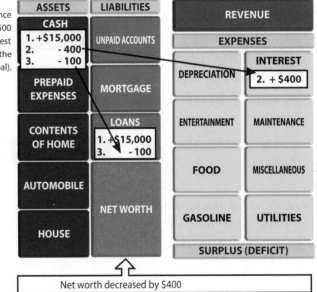

FIGURE 1.27

The transactions would appear on the T-accounts, as in Figure 1.28.

FIGURE 1.28

Even though your cash decreased by $500 when you made a payment to reduce the loan, your net worth decreased by $400 as a result of the expense.

Buying and Selling Assets

Buying or selling assets (according to the value stated in the balance sheet) has no impact on net worth. For example, you purchase a new car for $10,000; pay $3,000 cash and take a loan from the bank for the remaining $7,000.

The cash used to purchase the car is just an exchange of one asset for another (cash for the car), so there is no change in net worth. The loan is borrowed to pay for the car, so the liability increases as does the asset (car). Again there is no change in net worth. The affect on the accounts is shown in Figure 1.29. Although you now own a $10,000 car, there has been no change in your net worth.

ASSETS	LIABILITIES
CASH	**LOAN**
- $3,000	+ $7,000
AUTOMOBILE	
+ $10,000	

FIGURE 1.29

The transactions would appear on the T-accounts as shown in Figure 1.30. Cash decreases by $3,000 and your loan increases by $7,000. In the end, you have an increase to your automobile account for $10,000.

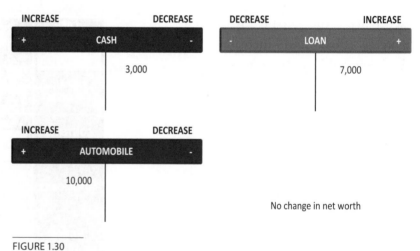

FIGURE 1.30

No change in net worth

If you exchange cash for an item, how do you know whether the item should be considered an asset or an expense? Typically, it is a question of how long it will provide a benefit to you and the cost of the item. The $10,000 car that was just purchased is an asset because it will benefit you for several years. On the other hand, spending $200 on food or entertainment would be an expense since they will only benefit you for a short period of time.

A CLOSER LOOK

Over time, the assets you own will change in value based on usage and changes in the market. The car you purchased for $10,000 will not always be worth that amount. After several years of use, it will be worth less than what you paid for it. Your house on the other hand may increase in value if you maintain it and the area you live in is desirable. On personal financial statements, there are no rules preventing you from changing the values of these assets as the market values change. In business, though, there are strict rules on how values of assets are recorded. This will be covered in later chapters.

So, borrowing and repaying debt principal does not impact net worth, and neither does buying or selling assets for the value stated in the balance sheet. The primary way you can change your net worth is to have revenue exceed expenses (net worth increases) or have expenses exceed revenue (net worth decreases).

Prepaid Expenses

It is a common practice to pay for various expenses in advance, for example, insurance and rent. These prepayments are not considered an expense at the time they are paid because the services have not been provided. The example illustrated in Figure 1.31 explains the prepayment of $1,200 for insurance for one year.

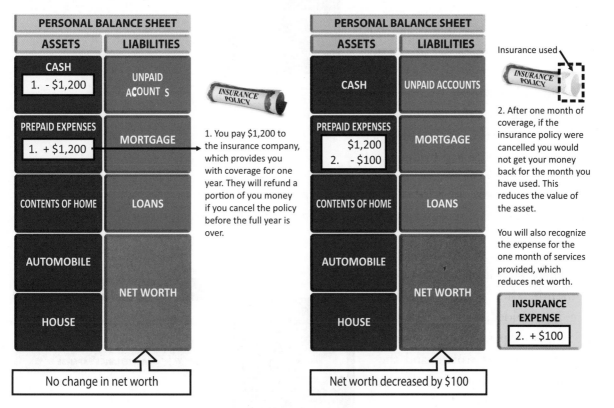

FIGURE 1.31

When you prepay your insurance, you might think intuitively that your net worth decreased because the cash is no longer in your bank account. However, what you have really done is purchase a one year insurance policy, which you now own. Anything you own and will benefit you in the future is considered an asset and recorded on the balance sheet. In this case the amount paid for the insurance policy is considered a prepaid expense. A **prepaid expense** occurs when you pay cash for an expense (like insurance) before you use it. You own the policy for one year and the insurance company must provide you with coverage for that period of time. If you cancel the insurance policy before the year is up, the company will have to refund your money for the amount of the policy that you did not use.

Figure 1.32 illustrates another example of a prepaid expense. Assume that you hire a gardening service that costs $600 per year ($50 per month). The service provider requests that you prepay the full $600 in January. In a perfect world, if you were to cancel the contract with the company the next morning, you would receive all the money back because the company has not yet provided the service. In effect, you have simply given the company an interest-free loan. Therefore, if you were to cancel the contract in three months, you would get back $450 [$600 – ($50 per month × 3 months)]; if it were cancelled in six months, you would get back $300: and so on.

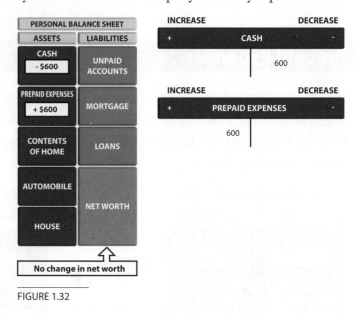

FIGURE 1.32

You have paid the $600 in advance but the service provider owes you the service which you will receive in the future. As a result, this payment is considered an asset (which is a prepaid expense). There is no expense (i.e. a decrease in net worth) until the service is provided.

As each month goes by, the value of the prepaid expense will decrease together with your net worth. In other words, you are recognizing the expense in the month in which it is used—not when it is paid.

If you prepare your financial statement each month, after the first month's service is provided, you will recognize $50 as an expense for that month (which decreases net worth) and the remaining prepaid portion will be $550 as shown in Figure 1.33.

An increase in expenses relates to a decrease in net worth. Cash does not have to be involved to increase an expense and decrease net worth. You will recognize $50 as an expense for each of the next 11 months as the supplier provides the service.

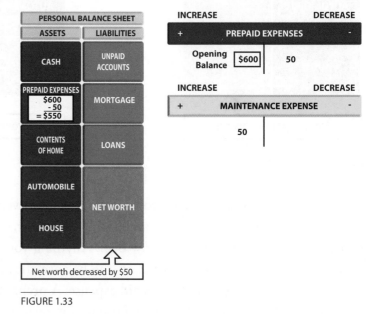

FIGURE 1.33

According to accrual-based accounting, expenses are always recorded when they are incurred. This has nothing to do with when the cash payment is made. If we assume an expense is $100, there are three possible timings the payment can be made in relation to the expense being incurred.

1. Pay before and recognize the expense when it is incurred (prepaid expense).
2. Pay as the expense is incurred (cash).
3. Pay after the expense is incurred (unpaid account).

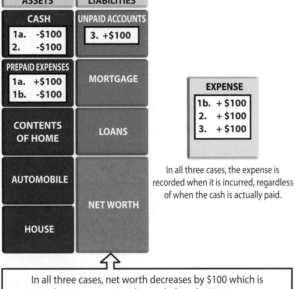

In all three cases, the expense is recorded when it is incurred, regardless of when the cash is actually paid.

In all three cases, net worth decreases by $100 which is recognized as an expense and recorded on the income statement

FIGURE 1.34

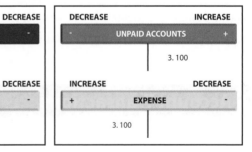

FIGURE 1.35

Capital

So far, we have discussed that the most common way to increase net worth is to earn revenue in an amount that exceeds your expenses. There are other ways to increase your net worth, such as winning the lottery or receiving a gift. These are not considered revenue since they were not earned, but they do increase your net worth. They are known as **capital**.

FIGURE 1.36

Part of the accounting function is to manage your finances by recording your monthly expenses and matching them to your monthly revenue. Capital items (such as gifts or lottery winnings) are not everyday revenues and are therefore recorded directly to net worth instead of the revenue account.

It is important to separate records of revenue received from regular activities (earning wages) from other infrequent increases to net worth (gifts) instead of pooling them all together. Keeping them separate will allow you to properly manage your finances month-to-month.

The accounting equation shows net worth at a particular point in time. However, net worth changes over time as you earn revenue, incur expenses or receive capital. The following formula shows how to calculate the ending or closing balance of net worth over a period of time.

Ending Net Worth = Beginning Net Worth + Capital + Surplus (Deficit)

You will recall that the beginning balance, or opening balance, is the balance at the beginning of the period. Capital is any transaction that increases your net worth which is not considered revenue. The surplus or deficit is from the income statement for the period. A surplus will increase net worth and a deficit will decrease net worth. At the end of the period, the accounting equation must still balance, so that assets must equal liabilities plus the ending net worth.

T-Account Transactions

To demonstrate how the T-accounts can be used to record the various financial transactions that happen during a period, and how the income statement is linked to the balance sheet, we will examine several transactions. A **transaction** is a trade or exchange with someone else in order to receive something of value.

We will begin the month with opening balances for assets, liabilities and net worth. These opening balances are the ending balances from the previous month. The opening balances of the asset accounts will normally appear on the left side of the T-accounts (increase side), and the opening balances of the liabilities and net worth will normally appear on the right side of the T-accounts (increase side).

The list of transactions is numbered and will be numbered in the T-accounts to help keep track of the transactions. Recall that the accounting equation must balance, so every transaction will affect at least two accounts.

The Process

① If applicable, enter the opening balances in the appropriate T-account. Then check that the accounting equation is in balance before you begin entering transactions. This step is highlighted for the opening balance of the cash account in the T-account worksheet.

② Enter both sides of the transaction in the correct account in the balance sheet and/or income statement. Be sure to record the transaction number so that you may check your work. This step is highlighted for the first transaction in the T-account worksheet.

③ Calculate the totals of the T-accounts on the income statement and calculate the surplus or deficit. A surplus will increase net worth and a deficit will decrease net worth.

④ Calculate the totals of the T-accounts on the balance sheet and complete the accounting equation at the bottom of the balance sheet to check that it balances.

Opening Balances as at April 1, 2016			
Cash	$1,000	Unpaid Accounts	$1,500
Prepaid Insurance	0	Mortgage	90,000
Contents of Home	6,000	Bank Loan	0
House	150,000	Net Worth	65,500

Transactions

1. Earned and deposited salary of $2,500.
2. Paid $1,200 cash for a one-year insurance policy.
3. Paid for $150 of entertainment with credit card.
4. Received a $4,000 loan from the bank.
5. Won $800 in a lottery.
6. Paid $1,000 for mortgage. Interest is $100 and the remainder is the principal.
7. Purchased new furniture worth $1,400 with credit card.
8. Bought food with $400 cash.

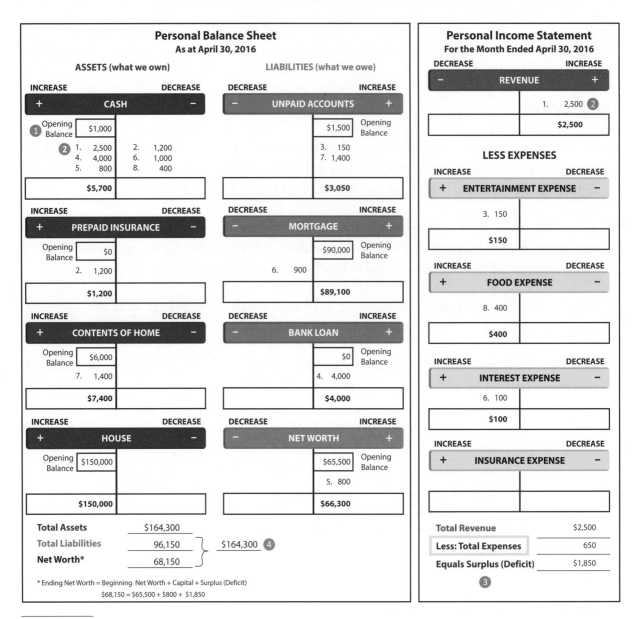

FIGURE 1.37

For the net worth calculation at the bottom of the balance sheet, we start with the the opening net worth of $65,500 and add the lottery winnings of $800. Since we show a surplus of $1,850 from the income statement, we will add this to net worth. This gives us a closing net worth balance of $68,150. Note that if we had a deficit on the income statement, this would be subtracted from net worth.

*Access **ameengage.com** for integrated resources including tutorials, practice exercises, the digital textbook and more.*

In Summary

Describe the purpose of accounting

✥ Accounting identifies, measures and communicates financial activities. This can be done for an individual or a business.

Describe the balance sheet and the income statement

✥ The balance sheet is a permanent record that records what you own (assets), what you owe (liabilities) and your net worth.

✥ The income statement is a temporary record and is used to determine the change in net worth (revenue minus expenses) over a period of time.

Define an accounting period

✥ An accounting period is the time frame in which the financial statements are prepared.

Explain how the accounting equations works

✥ The accounting equation: Assets = Liabilities + Net Worth. All transactions must be recorded in a way to ensure the accounting equation is always balanced.

Explain accrual-based accounting

✥ Accrual-based accounting recognizes revenue and expenses in the time period in which they occur, regardless of when the payment is received or made.

✥ The change in net worth is recognized when the activity occurs, not when cash is transferred.

Explain how to account for debt and assets

✥ Buying assets or selling them for the value shown on the balance sheet does not affect net worth, it is simply an exchange of one asset for another.

✥ Borrowing money and repaying debt will only affect assets and liabilities. The income statement and net worth will not be affected.

Explain how to account for prepaid expenses

✥ Prepaid expenses are expenses paid for before the expense is incurred. Initially they are recorded as an asset on the balance sheet. Once the expense has been incurred, the asset is reduced and an expense is recorded on the income statement.

Distinguish between capital and revenue

✥ Capital includes irregular items such as gifts that increase net worth. Revenue items also increase net worth but are earned and are recorded on the income statement.

Demonstrate how double entries are recorded in T-accounts

✥ T-accounts are used to track the increases and decreases in the value of assets, liabilities, net worth, revenue and expenses.

Review Exercise

Complete the T-account worksheet on the opposite page for the following transactions and calculate ending net worth.

Opening balances

Cash	$3,000
Contents of Home	3,000
House	100,000
Mortgage	70,000
Net Worth	36,000

Transactions for the month of January

1. Earned and deposited $2,000 salary
2. Earned and deposited $300 from providing tutoring services
3. Paid $300 cash for food
4. Went out for dinner and a show and spent $200 cash
5. Purchased new clothes with $100 cash
6. Paid $500 cash for maintenance on the house
7. Paid $100 cash for utilities
8. Deposited lottery winnings of $600
9. Received cash gift of $150

Review Exercise

See Appendix I for solutions.

T-account Worksheet

Personal Balance Sheet
As at January 31, 2016

ASSETS (what we own)

INCREASE			DECREASE
+	CASH		−

Opening Balance

LIABILITIES (what we owe)

DECREASE			INCREASE
−	UNPAID ACCOUNTS		+

Opening Balance

INCREASE			DECREASE
+	CONTENTS OF HOME		−

Opening Balance

DECREASE			INCREASE
−	MORTGAGE		+

Opening Balance

INCREASE			DECREASE
+	HOUSE		−

Opening Balance

DECREASE			INCREASE
−	NET WORTH		+

Opening Balance

Total Assets _____

Total Liabilities _____

Net Worth* _____

} _____

*Ending Net Worth = Beginning Net Worth + Capital + Surplus (Deficit)

Personal Income Statement
For the Month Ended January 31, 2016

DECREASE			INCREASE
−	REVENUE		+

LESS EXPENSES

INCREASE			DECREASE
+	CLOTHING EXPENSE		−

INCREASE			DECREASE
+	ENTERTAINMENT EXPENSE		−

INCREASE			DECREASE
+	FOOD EXPENSE		−

INCREASE			DECREASE
+	MAINTENANCE EXPENSE		−

INCREASE			DECREASE
+	UTILITIES EXPENSE		−

Total Revenue _____

Less: Total Expenses _____

Equals Surplus (Deficit) _____

Notes

Chapter 2

LINKING PERSONAL ACCOUNTING TO BUSINESS ACCOUNTING

LEARNING OUTCOMES

❶ List the differences between personal accounts and business accounts

❷ Describe the sequence of assets and liabilities as they appear on the balance sheet

❸ Define equity and calculate the balance of the capital account

❹ Describe the three main types of businesses

❺ Record revenue based on the concept of accruals

❻ Record expenses based on the concept of accruals

❼ Record business transactions in T-accounts

AMEENGAGE™ *Access **ameengage.com** for integrated resources including tutorials, practice exercises, the digital textbook and more.*

Business Accounts

Most of what you have learned about accounting in the personal context is similar to accounting in a business context. As you may guess, business accounting is more complex than personal accounting. To begin examining the differences, we will look at some of the differences in terminology between personal and business accounting.

1. The personal balance sheet and the personal income statement are now just called the Balance Sheet and the Income Statement.

2. Cash in a business is like cash in personal accounting. However, businesses may have several different bank accounts and all these amounts are included in cash.

3. Accounts receivable is a new business asset account. This is used when the business sells services or products to a customer and allows the customer to pay later. **Accounts receivable** is the amount owed to the business by its customers.

4. Inventory is an asset account used when a business sells products to customers. This account will be discussed in detail in later chapters.

5. Equipment, buildings, land and other similar assets that provide the business with benefits for a long period of time are called **property, plant and equipment** or long-term assets. These items are not intended to be sold to customers.

6. Unpaid accounts in the personal context are called accounts payable in a business. **Accounts payable** is the obligation the business owes to others.

7. **Unearned revenue** is an obligation the business has to provide products or service to a customer. It is used when a customer prepays the business for services or products.

8. Just as a person may have loans or mortgages, a business may also have long-term debt such as loans.

9. The category of net worth is referred to as **equity**. The equity may belong to the business owner, the partners or shareholders, depending on the organization of the business. Business organization will be discussed later.

10. Revenue will be called either service revenue or sales revenue. If a business provides services to its customers, it will use **service revenue**. If it sells products to its customers, it will use **sales revenue**. Some businesses will provide both and use both accounts on the income statement.

11. Although there are some similarities in the expense items on the income statement, a business will usually have more types of expenses. We will discuss these new expenses as they appear in the textbook. A business will typically list its expenses on the income statement in alphabetical order.

12. Surplus (deficit) on the personal income statement is now called net income (loss). **Net income** occurs when revenue exceeds expenses for the period and will increase equity. A **net loss** occurs when expenses exceed revenue for the period and will decrease equity.

Figure 2.1 shows the comparison between the personal balance sheet and the business balance sheet, and between the personal income statement and the business income statement.

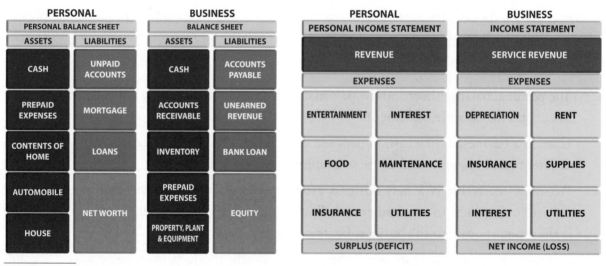

FIGURE 2.1

Sequence of Assets and Liabilities

The assets of a business are listed in sequence according to their liquidity. **Liquidity** is the ease with which the asset can be converted to cash. Cash is the most **liquid asset** and is therefore listed first on the balance sheet, followed by accounts receivable (the amount of money owed by customers to the business), inventory, and so on. Property, plant and equipment, such as buildings and machinery, are the least liquid and are therefore listed last.

Liabilities are also listed in sequence in a similar way. Those that are payable within the shortest amount of time are listed first (e.g. accounts payable). These amounts are usually due within one year of the balance sheet date. Debts that will last longer, such as bank loans, are listed last.

BUSINESS

BALANCE SHEET	
ASSETS	**LIABILITIES**
CASH	ACCOUNTS PAYABLE
ACCOUNTS RECEIVABLE	UNEARNED REVENUE
INVENTORY	BANK LOAN
PREPAID EXPENSES	
PROPERTY, PLANT & EQUIPMENT	

FIGURE 2.2

Equity vs. Net Worth

Equity is the net worth of a business, after all assets have been sold and all liabilities have been paid. Different business organizations classify who this equity belongs to in the following ways

- In a proprietary business (owned by a single person), it is referred to as **owner's equity**.
- In a partnership, it is referred to as **partners' equity**.
- In a corporation, it is referred to as **shareholders' equity**. Owners of a corporation buy shares to indicate ownership and own a percentage of the company.
- Some government institutions refer to it as **accumulated surplus (deficit)**.

All these terms represent equity of an organization, which is similar to net worth introduced in personal accounting. For the next few chapters in this textbook, we will focus on a proprietary business and will use the term owner's equity to describe the equity of the business. At the end of the accounting period, the ending owner's equity balance can be calculated as follows.

WORTH REPEATING

The accounting equation is
Assets = Liabilities + Owner's Equity

Ending Owner's Equity = Beginning Owner's Equity + Owner's Contributions + Net Income (Loss) - Owner's Withdrawals

Owner's contributions is the amount of cash or assets invested in the business by the owner. **Owner's withdrawals** is the amount of cash or assets taken by the business owner for personal use. If a company is brand new and has just started operations, then beginning owner's equity will be equal to $0. If a company has been established for at least one accounting period, then the beginning owner's equity is equal to the previous period's ending owner's equity.

In business accounting, owner's equity is a category on the balance sheet but not an account. Separate accounts are required to record transactions such as owner's contribution and owner's withdrawals.

The **owner's capital account** is used to record the amount of the owner's equity including owner's contributions. Owner's contributions are added directly into owner's capital. The owner can also withdraw cash from the business to pay for personal items. These withdrawals are called **owner's drawings** and decrease the business' assets and the value of owner's equity. Owner's drawings are never an expense and will never appear on the income statement. Owner's drawings, although a part of equity, does not appear on the balance sheet. Instead it appears on its own statement, which will be introduced later in the chapter.

In the personal T-account worksheet from the previous chapter, we used a single T-account to track the net worth transactions of an individual. In the context of a business, this single T-account is now represented by owner's capital. A separate T-account will be used for owner's drawings to track the amount removed from the business for personal use. The two T-accounts in Figure 2.3 below are the generic capital and drawings account. In an actual proprietary business, these accounts will typically have the owner's name attached to them. For example, if John Smith was the owner, the accounts would be called "Smith, Capital" and "Smith, Drawings."

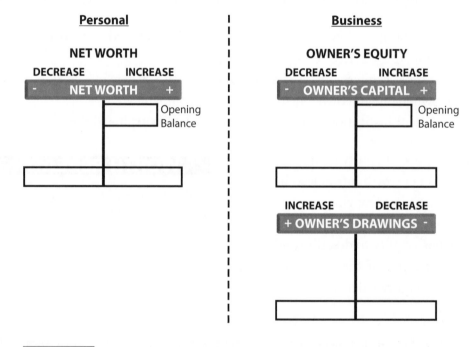

FIGURE 2.3

With these new T-accounts that make up owner's equity, the T-account increase and decrease map introduced in the previous chapter will be modified slightly to accommodate capital and drawings. This new T-account map, shown in Figure 2.4, will be the basis we follow for the remainder of this chapter. Notice that owner's drawings increases on the left side of the T-account, like an expense, and owner's capital increases on the right side of the T-account, like revenue.

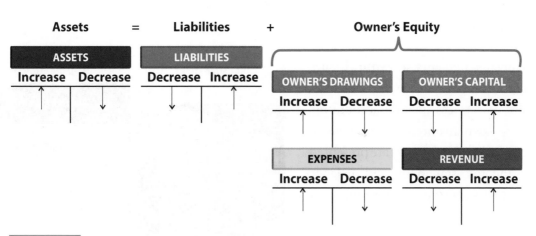

FIGURE 2.4

We will illustrate the T-account entries related to the owner's capital and owner's drawings with an example. Suppose that the owner of a newly formed company invested $10,000 in cash into the company (transaction 1). This will increase owner's capital and increase cash. For simplicity, assume that all opening account balances are $0.

Also suppose that the owner withdrew $1,000 from the company for personal use (transaction 2). This transaction will cause cash to decrease and owner's drawings to increase. These transactions related to owner's equity are summarized in Figure 2.5.

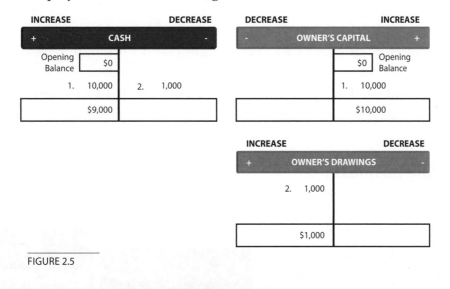

FIGURE 2.5

Financial Statements of Different Types of Businesses

Different types of businesses use different financial statement layouts: a small consulting firm would use a very simple income statement and balance sheet compared to a complex manufacturing company that produces goods. The manufacturing company requires a more detailed set of financial statements, which provide the information a manager needs to know to operate the business effectively.

The following examples display financial statements for three main types of businesses.

Service Business

The financial statements shown in Figure 2.6 represent a simple service business. Examples of services include accounting, consulting, lawn maintenance or general contracting. A few new items are presented on the income statement and balance sheet: cost of sales, gross profit and work in progress.

Cost of sales are the expenses directly tied to the service revenue earned. In a consulting firm, this would be the salary of the consultants. All other expenses would be part of the operating expenses (i.e. rent, insurance, depreciation, etc.).

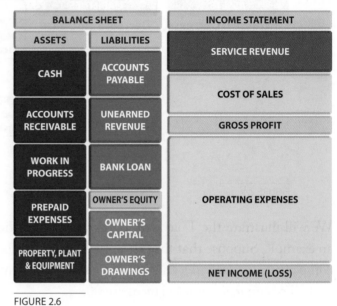

FIGURE 2.6

The difference between service revenue and cost of sales is called gross profit. **Gross profit** is used to pay for all other expenses and will be discussed in detail later in the text. Not all service businesses will use cost of sales, in which case every expense is considered an operating expense and there is no gross profit.

On the balance sheet, there may be an asset account called work in progress. This represents jobs that are currently being worked on but are not yet complete. For example, a training company in the middle of developing a training program. This partially completed work would be eventually recognized as cost of sales and matched to revenue when the service is delivered to the client.

Merchandising Business

The financial statements shown in Figure 2.7 represent a merchandising business. Any company that buys goods to resell to customers is considered a merchandising business. A common example is a retail store. Examples of retail stores include hardware, clothing, toy and convenience stores.

On the balance sheet, there is a new asset called inventory. This account tracks the value of all the goods the store has purchased and intends to sell to its customers. Once these items are sold, the

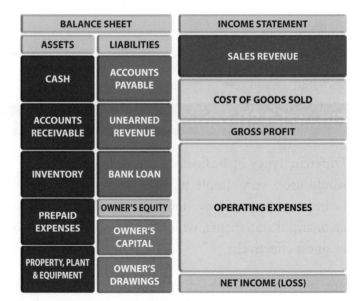

FIGURE 2.7

value of the inventory is transferred to cost of goods sold on the income statement. **Cost of goods sold** is the value of all the goods sold and is subtracted from sales revenue to determine gross profit. Inventory and cost of goods sold will be covered in later chapters.

Manufacturing Business

The financial statements of a manufacturing company are shown in Figure 2.8. A manufacturing company makes the products that it sells. Examples of manufacturers include auto makers, steel mills and furniture makers.

The balance sheet has an asset account called inventory, similar to a retail store. However, a manufacturer will have different types of inventory at various stages of production. Raw material represents the items that will be transformed into the product that can be sold (e.g. lumber used to make furniture). Work in progress represents partially completed

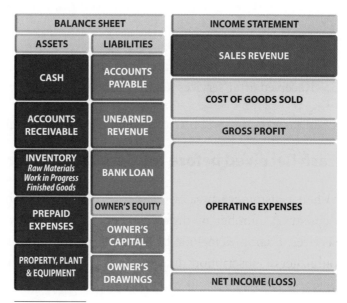

FIGURE 2.8

products and finished goods represent products that are complete and can be sold to customers. Once the items are sold, they are recorded in cost of goods sold.

IN THE REAL WORLD

It is simple to grasp the nature of a particular business by labelling it as either a service, merchandising or manufacturing business. However, some companies that operate as a combination of two or more of these types of businesses. Consider Apple Inc. which is well known as a manufacturer of breakthrough technology such as the Macintosh operating system, iPod, iPhone and iPad.

The company also has a merchandising segment: it operates an online store and a retail store. These stores predominantly sell its own self-manufactured products, but also sell complementary products produced by other manufacturers such as security software and computer speakers.

Apple is also in part a service business because the company provides online support as well as warranty and repair services for its products. It also provides online services such as MobileMe, a subscription-based service that allows users to store personal data on a server, create web pages, back up key files and so on.

Therefore, Apple is a hybrid of a service, merchandising and manufacturing business. However, it is reasonable to deem the company as primarily a manufacturing business since sales of its own products represent the majority of its total sales.

Recording Revenue

In business accounting, as in personal accounting, accrual-based accounting is used to record transactions. Revenues are recorded or recognized when they are earned regardless of when cash payment is received from the customer. Cash received for selling services or products is a timing issue, and cash for revenue can be received from customers at three different times.

1. Received before services are performed
2. Received when services are performed
3. Received after services are performed

In all cases, equity will increase when revenue is recognized.

Cash Received before the Service is Performed

When a customer pays a business for services before they are performed, it is known as a **customer deposit**. A number of different types of businesses require deposits or prepayments for their services. Examples include banquet halls (hall rental fees), health clubs (memberships), magazine publishers (subscription dues) and insurance companies (insurance premiums). In each case, the business receives cash up front and provides a service at a later date.

Since services have not been performed at the time the cash is received, service revenue cannot be affected. Instead, the business has an obligation to provide services in the future. You will recall that an obligation of a business is a liability. Thus, a new liability account known as unearned revenue must be used.

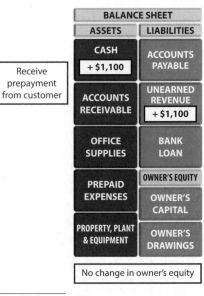

FIGURE 2.9

Suppose a business receives a deposit of $1,100 from a customer one month before services must be provided. Figure 2.9 illustrates the impact on the accounts of the business at the time the customer paid for the services (one month in advance). The prepayment by the customer is a liability for the business (unearned revenue) because the business now has an obligation to provide services to the customer. The payment is essentially held in trust on behalf of the customer. At this point, there is no impact on equity because even though cash is received, revenue is not recognized since no work has been completed. If the business fails to provide the services, they must return the deposit to the customer.

It is only when work is completed in the next month that revenue can be recognized. The transaction to record this will be covered in a later chapter.

Cash Received when the Service is Performed

When a company performs a service and the customer pays for it immediately, the transaction is fairly straightforward. From the service provider's perspective, cash increases and equity increases. The increase in equity is recognized as revenue and increases net income.

If a client pays $1,100 cash immediately when the business provides the service, then cash and service revenue will be affected. The impact on cash and service revenue is shown in Figure 2.10. Remember that recognizing revenue results in an increase to equity.

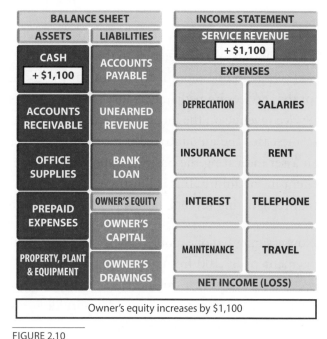

FIGURE 2.10

Cash Received after the Service is Performed

Most businesses provide customers with payment terms which allow customers to pay after they have received the product or service (e.g. 30 days to pay the balance owing). This form of making sales is sometimes referred to as "selling on account." You may mistakenly think that the value of equity would not change when selling with payment terms because no cash was received from the sale. However, revenue must be recorded at the time the product is sold or the service is delivered, regardless of when the payment is received.

When a company provides payment terms to sell its products or services, the money owed by its customers is recorded as an asset, called accounts receivable. After a service is provided, the seller issues an **invoice** to the buyer. The invoice includes the details of the service rendered and the agreed-upon price. This indicates that the customer now owes the balance and needs to pay the seller by the date stated on the invoice. From the seller's perspective, this indicates an increase in accounts receivable (an asset) and an increase in equity (recognized as revenue). Later, when the customer actually pays the outstanding amount, the issuing company increases cash and decreases accounts receivable. The

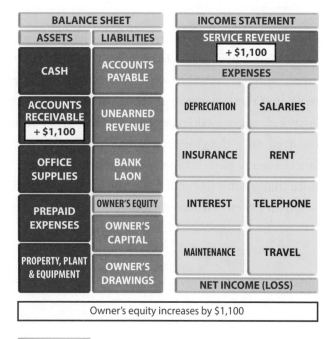

FIGURE 2.11

decrease in accounts receivable shows that the service provider received cash and is no longer owed any amount from the customer (i.e. nothing is "receivable").

For example, suppose a business provides services valued at $1,100 and has sent an invoice to the client. The client has promised to pay in one month. Even though this client is not paying for the services immediately, equity increases and is recognized as service revenue on the income statement. This causes net income to increase. The amount is also recorded in accounts receivable, an asset indicating the business expects to receive cash from the client in the future. This is illustrated in Figure 2.11. Remember that recognizing revenue results in an increase to equity.

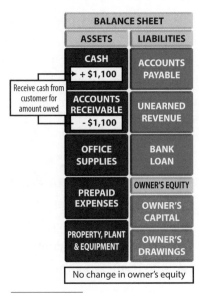

FIGURE 2.12

Now assume that one month has passed and the business receives payment of $1,100 from the client. Figure 2.12 illustrates the accounting impact of this transaction. This transaction is often referred to as "receipt of account." Equity does not change since one asset is exchanged for another.

Recording Expenses

Expenses, similar to revenues, are recorded when they are incurred, not necessarily when they are paid. This led to three different timings of the cash payments for expenses.

1. Pay before the expense is incurred
2. Pay when the expense is incurred
3. Pay after the expense is incurred

Notice we use the term "incurred" in all three scenarios. An expense is incurred by a company if the activities related to the expense have been used or consumed. You may also see the term "recognized" when it comes to expenses and revenue. **Recognizing** an expense or revenue simply means recording the expense or revenue on the income statement. For example, if a company has hired a lawn care service company to water the grass on its premises on August 16, the expense has been incurred once the grass has actually been watered. The expense would be recognized at that time. If a company pays for internet services, the internet expense for a given month has been incurred once that month has ended (i.e. the internet services for one month have been used up). In all cases, when an expense is recognized, this means that equity will decrease.

Pay Cash before the Expense is Incurred

When a company pays before the expense has been incurred, this is a supplier prepayment. This scenario requires increasing an asset account called a prepaid expense, which was discussed in the context of personal accounting. These prepayments are not considered an expense at the time they are paid because the service or the product has not been used.

For example, if a company pays its insurance premiums one year in advance, it is paying for services not yet received. The premiums should only be expensed in the months to which they apply—hence they are called prepaid expenses. Other common examples of prepaid expenses are rent and office supplies, although any time a company pays for products or services in advance, they can be considered prepaid expenses.

A business paid cash ahead of time to the insurance company for insurance coverage to be provided for the upcoming year. At the time of the payment, cash decreases and a prepaid expense called prepaid insurance increases. This prepaid expense is considered an asset because it could be turned back into cash if the entire year of insurance is not used up (e.g. the policy is cancelled).

The business paid $3,600 for insurance on January 1, 2016 for insurance coverage throughout 2016. On January 1, 2016, when the payment is made, the business' cash (an asset) decreases by $3,600 and prepaid insurance (another asset) increases by $3,600. At this point, equity is not affected. One asset was exchanged for another asset. This is shown in Figure 2.13.

Notice that expenses, and thus equity, have not been affected yet. Only as the asset is used up will an expense be recorded. If the insurance company fails to provide the services, or the business cancels the policy, the insurance company would have to return cash to the business for the unused portion of the policy. In this example, as each month passes, the prepaid insurance will gradually become an expense. The details for this transaction will be covered in a later chapter.

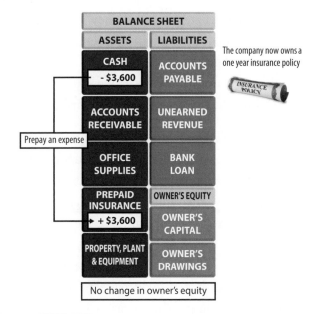

FIGURE 2.13

Pay Cash when the Expense is Incurred

When a company incurs an expense and pays for it immediately, the transaction is fairly straightforward. From the company's perspective, cash decreases and equity decreases. The decrease in equity is recorded as an expense on the income statement, which reduces net income. Suppose a business paid $800 cash for the cost to travel to a client's head office. Figure 2.14 illustrates the accounting treatment when paying immediately in cash for travel expenses. Remember that recognizing an expense results in a decrease to equity.

Pay Cash after the Expense is Incurred

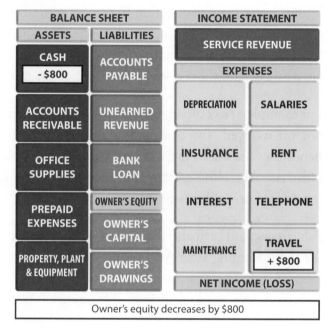

FIGURE 2.14

Many expenses are paid after they have been incurred. This form of paying expenses is sometimes referred to as "paying on account." You may mistakenly think that the value of equity would not change until the expense is paid for. However, accounting standards require expenses to be recorded at the time they are incurred, regardless of when the payment is made.

A business that provides products or services to another business is known as a supplier. When a company owes a supplier for a product or service, the money owed is recorded as a liability called accounts payable. When an invoice is issued to the company by the supplier (after the expense has been incurred), the value of the invoice is treated as an increase to the accounts payable account and an increase to the appropriate expense account. Later, when the company actually pays the outstanding amount, the transaction is a decrease to cash and a decrease to accounts payable. The company used cash to pay and it no longer owes any amount to the supplier (i.e. nothing is "payable").

Suppose a business will pay for a maintenance expense two months after it has been incurred. Even though the business is not paying for the services immediately, the supplier will issue an invoice as soon as the maintenance work is done. Assume that the supplier is charging $700 for its maintenance services. Figure 2.15 shows the impact on the applicable

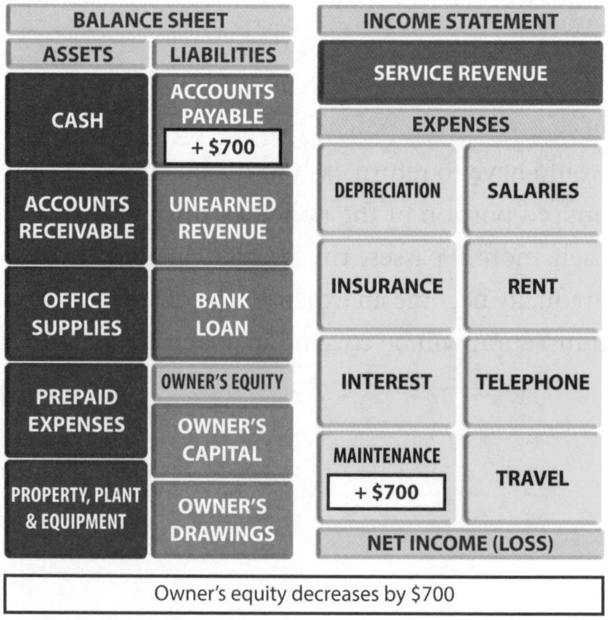

FIGURE 2.15

accounts of the business when the invoice is received from the supplier. Equity decreases and it is recorded as an expense on the income statement, which also decreases net income. Remember that recognizing an expense results in a decrease to equity.

Now assume that two months have passed and the business pays the $700 owed to the maintenance supplier. Figure 2.16 illustrates the accounting impact of this transaction. This transaction is often referred to as a "payment of account." Equity does not change. Only an asset (cash) and a liability (accounts payable) are affected.

BALANCE SHEET	
ASSETS	**LIABILITIES**
CASH - $700	ACCOUNTS PAYABLE - $700
ACCOUNTS RECEIVABLE	UNEARNED REVENUE
OFFICE SUPPLIES	BANK LOAN
PREPAID EXPENSES	**OWNER'S EQUITY**
	OWNER'S CAPITAL
PROPERTY, PLANT & EQUIPMENT	OWNER'S DRAWINGS

No change in owner's equity

FIGURE 2.16

Business Transactions

The ultimate goal of recording business transactions is to be able to create financial statements and assess how well the business is performing. However, not everything the business does will be recorded in the T-accounts and appear on the financial statements. A transaction occurs when the business trades something of value with another person or business and this causes a change in assets, liabilities or equity. The thing of value could include services, products, cash, a promise to pay money, or the right to collect money.

An **event**, on the other hand, does not involve trading something of value. Since assets, liabilities and equity are not affected by an event, nothing is recorded in the T-accounts. An event can lead to a transaction at a later date, but it is only at that later date that anything would be recorded in the T-accounts. For example, signing a contract with a customer to provide service in two months' time is an event. At the signing, nothing of value has been traded, therefore nothing is recorded in the T-accounts. However, two months later after the services have been provided, a transaction has occurred and will be recorded in the T-accounts.

We will examine several business transactions and how they are recorded in the T-accounts. Keep in mind that every transaction must leave the accounting equation in balance, so every transaction must be recorded in at least two accounts. We will explain each transaction and illustrate how the transaction will be recorded in the T-accounts. We will also illustrate how the accounting equation will remain in balance and explain any changes to equity. The reason for the change to equity will be listed under the explanation column and will be colour coded to match revenue, expense or equity accounts. If there is no change to equity, the explanation column will remain empty.

John Smith created Ace Bookkeepers as a proprietary business. During the month of March 2016, he made the following transactions.

1. John Smith deposited $30,000 cash into the new business' bank account.
2. Borrowed $10,000 from the bank.
3. Bought $8,000 worth of furniture with cash.
4. A customer paid $2,000 cash for bookkeeping services to be provided next month.
5. Provided services to customers and received $15,000 cash.
6. Provided bookkeeping services for $4,000 on account.
7. Paid $6,000 cash for a one-year insurance policy which started on the first of the month.
8. Paid $1,100 cash for rent for the month.
9. Paid $6,000 cash to employees for salary.
10. Paid $200 cash for interest on the bank loan.
11. Received a telephone bill for $300 which will be paid later.
12. Paid travel expenses of $2,000 with a credit card, which will be paid next month.
13. Paid $3,000 toward the bank loan.
14. John Smith withdrew $2,000 cash for personal use.
15. A customer paid $500 cash for the amount owing for bookkeeping services provided earlier in the month.
16. Paid the telephone bill received earlier in the month.

Transaction 1: The owner deposited cash into the business

When an owner invests his or her own cash into a proprietary business, the cash is recorded directly in the owner's capital and is regarded as owner's equity. This transaction increases cash and increases owner's capital and leaves the accounting equation balanced, as shown in Figure 2.17.

Record the transaction in the T-accounts

Analyze the impact on the accounting equation

*Explanation of changes to Owner's Equity

FIGURE 2.17

Transaction 2: Borrowed cash from the bank

The business has increased its debt by getting a loan from the bank. This transaction is recorded by increasing cash (an asset) and increasing the value of bank loan (a liability). The transaction has no impact on owner's equity; therefore nothing is recorded on the income statement. Again, the accounting equation will remain in balance.

WORTH REPEATING

A bank loan increases an asset and a liability without affecting the balance of owner's equity.

Record the transaction in the T-accounts

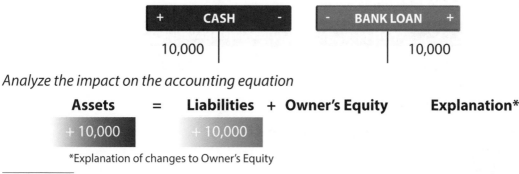

Analyze the impact on the accounting equation

Assets	=	Liabilities	+ Owner's Equity	Explanation*
+ 10,000		+ 10,000		

*Explanation of changes to Owner's Equity

FIGURE 2.18

Transaction 3: Bought furniture with cash

Furniture, computers, cars and other similar assets are considered to be property, plant and equipment and are long-term assets. These assets are used to run the business and generate sales and should not be sold to customers or sold to raise cash to pay for day-to-day expenses. Each type of property, plant and equipment is given its own T-account. This transaction is simply an exchange of one asset for another, and is recorded by increasing furniture and decreasing cash as shown in Figure 2.19.

Record the transaction in the T-accounts

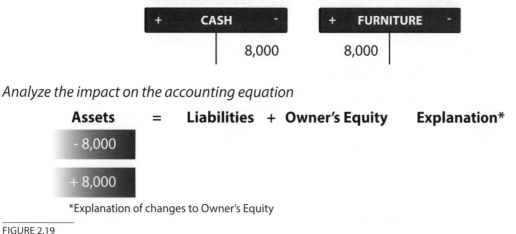

Analyze the impact on the accounting equation

Assets	=	Liabilities	+ Owner's Equity	Explanation*
- 8,000				
+ 8,000				

*Explanation of changes to Owner's Equity

FIGURE 2.19

Transaction 4: Customer prepays for services

One way to receive payment for services is for the customer to pay for services before they are performed. In this case, when the customer pays cash no work has been performed. In fact, the services will not be provided until next month. This means that service revenue cannot be affected. Ace Bookkeepers has now accepted an obligation to provide services in one month. An obligation is a liability, meaning we must record the amount received as an increase to cash and an increase to a liability account called unearned revenue. Unearned revenue represents the obligation the business has to provide services or products to customers in the future. If services are not performed by the business, the cash must be returned to the customer. The transaction is illustrated in Figure 2.20. The transaction to turn this liability into revenue will be covered in a later chapter.

Record the transaction in the T-accounts

+ CASH -	- UNEARNED REVENUE +
2,000	2,000

Analyze the impact on the accounting equation

Assets	=	Liabilities	+	Owner's Equity	Explanation*
+ 2,000		+ 2,000			

*Explanation of changes to Owner's Equity

FIGURE 2.20

Transaction 5: Provided services for cash

The sale of services is called revenue and it is the primary way a service business increases owner's equity. This transaction is recorded by increasing cash and increasing service revenue. The equity in the business increases and is recorded as an increase to service revenue.

Record the transaction in the T-accounts

+ CASH -	- SERVICE REVENUE +
15,000	15,000

Analyze the impact on the accounting equation

Assets	=	Liabilities	+	Owner's Equity	Explanation*
+ 15,000				+ 15,000	Revenue earned

*Explanation of changes to Owner's Equity

FIGURE 2.21

Transaction 6: Provided services on account

An alternate way to receive payment for services provided is to allow a customer to pay at a later date. Services were provided so revenue must be affected, however cash cannot be affected since there has been no payment. Instead, another asset called accounts receivable will increase. Recall that accounts receivable is the amount owing to the business from its customers. Since accounts receivable will eventually be collected and become cash, it is regarded as an asset. Since services were provided at this time, the equity in the business increases and is recorded as an increase to service revenue. A customer payment for this service will be shown in transaction 15.

Record the transaction in the T-accounts

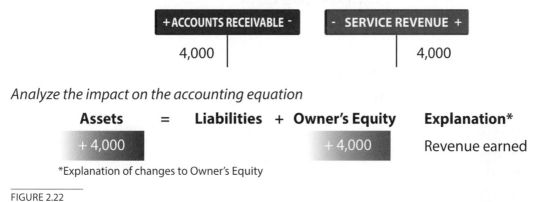

Analyze the impact on the accounting equation

Assets	=	Liabilities	+	Owner's Equity	Explanation*
+ 4,000				+ 4,000	Revenue earned

*Explanation of changes to Owner's Equity

FIGURE 2.22

Transaction 7: Prepaid insurance for one year with cash

It is common for a business to prepay various expenses such as insurance, web-hosting fees, consulting fees and legal fees. Recall from the previous chapter how prepaid expenses are recorded. The same concept is practiced in business. The item that is prepaid is initially recorded as an asset on the balance sheet. Figure 2.23 shows how the prepayment for insurance is recorded by decreasing cash and increasing prepaid insurance. The transaction to convert this asset to an expense will be covered in a later chapter.

Record the transaction in the T-accounts

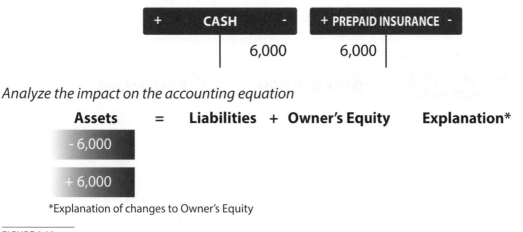

Analyze the impact on the accounting equation

Assets	=	Liabilities	+	Owner's Equity	Explanation*
- 6,000					
+ 6,000					

*Explanation of changes to Owner's Equity

FIGURE 2.23

Transactions 8 through 10: Paid cash for expenses

All these transactions relate to cash expenses. The transactions are recorded by decreasing the value of the cash account and increasing the value of the appropriate expense account. These expenses were incurred by the business in order to run the business and help generate revenue. Remember, the equity in the business decreases and is recorded as an increase to expenses.

Record the transaction in the T-accounts

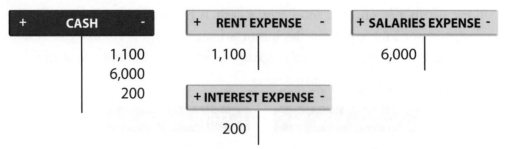

Analyze the impact on the accounting equation

Assets	=	Liabilities	+	Owner's Equity	Explanation*
- 1,100				- 1,100	Rent expense
- 6,000				- 6,000	Salaries expense
- 200				- 200	Interest expense

*Explanation of changes to Owner's Equity

FIGURE 2.24

Transactions 11 and 12: Incurred expenses to be paid later

The telephone expense is due to be paid next month and travel expenses were billed to a credit card that is also to be paid next month. These expenses must be recorded this month because they were incurred and used to generate sales this month. In other words, expenses incurred are matched to revenue earned in the same period. This transaction is recorded by increasing accounts payable and increasing the appropriate expense account, as illustrated in Figure 2.25. Remember, the equity in the business decreases and is recorded as an increase to expenses.

Record the transaction in the T-accounts

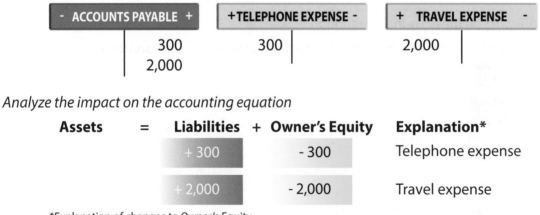

Analyze the impact on the accounting equation

Assets	=	Liabilities	+	Owner's Equity	Explanation*
		+ 300		- 300	Telephone expense
		+ 2,000		- 2,000	Travel expense

*Explanation of changes to Owner's Equity

FIGURE 2.25

Transaction 13: Repaid a portion of the bank loan principal

This transaction is the opposite of what was recorded in transaction 2. To pay back part of the bank loan principal we will decrease cash and decrease the bank loan with no impact on the owner's equity. Repaying any debt, including accounts payable, will be recorded in a similar manner. It is important to be able to pay back loans when they are due. Failure to pay loans on time is called defaulting on the loan and can make it more difficult to borrow in the future. In some cases, defaulting may also cause the business to close down.

Record the transaction in the T-accounts

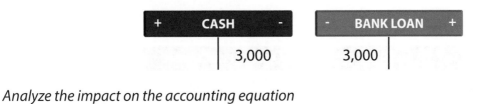

Analyze the impact on the accounting equation

*Explanation of changes to Owner's Equity

FIGURE 2.26

Transaction 14: The owner withdrew cash for personal use

In a proprietary business, the owner is not an employee and does not receive a salary the way that other employees do. If the owner withdraws cash from the business for personal items, such as grocery bills or mortgage payments on their house, these withdrawals are called drawings. As discussed earlier, owner's drawings are a direct decrease to owner's equity and are not recorded as expenses. This transaction is recorded by decreasing cash and increasing owner's drawings, and is shown in Figure 2.27. The decrease in equity is recorded as an increase to owner's drawings.

Record the transaction in the T-accounts

Analyze the impact on the accounting equation

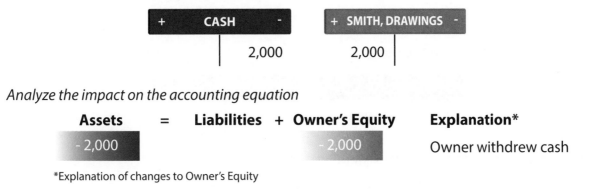

*Explanation of changes to Owner's Equity

FIGURE 2.27

Transaction 15: A customer pays the amount owing

In transaction 6, Ace Bookkeepers provided services to a customer and allowed them to pay later. Cash will only increase as payment is received. Recall that amounts owed by customers are recorded in the asset accounts receivable. Thus, when a customer decides to pay their bill, accounts receivable must decrease, since the amount has now been collected by the business. Notice that service revenue is not affected by this transaction. Service revenue increased in transaction 6 when the service was performed. This transaction is just an exchange of one asset for another, as shown in Figure 2.28.

Record the transaction in the T-accounts

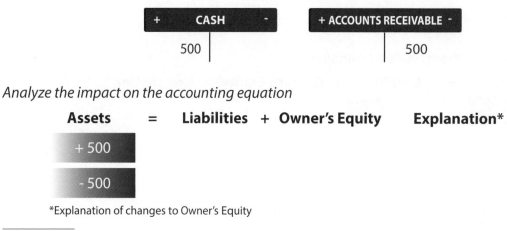

Analyze the impact on the accounting equation

FIGURE 2.28

Transaction 16: Paying a supplier the amount owing

In transaction 11, a telephone bill was received but not paid immediately. Cash will only decrease when payment is made. Recall that amounts owed to suppliers are recorded in the liability accounts payable. Thus, when Ace Bookkeepers pays the bill, accounts payable must decrease, since the amount has now been paid to the supplier. Notice that telephone expense is not affected by this transaction. Telephone expense increased in transaction 11 when the bill was received. This transaction is just paying off debt, as shown in Figure 2.29.

Record the transaction in the T-accounts

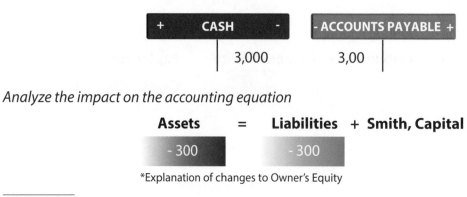

Analyze the impact on the accounting equation

FIGURE 2.29

All the transactions have been compiled in the T-account worksheet shown in Figure 2.30. Notice that the net income from the income statement is calculated first so it can be added to owner's equity. The owner's equity calculation is shown at the bottom of the balance sheet and shows an ending balance of $37,400. This calculation will be discussed in more detail in the next section.

Ace Bookkeepers
Balance Sheet
As at March 31, 2016

ASSETS (what we own)

CASH

INCREASE +		DECREASE -	
1.	30,000	3.	8,000
2.	10,000	7.	6,000
4.	2,000	8.	1,100
5.	15,000	9.	6,000
15.	500	10.	200
		13.	3,000
		14.	2,000
		16.	300
$29,900			

ACCOUNTS RECEIVABLE

INCREASE +		DECREASE -	
6.	4,000	15.	500
$3,500			

PREPAID INSURANCE

INCREASE +		DECREASE -	
7.	6,000		
$6,000			

FURNITURE

INCREASE +		DECREASE -	
3.	8,000		
$8,000			

LIABILITIES (what we owe)

ACCOUNTS PAYABLE

DECREASE -		INCREASE +	
16.	300	11.	300
		12.	2,000
		$2,000	

UNEARNED REVENUE

DECREASE -		INCREASE +	
		4.	2,000
		$2,000	

BANK LOAN

DECREASE -		INCREASE +	
13.	3,000	2.	10,000
		$7,000	

OWNER'S EQUITY

SMITH, CAPITAL

DECREASE -		INCREASE +	
		1.	30,000
		$30,000	

SMITH, DRAWINGS

INCREASE +		DECREASE -	
14.	2,000		
$2,000			

Total Assets	$48,400	
Total Liabilities	11,000	$48,400
Owner's Equity*	$37,400	

*Ending Owner's Equity Balance = Beginning Owner's Equity Balance
+ Owner's Contributions + Net Income (Loss) - Owner's Withdrawals
$37,400 = $0 + $30,000 + $9,400 - $2,000

Ace Bookkeepers
Income Statement
For the Month Ended March 31, 2016

SERVICE REVENUE

DECREASE -		INCREASE +	
		5.	15,000
		6.	4,000
		$19,000	

LESS EXPENSES

INTEREST EXPENSE

INCREASE +		DECREASE -	
10.	200		
$200			

RENT EXPENSE

INCREASE +		DECREASE -	
8.	1,100		
$1,100			

SALARIES EXPENSE

INCREASE +		DECREASE -	
9.	6,000		
$6,000			

TELEPHONE EXPENSE

INCREASE +		DECREASE -	
11.	300		
$300			

TRAVEL EXPENSE

INCREASE +		DECREASE -	
12.	2,000		
$2,000			

Total Revenue	$19,000
Less: Total Expenses	9,600
Net Income (Loss)	$9,400

FIGURE 2.30

Financial Statements

Now that the T-account worksheet is complete, we can prepare formal financial statements. All financial statements follow certain formatting standards when being created.

- Each statement will have three lines at the top to identify the company (e.g. Ace Bookkeepers), the statement (e.g. Income Statement) and the time period or date the statement covers (e.g. For the Month Ended March 31, 2016).

- The first number in each column will have a dollar sign to indicate the currency of values presented in the statement.

- The last number in a calculated column will have a single underline to indicate a total or subtotal is being calculated.

- The final number on the financial statement, or in the case of the balance sheet the total assets and the total liabilities and owner's equity figures, will have a dollar sign and be double underlined.

The first statement to complete is the income statement shown in Figure 2.31. Recall that this reports on the revenue earned and expenses incurred during the period. For Ace Bookkeepers, this income statement is for the month ended March 31, 2016 and shows a net income of $9,400.

Ace Bookkeepers Income Statement For the Month Ended March 31, 2016		
Revenue		
Service Revenue		$19,000
Expenses		
Interest Expense	$200	
Rent Expense	1,100	
Salaries Expense	6,000	
Telephone Expense	300	
Travel Expense	2,000	
Total Expenses		9,600
Net Income		$9,400 ①

FIGURE 2.31

The **Statement of Owner's Equity** is the formal statement to show how owner's equity changed during the month. It will cover the same reporting period as the income statement, so Ace Bookkeepers will prepare the statement of owner's equity for the month ended March 31, 2016. The basic calculation for the change in equity was shown at the bottom of the T-account worksheet in Figure 2.30. The statement of owner's equity is the formal presentation of this calculation and is shown in Figure 2.32.

Ace Bookkeepers Statement of Owner's Equity For the Month Ended March 31, 2016		
Smith, Capital, March 1, 2016		$0
Add: Investment		30,000
Net Income		9,400 ①
Less: Smith, Drawings		2,000
Smith, Capital, March 31, 2016		$37,400 ②

FIGURE 2.32

Since the business was started this month, the balance of the owner's capital account was $0 at the beginning of the month. The investment made in the first transaction is added, as is the net income we calculated from the income statement (indicated by the number 1). The amount of drawings by the owner is subtracted to give us a final balance of the owner's capital of $37,400. The closing balance for March will be the opening balance shown on April's statement of owner's equity.

Lastly, the balance sheet can be created to report on the balances of assets, liabilities and owner's equity on March 31, 2016. The balance sheet is shown in Figure 2.33. Notice how the value of the owner's capital is taken from the statement of owner's equity (indicated by the number 2). Also the total of the assets is equal to the total of liabilities plus owner's equity. These totals must be the same, otherwise the accounting equation is not balanced and there is an error either in recording the transactions in the T-accounts or in the calculation of the financial statements.

Ace Bookkeepers Balance Sheet As at March 31, 2016			
Assets		**Liabilities**	
Cash	$ 29,900	Accounts Payable	$ 2,000
Accounts Receivable	3,500	Unearned Revenue	2,000
Prepaid Insurance	6,000	Bank Loan	7,000
Furniture	8,000	**Total Liabilities**	11,000
		Owner's Equity	
		Smith, Capital	37,400 ②
Total Assets	$ 48,400	**Total Liabilities & Owner's Equity**	$ 48,400

FIGURE 2.33

Ethics

Owners and managers of businesses have control over how revenue and expenses are recorded and reported on the income statement. Perhaps the most famous example of misrepresenting revenue comes from Enron, a large energy company in the United States. Over a period of five years, Enron reported an increase in revenue of more than 750%. This massive increase in revenue was partly due to counting the full amount of trading contracts, instead of just brokerage fees, as revenue.

Another example of corporate fraud was committed by WorldCom, a telecommunication company. In addition to misrepresenting revenue, it also took certain expenses and recorded them as assets on the balance sheet. Thus, by increasing revenue and eliminating certain expenses, WorldCom was able to show very large profits. In both the Enron and WorldCom cases, executives were charged and went to jail for their involvement in fraud.

On a smaller business level, the owner of a banquet hall may receive deposits from customers to book the hall months in advance. As we learned, customer deposits must be treated as a liability (unearned revenue) until the service is actually performed.

Suppose the owner requires additional financing from the bank to help pay for an expansion to the hall and feels her income may not be enough to get the loan. To make her net income appear higher, the owner may decide to record the customer deposits as revenue instead of a liability. By inflating her revenue and profits, she hopes the bank will grant her the loan she needs. This action is unethical.

Consider a sole proprietor who is attempting to minimize the amount of taxes he must pay to the government on his business income. If he has a significant amount of prepaid expenses recorded as assets, he may be tempted to report them all as expenses. He may also be tempted to overstate the expenses by including personal expenses in his business records. All these would reduce the net income and the amount of taxes to be paid. Including personal expenses in business records is illegal, and can lead to charges and penalties imposed by the government.

In Summary

List the differences between personal accounts and business accounts

⮑ Some differences include: surplus (deficit) is called net income (loss); revenue is classified as sales revenue or service revenue; the net worth section is replaced with the owner's equity section.

Describe the sequence of assets and liabilities as they appear on the balance sheet

⮑ The assets of a business are listed in sequence, cash first and then all the other assets according to their liquidity.

⮑ The liabilities of a business are listed in sequence, starting with those that are payable within the shortest amount of time and ending with long-term debts.

Define equity and calculate the balance of the capital account

⮑ Owner's equity represents the net worth of a business.

⮑ The capital account tracks changes in owner's equity including owner contributions. Owner withdrawals are tracked separately in the owner's drawings account.

⮑ Ending Owner's Equity = Beginning Owner's Equity + Owner's Contributions + Net Income (Loss) - Owner's Withdrawals

Describe the three main types of businesses

⮑ A service business will provide services to clients. A merchandising business will buy inventory and resell the inventory to customers. A manufacturing business makes its own products and sells them to customers.

Record revenue based on the concept of accruals

⮑ Revenue is recorded when services have been provided to customers, regardless of when cash is received. Unearned revenue is used to record cash receipts before services are performed and accounts receivable is used when a customer will pay after services are performed.

Record expenses based on the concept of accruals

⮑ Expenses are recorded when they are incurred, regardless of when cash is paid. Prepaid expenses are used to record cash payments before expenses are incurred and accounts payable is used when suppliers will be paid after expenses are incurred.

Record business transactions in T-accounts

⮑ When recording transactions in T-accounts, remember that every transaction must be recorded in at least two accounts and the accounting equation must always remain in balance.

⮑ Revenues and expenses must be recorded when they are incurred, not necessarily when cash is transferred. This creates a need for additional accounts such as accounts receivable, prepaid expenses, accounts payable, and unearned revenue.

Review Exercise

Miranda Jones owns a salon called Style House. Record the following transactions for Miranda's business on the T-account worksheet provided on the opposite page, and then complete the income statement, the statement of owner's equity, and balance sheet. Below are the balances of the accounts on March 1, 2016.

Cash	$3,000
Equipment	12,000
Accounts payable	5,000
Jones, Capital	10,000

Transactions for the month of March

1. Borrowed $12,000 from the bank.
2. Purchased chairs and dryers with $8,000 cash.
3. Paid $333 cash toward the principal of the bank loan.
4. Paid $50 cash for interest on the bank loan.
5. Prepaid $600 cash for a monthly maintenance contract that will last six months.
6. Provided services to customers and received $8,000 cash.
7. Paid $4,000 cash to employees for salaries for the month.
8. Received a telephone bill for $250 which will be paid next month.
9. Received a bill for $300 for advertising and a bill for $500 for travel, both of which will be paid later.
10. Paid monthly rent with $2,000 cash.
11. Paid $1,000 owing to a supplier.
12. Miranda withdrew $3,000 cash from the business for personal use.
13. Provided $400 worth of services to customers on account.
14. Received $100 cash from a customer for services to be provided next month.

Review Exercise

See Appendix I for solutions.

T-account Worksheet

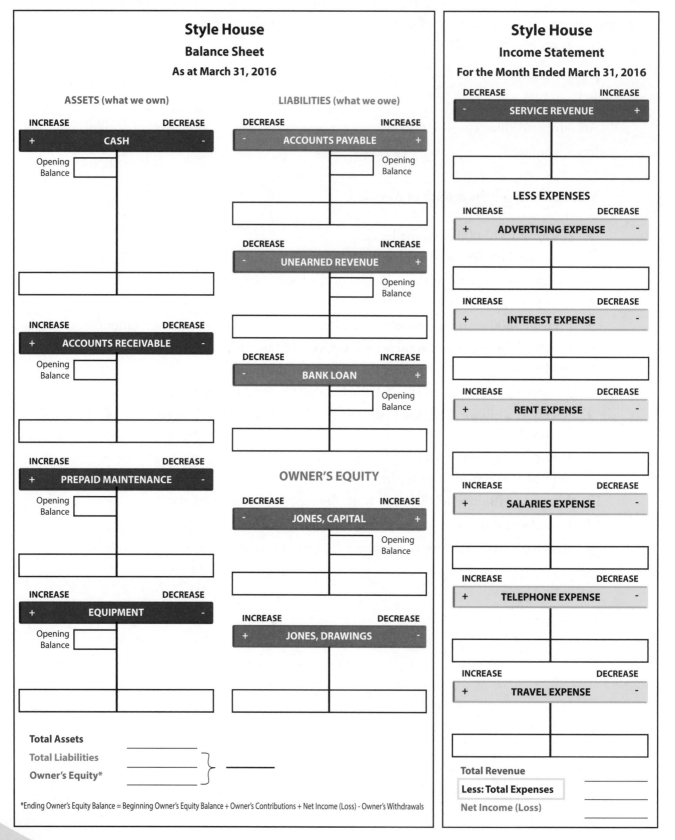

Complete the income statement, statement of owner's equity and balance sheet for this exercise.

Style House Income Statement For the Month Ended March 31, 2016		

Style House Statement of Owner's Equity For the Month Ended March 31, 2016	

Style House Balance Sheet As at March 31, 2016			

Notes

Chapter 3

THE ACCOUNTING FRAMEWORK

AMEENGAGE™ Access **ameengage.com** for integrated resources including tutorials, practice exercises, the digital textbook and more.

LEARNING OUTCOMES

❶ Describe the users of accounting information

❷ Describe the fields of accounting

❸ Compare the different forms of business organization

❹ Discuss the qualitative characteristics of financial information

❺ List and apply basic accounting assumptions and principles

❻ Illustrate the similarities and differences between ASPE and IFRS

❼ Explain the importance of ethics in accounting

Users of Accounting Information

The fundamental objective of accounting is to prepare financial statements that a wide variety of users can use to make decisions. Readers of financial statements rely on accurate information about an organization to make appropriate decisions. Users of accounting information can be divided into two categories.

1. **Internal users**, people who own the business and/or work in the business
2. **External users**, people or organizations outside the business, such as suppliers, banks and external accountants

Internal users rely on financial statements to manage the business efficiently. They assess the business by examining the financial results on a regular basis. To an internal user, financial statements serve the same purpose as a scoreboard does to a sports team.

Typically, external users need financial statements to ensure that their investment in the business is protected, whether they provide loans or supply products or services on credit. If a business is poorly managed or is not operating profitably, external users can decide whether or not to associate themselves with the business. They want to ensure that their loans can be repaid or that they receive a sufficient return on their investment.

There are also indirect external users of financial statements. For example, tax authorities look at the financial statements to ensure that the business is paying the appropriate amount of taxes. Indirect external users include customers and trade unions.

Fields of Accounting

Businesses large and small need **accountants** to ensure that internal and external users have the information they need to make informed decisions. There are two general fields of accounting which focus on the needs of different users: financial accounting and managerial accounting.

Financial Accounting

Financial accounting is concerned with the recordkeeping of the business and preparing the financial statements, similar to what has been discussed so far. Financial accounting serves the decision-making needs of external users of the business. Investors, suppliers, customers, and lenders all use financial accounting information to make decisions. For example, an investor may decide to invest more money into a business that reports growing profits, or a supplier may decide to cut ties with a business that reports low cash flows.

Financial accountants ensure that the information in financial statements (income statement, balance sheet, etc.) is accurate and up-to-date so that users can make informed decisions. Financial accountants may be employees of the business they work for, or they may work for an accounting firm which services many businesses.

Managerial Accounting

Managerial accounting serves the internal users of the business by preparing specialized reports to assist in decision making inside the business. Managerial accountants track and classify costs, prepare and analyze budgets and assist with strategic decision making. Managers and executives use cost reports and budgets generated by managerial accountants to determine whether certain products, services, or business functions are still profitable and how to improve if necessary. Managerial accountants are often employees of the business they work for.

Accounting Designations

An accounting-related education is required to work in the accounting field. Becoming an accounting clerk requires a college diploma, but many accounting positions (financial or managerial) require further specialized education to obtain an accounting certification. Several different accounting certifications recognized in Canada recently merged.

In the past, the major accounting certifications were

- Chartered Accountant (CA)
- Certified General Accountant (CGA)
- Certified Management Accountant (CMA)

These certifications were each governed by separate provincial organizations across Canada. On October 1, 2014, the three designations merged into a single unified designation, the Chartered Professional Accountant (CPA), reducing the number of governing accounting bodies from 40 to 14. The primary reason for this merger was to simplify Canadian accounting communities and allow accounting professionals across the country to more easily understand each other. The unification better serves the public under a strong and globalized brand of one Canadian accounting profession.

Obtaining a CPA designation requires successful completion of the CPA Professional Education Program, a final evaluation exam and the required practical experience.

Accountants may work for a single organization, or they may work in a firm which provides accounting services for many other organizations or individuals. Typical functions that accountants perform include financial statement preparation, tax return preparation, auditing, and consulting.

Forms of Business Organization

So far we have dealt with accounting for sole proprietorships. However, a business could be organized as a partnership, corporation, or a not-for-profit organization. The form of organization is important because that determines the laws and accounting standards that must be adhered to. Each form of organization is discussed in detail below.

Sole Proprietorship

A **sole proprietorship** is owned and generally operated by one owner. A proprietorship is usually a small business, and could provide services such as bookkeeping, gardening, painting or general contracting. Many proprietorships have only a small amount of money invested by the owner. Starting a proprietorship can be an easy process; often it is enough to register a business name and obtain a business licence. The proprietorship will last as  long as the owner wishes to run the business, or as long as the owner is alive. Sole proprietorships are examples of private enterprises because ownership of the business is restricted to one person. A **private enterprise** is any business or organization in which ownership is restricted to a select

group of people. In other words, the general public does not have the ability to acquire ownership of the business.

From an accounting perspective, the financial affairs of the business must be separate from the financial affairs of the owner. For example, the proprietor cannot list personal assets such as the contents of her home on the same statement as the business' assets. From a legal perspective, however, a sole proprietorship is *not* a separate entity from its owner. This means that the assets and liabilities of the business legally belong to the owner, even though the financial activi-

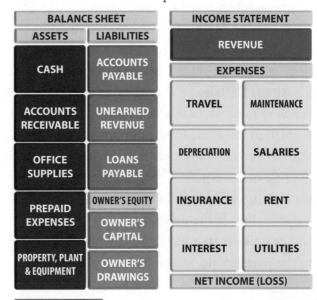

FIGURE 3.1

ties are recorded separately. If the business is unable to pay its debts, creditors of the business can force the owner to sell his or her personal assets to pay the business debts. This is called **unlimited liability**.

In other words, the owner will receive all the net income, suffer any net loss and be personally liable for all financial obligations of the business.

We will be using a proprietorship to illustrate various transactions. Figure 3.1 shows the names of some typical accounts used in a proprietary service business.

A CLOSER LOOK

Often a proprietary business owner incorrectly records business transactions in the same set of records as his personal records. This practice makes it very difficult, if not impossible, to monitor the activities of the business to evaluate its performance.

Consider this scenario: Emilio operates a gardening service and combines all his business and personal records. He also has a job at night to make more money to pay for personal expenses and to finance the gardening business. The gardening business has become very busy and he needs to hire some help and arrange a bank loan to buy more equipment and supplies. By maintaining personal and business records together, Emilio faces the following challenges.

1. He does not know how much the night job and the gardening business are contributing toward his income.

2. By not separating business and personal expenses, he will not know which expenses are being used to generate sales. This is important because business expenses can be tax deductible.

3. He also needs to establish how much is spent to complete each gardening job to help identify the profitability of the business. These expenses could include insurance, gas for the truck, etc.

Before lending money to Emilio, the bank will want to see financial statements to assess if the business is capable of servicing the loan. This will be a problem for Emilio in the current situation.

Partnership

A **partnership** is a business owned by two or more people called partners. As in a proprietorship, the only legal requirements that must be met to start a partnership are registering the business name and obtaining a business licence. To manage a business together, the partners need an oral or a written partnership agreement that sets out how profits and losses are to be shared. Partnerships use the term partners' equity as the title of the equity section on the balance sheet. The  partnership will last as long as the partners continue to run the business, or as long as all partners are still alive. If the partners decide to end the business, they will sell all the partnership's assets and pay all existing liabilities. The remaining cash will be divided among the partners according to the partnership agreement.

Partnerships are private enterprises. A partnership, like a proprietorship, is not legally separated from its owners. Depending on the type of partnership, partners may be subject to unlimited liability, which means that the partners are jointly responsible for all the debts of the partnership. In a partnership, **mutual agency** exists. Mutual agency means that each partner is able to speak for the other partners and bind them to business contracts. In other words, each partner is bound by the business actions of the other partners.

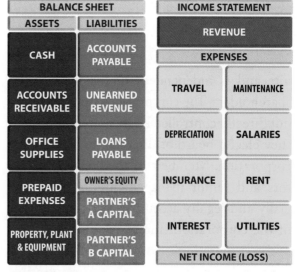

There are three types of partnerships that can be created.

FIGURE 3.2

1. A **general partnership** is a partnership in which all partners are subject to unlimited liability. All partners are considered to be general partners. Unless special provisions are made (as described below), all partnerships are general partnerships.

2. A **limited partnership** includes at least one general partner who accepts unlimited liability and one or more limited partners with liability limited to the amount they invested. All partnerships must have at least one general partner. The limited partners are sometimes referred to as silent partners, because they are not allowed to provide management input for the business.

3. A **limited liability partnership** (LLP) allows partners to have limited liability regarding the misconduct or negligence of the other partners. For example, if a partner in a law firm that is an LLP is sued for misconduct, only the partner in question will be responsible for paying damages. However, all partners remain personally liable for all other debts of the business.

Corporation

A **corporation** is a business that is registered with the provincial or federal government as a separate legal entity from its owners, the shareholders. As a separate legal entity, the corporation has all the rights of a person and is responsible for its own activities and is liable for its own debts. It can enter into contracts and buy and sell products or assets. It can also sue others and be sued.

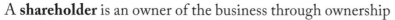

A **shareholder** is an owner of the business through ownership of **shares**. Each share provides partial ownership of the business. For example, if a person owns one share and there are 100 shares available, the person owns 1/100th of the corporation. If a shareholder owns more than 50% of all the shares of a corporation, they can control the business. Shareholders are legally distinct from the business and their financial risk is limited to the amount they have invested in the form of shares. Thus, owners or shareholders have limited liability.

Moreover, the life of a corporation is indefinite and is independent of the lives of the shareholders. The corporation's operations are not directly controlled by its shareholders, but they elect a board of directors to oversee the corporation. Members of the board of directors and senior management can be financially and legally accountable for the actions of the corporation. The behaviour of officers of the corporation is governed by a number of rules including those relating to responsible accounting and cash management.

The balance sheet of a corporation uses the term shareholders' equity for the equity

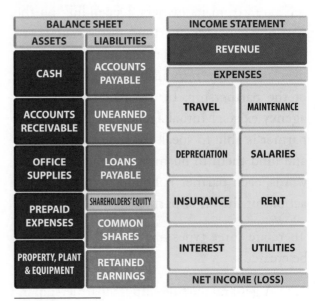

FIGURE 3.3

section, and it is equal to the difference between assets and liabilities, just like a sole proprietorship or partnership. For example, if the assets are worth $100,000 and the liabilities are worth $60,000, the shareholders' equity is equal to $40,000. If the corporation were to sell all its assets for $100,000 and use some of the cash to pay the liabilities of $60,000, the remaining $40,000 cash would represent the shareholders' equity and would belong to the shareholders. If there were two equal shareholders, each one would be paid $20,000. If there were 20 equal shareholders, each would be paid $2,000. In other words, the shareholders' equity is divided among the shareholders in proportion to the number of shares that they own.

Corporations can be set up as either public or private enterprises. A public corporation allows its shares to be sold to anyone in the general public who wishes to buy them. This gives the public corporation access to a large amount of cash to help grow the business. Typically, a public corporation will have thousands of individual shareholders. Stock exchanges such as the Toronto Stock Exchange or the New York Stock Exchange allow buyers and sellers to trade shares of public corporations.

A private corporation does not allow its shares to be sold to just anyone, and often the shares are held by a few individuals. Private corporations are subject to less stringent reporting requirements than public corporations, and private corporations in Canada sometimes receive income tax benefits that are unavailable to public corporations.

The major differences between the three forms of organization are summarized in Figure 3.4.

	Sole Proprietorship	Partnership	Corporation
Title of Owners	Proprietor (One)	Partners (Two or More)	Shareholders (One or More)
Public or Private	Private	Private	Public or Private
Equity Section	Owner's Equity	Partners' Equity	Shareholders' Equity
Owner's Liability	Unlimited	Limited or Unlimited	Limited

FIGURE 3.4

Not-for-Profit Organizations

Unlike regular businesses, profits made by **not-for-profit organizations** are paid out (redistributed) to the community by providing services. While the primary objective of other forms of organization is to maximize profits, not-for-profit organizations aim to improve society in some way. They usually obtain funding from donations and government grants. Not-for-profit organizations include religious organizations, community care centres, charitable organizations and hospitals. They do not have an identifiable owner but require financial statements because they are accountable to donors, sponsors, lenders, tax authorities, etc.

Accounting records provide key information pertaining to the activities of not-for-profit organizations, enabling them to operate as permitted. This textbook will not focus on not-for-profit organizations.

The Conceptual Framework of Accounting

Imagine a hockey or a football game with no rules or consistent method to keep score. The players and spectators would quickly become frustrated because of the lack of consistency. By having rules to follow and a consistent method to keep score, players know how to play the game and spectators know what to expect as they watch.

Accounting in a business is similar. If there were no rules to follow, business owners and accountants could make up rules regarding what to report. External users would find the reports to be unreliable and inconsistent. Thus, the accounting profession has created standards which provide guidance on how financial information should be reported. These standards are commonly referred to as **generally accepted accounting principles (GAAP)**.

In Canada, the Accounting Standards Board (AcSB) is responsible for setting accounting standards. In the past, Canadian GAAP was used as the standard for all companies in Canada. However, in recent years, there has been recognition of the different reporting needs of public companies and private companies. Therefore, the AcSB decided that Canadian businesses must adhere to one of two sets of standards, depending on the form of the organization.

Public enterprises must prepare financial information in accordance with the **International Financial Reporting Standards (IFRS)**. IFRS was developed by the International Accounting Standards Board (IASB) and is used globally.

Private enterprises may choose to adhere to IFRS, or may follow the **Accounting Standards for Private Enterprises (ASPE)**, developed by the AcSB. These standards are less complex and are used only by private companies in Canada.

Both ASPE and IFRS conform to an underlying **conceptual framework**. This framework forms the basis to determine how business transactions should be measured and reported. It ensures the external users (e.g. shareholders) have the most consistent, reliable and useful information when reviewing a company's financial reports. Although it is not possible to create a specific rule for every situation, the principles under the conceptual framework allow accountants to make appropriate decisions under different circumstances. This is referred to as **principles-based accounting**. In other words, ASPE and IFRS are designed as guidelines and accountants are allowed to flexibly apply these standards when preparing financial information. On the other hand, under **rules-based accounting**, the accounting standards are stated as a list of specific, detailed rules that must be followed when preparing financial information. To apply these rules, accountants have little room to make their own judgments. Not every country adopts principles-based accounting. For example, U.S. GAAP is primarily rules-based.

Next, we will examine the important characteristics, assumptions, and principles that form the conceptual framework of accounting. Figure 3.5 illustrates the framework.

The Conceptual Framework of Accounting

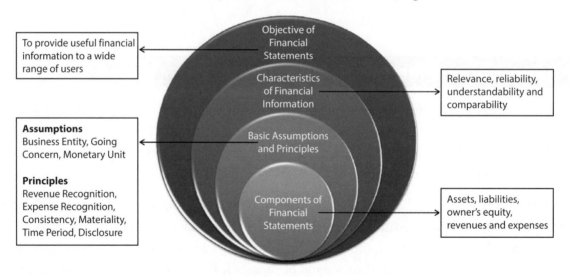

FIGURE 3.5

The fundamental objective of financial reporting is to provide useful and complete information to the users. However, an underlying constraint in the accounting framework is the **cost constraint**. It ensures that the value of reported financial information outweighs the costs incurred to report it, even if the information would improve the accuracy and completeness of the financial statements. For example, a company may find some information that is not required by accounting standards to be somewhat useful, however it is costly to prepare. If the value of this information does not outweigh the costs, the company should not prepare it.

Qualitative Characteristics of Financial Information

There are fundamental characteristics in the accounting framework upon which accounting standards are based. These characteristics form the foundation of the conceptual framework and define how information should be presented in financial statements. For financial statements to be effective, financial information should be relevant, reliable, understandable, and comparable.

Relevance

Relevance means that all information useful for decision making is present in the financial statements. Information is relevant if it helps users predict future performance or confirms previous predictions. For example, if an investor wants to predict the future cash flows of a company, and the company deliberately avoided reporting a bank loan, the investor would not understand the company's debt correctly. Therefore, the investor would not be able to accurately predict the company's interest expenses and available cash flow. This means the balance of the bank loan would be considered relevant financial information.

Another component of relevance is **timeliness**. Information is timely if there is no delay in reporting crucial information. To be useful to a decision maker, information must be received before it is no longer able to influence decisions. For instance, a business owner may prefer to have monthly statements prepared to help monitor the company's performance. If the business only prepares annual statements, the information may be available too late to correct problems with the company.

Reliability

Reliability means that information is free from significant error and bias. In other words, different independent people looking at the evidence will arrive at the same values. The activities that a business records must be based on objective evidence. A component of reliability is **verifiability**. For example, if a company records an expense transaction in its financial records, an invoice must be provided to back it up (i.e. the expense can be verified).

Another component of reliability is **conservatism**. Whenever an accountant needs to exercise their own interpretation or judgment in applying an accounting standard and has several options, the least optimistic option should be selected. In other words, the accountant should choose the option that results in a lower balance of assets, lower net income or a higher balance of debt.

Reliability also relies on the **representational faithfulness** of the information. This means that transactions must be presented as their true economic substance rather than their legal form. For example, a company that leases a machine for its entire useful life may list the machine as an asset even though it does not legally own the machine.

The concept of **neutrality** also states that financial information must be free from bias. Bias occurs when the information is influenced by the interests of particular users. For example, managers may be tempted to report higher sales and profit figures if they are paid a bonus based on the success of their department.

Understandability

Understandability means that the financial information can be reasonably understood by its users if the users have knowledge of the business and a basic knowledge of accounting. To be understandable, companies often include notes in the financial statements to explain many of the numbers, especially those that are based on company policy. For example, details of long-term debt such as the principal, interest rate and term would be outlined in the notes.

Comparability

Comparability means that the financial statements of a company must be prepared in a similar way year after year. The accounting policies used should be consistent to prevent misconceptions. This allows a comparison of this year's performance to past years. By comparing yearly statements, users can identify trends in the company's financial position and performance. For example, an investor may be interested in observing the change in a company's debt balance from one year to the next to see if the company incurred additional debt or was able to pay off its creditors. The financial information should also be comparable between companies.

Trade-Offs of Qualitative Characteristics

As discussed, accounting standards dictate that financial information should be relevant, reliable, understandable and comparable. However, sometimes it is difficult to fully represent all of these characteristics. There could be a trade-off among some of the characteristics. A trade-off is an exchange of part of one characteristic for part of another.

A frequently discussed trade-off is the one between relevance and reliability. For information to be relevant, it needs to be timely. For example, presenting information that is a few years old on today's financial statements is likely not very relevant. However, reliable information often requires time to gather.

Suppose that a company chooses to prepare financial statements on a monthly basis instead of on a quarterly or semi-annual basis. In this case, the financial statements are very timely and relevant. However, some reliability may be given up since there is less time for the accounting staff to scrutinize and make necessary adjustments to the monthly financial figures. If the financial statements were less frequent (such as quarterly or semi-annually), the accounting staff can allocate more time to verify the accuracy and effectiveness of the statements.

Basic Assumptions and Principles

The conceptual framework of accounting also includes several basic accounting assumptions and principles. Accountants must use their judgment to ensure that these assumptions and principles are met by all of the financial information presented by the business.

Assumptions

There are three basic assumptions underlying all accounting information that is prepared in accordance with either ASPE or IFRS. These assumptions are necessary for users to rely on the information presented.

The **business entity assumption** states that accounting for a business must be kept separate from the personal affairs of its owner or any other business. The owner of a business cannot record personal transactions on the income statement or the balance sheet of the business. The financial statements of the business must reflect the financial position of the business alone. Any personal expenses of the owner are charged to the owner and are not allowed to affect the operating results of the business. Financial statements of a business can be assumed to only contain items that pertain to the business.

The **going concern assumption** assumes that a business will continue to operate into the foreseeable future. Determining the value of the assets belonging to a business that is alive and well is not complicated. For example, items such as property, plant and equipment are listed on the balance sheet at their cost, or original purchase price. However, if an accountant deems that the business will not be able to continue operating into the foreseeable future, the balance sheet must instead show the value for which the property, plant and equipment could realistically be sold. When a company is going out of business, the value of the assets usually suffers because they have to be sold under unfavourable circumstances. Companies at risk of going out of business must include this information in the notes to their financial statements.

The **monetary unit assumption** requires that accounting records are expressed in terms of money. Accounting records should all be reported in a single currency, such as Canadian dollars or euros. This allows accountants to assign monetary values to business events. For instance, suppose that a company hires a salesman. The event of officially hiring the employee is not reflected in the company's accounting records since a value cannot be easily assigned to the event (i.e. expressed in terms of money). However, over time, the financial impact of the hiring will be evident (e.g. recognizing the salary expense for the salesman and realizing an increase in sales). Furthermore, it is also assumed that the unit of measure used in the accounting records remains fairly constant over time and that transactions can be measured relevantly in current monetary units. That is, inflation (a rise in prices) or deflation (a drop in prices) is ignored when comparing dollars of different years.

Principles

The following section will outline some of the basic accounting principles outlined by the conceptual framework of accounting. Accountants may need to use their professional judgment from time to time to apply these principles. The judgments must be in line with the objective of financial reporting and provide the most useful information for the users.

The **time period concept** requires that accounting takes place over specific time periods known as fiscal periods. These fiscal periods are of equal length, and are used when measuring the financial progress of a business.

Measurement is the process of determining the amount at which an item is recorded in the financial statements. Primarily, items must be recorded at their historical cost. This is sometimes referred to as the cost principle. In almost all cases, the historical cost is the amount that appears on the source document for the transaction. If the owner purchased office furniture on sale for $5,000, but knew the furniture was actually worth $7,000 (the price before the sale), the furniture would be recorded as $5,000, as shown on the receipt. There are times when the historical cost of an item is not appropriate. For example, a building could be received as a gift. In such a case, the transaction would be recorded at fair market value, which must be determined by some independent means.

Revenue recognition states that revenue can only be recorded (recognized) when goods are sold or when services are performed. This means that the item sold must be transferred to the buyer and the buyer has agreed to pay, or has already paid the price for the item. If the transaction involves a large project such as building a dam, it may take a construction company a number of years to complete. The construction company does not usually wait until the project is entirely completed before it recognizes the revenue. Periodically, it bills for work completed and recognizes revenue for the work completed since the last bill was sent.

Expense recognition states that an expense must be recorded in the same accounting period in which it was used to produce revenue. For example, suppose a manufacturing business spent $20,000 to produce 1,000 units of inventory in the current accounting period. If 500 units are sold in each of the following two accounting periods, $10,000 would be expensed in each period. This concept is commonly referred to as the "matching principle" because expenses must be matched to the same period as the revenue that they helped to generate. If an expense cannot be tied to revenue, then it should be recorded in the current period.

Consistency prevents businesses from changing accounting methods for the sole purpose of manipulating figures on the financial statements. Accountants must apply the same methods and policies from period to period. For example, a merchandising business must have a method to assign values to its products and use the same method from year to year. When a method changes from one period to another, the change must be clearly explained in the financial statements. The readers of financial statements have the right to assume that consistency has been applied if there is no statement to the contrary.

Materiality refers to the significance of information to users. A piece of information is considered material if it could influence or change a user's decision. Material amounts must be recorded correctly on financial statements. For example, suppose a company paid cash for $100 worth of office supplies. The supplies could be recorded as an asset and expensed as they are used, or they can simply be expensed immediately. While recording them as an asset is more accurate, it is also more complex and more costly to account for. Is this $100 a material amount? It depends on the size of the company and the judgment of the accountant. If the company typically lists more than $100,000 in assets, the $100 is not likely to affect any user's decision and is therefore immaterial. On the other hand, if the company typically lists total assets of $1,000, the treatment of $100 in office supplies may impact the decision of an investor.

Disclosure states that any and all information that affects the full understanding of a company's financial statements must be included with the financial statements. Some items may not affect the accounting records directly. These items would be included in the notes accompanying the statements. Examples of such items are outstanding lawsuits, tax disputes and company takeovers.

ASPE or IFRS?

Although both ASPE and IFRS have very similar accounting frameworks, the decision of choosing which to implement is an important one. Public companies do not have a choice and must report accounting information under IFRS. Advantages of IFRS include allowing for better comparability among and more streamlined reporting of multinational corporations.

On the other hand, IFRS can be costly to implement and is generally more rigorous in its reporting requirements than ASPE.

Private companies in Canada have a choice of whether to implement ASPE or IFRS. If the company plans to become a public corporation at some point in the future, it would be better to implement IFRS now rather than needing to switch from ASPE to IFRS later. If there are no plans to become a public corporation, then ASPE is likely the best choice because it is easier to implement and maintain. See Figure 3.7 for a more detailed comparison of ASPE and IFRS.

ASPE	IFRS
When to Use • Private organization (sole proprietorship, partnership, private corporation) • No plans to become public in the near future • Competitors also use ASPE	When to Use • Public corporation or owned by a public company • Private organization has plans to become public in the near future • Competitors have already adopted IFRS • Private enterprises can elect to use IFRS
Advantages • Less costly and simpler to implement • Fewer disclosures are required	Advantages • More relevant, reliable and comparable on a global scale • Long-term accounting standards
Disadvantages • Banks may require statements to conform to IFRS before offering a loan • ASPE may eventually evolve into IFRS in the future	Disadvantages • Can be costly to implement • Fewer hard-and-fast rules; more judgments required • More disclosures are required

FIGURE 3.7

Ethics of Accounting

Users place significant trust in the accuracy of financial records to enable them to make sensible decisions regarding a business. It is an accountant's responsibility to ensure that the financial status of the business is accurately reported. The standards by which these actions are judged as being honest versus dishonest, right or wrong, fair or unfair, are also known as **accounting ethics**.

Professional accounting bodies have strict rules governing the behaviour of their members. Some cases have resulted in jail sentences for violating these rules. Two of the most infamous examples are Enron and Worldcom. The senior executives of these companies were found guilty of various offences, including using company funds for their own personal use, and covering up certain negative financial information.

Typical ethical standards for accountants state that

- Members shall act with trustworthiness, integrity and objectivity.

- Members shall not participate in any activity or provide services to any company that the member, or a reasonably prudent person, would believe to be unlawful.

- Members shall not engage in a discriminatory practice on prohibited grounds for discrimination, as those terms are defined in the Canadian Human Rights Act.

- Members shall not criticize another professional colleague without first submitting this criticism to that colleague for explanation.

- Members shall act in the interest of their clients, employers, and interested third parties, and shall be prepared to sacrifice their self-interest to do so. Members shall honour the trust bestowed upon them by others, and shall not use their privileged position without their principal's knowledge and consent. Members shall avoid conflicts of interest.

- Members shall not disclose or use any confidential information concerning the affairs of any client, former client, employer or former employer.

- Members shall, when engaged to audit or review financial statements or other information, be free of any influence, interest or relationship with respect to the client's affairs, which impairs the member's professional judgment or objectivity, or which, in the view of a reasonable observer, may have that effect.

- Members shall not, without an employer's or client's consent, use confidential information relating to the business of the member's employer or client to directly or indirectly obtain a personal advantage. Members shall not take any action, such as acquiring any interest, property or benefit, that is for unauthorized use, or is confidential relating to an employer's or client's affairs, based on information obtained in the course of his or her duties.

- Members shall strive to continually upgrade and develop their technical knowledge and skills in the areas in which they practice as professionals. This technical expertise shall be employed with due professional care and judgment.

- Members shall adhere to acknowledged principles and standards of professional practice.

- Members shall not be associated with any information that the member knows, or ought to know, to be false or misleading, whether by statement or omission.

- Members shall always act in accordance with the duties and responsibilities associated with being members of the profession, and shall work in a manner that will enhance the image of the profession and the association.

Some of the common concerns about ethics in a business are issues related to

- cash discounts
- operation of a petty cash fund
- manipulation of expenses to manage earnings
- trading a company's shares based on insider information (insider trading)

There is often a fine line between the law and ethics. A behaviour can be quite legal, but unethical. For example, a manager may employ his nephew in the company where he is working. He decides to pay his nephew a higher salary than others in a similar position in the business. While this practice may not be illegal, it could be considered unethical. Many organizations create their own set of rules pertaining to ethics and morals.

AMEENGAGE™ Access **ameengage.com** for integrated resources including tutorials, practice exercises, the digital textbook and more.

In Summary

Describe the users of accounting information

↪ Internal users include owners and employees of the business. They use accounting information to make internal strategic decisions regarding products, services, and business departments.

↪ External users include investors, suppliers, lenders, and customers of the business. Financial statements help these users make important business decisions.

Describe the fields of accounting

↪ Financial accounting serves the needs of external users by preparing financial statements.

↪ Managerial accounting provides valuable information to internal users to make decisions regarding the future of the business.

Compare the different forms of organization

↪ A small business that is owned by one person is generally structured in the form of a sole proprietorship. Sole proprietorships are private enterprises.

↪ A partnership is a business owned by two or more persons operating under a partnership agreement. Partnerships are private enterprises.

↪ A corporation is a business that is registered with the provincial or federal government and sells ownership of the company to individuals in the form of shares. Corporations may be private or public.

↪ Sole proprietorships and partnerships are subject to unlimited liability, which means that one or more owners are personally and legally accountable for the liabilities of the business. Corporations (both private and public) are subject to limited liability, which means that their risk is limited to their monetary investment in the business.

↪ Unlike other businesses, profits made by not-for-profit organizations may be paid out (redistributed) to the community by providing services.

Identify the qualitative characteristics of financial information

↪ The four qualitative characteristics of financial information are relevance, reliability, understandability, and comparability.

↪ Accountants may face a trade-off between two or more characteristics (e.g. relevance and reliability).

List and apply basic accounting assumptions and principles

↪ The assumptions of the accounting framework are the business entity, going concern, and monetary unit assumptions.

⇨ The basic principles of the accounting framework are revenue recognition, expense recognition, consistency, materiality, time period concept, and disclosure.

Illustrate the similarities and differences between ASPE and IFRS

⇨ Both ASPE and IFRS are principles-based standards used in Canada. Many of the principles in the two sets of standards are very similar.

⇨ ASPE requires fewer disclosures and is used only in Canada. Private enterprises in Canada have a choice whether to use ASPE or IFRS.

⇨ IFRS has more disclosure requirements and is used globally. Public enterprises are required to use IFRS.

Explain the importance of ethics in accounting

⇨ Accountants must adhere to a high standard of ethics to ensure that the financial information of a business is accurately reported.

⇨ All of a business' users rely on this information to make decisions.

Review Exercise

Hollinger Runners Inc. (HRI) is a publicly traded manufacturer of high quality, stylish sneakers with hundreds of shareholders. The company has been in business for more than 20 years and has experienced good and bad economic times. The company's financial performance has usually been aligned with the state of the economy. Lately the economy has been booming.

The company has a year-end of April 30. It is now May 31, 2016. HRI produces financial statements on an annual basis. The company's accountant has prepared the balance sheet as at April 30, 2016 using ASPE. A portion of this balance sheet (i.e. the assets portion) is shown below.

Hollinger Runners Inc.
Balance Sheet
As at April 30, 2016

	2016	2015
ASSETS		
	(in thousands)	
Current Assets		
Cash	10	500
Accounts receivable	10	140
Inventory	5	120
Other current assets	60	70
Total Current Assets	85	830
Long-Term Assets		
Available-for-sale investments	60	65
Property, plant and equipment	1,210	2,120
Goodwill	40	50
Total Long-Term Assets	1,310	2,235
TOTAL ASSETS	1,395	3,065

On May 1, 2015, the company changed the location of its headquarters from Europe to Canada. Therefore, the 2015 column in the balance sheet is presented in the currency unit of euros and the 2016 column is presented in Canadian dollars. The company did not disclose this information in the notes to the financial statements. The euro was much stronger than the Canadian dollar during 2015 and 2016.

Additional information regarding HRI's financial statements and accounting records is shown below.

- HRI indicated in the notes to the financial statements that in 2016 it changed the accounting policy it used for depreciating assets. However, it did not justify its reason for doing so.

- The cash account is comprised of two sub-accounts: cash related to the business and personal cash savings of a few of the shareholders.

- Purchases have all been valued at fair market value at the year-end date.

- Regarding expenses, there are numerous invoices which did not match the cost amounts reported in the accounting records. The amounts on the invoices are significantly greater than the amounts in the accounting records.

- The company's income statement has shown a significant net loss for the past three years.

See Appendix I for solutions.

Part 1

Which of the four fundamental characteristics of financial information has HRI failed to apply? Explain.

Part 2

Which of the basic accounting principles and/or assumptions has HRI violated? Explain.

_____

_____

_____

_____

_____

_____

_____

_____

_____

_____

_____

_____

_____

_____

_____

_____

_____

_____

_____

_____

Notes

Chapter 4

THE ACCOUNTING CYCLE: JOURNALS AND LEDGERS

LEARNING OUTCOMES

❶ Distinguish between debits and credits

❷ Describe the accounting cycle

❸ Explain how to analyze a transaction

❹ Record transactions in the general journal

❺ Post journal entries to the general ledger

❻ Prepare a trial balance

AMEENGAGE™ *Access **ameengage.com** for integrated resources including tutorials, practice exercises, the digital textbook and more.*

Transition to Debits and Credits

We have been using the terms increase and decrease to record transactions in T-accounts, but formal accounting requires the use of debits and credits. In the debit and credit system (unlike increases and decreases), a **debit** is always recorded on the left-hand side of an account and a **credit** is always recorded on the right-hand side. DR represents debits and CR represents credits.

Debit DR	Credit CR

Remember that debit and credit do not always mean increase or decrease. A credit means an entry on the right side of the account, and it may cause the account to increase or decrease, depending on the type of account it is. Similarly, a debit means an entry on the left side of the account and it may cause the account to increase or decrease, depending on the type of account it is. Remember, the accounting equation is

WORTH REPEATING

In accounting, there are always at least two parts to a transaction. For each transaction, the total value of debits equals the total value of credits. This is known as **double entry**.

Assets = Liabilities + Owner's Equity

For the accounting equation to be correct and for the balance sheet to stay in balance, the total value of the debits must always equal the total value of the credits. Use the Debit and Credit Reference Guide shown in Figure 4.1 to help when analyzing transactions.

Debit and Credit Reference Guide

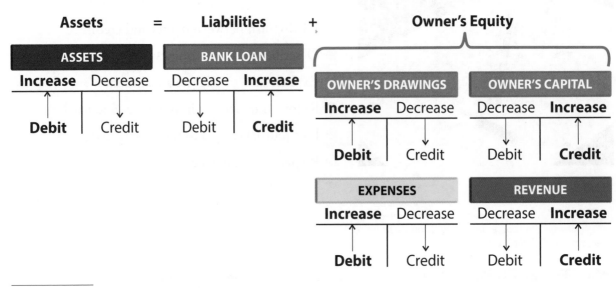

FIGURE 4.1

Every transaction will have at least one debit and one credit. The total of all debits in a transaction must equal the total of all credits. If debits do not equal credits, the accounting equation will not balance.

Each type of account also has a normal balance. A **normal balance** will correspond to the side of the T-account that records the increase and is shown in bold in Figure 4.1. A normal balance indicates a positive balance for the account. For instance, the cash account (an asset) has a debit normal balance.

Using the Debit and Credit Reference Guide, let us look at a few sample transactions and see how to translate increases and decreases into debits and credits.

1.   Provided services to a customer who pays cash.

2.   Paid cash to reduce the principal of the bank loan.

3.   Paid cash for a one-year insurance policy.

4.   Record maintenance expense, which will be paid later.

These transactions are summarized in a table and illustrated in T-accounts in Figure 4.2.

1.	Cash	Increase	Debit
	Service Revenue	Increase	Credit

CASH
↑ Debit

SERVICE REVENUE
↑ Credit

2.	Bank Loan	Decrease	Debit
	Cash	Decrease	Credit

BANK LOAN
↓ Debit

CASH
↓ Credit

3.	Prepaid Insurance	Increase	Debit
	Cash	Decrease	Credit

PREPAID INSURANCE
↑ Debit

CASH
↓ Credit

4.	Maintenance Expense	Increase	Debit
	Accounts Payable	Increase	Credit

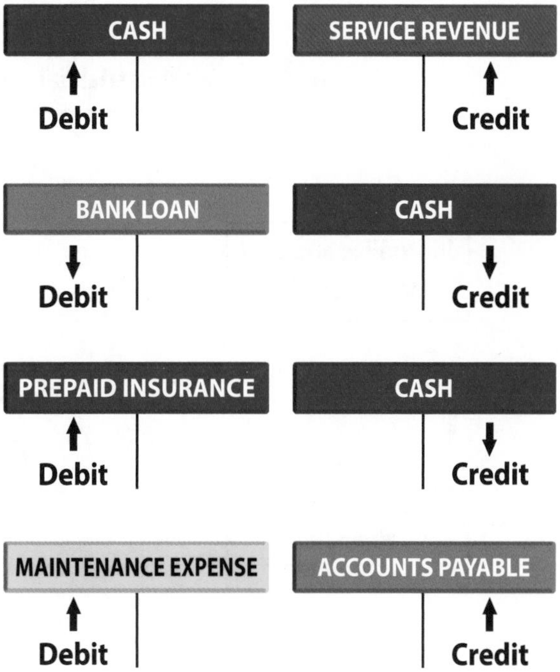

MAINTENANCE EXPENSE
↑ Debit

ACCOUNTS PAYABLE
↑ Credit

FIGURE 4.2

The Accounting Cycle

As discussed in the previous chapter, the purpose of accounting is to prepare financial statements which help users to make informed decisions. There are many transactions during an accounting period and it is important to summarize them all within the financial statements. The framework to make sure this is done properly is called the accounting cycle.

The **accounting cycle** refers to the steps required to complete the financial statements. Businesses prepare financial statements at the end of each accounting period, whether it is a month, quarter, year, etc. Every period, the cycle repeats. Over the next three chapters, the accounting cycle will be illustrated using a monthly period for a sample company.

Figure 4.3 shows the steps required to generate a formal set of financial statements for a given period. A computerized system will either perform most of these steps automatically or have them available immediately, while a manual system requires each step to be completed by hand. The first three steps (in blue) are performed repeatedly during the accounting period while the remaining steps are all completed at the end of the current period and prepare the accounts for the next period. This chapter will cover the first four steps of the accounting cycle.

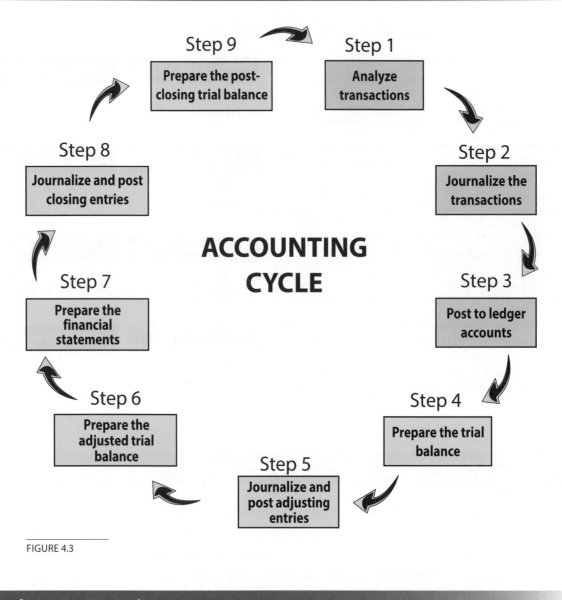

FIGURE 4.3

Analyze Transactions

The first part of the accounting cycle is to gather and analyze what must be recorded as transactions. All transactions must have **source documents** or evidence that they actually happened. Source documents can include sales receipts, bills, cheques, bank statements, etc.

As discussed earlier we must determine which accounts will be affected, what parts of the accounting equation the accounts belong to and identify whether these accounts will increase or decrease as a result of this transaction. The extra step now is to match the increase or decrease of each account with a debit or credit entry to the account. Use the Debit and Credit Reference Guide in Figure 4.1 to help with this.

For example, suppose you pay a $100 utility bill with cash. To analyze this, first determine which accounts will be affected. In this example, the accounts would be utilities expense and cash. Now, for each account, answer the following questions

- What category does the account belong to?
- Is the account increasing or decreasing?
- Is the increase or decrease a debit or credit?

The full analysis for the transaction is shown in the table below. It is important to note that the analysis is just to determine whether the account will be debited or credited. At this point, which account is analyzed first is irrelevant. Later, in step two of the accounting cycle, we will record the accounts in a standardized format.

Which accounts will be affected?	Utilities Expense	Cash
What category does the account belong to?	Expense	Asset
Is the account increasing or decreasing?	Increasing	Decreasing
Is the increase or decrease a debit or credit? (Use the Debit and Credit Reference Guide)	Debit	Credit

From this analysis, we can illustrate how the accounts would be affected. Notice in Figure 4.4 that utilities expense increases with a debit and cash decreases with a credit.

This type of analysis can be done for any transaction. Keep this in mind as you progress and come across new accounts and new types of transactions. To help you analyze how increases and decreases translate into debits and credits, consider these common transactions

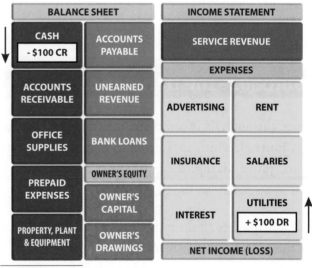

FIGURE 4.4

1. Provided consulting services for a customer for cash.
2. Received a bill for advertising, which will be paid later.
3. Received cash from a customer for work to be completed next month.
4. Paid cash toward the principal of a bank loan.
5. Prepaid cash for four months' rent.
6. Purchased office furniture with cash.
7. Provided consulting services to a customer on account.
8. Paid cash toward the advertising bill received in transaction 2.
9. A customer paid an amount they owed.

Using the steps illustrated above on these transactions, we can create a table to determine which accounts will be debited and credited. The table for the nine transactions are shown in Figure 4.5.

	Account Name	Category	Increase or Decrease	Debit or Credit
1	Cash Service Revenue	Asset Revenue	Increase Increase	Debit Credit
2	Advertising Expense Accounts Payable	Expense Liability	Increase Increase	Debit Credit
3	Cash Unearned Revenue	Asset Liability	Increase Increase	Debit Credit
4	Bank Loan Cash	Liability Asset	Decrease Decrease	Debit Credit
5	Prepaid Rent Cash	Asset Asset	Increase Decrease	Debit Credit
6	Furniture Cash	Asset Asset	Increase Decrease	Debit Credit
7	Accounts Receivable Service Revenue	Asset Revenue	Increase Increase	Debit Credit
8	Accounts Payable Cash	Liability Asset	Decrease Decrease	Debit Credit
9	Cash Accounts Receivable	Asset Asset	Increase Decrease	Debit Credit

FIGURE 4.5

Journalize the Transaction

Once the analysis is complete, the transaction must be recorded. The transaction will be recorded in a **journal**, which is referred to as a book of original entry. The act of recording in the journal is called **journalizing**. There are various journals available for a company to use, but at this point we will focus solely on the **general journal**.

The journal lists all the transactions of the business in one place and in chronological order. Keeping all transactions in one place makes them easier to follow and makes it easier to trace any mistakes, compared to only recording them in T-accounts.

As an example, consider a business called MP Consulting, owned by Mark Parish. Mark runs the business as a sole proprietorship and provides financial consulting to his clients. On January 2, 2016 he completed some work for a client and the client paid $1,500 cash. Our analysis indicates that cash should be debited and service revenue should be credited. Figure 4.6 on the next page shows how this would be recorded in the journal. The circled numbers explain how to properly create a journal entry.

JOURNAL				Page 1
❶ Date	**Account Titles and Explanation ❷**	**PR ❸**	**Debit ❹**	**Credit**
2016				
Jan 2	Cash ❷ⓐ		1,500	
	Service Revenue ❷ⓑ			1,500
	Completed work for client ❷ⓒ			
	❺			

FIGURE 4.6

❶ Date

The date column includes the current year at the top of the column, followed by the month and day of the transaction. The journal entries are entered in chronological order.

❷ Account Titles and Explanation

This column indicates the names of the accounts being affected. The logic you have been using to indicate the accounts to be used has not changed. For example, if revenue is being earned and cash is received, cash will increase (debit) and service revenue will increase (credit). The journal merely places this information in a standard order to keep information organized.

❷ⓐ   Any accounts that will be debited in the transaction will be listed first.

❷ⓑ   Any accounts that will be credited in the transaction will be listed after the debited accounts and indented slightly. This is a formatting standard which makes it easier to read long lists of transactions.

❷ⓒ   A brief explanation will be listed immediately after the transaction.

If you are given a list of accounts to choose from, use accounts from that list. If you are not provided with a list, use an appropriate name that accurately describes what the account is tracking. For example, repairs performed in the office may be called Repairs Expense, Maintenance Expense or Repairs & Maintenance Expense. However once an account name has been used, the same name should be used for all similar transactions.

❸ PR (Posting Reference)

The posting reference column is initially left blank when the journal entry is prepared. We will use this column when we start the third step of the accounting cycle, posting to the ledger accounts.

❹ Debit or Credit

These two columns are used to record the amount of the transaction in the appropriate side—debit or credit.

❺   Leave a space between journal entries to make it easier to read and separate them.

If a journal entry only affects two accounts, one account will be debited and one account will be credited. This type of entry is fairly straightforward to complete. However, some journal entries may affect three or more accounts. These entries are called **compound journal entries** and will have multiple debits or multiple credits.

To illustrate a compound journal entry, suppose you purchase equipment for $5,000 on May 25. You will pay $1,000 cash at the time of the purchase, but will not pay the remainder until sometime later (accounts payable). This transaction will increase equipment, increase accounts payable and decrease cash. The journal entry is illustrated in Figure 4.7 below.

JOURNAL					Page 1
Date 2016	**Account Titles and Explanation**		**PR**	**Debit**	**Credit**
May 25	Equipment			5,000	
	Accounts Payable				4,000
	Cash				1,000
	Purchased equipment				

FIGURE 4.7

Post to Ledger Accounts

Although all the activities for the month have been recorded in the general journal, the ending balance for each account has not yet been determined. For example, there may have been several transactions relating to cash. To calculate the closing cash balance, the accounts need to be sorted into a manageable format where all transactions affecting that account will be recorded.

The **general ledger** organizes the accounts used by the business. Each account is given a unique number to help identify it and is assigned a separate page to track the balance of the account. The list of all the accounts in the general ledger is called a **chart of accounts**. Combined with the journal introduced in the previous section, the journal and ledger can be referred to as the books of the business.

To set up a chart of accounts, first define the various accounts to be used by the business and then give each account an identifying number. For small businesses, three-digit account numbers may be sufficient, although more digits allow for new accounts to be added as the business grows. Large organizations may have thousands of accounts and require longer account numbers.

It is important to assign account numbers in a logical manner and to follow specific industry standards. One example of a numbering system is

Account Numbering
100–199: **Asset** accounts
200–299: **Liability** accounts
300–399: **Equity** accounts
400–499: **Revenue** accounts
500–599: Expense accounts

Separating each account by several numbers will allow new accounts to be added while maintaining the same logical order. Note that the account numbering follows the order of the financial statements: balance sheet (assets, liabilities and equity); income statement (revenue and expenses).

Different types of businesses utilize different types of accounts. For example, a manufacturing business will require various accounts for reporting manufacturing costs. A retail business, however, will have accounts for the purchase of inventory.

Figure 4.8 shows how a service company may set up its accounts. Some of the accounts listed here will be introduced in later chapters. Other accounts can be set up as needed. For example, if the business has more than one bank account, the chart of accounts would include an account for each bank account.

Account Description	Account #		Account Description	Account #
ASSETS			**REVENUE**	
Cash	101		Service Revenue	400
Accounts Receivable	105			
Prepaid Insurance	110		**EXPENSES**	
Office Supplies	115		Advertising Expense	500
Equipment	120		Bad Debt Expense	505
Accumulated Depreciation	125		Depreciation Expense	510
			Insurance Expense	515
LIABILITIES			Interest Expense	520
Accounts Payable	200		Maintenance Expense	525
Interest Payable	205		Office Supplies Expense	530
Unearned Revenue	210		Professional Fees Expense	535
Bank Loan	215		Rent Expense	540
			Salaries Expense	545
OWNER'S EQUITY			Telephone Expense	550
Owner's Capital	300		Travel Expense	555
Owner's Drawings	310			
Income Summary	315			

FIGURE 4.8

Each of the accounts listed above will have its own ledger account. Think of the ledger as an expanded T-account. In Figure 4.9, notice the red "T" under the debit and credit columns. This is shown to illustrate its similarity to the T-accounts you have been working with.

Account: Cash					GL No. 101	
Date	Description	PR	DR	CR	Balance	

FIGURE 4.9

Each entry in the journal must be posted to the appropriate ledger account. To maintain up-to-date records, posting to the ledger accounts should be completed regularly, whether daily, weekly or monthly. The posting of the first journal entry to the general ledger is completed in Figure 4.10. The cash account has an opening balance of $3,000.

JOURNAL   **PAGE 1**

Date 2016	Account Titles and Explanation	PR	Debit	Credit
Jan 2	Cash	101 	1,500	
	Service Revenue	400		1,500
	Completed work for client			

Account: Cash					GL No. 101	
Date	**Description**	**PR**	**DR**	**CR**	**Balance**	
2016						
Jan 1	Opening Balance				3,000	DR
❶ Jan 2	❷	❸ J1	❹ 1,500		❺ 4,500	DR

Account: Service Revenue					GL. No. 400	
Date	**Description**	**PR**	**DR**	**CR**	**Balance**	
2016						
Jan 2		J1		1,500	1,500	CR

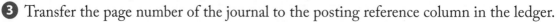

❼

FIGURE 4.10

There are a number of steps to complete when posting items from the journal to the general ledger.

❶ Transfer the date of the transaction.

❷ The description in the ledger does not have to be completed for every transaction, provided you have a description already recorded in the journal.

❸ Transfer the page number of the journal to the posting reference column in the ledger.

❹ Enter the transaction amount into the appropriate debit or credit column.

❺ Calculate the new account balance (i.e. the ending, or closing balance). Increase and decrease the previous balance according to the debit and credit rules in Figure 4.1.

6 Enter the ledger number into the posting reference in the journal as a checking process once the amount has been posted.

7 Repeat the steps for all lines in the journal entry.

IN THE REAL WORLD

Accounting software such as QuickBooks® and Sage automatically perform the functions of double entries. For example, assume that a cash payment is received by the company and the user defines the payment as a payment for services or goods provided. The user is usually the company's bookkeeper or accountant. The software will automatically realize that an asset account must be debited and the revenue account must be credited. After the entry is journalized by the software, the amounts are automatically posted to the general ledger and the trial balance. There is a significant level of automation provided by accounting software, which can reduce the number of accounting errors and misstatements if used correctly.

It is good practice to double check that the balance shown in the ledger for each account is a normal balance (e.g. cash is an asset and assets have a debit normal balance). If an account does not have a normal balance, this may indicate that an error has occurred. Double check that the balance was calculated correctly, the amount in the ledger was correctly copied from the journal and the journal entry was created correctly.

In the modern accounting system, the posting process is automatically done by the computer system. Accountants no longer need to refer to a specific page in the journal book to look for transactions.

Return to Mark Parish's company, MP Consulting, to see how a full set of journals would be prepared and posted to the ledger accounts. First examine the opening balances of the company from the previous period's balance sheet in Figure 4.11.

MP Consulting Balance Sheet As at December 31, 2015			
Assets		**Liabilities**	
Cash	$3,000	Accounts Payable	$1,000
Accounts Receivable	1,200	Unearned Revenue	900
Equipment	6,000	Bank Loan	3,000
		Total Liabilities	4,900
		Owner's Equity	
		Parish, Capital	5,300
Total Assets	$10,200	**Total Liabilities & Equity**	$10,200

FIGURE 4.11

Note that the above balance sheet is dated December 31, 2015. It shows the ending account balances for the month of December 2015, which are also the beginning balances for the month of January 2016. In general, a balance sheet account's ending balance for a given accounting period is the beginning balance of the next period. In this textbook, the term "opening balance" will be used synonymously with "beginning balance" and "closing balance" is synonymous with "ending balance." These opening balances are already recorded in the ledger accounts.

The income statement is only prepared for the period (the month or year) and always starts the new period with no balances in the accounts. This idea will be expanded on and explained in a later chapter.

MP Consulting had the following transactions for the month of January 2016. The transactions have been entered in the journal in Figure 4.12.

Jan 2	Completed work for a client and the client paid $1,500 cash.
Jan 3	Paid $800 cash for January's rent.
Jan 4	Prepaid $1,200 cash for a one-year insurance policy.
Jan 5	Mark invested $5,000 cash into the business.
Jan 7	Paid $2,300 cash for equipment.
Jan 10	Completed work for a client who will pay $1,800 next month.
Jan 16	Paid $500 toward the principal of the bank loan.
Jan 19	Received $1,100 cash from a client for work to be completed next month.
Jan 20	Received a telephone bill telephone for $250. This will be paid next month.
Jan 30	Mark withdrew $2,000 cash for personal use.

JOURNAL				Page 1
Date 2016	**Account Titles and Explanation**	**PR**	**Debit**	**Credit**
Jan 2	Cash	101	1,500	
	Service Revenue	400		1,500
	Completed work for client			
Jan 3	Rent Expense	540	800	
	Cash	101		800
	Paid rent for month of January			
Jan 4	Prepaid Insurance	110	1,200	
	Cash	101		1,200
	Prepaid annual insurance policy			
Jan 5	Cash	101	5,000	
	Parish, Capital	300		5,000
	Owner invested cash			
Jan 7	Equipment	120	2,300	
	Cash	101		2,300
	Bought equipment			
Jan 10	Accounts Receivable	105	1,800	
	Service Revenue	400		1,800
	Completed work on account			
Jan 16	Bank Loan	215	500	
	Cash	101		500
	Paid bank loan principal			
Jan 19	Cash	101	1,100	
	Unearned Revenue	210		1,100
	Received customer deposit			
Jan 20	Telephone Expense	550	250	
	Accounts Payable	200		250
	Received telephone bill			
Jan 30	Parish, Drawings	310	2,000	
	Cash	101		2,000
	Owner took cash for personal use			

FIGURE 4.12

Figure 4.13 shows how the general ledger would look after posting all the journal entries from Figure 4.12.

GENERAL LEDGER

Account: Cash   GL. No. 101

Date	Description	PR	DR	CR	Balance	
2016						
Jan 1	Opening Balance				3,000	DR
Jan 2		J1	1,500		4,500	DR
Jan 3		J1		800	3,700	DR
Jan 4		J1		1,200	2,500	DR
Jan 5		J1	5,000		7,500	DR
Jan 7		J1		2,300	5,200	DR
Jan 16		J1		500	4,700	DR
Jan 19		J1	1,100		5,800	DR
Jan 30		J1		2,000	3,800	DR

Account: Accounts Receivable   GL. No. 105

Date	Description	PR	DR	CR	Balance	
2016						
Jan 1	Opening Balance				1,200	DR
Jan 10		J1	1,800		3,000	DR

Account: Prepaid Insurance   GL. No. 110

Date	Description	PR	DR	CR	Balance	
2016						
Jan 1	Opening Balance				0	DR
Jan 4		J1	1,200		1,200	DR

Account: Equipment   GL. No. 120

Date	Description	PR	DR	CR	Balance	
2016						
Jan 1	Opening Balance				6,000	DR
Jan 7		J1	2,300		8,300	DR

Account: Accounts Payable   GL. No. 200

Date	Description	PR	DR	CR	Balance	
2016						
Jan 1	Opening Balance				1,000	CR
Jan 20		J1		250	1,250	CR

Account: Unearned Revenue					GL. No.	210
Date	Description	PR	DR	CR	Balance	
2016						
Jan 1	Opening Balance				900	CR
Jan 19		J1		1,100	2,000	CR

Account: Bank Loan					GL. No.	215
Date	Description	PR	DR	CR	Balance	
2016						
Jan 1	Opening Balance				3,000	CR
Jan 16		J1	500		2,500	CR

Account: Parish, Capital					GL. No.	300
Date	Description	PR	DR	CR	Balance	
2016						
Jan 1	Opening Balance				5,300	CR
Jan 5		J1		5,000	10,300	CR

Account: Parish, Drawings					GL. No.	310
Date	Description	PR	DR	CR	Balance	
2016						
Jan 30		J1	2,000		2,000	DR

Account: Service Revenue					GL. No.	400
Date	Description	PR	DR	CR	Balance	
2016						
Jan 2		J1		1,500	1,500	CR
Jan 10		J1		1,800	3,300	CR

Account: Rent Expense					GL. No.	540
Date	Description	PR	DR	CR	Balance	
2016						
Jan 3		J1	800		800	DR

Account: Telephone Expense					GL. No.	550
Date	Description	PR	DR	CR	Balance	
2016						
Jan 20		J1	250		250	DR

FIGURE 4.13

To summarize, the first three steps of the accounting cycle (analyze transactions, journalize transactions, and post to the general ledger) are done repeatedly during the period. There may be hundreds of journal entries each period, depending on the size of the business. Once the period ends, then the accountant will move on to the rest of the accounting cycle, starting with step 4.

Prepare the Trial Balance

Remember that in every journal entry, the total value of the debits must equal the total value of the credits (at *all* times). To ensure that this rule has been adhered to, we need to create a trial balance. A **trial balance** lists all accounts in the general ledger and their balances at a specific date. If the total debits equals total credits, then the trial balance balances. The trial balance is created at the end of the accounting cycle and is used as an internal report for the preparation of financial statements. Some accountants choose to total the debit and credit columns in journals as well, as an added control.

The trial balance has a title which indicates the company name, the name of the report (Trial Balance) and the date the trial balance was prepared. It then lists each account in the order they appear in the general ledger and their final balances in the debit or credit column. The trial balance in Figure 4.14 is based on the accounts and balances from Figure 4.13. Only accounts that have a balance are listed in the trial balance.

MP Consulting Trial Balance January 31, 2016		
Account	DR	CR
Cash	$3,800	
Accounts Receivable	3,000	
Prepaid Insurance	1,200	
Equipment	8,300	
Accounts Payable		$1,250
Unearned Revenue		2,000
Bank Loan		2,500
Parish, Capital		10,300
Parish, Drawings	2,000	
Service Revenue		3,300
Rent Expense	800	
Telephone Expense	250	
Total	$19,350	$19,350

FIGURE 4.14

If the trial balance does not balance, the financial statements cannot be prepared because there is an error somewhere in the accounts. Double check the following items to identify the error.

1. Do all accounts on the trial balance show a normal balance?

2. Were the balances on the trial balance copied correctly from the ledger accounts?

3. Was the calculation of the ledger account balances done correctly?

4. Were the amounts in the ledger accounts copied correctly from the journal?

5. Were the journal entries created correctly?

The fact that a trial balance balances does not necessarily mean that all transactions were correctly recorded. For example, the following errors can be made but still leave the trial balance in balance.

- The wrong account was used. For example, debiting an asset instead of debiting an expense.
- An entire journal entry may have been omitted.
- An entire journal entry may have been recorded or posted twice.
- Incorrect amounts may have been used for the journal entry.
- Debits and credits were placed on the wrong side of the entry. For example, instead of debiting cash and crediting revenue, the entry may have debited revenue and credited cash.

Locating errors can be a frustrating experience, so it is important to ensure that entries are made correctly the first time.

A CLOSER LOOK

A common error that leaves the trial balance unbalanced is transposition. A transposition error occurs when two numbers are switched, for example 530 may be written as 350. If the difference between the total debits and total credits is evenly divisible by 9, then it is likely a transposition error has been made.

Ethics and Controls

Regardless of whether the company uses accounting software or records transactions manually, there is ample opportunity to manipulate the books. Computerized accounting information is only as reliable and accurate as the information that goes into the system. Most of the time, the accounting system used by a company is not fully automated. This means that the user must input information into the system or interact directly with the software at one point or another, which provides opportunity for inaccurate reporting.

For instance, certain accounting software allow automated recurring entries. In other words, they can be set up to repeat the same entry at various time intervals. Consider GG Property Management, which manages and rents out offices in high-rise buildings. Since the company receives rent from its tenants on a monthly basis, it set up its accounting software to record rent revenue automatically at the beginning of each month. Suppose that a

tenant decides to move out and stops paying rent to GG. However, the rent revenue for the tenant continues to be recorded in GG's accounting system for every subsequent month after the office has been vacated. Allowing the entries to continue being recorded automatically is inaccurate. The additional entries for rent revenue will automatically flow to the general ledger, the trial balance, the income statement and ultimately the balance sheet. Earnings for the period will be inflated. The financial statements will be misstated and this significant error will mislead the users of the financial statements if it goes undetected.

If the above behaviour is intentional and management conceals the misstatement, then it is considered highly unethical and fraudulent. However, assume the error was unintentional and the business wants to ensure it does not happen again. A possible control that may detect the error is to compare the current list of tenants to the transaction details in the journal at regular intervals (such as at month end). Another method of preventing this error is to program the software to automatically prompt the software administrator to authorize each entry or avoid using automated recurring entries entirely.

 *Access **ameengage.com** for integrated resources including tutorials, practice exercises, the digital textbook and more.*

In Summary

Distinguish between debits and credits

↬ Debits are recorded on the left side of an account and credits are recorded on the right side. For the accounting equation to be correct, the total value of the debits must equal the total value of the credits. This will ensure that the accounting equation stays in balance.

↬ Assets, expenses, and owner's drawings increase with debits and decrease with credits. Liabilities, revenues, and owner's capital increase with credits and decrease with debits.

Describe the accounting cycle

↬ The accounting cycle consists of the steps required to prepare financial statements. The cycle repeats every period.

Explain how to analyze a transaction

↬ Analysis of transactions begins with source documents which indicate a transaction has occurred. The analysis helps to determine which accounts are affected, whether they are increasing or decreasing, and whether they are debited or credited.

Record transactions in the general journal

↬ A journal is a record in which transactions are recorded before they are posted. Journals are known as books of original entry.

↬ Double-entry transactions are called journal entries. Every journal entry must have at least one debit and one credit entry so that the total of the debits equals the total of the credits.

↬ Journal entries are dated and are listed in chronological order. Accounts which are debited in a journal entry are listed first, followed by the accounts which are credited (indented). A short explanation is included for every journal entry.

Post journal entries to the general ledger

↬ The general ledger is a book used to record all the accounts and balances of the business. These accounts represent the complete financial position of the business. They also make up the accounting data from which all reports are generated.

↬ The listing of all the accounts being used by a business is called a chart of accounts.

↬ The general ledger is similar to a collection of T-accounts. The debits and credits of each account are shown along with the current balance of the account.

Prepare a trial balance

↬ The trial balance lists all accounts in the general ledger and their balances. If the total debits equals total credits, then the trial balance is balanced.

↬ If the trial balance is not balanced, an error has occurred and must be fixed before continuing with the accounting cycle.

Review Exercise

Catherine Gordon is running her own proprietary business called CG Accounting. CG Accounting provides bookkeeping services to small and mid-sized companies. The company prepares financial statements on a monthly basis and had the following closing balances at the end of May 2016.

CG Accounting Balance Sheet As at May 31, 2016			
Assets		**Liabilities**	
Cash	$4,200	Accounts Payable	$2,300
Accounts Receivable	3,100	Unearned Revenue	600
Equipment	6,000	Bank Loan	4,000
		Total Liabilities	6,900
		Owner's Equity	
		Gordon, Capital	6,400
Total Assets	$13,300	**Total Liabilities & Owner's Equity**	$13,300

CG Accounting uses a variety of accounts and account numbers in its accounting records.

Account Description	Account #		Account Description	Account #
ASSETS			**REVENUE**	
Cash	101		Service Revenue	400
Accounts Receivable	105			
Prepaid Insurance	110		**EXPENSES**	
Equipment	120		Advertising Expense	500
Accumulated Depreciation	125		Bad Debt Expense	505
			Depreciation Expense	510
LIABILITIES			Insurance Expense	515
Accounts Payable	200		Interest Expense	520
Interest Payable	205		Maintenance Expense	525
Unearned Revenue	210		Office Supplies Expense	530
Bank Loan	215		Professional Fees Expense	535
			Rent Expense	540
OWNER'S EQUITY			Salaries Expense	545
Gordon, Capital	300		Telephone Expense	550
Gordon, Drawings	310		Travel Expense	555
Income Summary	315			

During the month of June 2016, CG Accounting made the following transactions

Jun 1	Paid $900 cash for rent incurred.
Jun 3	Prepaid $1,200 cash for a one-year insurance policy.
Jun 6	Completed work for a client who immediately paid $2,100 cash.
Jun 11	Received a bill for advertising for $450 which will be paid next month.
Jun 13	Catherine contributed an extra $3,000 cash to the business.
Jun 16	Received $300 from a client for work to be completed in July.
Jun 18	Completed work for a client who will pay $1,500 next month.
Jun 23	Paid $950 cash toward the principal portion of the bank loan.
Jun 30	Catherine withdrew $1,000 cash for personal use.

Required

a) Complete the journal entries.

b) Post the journal entries to the general ledger.

c) Prepare a trial balance.

See Appendix I for solutions.

a) Journal Entries

JOURNAL				Page 1
Date	**Account Titles and Explanation**	**PR**	**Debit**	**Credit**

b) General Ledger

GENERAL LEDGER

Account: Cash					GL. No.	101
Date	**Description**	**PR**	**DR**	**CR**	**Balance**	

Account: Accounts Receivable					GL. No.	105
Date	**Description**	**PR**	**DR**	**CR**	**Balance**	

Account: Prepaid Insurance					GL. No.	110
Date	**Description**	**PR**	**DR**	**CR**	**Balance**	

Account: Equipment					GL. No.	120
Date	**Description**	**PR**	**DR**	**CR**	**Balance**	

Account: Accounts Payable					GL. No.	200
Date	**Description**	**PR**	**DR**	**CR**	**Balance**	

Account: Unearned Revenue					GL. No.	210
Date	**Description**	**PR**	**DR**	**CR**	**Balance**	

Account: Bank Loan					GL. No. 215	
Date	Description	PR	DR	CR	Balance	

Account: Gordon, Capital					GL. No. 300	
Date	Description	PR	DR	CR	Balance	

Account: Gordon, Drawings					GL. No. 310	
Date	Description	PR	DR	CR	Balance	

Account: Service Revenue					GL. No. 400	
Date	Description	PR	DR	CR	Balance	

Account: Advertising Expense					GL. No. 500	
Date	Description	PR	DR	CR	Balance	

Account: Rent Expense					GL. No. 540	
Date	Description	PR	DR	CR	Balance	

c) Trial Balance

Account Titles	DR	CR

Notes

Chapter 5

THE ACCOUNTING CYCLE: ADJUSTMENTS

LEARNING OUTCOMES

❶ Describe the purpose of adjustments

❷ Prepare adjusting entries for accrued revenue

❸ Prepare adjusting entries for accrued expenses

❹ Prepare adjusting entries for unearned revenue

❺ Prepare adjusting entries for prepaid expenses

❻ Prepare adjusting entries for depreciation

❼ Prepare an adjusted trial balance

Appendix

❽ Prepare correcting entries

AMEENGAGE *Access ameengage.com for integrated resources including tutorials, practice exercises, the digital textbook and more.*

Introduction to Adjustments

Accrual-based accounting is designed to record revenues when earned and expenses when incurred. However, cash receipts and cash payments do not always coincide with the recording of revenues and expenses. Thus, cash can change hands in a period before or after recording revenues or expenses.

For example, if you prepaid $3,000 for one year's insurance in January, in July the true value of the insurance has decreased by six months and is now worth only $1,500. The value of the prepaid asset must be adjusted to reflect its true value. The decrease in value of the assets will decrease equity, which is recorded as an expense on the income statement.

Alternatively, you may have received cash from a customer for work to be done in the future. This cash was initially recorded as unearned revenue. As time passes and you provide service for the customer, the amount of work remaining to be completed (unearned revenue) decreases. The value of unearned revenue must be adjusted to reflect its true value. The decrease in value of this liability will increase equity, which is recorded as revenue on the income statement.

There are a number of such adjustments that need to be made to update the values of the assets and liabilities. The process to ensure that all accounts are reported accurately at the end of the period is called the adjusting process and is the fifth step in the accounting cycle shown in Figure 5.1.

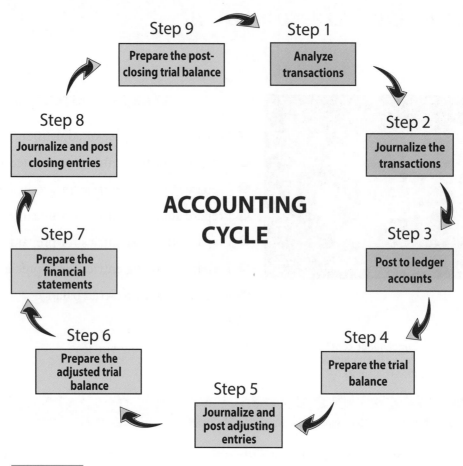

FIGURE 5.1

An accounting period is the period of time covered by the financial statements. A company will have a **fiscal year**, which is usually a one-year time frame. A company's fiscal year may cover the same time as the calendar year from January 1 to December 31; however some companies have a fiscal year that ends during a slow time of the year. For example, a retail store may have its fiscal year end at the end of January, after the Christmas rush is finished. In this case, the fiscal year is from February 1 to January 31.

A company will usually prepare a set of financial statements at the end of each fiscal year, although some prepare the statements more frequently to better manage the business. Whenever these statements are prepared, remember that accrual-based accounting states that revenue and expenses should be recognized in the accounting period when they occur, regardless of when the cash payment is received or made.

Adjusting entries are made at the end of the accounting period to record assets, liabilities, equity, revenue and expenses according to revenue and expense recognition. Every adjustment will affect both a balance sheet account and an income statement account. Adjusting entries typically fall under five broad categories

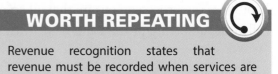

WORTH REPEATING

Revenue recognition states that revenue must be recorded when services are performed, regardless of when cash is received. Expense recognition requires that expenses must be recorded in the same period in which they were used to generate revenue.

1. Accrued revenue
2. Accrued expenses
3. Unearned revenue
4. Prepaid expenses
5. Depreciation

We will examine each category in detail and provide examples of the types of adjustments that apply to each category. It is important to note that all adjustments presented in this chapter are just changes made to the recorded values in the books. At no time will cash be received from customers or paid to suppliers. Therefore, adjusting entries will never use the cash account.

Accrued Revenue

Accrued revenue is revenue that has been earned but not yet recorded. There is nothing in the ledger accounts to show for this yet. Revenue can accrue or accumulate over a period of time, such as interest on money loaned to someone else or rent (if the business is a landlord). Other examples of accrued revenue are where completed services have not been billed or there is a contract with a client for work to be performed over a long period of time. Accrued revenues will always increase a receivable asset account and increase a revenue account.

Suppose you have a contract with a client, stating you will provide them with services for 30 days. At the end of the contract, you will bill the client and they will pay you. The contract starts on September 21 and is worth $6,000. On September 21, you will not make a journal entry, since you have not yet completed any work and no cash has been paid to you.

At the end of September you want to prepare your financial statements. At this point, there is nothing in the books to indicate that you have done work for this client and that the client owes you money for the work completed so far. Thus, service revenue and accounts receivable are not stated correctly. Accounts receivable is used to record the amount owing because this is a binding contract and the customer will pay in the future. An adjusting entry to record this accrued revenue is required. You have completed 10 out of 30 days, or one-third of the contract, so you have earned one-third of the $6,000, which is $2,000. Figure 5.2 illustrates the adjusting entry that must be made.

JOURNAL				Page 1
Date 2016	**Account Title and Explanation**	**PR**	**Debit**	**Credit**
Sep 30	Accounts Receivable		2,000	
	Service Revenue			2,000
	To accrue revenue on contract			

FIGURE 5.2

BALANCE SHEET		INCOME STATEMENT
ASSETS	LIABILITIES	SERVICE REVENUE + $2,000 CR
CASH	ACCOUNTS PAYABLE	EXPENSES
ACCOUNTS RECEIVABLE + $2,000 DR	UNEARNED REVENUE	DEPRECIATION / SALARIES
OFFICE SUPPLIES	LOAN PAYABLE	INSURANCE / RENT

Owner's equity increases by $2,000

Once the contract is completed on October 20, you can bill the client. If they pay you immediately, you will receive the full $6,000 cash. You will only record $4,000 worth of revenue earned for the month of October since the other $2,000 worth of revenue was already recorded on September 30. There will also be a $2,000 decrease to accounts receivable to indicate that the client has now paid you the amount owed. This is illustrated in Figure 5.3.

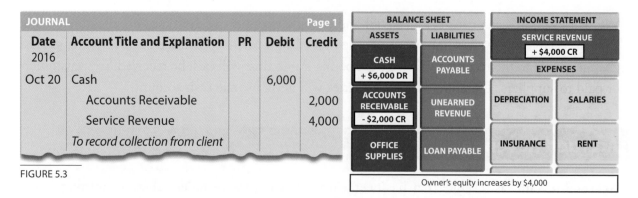

FIGURE 5.3

IN THE REAL WORLD

In most cases, sales are entered from a sales invoice directly into the accounting records, without looking back to see if there were any adjustments made in the previous period. Thus, the transaction on October 20 could be recorded incorrectly if the adjusted amount in accounts receivable is forgotten and not applied to the transaction. If accounts receivable is not applied, $6,000 would be recorded as service revenue for October instead of $4,000. To eliminate the risk of forgetting about the adjustment for accrued revenue and making an error, an optional step is to record a reversing entry. This would be done on the first day of the new accounting period; in this example it would be made on October 1, 2016 so it would not affect the reporting in September. The reversing entry would be the opposite of the adjustment on September 30, 2016.

| Oct 1 | Service Revenue | 2,000 | |
| | Accounts Receivable | | 2,000 |

By creating this reversing entry, the effect of the adjustment of the previous month is undone for the current month and leaves the revenue account with a negative (debit) balance of $2,000. On October 20, the full amount of the contract of $6,000 can be recorded, but since service revenue already has a negative balance of $2,000, only $4,000 of revenue will be recognized in the month of October.

| Oct 20 | Cash | 6,000 | |
| | Service Revenue | | 6,000 |

It is important to note that a reversing entry is just an option businesses can use to make their bookkeeping easier. It does not change anything about the accrual-based accounting and it typically occurs only at the beginning of an accounting period.

Accrued Expenses

Similar to accrued revenue, **accrued expenses** are expenses that have been incurred but have not yet been recorded. Examples of expenses that may accrue at month end include property taxes, salaries, interest on a loan and rent. In some cases, a business may have to estimate the accrued expense because the bill may not be received until later in the following month. Two examples of this are electricity or water bills. An accrued expense will always increase a liability and increase an expense account.

For accrued expenses, the end of the period will not report the correct amount of expenses on the income statement without an adjustment. Also, since this expense represents an amount owed, liabilities on the balance sheet will also be incorrectly stated. The adjusting entry for an accrued expense will correct this. We will examine two examples of accrued expenses: salaries and interest.

Salaries Expense

Salaries to employees are paid after the work has been completed. If the work and the payment for the work occur within the same period, no adjustment will have to be made. However, if the work done by the employee occurs in a different period than the payment, an adjustment must be made at the end of the period.

For example, suppose an employee is paid every two weeks. From the calendar in Figure 5.4, we see the first pay period starts on September 12 and ends on September 23 when the employee gets paid. Since the payment on September 23 is for work done in the same month, this will be a transaction similar to what you have learned to pay salaries expense with cash.

The employee will then work the last week of September and the business will not pay until October 7, which is the next pay date. The business accrues a salary expense for the employee for the week worked in September. This expense must be recorded in September, even though the employee will not be paid until October.

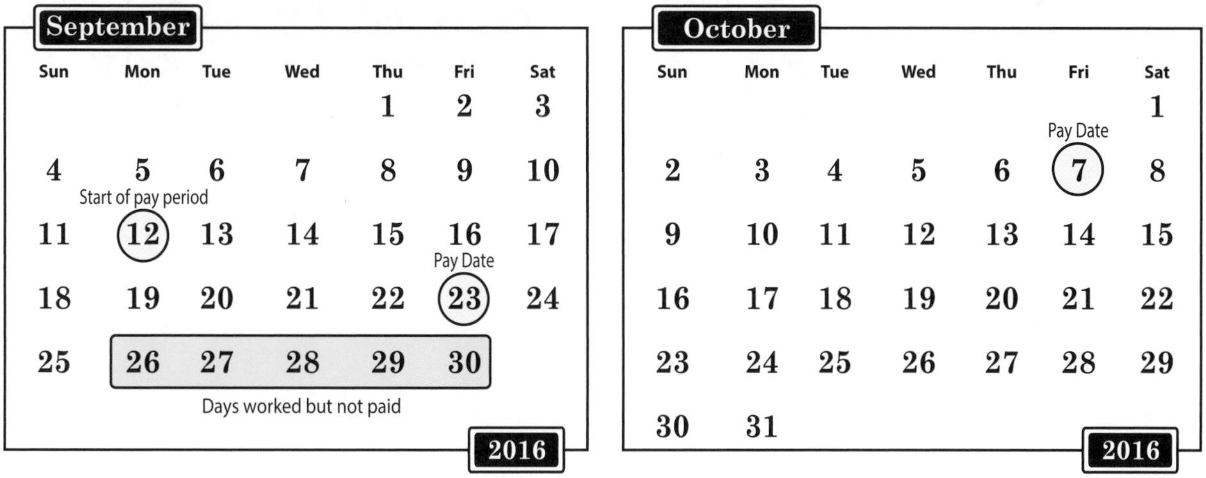

FIGURE 5.4

If the employee earns $1,000 every two weeks, they earn $100 per day ($1,000 ÷ 10 working days). Thus, the business must create an adjusting entry for salaries expense for $500 ($100 per day × 5 days). Figure 5.5 illustrates the adjusting entry. Equity decreases, which is recorded as an expense.

Since the salary payment is owed to the employee, we will use a liability account called salaries payable to track the amount owing.

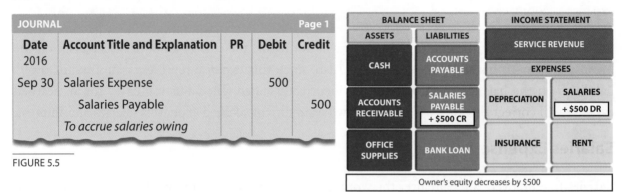

FIGURE 5.5

The $500 balance in the liability account will be paid at the next pay date. Thus, on October 7, the business will pay the employee their salary of $1,000. The accrued amount in the liability account will be cleared out since the business is paying the debt to the employee. Only $500 will be recorded as an expense, since we only need to record the salary expense for the time worked in October. The journal entry for this transaction is shown in Figure 5.6.

JOURNAL				Page 1
Date 2016	Account Title and Explanation	PR	Debit	Credit
Oct 7	Salaries Expense		500	
	Salaries Payable		500	
	Cash			1,000
	To record payment of salaries owing			

BALANCE SHEET

ASSETS | **LIABILITIES**

CASH - $1,000 CR | ACCOUNTS PAYABLE

ACCOUNTS RECEIVABLE | SALARIES PAYABLE - $500 DR

OFFICE SUPPLIES | BANK LOAN

INCOME STATEMENT

SERVICE REVENUE

EXPENSES

DEPRECIATION | SALARIES + $500 DR

INSURANCE | RENT

Owner's equity decreases by $500

FIGURE 5.6

IN THE REAL WORLD

In most cases, expenses are entered from a purchase invoice or other source documents directly into the accounting records, without looking back to see if there were any adjustments made in the previous period. Thus, the transaction on October 7 could be recorded incorrectly if the adjusted amount in salaries payable is forgotten and not applied to the transaction. If salaries payable is not applied, $1,000 would be recorded as salaries expense for October instead of $500. To eliminate the possibility of forgetting about the adjustment for accrued expenses and making an error, an optional step is to record a reversing entry. This would be done on the first day of the new accounting period; in this example it would be made on October 1, 2016 so it would not affect the reporting in September. The reversing entry would be the opposite of the adjustment on September 30, 2016.

Oct 1	Salaries Payable	500	
	Salaries Expense		500

By creating this reversing entry, the effect of the adjustments of the previous month is undone for the current month and leaves the expense account with a negative (credit) balance of $500. On October 7, the salary payment would be made as usual for $1,000, but since salaries expense already has a negative balance of $500, only $500 of salaries expense will be recognized in the month of October.

Oct 7	Salaries Expense	1,000	
	Cash		1,000

Some accounting software can create reversing entries for accrued revenue and accrued expenses, thus removing the possibility of double counting revenue and expenses that have already been accrued.

Interest Expense

Borrowing cash is usually not free. The lender will charge interest on the amount borrowed and expect payment at regular intervals. Interest accumulates, or accrues, during the interval before it is paid. At the end of an accounting period, the borrower must calculate and record the amount of interest that has accumulated to date as an accrued expense. Since it is owed to the lender, it will be recorded in a liability account as well.

To calculate interest, three pieces of information must be known

1. The principal amount (the amount that was originally borrowed)
2. The interest rate (an annual percentage of interest charged on the principal)
3. The term of the loan (how long the debt will last)

For example, suppose a business borrowed $10,000 from the bank on July 1 and must repay the loan in three months on October 1. The bank is charging 5% interest on the loan. Keep in mind that interest rates are always expressed as an annual rate, so any duration that is less than one year must be adjusted accordingly. If the business prepares its statements on September 30, and has not prepared any statements since the loan was received, the entire amount of interest that has accrued on the loan in the three months from July 1 to September 30 must be recorded. The calculation is shown below.

$$\text{Accrued Interest} = \text{Principal} \times \text{Interest Rate} \times \text{Time in Years}$$
$$\text{Accrued Interest} = \$10,000 \times 5\% \times \tfrac{3}{12} = \$125$$

The $125 worth of interest will be recorded in interest expense and in a liability account called interest payable. This account tracks all the interest owed. The adjusting entry is shown in Figure 5.7.

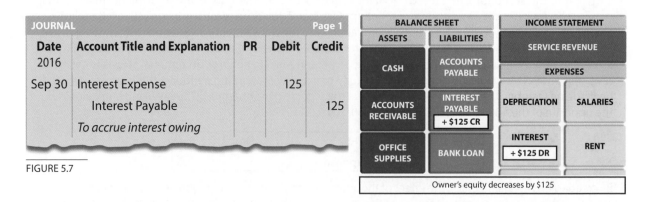

FIGURE 5.7

After the accrued interest for the loan has been recorded, the statements will be up-to-date and accurate. When it comes time to pay back the loan and interest on October 1, there will not be any interest expense to record. The payment will simply be a reduction of the bank loan and the interest payable, as shown in Figure 5.8.

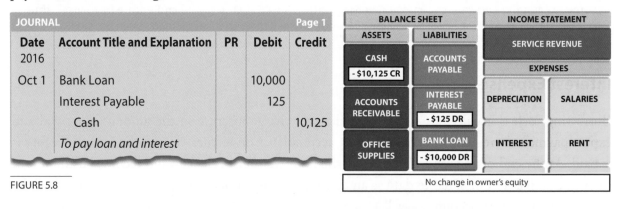

FIGURE 5.8

Unearned Revenue

You will recall from earlier discussions that unearned revenue is a liability that arises when a customer pays for services or products in advance. When a customer pays in advance for a service or product, cash increases. Since the business now has an obligation to provide services or products to the customer, this amount is recorded in unearned revenue, a liability account, until the product or service is provided to the customer. The adjustment to unearned revenue is to account for the earning of revenue for the services which were paid for in advance. An adjustment to recognize unearned revenue as earned will always decrease unearned revenue and increase revenue.

To illustrate the concept of adjustments related to unearned revenue, consider Raina Property Management (Raina). Raina recently bought a large office building which it rents out as separate offices to tenants. The company has a policy of collecting the first three months' rent in advance when a new tenant moves in. For each office, Raina charges $2,200 per month for rent. On March 1, 2016, a new tenant moved in and paid $6,600 immediately to Raina to cover rent for March,

April and May. Raina makes adjustments to its accounting records at the end of each month because it produces financial statements internally on a monthly basis.

In Raina's books, on March 1 when the payment is received, Raina will increase cash (an asset) by $6,600 and increase unearned revenue (a liability) by $6,600. This is shown in Figure 5.9.

JOURNAL — **Page 1**

Date	Account Title and Explanation	PR	Debit	Credit
2016				
Mar 1	Cash		6,600	
	Unearned Revenue			6,600
	Receive cash for 3 months rent			

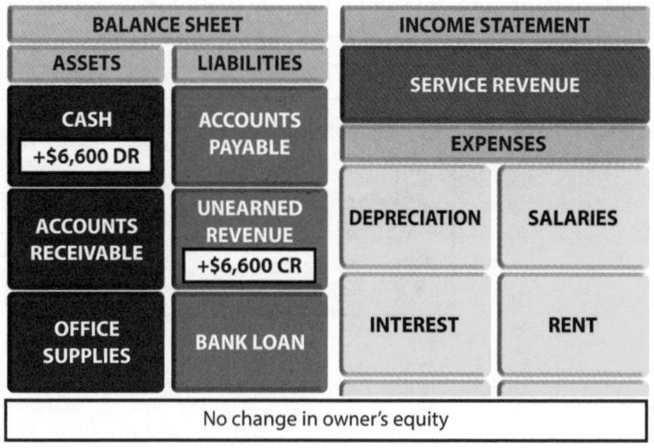

FIGURE 5.9

As of March 31, Raina has earned one month of revenue. On this date, the company will decrease unearned revenue (a liability) by $2,200 and increase owner's equity by $2,200 with an increase to rent revenue (an income statement account). After this adjustment is made on March 31, Figure 5.10 shows that Raina still owes $4,400 worth of rent to the tenant.

	- UNEARNED REVENUE	+	- RENT REVENUE	+
Adjustment	2,200	6,600		2,200
		4,400		

JOURNAL — **Page 1**

Date	Account Title and Explanation	PR	Debit	Credit
2016				
Mar 31	Unearned Revenue		2,200	
	Rent Revenue			2,200
	To adjust for 1 month rent earned			

FIGURE 5.10

The same adjustment will be made on April 30 (to recognize April's rent revenue) and May 31 (to recognize May's rent revenue). Figure 5.11 shows the timing of the transactions related to unearned revenue.

Transactions From Raina's Perspective

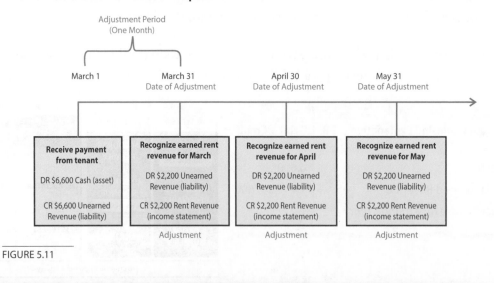

FIGURE 5.11

Prepaid Expenses

Similar to unearned revenue, accounting for prepaid expenses involves making adjustments for amounts used. Recall that when a prepaid expense is recognized as an actual expense, prepaid expenses (an asset) decreases and the expense (an income statement account) increases. This is the adjusting entry for prepaid expenses.

Prepaid Rent

We can apply this to the example of Raina Property Management which was illustrated in the unearned revenue section. Now examine the financial impact of the transactions from the perspective of the tenant who paid Raina three months of rent at $2,200 per month in advance. On March 1, the tenant would have recorded a cash payment to Raina for $6,600 as a prepayment for rent, as shown in Figure 5.12.

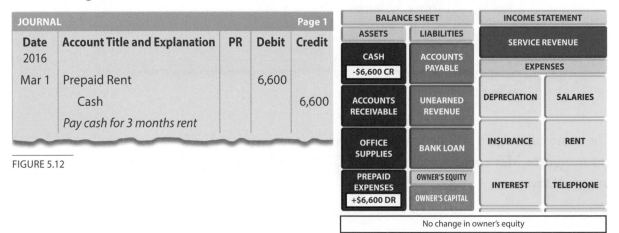

FIGURE 5.12

If the tenant also uses a monthly accounting period, then it will adjust the prepaid rent at the end of each month. In this case, the tenant is adjusting based on what has been used (one month) on March 31. The adjustment will decrease the prepaid rent account and increase rent expense on the income statement. As Figure 5.13 shows, after the adjustment on March 31, the prepaid rent account will be left with a balance of $4,400 representing the two months that are still prepaid.

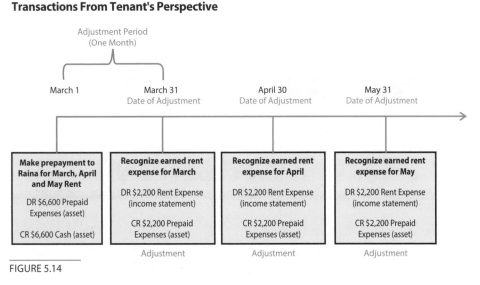

+ PREPAID RENT -			+ RENT EXPENSE -
6,600	2,200 *Adjustment*		2,200
4,400			

JOURNAL				Page 1
Date 2016	**Account Title and Explanation**	**PR**	**Debit**	**Credit**
Mar 31	Rent Expense		2,200	
	Prepaid Rent			2,200
	To adjust for 1 month rent used			

FIGURE 5.13

The same adjustment will be made on April 30 (to recognize April's rent expense) and May 31 (to recognize May's rent expense). Figure 5.14 shows the timing of the transactions related to the prepaid rent.

Transactions From Tenant's Perspective

Adjustment Period (One Month)

March 1	March 31 Date of Adjustment	April 30 Date of Adjustment	May 31 Date of Adjustment
Make prepayment to Raina for March, April and May Rent DR $6,600 Prepaid Expenses (asset) CR $6,600 Cash (asset)	**Recognize earned rent expense for March** DR $2,200 Rent Expense (income statement) CR $2,200 Prepaid Expenses (asset)	**Recognize earned rent expense for April** DR $2,200 Rent Expense (income statement) CR $2,200 Prepaid Expenses (asset)	**Recognize earned rent expense for May** DR $2,200 Rent Expense (income statement) CR $2,200 Prepaid Expenses (asset)
	Adjustment	Adjustment	Adjustment

FIGURE 5.14

Prepaid expenses and unearned revenue are opposites. Usually, as in this example, the prepaid expense of one company (the tenant) is the unearned revenue of another company (Raina). The above example illustrated prepaid rent, however the same idea and transactions would apply for an item such as prepaid insurance or prepaid property taxes.

Office Supplies

Another type of prepaid expense is office supplies. Office supplies are the physical items used to run the office of a business and include paper, photocopy toner, printer toner, pens, etc. When they are initially purchased, these items are recorded as assets on the balance sheet. Instead of recording each item as an expense when it is used, a single adjusting entry is made for the total office supplies used.

At the end of the period, a count is made to determine the value of the remaining office supplies and an adjusting entry is created to record the amount of office supplies used as an expense.

To illustrate, suppose a business paid $1,200 cash for office supplies on September 4. This initial purchase of office supplies is just a transfer of one asset (cash) for another (office supplies) and is shown in Figure 5.15.

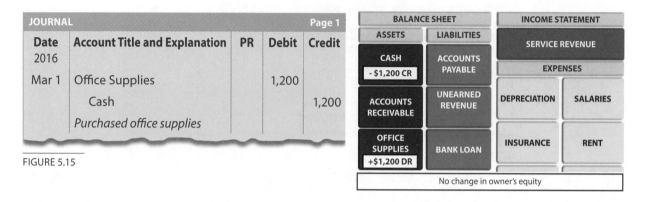

FIGURE 5.15

At the end of the month, a count shows that only $700 worth of office supplies remain on hand. This means that office supplies of $500 ($1,200 – $700) must have been used and must be recorded as an expense. The adjustment is shown in Figure 5.16. Notice that the ending balance of the office supplies account is equal to $700, matching the count that was taken.

+ OFFICE SUPPLIES –		+ OFFICE SUPPLIES EXPENSE –
1,200	500 *Adjustment*	500
Count 700		

JOURNAL				Page 1
Date 2016	Account Title and Explanation	PR	Debit	Credit
Sep 30	Office Supplies Expense		500	
	Office Supplies			500
	To adjust office supplies used			

FIGURE 5.16

IN THE REAL WORLD

Office supplies are often low-value items, such as paper and pens. In many businesses, keeping track of these small amounts as an asset, then counting them to see what was used is not viewed as an important procedure. The materiality principle introduced earlier indicates that if a piece of information could influence a user's decision, it is material and must be accounted for properly according to ASPE. For many businesses, it is easier to simply record office supplies as an expense immediately instead of as an asset first. This is done when the amount is not material, since the extra work and detail would not affect the users' decisions.

Depreciation

We learned that items such as land, furniture, computers and automobiles fall under the property, plant and equipment category. These assets are used to run the business and generate sales. However, with the exception of land, these assets will eventually become obsolete, unusable or broken. This may not happen for several years, but however long it is, the length of time the asset can be used is called the **useful life**.

In a sense, these long-term assets are like prepaid expenses in that the asset is purchased and then used up over time. **Depreciation** is how accountants allocate the cost of a long-term asset over its useful life. The reason that land does not depreciate is that land does not have a limited useful life. Depreciation matches the expense of the long-term asset to the period in which it generates revenue for the business.

For example, suppose a machine was purchased for $10,000 one year ago and depreciation of $2,000 must be recorded. The $2,000 of depreciation is a reduction of the value of the machine which gives us the net book value of the machine. The **net book value** of the asset is its original value less the total depreciation that has been recognized. This does not represent what it could be sold for; net book value is just the accounting value of the asset. Thus, the net book value of the machine after recording depreciation will be $8,000. However, ASPE requires the original amount (or historical cost) of the asset to be recorded on the balance sheet. Accounting for depreciation requires a special account called a contra account.

Contra Account

Contra means opposite. A **contra account** is linked to another account and records decreases in the value of that account. This is done so that the original value of the related account remains unchanged. The value of the contra account is subtracted from the related account to arrive at a net book value for the item. In the case of property, plant and equipment (PPE), the contra account is called **accumulated depreciation**. This contra asset account will reflect the decrease in the net book value of PPE without changing the original cost of the asset.

With the exception of land, every asset that is considered part of property, plant and equipment will have its own separate accumulated depreciation account to track the decrease in net book value.

Suppose an asset was purchased for $10,000 and since it was purchased, $2,000 worth of depreciation has been recorded. To preserve the original amount paid of $10,000, the asset account under PPE is not directly adjusted. Instead, as illustrated in Figure 5.17, accumulated depreciation records the total decrease in net book value of the asset. The contra asset account is called accumulated depreciation because the depreciation accumulates as the asset's cost is allocated to each period. This is different from depreciation expense, an income statement account which only shows the depreciation for the current period.

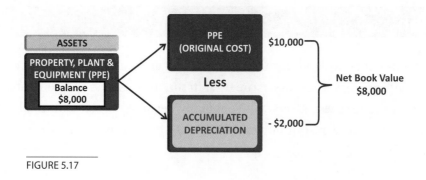

FIGURE 5.17

The contra asset account behaves in a manner opposite to the way a regular asset account behaves. Recall that an asset account will increase with a debit and decrease with a credit. The contra asset account (accumulated depreciation) will increase with a credit and decrease with a debit. Figure 5.18 illustrates the T-accounts for property, plant and equipment and accumulated depreciation.

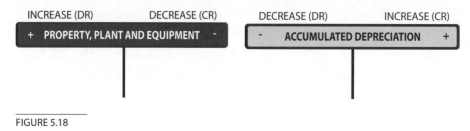

FIGURE 5.18

Calculation of Depreciation

There are a number of ways to calculate depreciation for the period. We are going to use a simple method called straight-line depreciation. **Straight-line depreciation** is a method to allocate the cost of the asset evenly over the life of the asset. The calculation for straight-line depreciation is shown below.

$$\text{Straight-Line Depreciation} = \frac{\text{Cost of Asset} - \text{Residual Value}}{\text{Useful Life}}$$

There are three parts of this calculation that must be explained.

1. The cost of the asset is the original purchase price of the asset. This is the value shown on the balance sheet in the asset account.
2. **Residual value** is the estimated value of the asset at the end of its useful life. By subtracting the residual value from the original cost of the asset, we determine the cost that will be allocated over the life of the asset. It is possible for an asset to have a residual value of $0, meaning the asset will be fully depreciated and worthless at the end of its useful life.
3. The useful life is how long the asset is expected to be used by the business. Like residual value, this is also an estimate. The useful life can be expressed in years or months, depending on how often depreciation will be recorded.

For example, suppose a machine was purchased on January 1, 2016 for $10,000. The machine is expected to last for five years, and after five years the machine is expected to have a residual value of $1,000. The calculation for yearly depreciation under the straight-line method is shown below.

$$\text{Depreciation} = \frac{\$10,000 - \$1,000}{5 \text{ Years}} = \$1,800 \text{ per year}$$

The cost we are allocating over 5 years is $9,000, which is the original purchase price minus the estimated residual value. Each year we will record $1,800 as a depreciation expense and each year we will add $1,800 to accumulated depreciation. The journal entry is shown in Figure 5.19.

- ACCUMULATED DEPRECIATION +	+ DEPRECIATION EXPENSE -
1,800	1,800

JOURNAL					Page 1
Date 2016	Account Title and Explanation	PR	Debit	Credit
Dec 31	Depreciation Expense		1,800	
	Accumulated Depreciation			1,800
	To adjust for depreciation			

FIGURE 5.19

Since each year the income statement resets and starts from scratch, depreciation expense of $1,800 will be recorded each year. The accumulated depreciation account, on the other hand, will increase by $1,800 each year. As the accumulated depreciation account increases, the net book value of the machine will decrease. Net book value is the original cost of the asset less accumulated depreciation. The above transaction will be recorded at the end of each year. The amount of accumulated depreciation and the net book value of the machine over the five-year useful life are shown in the table in Figure 5.20.

Year	Original Cost of Machine	Depreciation Expense	Accumulated Depreciation	Net Book Value
2016	10,000	1,800	1,800	8,200
2017	10,000	1,800	3,600	6,400
2018	10,000	1,800	5,400	4,600
2019	10,000	1,800	7,200	2,800
2020	10,000	1,800	9,000	1,000
Total	$10,000	$9,000	$9,000	$1,000

FIGURE 5.20

The net book value at the end of 2020 is equal to $1,000, which is the estimated residual value of the machine. This means that $9,000 of the cost of the machine was allocated over 5 years.

In addition to the above example, it is possible that depreciation may be recorded for periods of time that are less than one year. For example, suppose the machine was purchased on September 1, 2016 and the business records adjustments at year end, December 31, 2016. In this case, depreciation should only be recorded for four months. The calculation of depreciation in this example is shown below.

$$\text{Depreciation} = \frac{\$10,000 - \$1,000}{5 \text{ Years}} \times \frac{4}{12} = \$600 \text{ for 4 months}$$

The same accounts would be used as the ones in the journal entry in Figure 5.19, but the amount of depreciation would only be $600.

Adjusted Trial Balance

The sixth step of the accounting cycle is to prepare the adjusted trial balance. To help illustrate this step, return to the sample company MP Consulting introduced in the previous chapter. At the end of the fourth step of the accounting cycle, we had prepared the trial balance for the business, shown in Figure 5.21.

MP Consulting Trial Balance January 31, 2016		
Account Titles	**DR**	**CR**
Cash	$3,800	
Accounts Receivable	3,000	
Prepaid Insurance	1,200	
Equipment	8,300	
Accounts Payable		$1,250
Unearned Revenue		2,000
Bank Loan		2,500
Parish, Capital		10,300
Parish, Drawings	2,000	
Service Revenue		3,300
Rent Expense	800	
Telephone Expense	250	
Total	$19,350	$19,350

FIGURE 5.21

This trial balance is the balance of the general ledger accounts after all the regular day-to-day transactions have been recorded in the general journal and posted to the general ledger. It is from these balances that MP Consulting will make adjusting entries. Suppose the company has the following adjustments to make at the end of the month

❶ The company borrowed cash from the bank at a 12% rate of interest. Using the interest calculation introduced earlier in the chapter, accrued interest for the month is calculated as

$$\text{Interest} = \$2,500 \times 12\% \times \frac{1}{12} = \$25 \text{ per month}$$

❷ One month of the prepaid insurance has been used. Since the balance of $1,200 represents a one-year policy, $100 ($1,200 ÷ 12 months) must be adjusted as an expense.

❸ Based on the records of MP Consulting, $200 worth of the unearned revenue had been earned by the end of the month. This amount must be recognized as revenue.

❹ All the equipment that MP Consulting owns has an estimated useful life of four years and an estimated residual value of $1,100. Using the depreciation calculation shown earlier, depreciation for the month is calculated as

$$\text{Depreciation} = \frac{\$8,300 - \$1,100}{4\ \text{Years}} \times \frac{1}{12} = \$150\ \text{per month}$$

❺ On January 2, MP Consulting began a two-month contract with a client. The contract covers work for the months of January and February. On February 29, 2016, the contract will be completed and MP Consulting will bill the client $2,000. An adjusting entry must be made on January 31 to accrue the revenue earned during the month of January. MP Consulting will create an adjusting entry showing revenue of $1,000 earned during the month.

Before recording the adjustments in the general journal, it can be helpful to see the impact of the adjustments and to ensure that the accounts will still balance after adjustments are made. To assist in this process, a **worksheet** can be used to display the trial balance before the adjustments are made and a trial balance after the adjustments are made. The original trial balance is called the **unadjusted trial balance** because these values represent account balances before adjustments are made. The trial balance after the adjustments are made is called the **adjusted trial balance**.

The worksheet shown in Figure 5.22 shows the unadjusted trial balance at the end of January. Beside this trial balance is a set of debit and credit columns for the adjustments. The five adjustments are numbered to illustrate step-by-step how they are recorded. It is important to ensure the debit and credit columns of the adjustments column balance, otherwise the adjusted trial balance will not balance.

The last set of debit and credit columns is the adjusted trial balance. The amounts in the adjustment columns are added or subtracted from the original balances and placed in the adjusted trial balance columns. This shows what the ledger balances will be after the adjustments are made. If the debit and credit columns balance, then the financial statements can be prepared.

	MP Consulting Worksheet January 31, 2016					
	Unadjusted Trial Balance		Adjustments		Adjusted Trial Balance	
Account Titles	**DR**	**CR**	**DR**	**CR**	**DR**	**CR**
Cash	$3,800				$3,800	
Accounts Receivable	3,000		❺ $1,000		4,000	
Prepaid Insurance	1,200			❷ $100	1,100	
Equipment	8,300				8,300	
Accumulated Depreciation		$0		❹ 150		$150
Accounts Payable		1,250				1,250
Interest Payable		0		❶ 25		25
Unearned Revenue		2,000	❸ 200			1,800
Bank Loan		2,500				2,500
Parish, Capital		10,300				10,300
Parish, Drawings	2,000				2,000	
Service Revenue		3,300		❸ ❺ 1,200		4,500
Depreciation Expense	0		❹ 150		150	
Insurance Expense	0		❷ 100		100	
Interest Expense	0		❶ 25		25	
Rent Expense	800				800	
Telephone Expense	250				250	
Total	**$19,350**	**$19,350**	**$1,475**	**$1,475**	**$20,525**	**$20,525**

FIGURE 5.22

Once the worksheet is prepared and the adjusted trial balance is in balance, the journal entries for the above transactions would be recorded in the general journal and posted to the general ledger. The journal entries are shown in Figure 5.23. All the postings to general ledger accounts, including these adjustments, are shown in the next chapter.

JOURNAL				Page 1
Date 2016	**Account Title and Explanation**	**PR**	**Debit**	**Credit**
Jan 31	Interest Expense		25	
	Interest Payable			25
	Record one month of accrued interest			
Jan 31	Insurance Expense		100	
	Prepaid Insurance			100
	Record one month of insurance used			
Jan 31	Unearned Revenue		200	
	Service Revenue			200
	Record revenue now earned			
Jan 31	Depreciation Expense		150	
	Accumulated Depreciation			150
	Record depreciation for one month			
Jan 31	Accounts Receivable		1,000	
	Service Revenue			1,000
	Record accrued revenue			

FIGURE 5.23

The preparation of the worksheet is optional. It is possible to simply prepare the journal entries as shown in Figure 5.23 and post them to the general ledger, then create the adjusted trial balance without preparing a worksheet. However, in a manual accounting system, it is a good idea to constantly check to ensure all accounts remain in balance because going back to find errors can be a difficult process.

ASPE vs IFRS

ASPE states that private companies must prepare financial statements at least once per year. Therefore, the adjustments process must be completed just as often.

On the other hand, IFRS requires companies to prepare financial statements at least once per quarter. This means that the accounts will be adjusted at least four times per year.

Ethics

It is possible to intentionally manipulate adjustments to change how the financial performance and position of the company is presented. If the manipulation hides information from users, this is unethical. Consider the accrual of interest on a bank loan. Management should not wait until the interest is paid to record interest. Interest should be accrued at the end of an accounting period and thus reflected as interest expense on the income statement. If management fails to accrue interest at the end of an accounting period, the financial statements will understate liabilities (since interest payable is understated) and overstate net income (since interest expense is understated). This will provide investors and creditors an incorrect representation of the company's performance and debt position.

As an internal control, management should review the terms of the debt contracts for all outstanding long-term liabilities at the end of an accounting period. This will provide management with a reasonable idea of what the interest expense should be for the period after including accrued interest as well.

 *Access **ameengage.com** for integrated resources including tutorials, practice exercises, the digital textbook and more.*

In Summary

Describe the purpose of adjustment

⇨ Adjustments are made to ensure that all accounts are accurately reported at the end of the period.

⇨ Adjustments are made before the creation of the financial statements.

Prepare adjusting entries for accrued revenue

⇨ Accrued revenue is revenue that has been earned but has not yet been recorded. The adjustment is made by debiting (increasing) accounts receivable and crediting (increasing) service revenue.

Prepare adjusting entries for accrued expenses

⇨ Accrued expenses are expenses that have been incurred but have not yet been recorded. The adjustment is made by debiting (increasing) an expense and crediting (increasing) a liability.

Prepare adjusting entries for unearned revenue

⇨ Adjustments to unearned revenue is to account for revenue that has now been earned. The adjustment is made by debiting (decreasing) unearned revenue and crediting (increasing) service revenue.

Prepare adjusting entries for prepaid expenses

⇨ Adjustments to prepaid expenses is to account for expenses that have now been incurred. The adjustment is made by debiting (increasing) an expense and crediting (decreasing) the prepaid expense.

Prepare adjusting entries for depreciation

⇨ Adjustments for depreciation is to allocate the cost of a long-term asset over its useful life. The adjustment is made by debiting (increasing) depreciation expense and crediting (increasing) the contra account called accumulated depreciation.

Prepare an adjusted trial balance

⇨ The adjusted trial balance is prepared after the adjusting entries have been made. This is to ensure the accounts are still in balance and the financial statements can be prepared.

Review Exercise

Catherine Gordon is running her own proprietary business called CG Accounting. CG Accounting provides bookkeeping services to small and mid-sized companies. The company prepares financial statements on a monthly basis and was introduced in the review exercise in chapter 4. Before you begin this exercise, familiarize yourself with the review exercise in chapter 4 because this is a continuation.

The journal entries for the month of June have already been entered in the journal and posted to the ledger. The trial balance, before adjustments, is presented below.

CG Accounting Trial Balance June 30, 2016		
Account Titles	**DR**	**CR**
Cash	$5,550	
Accounts Receivable	4,600	
Prepaid Insurance	1,200	
Equipment	6,000	
Accounts Payable		$2,750
Unearned Revenue		900
Bank Loan		3,050
Gordon, Capital		9,400
Gordon, Drawings	1,000	
Service Revenue		3,600
Advertising Expense	450	
Professional Fees Expense	900	
Total	**$19,700**	**$19,700**

CG Accounting uses the following accounts and accounting numbers in its accounting records.

Account Description	Account #
ASSETS	
Cash	101
Accounts Receivable	105
Prepaid Insurance	110
Equipment	120
Accumulated Depreciation	125
LIABILITIES	
Accounts Payable	200
Interest Payable	205
Unearned Revenue	210
Bank Loan	215
OWNER'S EQUITY	
Gordon, Capital	300
Gordon, Drawings	310
Income Summary	315

Account Description	Account #
REVENUE	
Service Revenue	400
EXPENSES	
Advertising Expense	500
Bad Debt Expense	505
Depreciation Expense	510
Insurance Expense	515
Interest Expense	520
Maintenance Expense	525
Office Supplies Expense	530
Professional Fees Expense	535
Rent Expense	540
Salaries Expense	545
Telephone Expense	550
Travel Expense	555

At the end of June 2016, CG Accounting had to make the following adjustments.

Jun 30   The prepaid insurance represents a one-year policy that started in June. One month has now been used.

Jun 30   When examining the balance of unearned revenue, Catherine determined that $450 has now been earned.

Jun 30   Interest has accrued on the balance of the bank loan for the month. The loan interest rate is 10%. (For simplicity, round the interest to the nearest whole number.)

Jun 30   Depreciation on the equipment for the month must be recorded. The equipment is depreciated using the straight-line method. The equipment is expected to last five years and will have no residual value

Jun 30   Catherine started an audit for a new client. The contract is for 20 days of work starting June 21. At the end of the contract, the client will pay CG Accounting $1,800. Accrue the revenue earned for June.

Required

a) Complete the worksheet.

b) Complete the journal entries for the adjusting entries and post them to the general ledger.

See Appendix I for solutions.

a) Complete the worksheet.

	CG Accounting Worksheet June 30, 2016					
	Unadjusted Trial Balance		Adjustments		Adjusted Trial Balance	
Account Titles	DR	CR	DR	CR	DR	CR
Cash	$5,550					
Accounts Receivable	4,600					
Prepaid Insurance	1,200					
Equipment	6,000					
Accumulated Depreciation		$0				
Accounts Payable		2,750				
Interest Payable		0				
Unearned Revenue		900				
Bank Loan		3,050				
Gordon, Capital		9,400				
Gordon, Drawings	1,000					
Service Revenue		3,600				
Advertising Expense	450					
Depreciation Expense	0					
Insurance Expense	0					
Interest Expense	0					
Rent Expense	900					
Total	$19,700	$19,700				

b) Prepare the adjusting journal entries.

JOURNAL				Page 1
Date	**Account Titles and Explanation**	**PR**	**Debit**	**Credit**

GENERAL LEDGER

Account: Cash					GL. No. 101	
Date	**Description**	**PR**	**DR**	**CR**	**Balance**	
2016						
Jun 1	Opening Balance				4,200	DR
Jun 1		J1		900	3,300	DR
Jun 3		J1		1,200	2,100	DR
Jun 6		J1	2,100		4,200	DR
Jun 13		J1	3,000		7,200	DR
Jun 16		J1	300		7,500	DR
Jun 23		J1		950	6,550	DR
Jun 30		J1		1,000	5,550	DR

Account: Accounts Receivable　　　　　　　　　　　　　　　　　　　　　　GL. No.　105

Date	Description	PR	DR	CR	Balance	
2016						
Jun 1	Opening Balance				3,100	DR
Jun 18		J1	1,500		4,600	DR

Account: Prepaid Insurance　　　　　　　　　　　　　　　　　　　　　　　GL. No.　110

Date	Description	PR	DR	CR	Balance	
2016						
Jun 1	Opening Balance				0	DR
Jun 3		J1	1,200		1,200	DR

Account: Equipment　　　　　　　　　　　　　　　　　　　　　　　　　　GL. No.　120

Date	Description	PR	DR	CR	Balance	
2016						
Jun 1	Opening Balance				6,000	DR

Account: Accumulated Depreciation　　　　　　　　　　　　　　　　　　GL. No.　125

Date	Description	PR	DR	CR	Balance	

Account: Accounts Payable　　　　　　　　　　　　　　　　　　　　　　GL. No.　200

Date	Description	PR	DR	CR	Balance	
2016						
Jun 1	Opening Balance				2,300	CR
Jun 11		J1		450	2,750	CR

Account: Interest Payable　　　　　　　　　　　　　　　　　　　　　　GL. No.　205

Date	Description	PR	DR	CR	Balance	

Account: Unearned Revenue　　　　　　　　　　　　　　　　　　　　　GL. No.　210

Date	Description	PR	DR	CR	Balance	
2016						
Jun 1	Opening Balance				600	CR
Jun 16		J1		300	900	CR

Account: Bank Loan — GL. No. 215

Date	Description	PR	DR	CR	Balance	
2016						
Jun 1	Opening Balance				4,000	CR
Jun 23		J1	950		3,050	CR

Account: Gordon, Capital — GL. No. 300

Date	Description	PR	DR	CR	Balance	
2016						
Jun 1	Opening Balance				6,400	CR
Jun 13		J1		3,000	9,400	CR

Account: Gordon, Drawings — GL. No. 310

Date	Description	PR	DR	CR	Balance	
2016						
Jun 30		J1	1,000		1,000	DR

Account: Service Revenue — GL. No. 400

Date	Description	PR	DR	CR	Balance	
2016						
Jun 6		J1		2,100	2,100	CR
Jun 18		J1		1,500	3,600	CR

Account: Advertising Expense — GL. No. 500

Date	Description	PR	DR	CR	Balance	
2016						
Jun 11		J1	450		450	DR

Account: Depreciation Expense — GL. No. 510

Date	Description	PR	DR	CR	Balance	

Account: Insurance Expense — GL. No. 515

Date	Description	PR	DR	CR	Balance	

Account: Interest Expense					GL. No.	520
Date	Description	PR	DR	CR	Balance	

Account: Rent Expense					GL. No.	540
Date	Description	PR	DR	CR	Balance	
2016						
Jun 1		J1	900		900	DR

Appendix 5A: Correcting Entries

At any time during the accounting cycle, errors in a journal entry may be discovered in the accounting records. The error could be for the incorrect amount, or the wrong account may have been used. In either case, a correction must be made.

In accounting systems, there must always be a paper trail to document what has happened to affect the ledger balances. Errors should not be simply erased to be corrected. Instead, a correcting journal entry should be made to reverse the error and make the correction. It is important to clarify that these correcting entries are different from adjusting entries. Correcting entries can be made at any time during the accounting cycle and are meant to fix an error in a previous journal entry.

For example, suppose an entry was made on March 1, 2016 to prepay a one-year insurance policy for $1,800. Instead of debiting the prepaid insurance account, the prepaid rent account was debited instead. The incorrect journal entry is shown in Figure 5A.1.

| JOURNAL | | | | Page 1 |
Date 2016	Account Title and Explanation	PR	Debit	Credit
Mar 1	Prepaid Rent		1,800	
	Cash			1,800
	Pay for one-year insurance policy			

FIGURE 5A.1

This journal entry will overstate prepaid rent and understate the prepaid insurance. If the error is discovered a week later on March 8, 2016, a correction must be made. First, a reversing entry to reverse the original transaction from March 1 and then the correct journal entry. This is shown in Figure 5A.2.

| JOURNAL | | | | Page 2 |
Date 2016	Account Title and Explanation	PR	Debit	Credit
Mar 8	Cash		1,800	
	Prepaid Rent			1,800
	To reverse incorrect entry			
Mar 8	Prepaid Insurance		1,800	
	Cash			1,800
	To correctly pay for one-year insurace policy			

FIGURE 5A.2

After the correcting entries are made, they are posted to the appropriate general ledger accounts to update them. At this point, the ledger account balances will be correct.

In Summary

Prepare correcting entries

↪ Correcting entries are made to fix journal entry errors due to wrong accounts or incorrect amounts.

↪ Correcting entries are different from adjusting entries and they can be made at any time during the accounting cycle.

↪ The related general ledgers accounts should be updated after making correcting entries to update the ledger account balances.

Review Exercise

On June 28, Jeremy Preston reviewed the transactions that were made during the month. During his review, he came across two errors in the journals.

1. A cash payment of $400 for minor repairs on the company vehicle was debited to the automobile asset account instead of the maintenance expense account.

2. A cash payment of $200 for office supplies was debited to the equipment asset account instead of the office supplies asset account.

Prepare the journal entries to correct the two errors on June 28.

See Appendix I for solutions.

JOURNAL				Page 1
Date	Account Titles and Explanation	PR	Debit	Credit

Chapter 6

THE ACCOUNTING CYCLE: STATEMENTS AND CLOSING ENTRIES

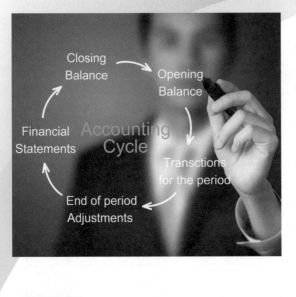

Closing Balance
Opening Balance
Accounting Cycle
Financial Statements
Transactions for the period
End of period Adjustments

LEARNING OUTCOMES

❶ Prepare financial statements using the adjusted trial balance

❷ Prepare closing journal entries and post them to the general ledger

❸ Prepare the post-closing trial balance to complete the accounting cycle

❹ Distinguish between current and long-term assets and liabilities

❺ Prepare the classified balance sheet

❻ Calculate working capital, the current ratio and the quick ratio

❼ Describe the benefits of a computerized accounting system over a manual system

Appendix

❽ Prepare a 10-column worksheet

AMEENGAGE *Access **ameengage.com** for integrated resources including tutorials, practice exercises, the digital textbook and more.*

Preparing the Financial Statements

At this point in the accounting cycle, day-to-day journal entries have been made, adjustments have been recorded, all transactions have been posted to the general ledger and the adjusted trial balance has been completed. It is now time to complete the final three steps of the accounting cycle, beginning with the preparation of financial statements. Recall the first three steps of the accounting cycle are repeated many times during the period, while the remaining six steps are only completed at the end of the period.

Step 9 Prepare the post-closing trial balance

Step 1 Analyze transactions

Step 2 Journalize the transactions

Step 3 Post to ledger accounts

Step 4 Prepare the trial balance

Step 5 Journalize and post adjusting entries

Step 6 Prepare the adjusted trial balance

Step 7 Prepare the financial statements

Step 8 Journalize and post closing entries

ACCOUNTING CYCLE

FIGURE 6.1

135

The final steps of the accounting cycle are illustrated using the MP Consulting example from the previous chapter. At the end of the previous chapter, we prepared a worksheet which shows the unadjusted trial balance, the adjustments made and the adjusted trial balance. This is shown in Figure 6.2. The adjusted trial balance shows the balance of the accounts after the adjustments have been made. At this point, the accounts are ready to be compiled into the financial statements.

MP Consulting Worksheet January 31, 2016						
	Unadjusted Trial Balance		Adjustments		Adjusted Trial Balance	
Account Titles	DR	CR	DR	CR	DR	CR
Cash	$3,800				$3,800	
Accounts Receivable	3,000		$1,000		4,000	
Prepaid Insurance	1,200			$100	1,100	
Equipment	8,300				8,300	
Accumulated Depreciation		$0		150		$150
Accounts Payable		1,250				1,250
Interest Payable		0		25		25
Unearned Revenue		2,000	200			1,800
Bank Loan		2,500				2,500
Parish, Capital		10,300				10,300
Parish, Drawings	2,000				2,000	
Service Revenue		3,300		1,200		4,500
Depreciation Expense	0		150		150	
Insurance Expense	0		100		100	
Interest Expense	0		25		25	
Rent Expense	800				800	
Telephone Expense	250				250	
Total	$19,350	$19,350	$1,475	$1,475	$20,525	$20,525

FIGURE 6.2

The worksheet is only a working paper for accountants, it is not meant to be read by external users of financial information. It is therefore important to create formal documents in the form of an income statement, a statement of owner's equity and a balance sheet.

The Income Statement

The income statement takes the values from the adjusted trial balance columns of the worksheet and organizes them into a format that shows the net income or loss. To illustrate the importance of preparing the adjustments, first look at the income statement in Figure 6.3. This income statement was prepared before any adjustments were made. Net income shows $2,250.

MP Consulting Income Statement (Pre-Adjustment) For the Month Ended January 31, 2016		
Service Revenue		$3,300
Expenses		
Rent Expense	$800	
Telephone Expense	250	
Total Expenses		1,050
Net Income (Loss)		$2,250

FIGURE 6.3

After the adjustments, the income statement can be prepared properly. In Figure 6.4, net income is properly reported as $3,175. If no adjustments were made, net income would have been understated, which would have caused owner's equity to also be understated.

MP Consulting Income Statement For the Month Ended January 31, 2016		
Service Revenue		$4,500
Expenses		
Depreciation Expense	$150	
Insurance Expense	100	
Interest Expense	25	
Rent Expense	800	
Telephone Expense	250	
Total Expenses		1,325
Net Income (Loss)		$3,175 ❶

FIGURE 6.4

Statement of Owner's Equity

The statement of owner's equity reports any changes in equity during the reporting period. The statement of owner's equity for MP Consulting is shown in Figure 6.5. The statement of owner's equity represents the change to owner's equity during the accounting period and is presented with a date format of an elapsed time period similar to the income statement.

MP Consulting Statement of Owner's Equity For the Month Ended January 31, 2016		
Parish, Capital at January 1		$5,300
Add:		
Additional Investment	$5,000	
Net Income	3,175 ❶	8,175
Subtotal		13,475
Less:		
Parish, Drawings		2,000
Parish, Capital at January 31		$11,475 ❷

FIGURE 6.5

The statement begins with the opening balance of the owner's capital account. In our example, the opening balance was $5,300 on January 1, 2016.

Owner's equity will increase if the owner invests more cash or assets into the business, or if the

business earned a profit during the period. In our example, the owner invested $5,000 into the business during the month. Notice the net income (marked 1) from the income statement in Figure 6.4 is also added.

The equity will decrease if the owner withdraws any capital (cash or assets) from the business for personal use, or if the business suffered a loss during the period. There was no loss in our example, but there was a $2,000 withdrawal, as shown in the worksheet under Parish, Drawings.

The final closing balance of the capital account (marked 2) is transferred to the owner's equity section of the balance sheet in Figure 6.6.

The Balance Sheet

The balance sheet is prepared using the values from the asset and liability accounts from the adjusted trial balance. Previous chapters showed the balance sheet organized horizontally, with assets beside liabilities and owner's equity. An alternate organization, and the way balance sheets are most commonly presented, is vertically. Assets are listed above liabilities and owner's equity.

MP Consulting Balance Sheet As at January 31, 2016		
Assets		
Cash		$3,800
Accounts Receivable		4,000
Prepaid Insurance		1,100
Equipment	$8,300	
Accumulated Depreciation	(150)	8,150
Total Assets		$17,050
Liabilities		
Accounts Payable	$1,250	
Interest Payable	25	
Unearned Revenue	1,800	
Bank Loan	2,500	
Total Liabilities		$5,575
Owner's Equity		
Parish, Capital		11,475 ❷
Total Liabilities and Owner's Equity		$17,050

FIGURE 6.6

Notice that the value of Parish, Capital (marked 2) comes directly from the statement of owner's equity in Figure 6.5 and not from the worksheet. The journal entries used to update the capital account will be demonstrated in the next section.

ASPE vs IFRS

ASPE uses the term "Balance Sheet", although the term "Statement of Financial Position" is also allowed.

IFRS uses the term "Statement of Financial Position", although it also allows the term "Balance Sheet".

Notice how equipment is presented. The accumulated depreciation is subtracted from the asset account, giving the net book value of $8,150.

Closing Entries

The statement of owner's equity shows the balance of the owner's capital account after it has been updated with the net income or loss from the period and any drawings. Although this presents the ending balance of owner's capital in the financial statements, the actual account in the general ledger does not yet reflect this new balance. The owner's capital balance must be updated to reflect these changes. This process is called closing the books. **Closing the books** updates owner's capital (the equity of the business) and starts a new income statement for the next accounting period.

In a manual accounting system, equity (owner's capital) is only updated at the end of the period. That means that all accounts that affect equity must have their balances transferred to owner's capital. Thus, revenue and expenses are considered to be **temporary accounts** because they are brought back to a zero balance at the end of each period. This is done so that a new income statement can be prepared for the next period with a fresh start.

An income statement reports net income (or net loss) for a specific period of time. For example, if MP Consulting had net income of $100,000 for a period ended December 31, 2016, this amount would relate exclusively to the period ended on that date and would not be carried over to the next period. Therefore, all revenue and expense accounts are classified as temporary. They must be cleared at the end of an accounting period to start a new fiscal year.

Besides revenue and expenses, owner's drawings is also a temporary account which needs to be closed at the end of the period. This is because owner's drawings measures the amount the owner takes from the business during a specific accounting period and is used to calculate the value of equity. Figure 6.7 illustrates which accounts are temporary and which are permanent.

FIGURE 6.7

There are two methods to close the books, and we will use MP Consulting to illustrate both methods.

Direct Method: Close Directly to Owner's Capital

Closing entries are those entries made to revenue and expenses at the end of an accounting period to close out the accounts. To illustrate the concept of **closing entries,** examine MP Consulting's balance sheet at the beginning of January 2016 (i.e. the end of December 2015). At the beginning of the period, MP Consulting's balance sheet was in balance, as shown in Figure 6.8. T-accounts are also used to illustrate the overall values of three categories: assets, liabilities and equity.

MP Consulting Balance Sheet As at December 31, 2015		
Assets		
Cash		$3,000
Accounts Receivable		1,200
Equipment		6,000
Total Assets		$10,200
Liabilities		
Accounts Payable	$1,000	
Unearned Revenue	900	
Bank Loan	3,000	
Total Liabilities		$4,900
Owner's Equity		
Parish, Capital		5,300
Total Liabilities and Owner's Equity		$10,200

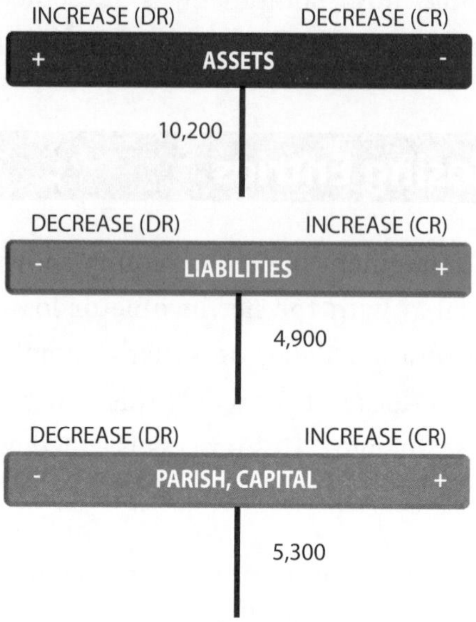

FIGURE 6.8

Notice what happens in Figure 6.9 when we provide services to a customer who pays cash.

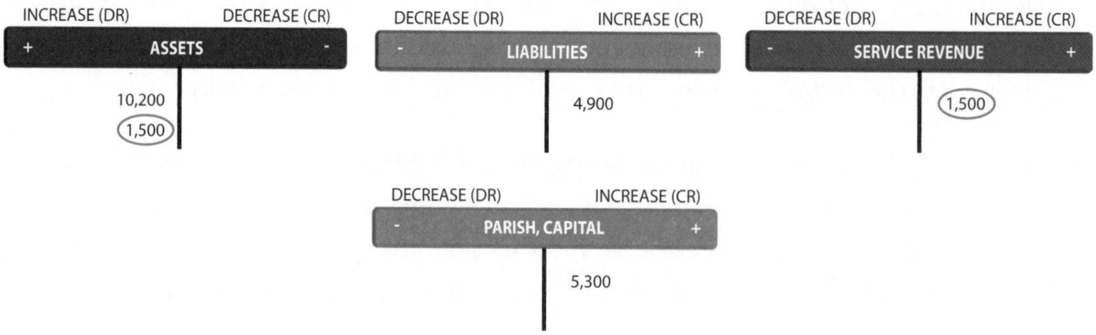

FIGURE 6.9

The balance sheet is now out of balance because assets have increased, but owner's capital has not been updated. A similar discrepancy occurs if a telephone bill is received and will be paid later, as shown in Figure 6.10.

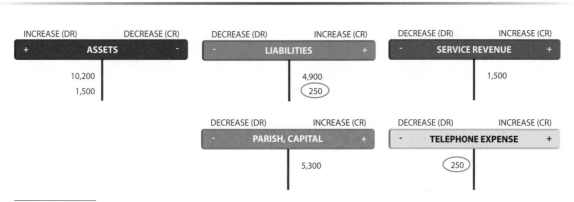

FIGURE 6.10

To get the balance sheet back into balance, owner's capital must be updated with the revenue and expense transactions. To do this, the revenue account must be closed by decreasing revenue and increasing owner's capital, as illustrated in Figure 6.11. The revenue account is now reduced to a zero balance.

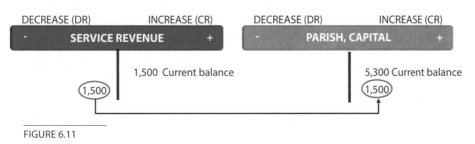

FIGURE 6.11

The expense account must also be closed by decreasing the expense and decreasing owner's capital, as illustrated in Figure 6.12. The expense account is now reduced to zero.

FIGURE 6.12

The end result is that owner's capital will have a new balance and assets will equal liabilities plus equity.

To see how to close the books for MP Consulting, we will use the adjusted trial balance on the worksheet, which shows all the balances we need. The adjusted trial balance is shown again in Figure 6.13.

MP Consulting Adjusted Trial Balance January 31, 2016		
Account Titles	**DR**	**CR**
Cash	$3,800	
Accounts Receivable	4,000	
Prepaid Insurance	1,100	
Equipment	8,300	
Accumulated Depreciation		$150
Accounts Payable		1,250
Interest Payable		25
Unearned Revenue		1,800
Bank Loan		2,500
Parish, Capital		10,300
Parish, Drawings	2,000	❸
Service Revenue		4,500 ❶
Depreciation Expense	150	
Insurance Expense	100	
Interest Expense	25	❷
Rent Expense	800	
Telephone Expense	250	
Total	**$20,525**	**$20,525**

FIGURE 6.13

Notice that the revenue balance is a credit, the expense balances are debits and the owner's drawings balance is also a debit. To reset (close) the balances back to zero to prepare for the next accounting period, we must decrease the value of each of these accounts. Thus, revenue will be debited, expenses will be credited and owner's drawings will be credited. In the context of closing entries, the terms "close," "reset" and "zero out" can be used interchangeably.

Figure 6.14 illustrates the journal entries to close the accounts directly to the capital account. The steps involved are explained.

JOURNAL				Page 3	
Date	**Account Title and Explanation**	**PR**	**Debit**	**Credit**
2016				
❶ Jan 31	Service Revenue	400	4,500	
	Parish, Capital	300		4,500
	To close revenue			
❷ Jan 31	Parish, Capital	300	1,325	
	Depreciation Expense	510		150
	Insurance Expense	515		100
	Interest Expense	520		25
	Rent Expense	540		800
	Telephone Expense	550		250
	To close expenses			
❸ Jan 31	Parish, Capital	300	2,000	
	Parish, Drawings	310		2,000
	To close owner's drawings			

FIGURE 6.14

❶ Zero out the revenue account

The transaction is recorded by debiting (decreasing) the current revenue balance with $4,500 and crediting (increasing) owner's capital with the same amount. The revenue account is now reduced to zero.

❷ Zero out the expense accounts

The transaction is recorded by crediting (decreasing) the current expense balances and debiting (decreasing) owner's capital with the total of all expense amounts. The expense accounts are now reduced to zero. Notice in Figure 6.14 that instead of closing each expense account individually to owner's capital, all expenses were listed in one transaction. This saves time and effort (imagine if the company had 50 or more expense accounts). The debit to owner's capital is the total of all the expenses.

❸ Zero out the owner's drawings account

The transaction is recorded by crediting (decreasing) the current owner's drawings balance with $2,000 and debiting (decreasing) owner's capital with the same amount. The owner's drawings account is now reduced to zero.

Net Result

Owner's capital has increased by the total revenue and decreased by the total expenses and owner's drawings. Figure 6.15 shows the new balance is $11,475. This is the same figure shown as the ending value on the statement of owner's equity from Figure 6.5.

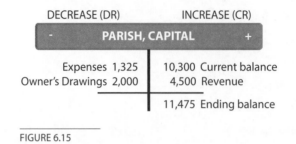

FIGURE 6.15

Income Summary Method: Close Using the Income Summary Account

Instead of debiting and crediting owner's capital directly, it is common to use a temporary holding account called **income summary** to close the revenue and expense accounts. Using our T-account example, Figure 6.16 shows how the income summary account is used.

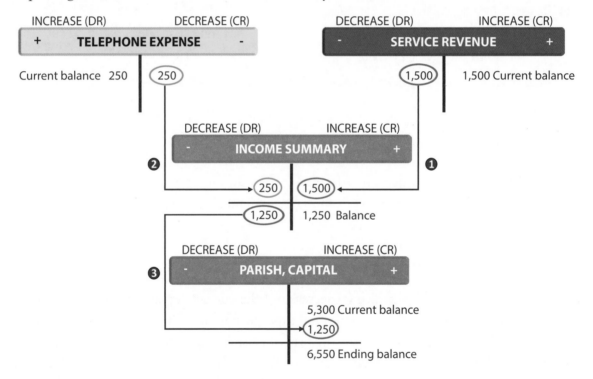

FIGURE 6.16

❶ Debit each revenue account to clear it and credit the income summary account for the total amount.

❷ Credit each expense account to clear it and debit the income summary account for the total amount.

❸ Calculate the balance of the income summary account. This is equal to the net income or loss for the period. Credit owner's capital and debit income summary with the net income amount, or debit owner's capital and credit income summary with the net loss amount.

The income summary is only used to close the revenue and expense accounts. The owner's drawings account is not closed through the income summary account because owner's withdrawals do not affect the amount of net income or net loss. The owner's drawings account is closed directly to the owner's capital account.

Using the adjusted trial balance amounts for our existing company (Figure 6.13), the closing entries are presented as shown in the journal in Figure 6.17 below.

JOURNAL				Page 3
Date	**Account Title and Explanation**	**PR**	**Debit**	**Credit**
2016				
❶ Jan 31	Service Revenue	400	4,500	
	Income Summary	315		4,500
	To close revenue			
❷ Jan 31	Income Summary	315	1,325	
	Depreciation Expense	510		150
	Insurance Expense	515		100
	Interest Expense	520		25
	Rent Expense	540		800
	Telephone Expense	550		250
	To close expenses			
❸ Jan 31	Income Summary	315	3,175	
	Parish, Capital	300		3,175
	To close Income Summary			
Jan 31	Parish, Capital	300	2,000	
	Parish, Drawings	310		2,000
	To close owner's drawings			

FIGURE 6.17

The first two transactions are nearly the same as shown in the direct method (Figure 6.14), except that the income summary account is used instead of owner's capital.

The third transaction is used to close the income summary to the capital account. The value of $3,175 is the difference between the revenue and expenses accounts. Note that this value is the same as the net income reported on the income statement in Figure 6.4.

The last transaction is identical to the one shown in the direct method (Figure 6.14).

Figure 6.18 summarizes how the temporary accounts are closed at the end of an accounting period under each method.

Direct Method

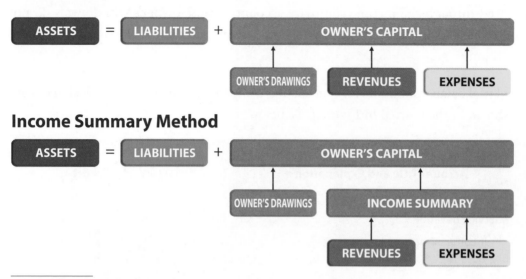

Income Summary Method

FIGURE 6.18

Remember, all journal entries must be posted to the general ledger. Assuming MP Consulting uses the income summary method to close its books, Figure 6.19 shows how the ledger accounts would look at the end of the period. All journal entries from the two previous chapters and the closing entries from this chapter are reflected here. Notice that adjustments and closing entries include a description to make them stand out in the ledger.

GENERAL LEDGER

Account: Cash						GL. No.	101
Date	**Description**	**PR**	**DR**	**CR**	**Balance**		
2016						
Jan 1	Opening Balance				3,000	DR
Jan 2		J1	1,500		4,500	DR
Jan 3		J1		800	3,700	DR
Jan 4		J1		1,200	2,500	DR
Jan 5		J1	5,000		7,500	DR
Jan 7		J1		2,300	5,200	DR
Jan 16		J1		500	4,700	DR
Jan 19		J1	1,100		5,800	DR
Jan 30		J1		2,000	3,800	DR

Account: Accounts Receivable						GL. No.	105
Date	**Description**	**PR**	**DR**	**CR**	**Balance**		
2016						
Jan 1	Opening Balance				1,200	DR
Jan 10		J1	1,800		3,000	DR
Jan 31	Adjustment	J2	1,000		4,000	DR

Account: Prepaid Insurance — GL. No. 110

Date	Description	PR	DR	CR	Balance	
2016						
Jan 1	Opening Balance				0	DR
Jan 4		J1	1,200		1,200	DR
Jan 31	Adjustment	J2		100	1,100	DR

Account: Equipment — GL. No. 120

Date	Description	PR	DR	CR	Balance	
2016						
Jan 1	Opening Balance				6,000	DR
Jan 7		J1	2,300		8,300	DR

Account: Accumulated Depreciation — GL. No. 125

Date	Description	PR	DR	CR	Balance	
2016						
Jan 31	Adjustment	J2		150	150	CR

Account: Accounts Payable — GL. No. 200

Date	Description	PR	DR	CR	Balance	
2016						
Jan 1	Opening Balance				1,000	CR
Jan 20		J1		250	1,250	CR

Account: Interest Payable — GL. No. 205

Date	Description	PR	DR	CR	Balance	
2016						
Jan 31	Adjustment	J2		25	25	CR

Account: Unearned Revenue — GL. No. 210

Date	Description	PR	DR	CR	Balance	
2016						
Jan 1	Opening Balance				900	CR
Jan 19		J1		1,100	2,000	CR
Jan 31	Adjustment	J2	200		1,800	CR

Account: Bank Loan   GL. No. 215

Date	Description	PR	DR	CR	Balance	
2016						
Jan 1	Opening Balance				3,000	CR
Jan 16		J1	500		2,500	CR

Account: Parish, Capital   GL. No. 300

Date	Description	PR	DR	CR	Balance	
2016						
Jan 1	Opening Balance				5,300	CR
Jan 5		J1		5,000	10,300	CR
Jan 31	Closing Entry	J3		3,175	13,475	CR
Jan 31	Closing Entry	J3	2,000		11,475	CR

Account: Parish, Drawings   GL. No. 310

Date	Description	PR	DR	CR	Balance	
2016						
Jan 30		J1	2,000		2,000	DR
Jan 31	Closing Entry	J3		2,000	0	DR

Account: Income Summary   GL. No. 315

Date	Description	PR	DR	CR	Balance	
2016						
Jan 31	Closing Entry	J3		4,500	4,500	CR
Jan 31	Closing Entry	J3	1,325		3,175	CR
Jan 31	Closing Entry	J3	3,175		0	CR

Account: Service Revenue   GL. No. 400

Date	Description	PR	DR	CR	Balance	
2016						
Jan 2		J1		1,500	1,500	CR
Jan 10		J1		1,800	3,300	CR
Jan 31	Adjustment	J2		200	3,500	CR
Jan 31	Adjustment	J2		1,000	4,500	CR
Jan 31	Closing Entry	J3	4,500		0	CR

Account: Depreciation Expense   GL. No. 510

Date	Description	PR	DR	CR	Balance	
2016						
Jan 31	Adjustment	J2	150		150	DR
Jan 31	Closing Entry	J3		150	0	DR

Account: Insurance Expense					GL. No.	515	
Date	Description	PR	DR	CR	Balance		
2016							
Jan 31	Adjustment	J2	100		100	DR	
Jan 31	Closing Entry	J3		100	0	DR	

Account: Interest Expense					GL. No.	520	
Date	Description	PR	DR	CR	Balance		
2016							
Jan 31	Adjustment	J2	25		25	DR	
Jan 31	Closing Entry	J3		25	0	DR	

Account: Rent Expense					GL. No.	540	
Date	Description	PR	DR	CR	Balance		
2016							
Jan 3		J1	800		800	DR	
Jan 31	Closing Entry	J3		800	0	DR	

Account: Telephone Expense					GL. No.	550	
Date	Description	PR	DR	CR	Balance		
2016							
Jan 20		J1	250		250	DR	
Jan 31	Closing Entry	J3		250	0	DR	

FIGURE 6.19

Post-Closing Trial Balance

Once the closing entries are completed, it is necessary to ensure that the balance sheet still balances. This is done by completing another trial balance called the post-closing trial balance. The **post-closing trial balance** only lists accounts that have a balance. Since the closing entries have been journalized and posted, only assets, liabilities and owner's capital should have a balance. The post-closing trial balance is shown in Figure 6.20.

MP Consulting Post-Closing Trial Balance January 31, 2016		
Account Titles	**DR**	**CR**
Cash	$3,800	
Accounts Receivable	4,000	
Prepaid Insurance	1,100	
Equipment	8,300	
Accumulated Depreciation		$150
Accounts Payable		1,250
Interest Payable		25
Unearned Revenue		1,800
Bank Loan		2,500
Parish, Capital		11,475
Total	$17,200	$17,200

FIGURE 6.20

Once the post-closing trial balance is complete, the entire accounting cycle for the period is done. The company is ready to begin the next accounting cycle for the upcoming accounting period.

Classified Balance Sheet

We have learned that the balance sheet lists assets, liabilities and equity. However, it is useful to group together similar assets and similar liabilities on the basis of their financial characteristics. Before we go into the details of a classified balance sheet, we will first discuss the groupings of assets and liabilities. Figure 6.21 shows the groupings of assets and liabilities on the balance sheet.

Current Assets vs. Long-Term Assets

Assets are divided into two categories

1. **Current assets** are those that are likely to be converted into cash or used up within the next 12 months through the day-to-day operations of the business. Some examples of current assets are cash, inventory (products sold to customers), accounts receivable and prepaid expenses.

2. **Long-term assets** are used to operate a business and are not expected to turn into cash or be used up within the next 12 months unless they are sold for reasons other than the day-to-day operations of the business. Any asset that is not included in the current asset category is assumed to be long-term. Thus our classified balance sheet will include two sections of assets. Current assets are presented under a current asset heading. Long-term assets (various types are discussed below) are presented separately.

Certain types of long-term assets must be presented separately on the classified balance sheet. Although not all of the long-term assets discussed below will be covered in detail in this textbook, you may come across these terms if you look at the balance sheet of other companies.

Property, plant and equipment are long-term physical assets used to help run the business. This category contains several types of long-term assets such as land, building, equipment and furniture. Each of these items must be presented separately along with any accumulated depreciation to show its net book value.

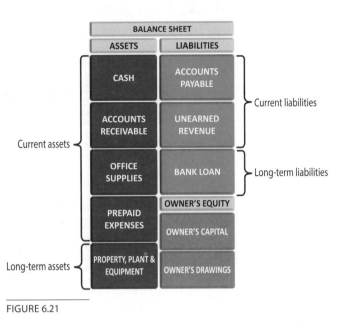

FIGURE 6.21

Long-term investments are investments by the business by buying debt (e.g. bonds) or equity (e.g. shares) of another company. These are assets because the business owns the investment and expects to receive benefits from owning them. Benefits are usually cash receipts of interest or dividends.

Intangible assets are long-term assets that lack a physical body. They provide legal rights and include items such as patents, trademarks or copyrights. Some intangible assets such as patents have their cost allocated across their useful life, similar to how depreciation is accounted for property, plant and equipment. These intangibles must show their net book value. Different types of intangible assets may require different methods of recording depreciation or reductions in their value.

Goodwill is a special type of intangible asset. It only arises when a business buys another company and pays more than the fair value of the company's net assets.

Current Liabilities vs. Long-Term Liabilities

Liabilities are divided into two categories

1. **Current liabilities** are amounts due to be paid within the next 12 months. Examples of current liabilities include accounts payable, interest payable and unearned revenue. (assuming the related revenue will be earned within the next 12 months).

2. **Long-term liabilities** are amounts due to be paid after 12 months. Examples of long-term liabilities include bank loans and mortgages.

Long-term liabilities usually have a portion that is considered current. That is, a portion must be repaid within the next 12 months. To properly plan for cash payments in the upcoming year, accountants will separate the current portion from the long-term portion on the classified balance sheet.

For example, if a company had a $50,000 bank loan that was supposed to be paid off in five equal installments, $10,000 ($50,000 ÷ 5 years) would be considered current and the rest ($40,000) would be considered long-term. In other words, $10,000 is due within one year and $40,000 is due after one year. This separation of current debt from long-term debt is done on the date of the balance sheet. Each year, the amount of long-term debt would decrease because a portion is classified as current debt. This is illustrated in Figure 6.22.

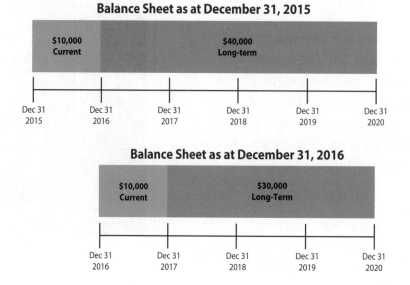

FIGURE 6.22

What is the reason for splitting the balance sheet assets and liabilities between current and long-term items? Readers of the financial statements are interested in the ability of the business to pay the upcoming debt, and where they will get the money to do so. Current liabilities indicate the upcoming debt and current assets indicate where the money will come from. The classified balance sheet also indicates how much the company has invested in itself by means of long-term assets. The amount of long-term liabilities and equity also provide a snapshot of how the company finances its operations.

Now that we have defined current and long-term assets, as well as current and long-term liabilities, we can demonstrate the difference between the balance sheet that we have been using so far and a classified balance sheet.

The classified balance sheet for a sample company is illustrated in Figure 6.23. It illustrates the categories used to classify the various assets and liabilities of the business. The order of presentation for the current assets is shown as most liquid (cash) to least liquid (prepaid insurance) followed by various long-term assets in order of liquidity. Liabilities are also shown in order of when they are due, with the debts due earlier listed first.

Both ASPE and IFRS do not prescribe the listing order of items on the balance sheet. Most companies that adopt ASPE list the items from most liquid to least liquid, as stated above. Interestingly, most companies that adopt IFRS, particularly European companies, take an opposite approach by listing least liquid assets first. On the other side of the balance sheet, those companies also tend to present equity first, followed by long-term liabilities and current liabilities.

Great Scot Classified Balance Sheet As at December 31, 2016			
Assets			
Current Assets			
Cash		$42,500	
Accounts Receivable		56,300	
Inventory		87,400	
Prepaid Insurance		11,600	
Total Current Assets			$197,800
Long-Term Investments			
Equity Investment		60,000	
Debt Investment		30,000	
Total Long-Term Investments			90,000
Property, Plant & Equipment			
Land		240,000	
Building	$680,000		
Less Accumulated Depreciation	(52,000)	628,000	
Equipment	123,000		
Less Accumulated Depreciation	(26,000)	97,000	
Total Property, Plant & Equipment			965,000
Patents			45,000
Goodwill			60,000
Total Assets			$1,357,800
Liabilities			
Current Liabilities			
Accounts Payable		$62,100	
Interest Payable		1,300	
Unearned Revenue		15,800	
Current Portion of Bank Loan		25,000	
Total Current Liabilities			$104,200
Long-Term Liabilities			
Mortgage		520,000	
Long-Term Portion of Bank Loan		120,000	
Total Long-Term Liabilities			640,000
Total Liabilities			744,200
Owner's Equity			
Scot, Capital			613,600
Total Owner's Equity			613,600
Total Liabilities and Owner's Equity			$1,357,800

FIGURE 6.23

Let us see how the sample company used in this chapter would prepare the classified balance sheet. The balance sheet for MP Consulting was shown in Figure 6.6. It was not a classified balance sheet, so all assets and liabilities were grouped as one. The company has a $2,500 bank loan, of which $1,000 will be paid off by January 31, 2017 (one year from the balance sheet date).

The classified balance sheet is shown in Figure 6.24. Notice that $1,000 of the bank loan is classified as current because it will be paid within the next one-year period.

MP Consulting Classified Balance Sheet As at January 31, 2016		
Assets		
Current Assets		
Cash	$3,800	
Accounts Receivable	4,000	
Prepaid Insurance	1,100	
Total Current Assets		$8,900
Property, Plant and Equipment		
Equipment	8,300	
Less Accumulated Depreciation	(173)	
Total Property, Plant and Equipment		8,127
Total Assets		$17,027
Liabilities		
Current Liabilities		
Accounts Payable	$1,250	
Interest Payable	25	
Unearned Revenue	1,800	
Current Portion of Bank Loan	1,000	
Total Current Liabilities		$4,075
Long-Term Liabilities		
Long-Term Portion of Bank Loan	1,500	
Total Long-Term Liabilities		1,500
Total Liabilities		5,575
Owner's Equity		
Parish, Capital		11,452
Total Owner's Equity		11,452
Total Liabilities and Owner's Equity		$17,027

FIGURE 6.24

Analyzing the Financial Statements

Financial statements can do more than just tell us how much profit was earned or the total of our assets or liabilities. Financial statement analysis includes calculating ratios between two values to provide insight into the business and how well it is operating. This topic will be covered in more detail later, but for now we will look at a few ratios that indicate how liquid the business is. Liquidity is the ability of the business to convert current assets to cash to pay its debts as they come due.

This presentation of the classified balance sheet, which separates current from long-term items, allows for the easy calculation of working capital, the current ratio and the quick ratio. Each of these looks at how well the company can pay its debts with its liquid, or current assets.

Working capital is the difference between current assets and current liabilities. This provides a dollar figure, which if positive, means the business has more current assets than current liabilities and should be able to pay its current debt. If current liabilities are greater than current assets, the business may have difficulty paying its debt as it comes due. Using the values in Figure 6.24, the working capital for MP Consulting is

$$\text{Current Assets} \quad - \quad \text{Current Liabilities} \quad = \quad \text{Working Capital}$$
$$\$8,900 \quad - \quad \$4,075 \quad = \quad \$4,825$$

MP Consulting has more than enough current assets to pay for the current liabilities and should have no trouble paying the debts as they come due.

The **current ratio** measures a company's ability to pay off short-term debt. The higher the current ratio, the more current assets the company has to pay off debt that is due within one year. The formula is shown below

$$\text{Current Ratio} \ = \ \frac{\text{Current Assets}}{\text{Current Liabilities}}$$

From the balance sheet in Figure 6.24, the current ratio is calculated as

$$\text{Current Ratio} = \frac{\$8,900}{\$4,075}$$
$$= \ 2.18$$

This indicates that the company has $2.18 in current assets for every $1.00 in current liabilities. MP Consulting is doing well, since it has enough current assets to cover its upcoming debt payments.

The **quick ratio** is similar to the current ratio, but only counts assets that can easily be turned into cash. Thus, assets such as prepaid items are omitted and only cash, accounts receivable and short-term investments are included. Short-term investments will not be covered in this textbook. The formula is shown below

$$\text{Quick Ratio} = \frac{\text{Cash} + \text{Short-Term Investments} + \text{Accounts Receivable}}{\text{Current Liabilities}}$$

From the balance sheet in Figure 6.24, the quick ratio is calculated as

$$\text{Quick Ratio} = \frac{\$3,800 + \$4,000}{\$4,075}$$
$$= 1.91$$

This shows that the company has $1.91 of very liquid current assets for every $1.00 of current liabilities. Again, MP Consulting is doing well. If the quick ratio were to drop below 1.00, it could indicate problems with paying back debts.

The Evolution from Manual to Computerized Accounting

One of the challenges in teaching a modern accounting course is the need to combine traditional concepts and methods with modern technology. However, the reality is that today's accounting students may never see or use a set of paper-based accounting journals and ledgers.

Although computerized systems are becoming more common, and while they make gathering and analyzing information easier for the accountant, having a sound knowledge of traditional paper-based systems provides a foundation for understanding what accounting is all about. It also allows for an understanding of how the computerized system will store the information and how to look for errors or anomalies in the data.

Before computers, bookkeepers used various types of journals to maintain company financial records. Special journals were used to track similar types of transactions, such as sales and purchases. The general journal was used for infrequent transactions, such as adjustments. All these journals were used to update the general ledger and other accounts.

In manual systems, recording procedures often provide the analytical structure for the accountant. If accounts receivable needed analyzing, the accountant would refer to all related journals and ledgers for accounts receivable. If, on the other hand, inventory was being analyzed, the paper trail from receipt to shipping would be tracked accordingly.

Similar to the manual system, a computerized system will typically have special sections or journals to enter similar types of transactions, such as sales and purchases. There will also be a general journal used for adjusting entries and other specific types of transactions. All these journals will update the general ledger and other accounts and this information is kept in a database for easy storage and retrieval.

In effect, all the accountant must worry about is analyzing and creating the journal entries for the day-to-day transaction, and journalizing the adjusting entries at the end of the period. The day-to-day transactions do not have to be entered in chronological order since the software will automatically order them when reports are prepared. All the posting to the general ledger, preparing the various reports, and even preparing the closing entries are done automatically by the computer.

It is the responsibility of management and the accounting department to work with information technology personnel to buy or design a system that meets organizational objectives. Manual systems help accountants learn the basics of their profession; however, in today's business world, a properly designed computer system, tailored to the needs of a specific company, can make accounting more efficient.

AMEENGAGE *Access **ameengage.com** for integrated resources including tutorials, practice exercises, the digital textbook and more.*

In Summary

Prepare financial statements using the adjusted trial balance

↪ The adjusted trial balance provides the updated balances that are used to create the financial statements. The income statement shows the net income or loss for the period. The statement of owner's equity shows the change in equity for the period. The balance sheet shows the financial standing of the business at the period end date.

Prepare closing journal entries and post to the general ledger

↪ Closing journal entries zero out the income statement accounts and the owner's drawing account. The entries are then posted to the general ledger. After closing these accounts, a new income statement can be started for the next accounting period.

↪ There are two ways to close the income statement accounts: close directly to owner's capital or close to an intermediary income summary account.

Prepare the post-closing trial balance to complete the accounting cycle

↪ A post-closing trial balance is created after the books are closed. It will only show accounts with a balance, which are assets, liabilities and owner's capital.

Distinguish between current and long-term assets and liabilities

↪ Current assets are assets that will be converted to cash or used up within one year. Long-term assets are typically used to run the business and will not be used up within one year.

↪ Current liabilities are liabilities that are due within one year. Long-term liabilities are due beyond one year.

Prepare the classified balance sheet

↪ The classified balance sheet presents assets and liabilities separated into current and long-term items.

Calculate working capital, the current ratio and the quick ratio

↪ Working capital is the difference between current assets and current liabilities.

↪ The current ratio is calculated as current assets divided by current liabilities.

↪ The quick ratio is calculated as liquid assets (cash and accounts receivable) divided by current liabilities.

Describe some benefits of a computerized accounting system over a manual system

↪ A computerized system automates many of the steps of the accounting cycle, such as posting to the general ledger and preparing reports. It also allows for easy retrieval of the data.

Review Exercise

Catherine Gordon is running her own proprietary business called CG Accounting. CG Accounting provides bookkeeping services to small and mid-sized companies. The company was introduced in the review exercises from chapter 4 and 5. Before you begin this exercise, familiarize yourself with the review exercise in chapter 5 because this is a continuation.

Journal entries for the month have already been completed, as have the adjustments at month end. The adjusted trial balance is presented below.

CG Accounting Trial Balance June 30, 2016		
Account Titles	DR	CR
Cash	$5,550	
Accounts Receivable	5,500	
Prepaid Insurance	1,100	
Equipment	6,000	
Accumulated Depreciation		$100
Accounts Payable		2,750
Interest Payable		25
Unearned Revenue		450
Bank Loan		3,050
Gordon, Capital		9,400
Gordon, Drawings	1,000	
Service Revenue		4,950
Advertising Expense	450	
Depreciation Expense	100	
Insurance Expense	100	
Interest Expense	25	
Rent Expense	900	
Total	**$20,725**	**$20,725**

The balance of owner's equity as at May 31, 2016 was $6,400. Also recall from the chapter 4 review exercise that during June the owner contributed $3,000 cash to the business and withdrew $1,000 cash for personal use. Assume that $800 of the bank loan must be paid by June 30, 2017.

CG Accounting uses the following accounts and accounting numbers in its accounting records.

Account Description	Account #
ASSETS	
Cash	101
Accounts Receivable	105
Prepaid Insurance	110
Equipment	120
Accumulated Depreciation	125
LIABILITIES	
Accounts Payable	200
Interest Payable	205
Unearned Revenue	210
Bank Loan	215
OWNER'S EQUITY	
Gordon, Capital	300
Gordon, Drawings	310
Income Summary	315

Account Description	Account #
REVENUE	
Service Revenue	400
EXPENSES	
Advertising Expense	500
Bad Debt Expense	505
Depreciation Expense	510
Insurance Expense	515
Interest Expense	520
Maintenance Expense	525
Office Supplies Expense	530
Professional Fees Expense	535
Rent Expense	540
Salaries Expense	545
Telephone Expense	550
Travel Expense	555

Required

a) Prepare the income statement, statement of owner's equity and the classified balance sheet.

b) Complete the closing entries using the income summary account and post them to the general ledger.

c) Prepare the post-closing trial balance.

See Appendix I for solutions.

a) Prepare the income statement, statement of owner's equity and the classified balance sheet.

b) Complete the closing entries using the income summary method and post them to the general ledger.

JOURNAL				Page 3
Date	Account Titles and Explanation	PR	Debit	Credit

GENERAL LEDGER

Account: Cash					GL. No. 101	
Date	Description	PR	DR	CR	Balance	
2016						
Jun 1	Opening Balance				4,200	DR
Jun 1		J1		900	3,300	DR
Jun 3		J1		1,200	2,100	DR
Jun 6		J1	2,100		4,200	DR
Jun 13		J1	3,000		7,200	DR
Jun 16		J1	300		7,500	DR
Jun 23		J1		950	6,550	DR
Jun 30		J1		1,000	5,550	DR

Account: Accounts Receivable					GL. No.	105
Date	Description	PR	DR	CR	Balance	
2016						
Jun 1	Opening Balance				3,100	DR
Jun 18		J1	1,500		4,600	DR
Jun 30	Adjusting Entry	J2	900		5,500	DR

Account: Prepaid Insurance					GL. No.	110
Date	Description	PR	DR	CR	Balance	
2016						
Jun 1	Opening Balance				0	DR
Jun 3		J1	1,200		1,200	DR
Jun 30	Adjusting Entry	J2		100	1,100	DR

Account: Equipment					GL. No.	120
Date	Description	PR	DR	CR	Balance	
2016						
Jun 1	Opening Balance				6,000	DR

Account: Accumulated Depreciation					GL. No.	125
Date	Description	PR	DR	CR	Balance	
2016						
Jun 30	Adjusting Entry	J2		100	100	CR

Account: Accounts Payable					GL. No.	200
Date	Description	PR	DR	CR	Balance	
2016						
Jun 1	Opening Balance				2,300	CR
Jun 11		J1		450	2,750	CR

Account: Interest Payable					GL. No.	205
Date	Description	PR	DR	CR	Balance	
2016						
Jun 30	Adjusting Entry	J2		25	25	CR

Account: Unearned Revenue					GL. No.	210
Date	Description	PR	DR	CR	Balance	
2016						
Jun 1	Opening Balance				600	CR
Jun 16		J1		300	900	CR
Jun 30	Adjusting Entry	J2	450		450	CR

Account: Bank Loan   GL. No.   215

Date	Description	PR	DR	CR	Balance	
2016						
Jun 1	Opening Balance				4,000	CR
Jun 23		J1	950		3,050	CR

Account: Gordon, Capital   GL. No.   300

Date	Description	PR	DR	CR	Balance	
2016						
Jun 1	Opening Balance				6,400	CR
Jun 13		J1		3,000	9,400	CR

Account: Gordon, Drawings   GL. No.   310

Date	Description	PR	DR	CR	Balance	
2016						
Jun 30		J1	1,000		1,000	DR

Account: Income Summary   GL. No.   315

Date	Description	PR	DR	CR	Balance	

Account: Service Revenue   GL. No.   400

Date	Description	PR	DR	CR	Balance	
2016						
Jun 6		J1		2,100	2,100	CR
Jun 18		J1		1,500	3,600	CR
Jun 30	Adjusting Entry	J2		450	4,050	CR
Jun 30	Adjusting Entry	J2		900	4,950	CR

Account: Advertising Expense   GL. No.   500

Date	Description	PR	DR	CR	Balance	
2016						
Jun 11		J1	450		450	DR

Account: Depreciation Expense					GL. No.	510	
Date	Description	PR	DR	CR	Balance		
2016							
Jun 30	Adjusting Entry	J2	100		100	DR	

Account: Insurance Expense					GL. No.	515	
Date	Description	PR	DR	CR	Balance		
2016							
Jun 30	Adjusting Entry	J2	100		100	DR	

Account: Interest Expense					GL. No.	520	
Date	Description	PR	DR	CR	Balance		
2016							
Jun 30	Adjusting Entry	J2	25		25	DR	

Account: Rent Expense					GL. No.	540	
Date	Description	PR	DR	CR	Balance		
2016							
Jun 1		J1	900		900	DR	

c) Prepare the post-closing trial balance.

Account Titles	DR	CR

Appendix 6A: The 10-Column Worksheet

Earlier, we introduced the six-column worksheet to help display the changes in account balances due to adjustments. Although this worksheet is optional, it shows the unadjusted trial balance, the adjustments and the adjusted trial balance all in one place. An extension of this is the optional ten-column worksheet. In this worksheet, the first six columns are identical to what we learned. The extra columns are to show the accounts and balances that will appear on the financial statements. One set of columns is for the income statement accounts and the other set is for the balance sheet and owner's equity accounts. The values shown in these columns are copied directly from the adjusted trial balance columns.

In Figure 6A.1, the income statement accounts are separated from the balance sheet and equity accounts. Notice that the initial debit and credit totals of the income statement accounts do not balance. This is expected because the company should report an income or loss. In this case, MP Consulting shows a greater credit balance (see numbers 1 and 2). Since the credit total is higher, they generated an income. Find the difference between the two figures and add the difference to the smaller total. In the case of MP Consulting, the difference is $3,175 (see number 3) and is added to the smaller debit total to get $4,500. This ensures the income statement columns balance. If the company had a net loss, the difference would be added to the credit column to ensure the income statement columns balance.

A similar process is completed for the balance sheet and equity columns. The difference is calculated and added to the smaller total (see number 4) to ensure the balance sheet and equity columns balance. Notice that the difference between the income statement columns and the difference between the balance sheet and equity columns are identical. This should always be the case. A net income will increase the capital account; therefore it will always be a credit to the balance sheet and equity accounts. Conversely, a net loss decreases equity and is placed on the debit side of the balance sheet and equity accounts.

MP Consulting
Worksheet
January 31, 2016

Account Titles	Unadjusted Trial Balance DR	Unadjusted Trial Balance CR	Adjustments DR	Adjustments CR	Adjusted Trial Balance DR	Adjusted Trial Balance CR	Income Statement DR	Income Statement CR	Balance Sheet & Equity DR	Balance Sheet & Equity CR
Cash	$3,800				$3,800				$3,800	
Accounts Receivable	3,000		$1,000		4,000				4,000	
Prepaid Insurance	1,200			$100	1,100				1,100	
Equipment	8,300				8,300				8,300	
Accumulated Depreciation		$0		150		$150				$150
Accounts Payable		1,250				1,250				1,250
Interest Payable		0		25		25				25
Unearned Revenue		2,000	200			1,800				1,800
Bank Loan		2,500				2,500				2,500
Parish, Capital		10,300				10,300				10,300
Parish, Drawings	2,000				2,000				2,000	
Service Revenue		3,300		1,200		4,500		$4,500		
Depreciation Expense	0		150		150		$150			
Insurance Expense	0		100		100		100			
Interest Expense	0		25		25		25			
Rent Expense	800				800		800			
Telephone Expense	250				250		❷ 250	❶		
Total	$19,350	$19,350	$1,475	$1,475	$20,525	$20,525	$1,325	$4,500	$19,200	$16,025
Net Income (Loss)							❸ 3,175			❹ 3,175
Total							$4,500	$4,500	$19,200	$19,200

FIGURE 6A.1

 Access **ameengage.com** *for integrated resources including tutorials, practice exercises, the digital textbook and more.*

In Summary

Prepare a 10-column worksheet

⇨ A ten-column worksheet is an extension of a six-column worksheet where the four additional columns are for the income statement, balance sheet and owner's equity accounts.

⇨ For the income statement columns, the difference between the initial debit and credit totals is equal to the company's reported income or loss.

⇨ The debit and credit columns of the balance sheet and equity should have the exact same difference as the income statement columns.

Review Exercise

Catherine Gordon is running her own proprietary business called CG Accounting. CG Accounting provides bookkeeping services to small and mid-sized companies. The company prepares financial statements on a monthly basis.

The journal entries for the month of June have already been entered in the journal and posted to the ledger.

At the end of June 2016, CG Accounting had to make the following adjustments.

Jun 30   The prepaid insurance represents a one-year policy that started in June. One month has now been used.

Jun 30   When examining the balance of unearned revenue, Catherine determined that $450 has now been earned.

Jun 30   Interest has accrued on the balance of the bank loan for the month. The loan interest rate is 10%. (For simplicity, round the interest to the nearest whole number.)

Jun 30   Depreciation on the equipment for the month must be recorded. The equipment is depreciated using the straight-line method. The equipment is expected to last five years and will have no residual value

Jun 30   Catherine started an audit for a new client. The contract is for 20 days of work starting June 21. At the end of the contract, the client will pay CG Accounting $1,800. Accrue the revenue earned for June.

Required

See Appendix I for solutions.

Complete the worksheet.

CG Accounting
Worksheet
June 30, 2016

Account Titles	Unadjusted Trial Balance DR	Unadjusted Trial Balance CR	Adjustments DR	Adjustments CR	Adjusted Trial Balance DR	Adjusted Trial Balance CR	Income Statement DR	Income Statement CR	Balance Sheet & Equity DR	Balance Sheet & Equity CR
Cash	$5,550									
Accounts Receivable	4,600									
Prepaid Insurance	1,200									
Equipment	6,000									
Accumulated Depreciation		$0								
Accounts Payable		2,750								
Interest Payable		0								
Unearned Revenue		900								
Bank Loan		3,050								
Gordon, Capital		9,400								
Gordon, Drawings	1,000									
Service Revenue		3,600								
Advertising Expense	450									
Depreciation Expense	0									
Insurance Expense	0									
Interest Expense	0									
Rent Expense	900									
Total	$19,700	$19,700								
Net Income (Loss)										
Total										

Chapter 7
INVENTORY: MERCHANDISING TRANSACTIONS

LEARNING OUTCOMES

❶ Define a merchandising business

❷ Differentiate between the perpetual and the periodic inventory systems

❸ Record journal entries related to inventory purchases under the perpetual inventory system

❹ Record journal entries related to inventory sales under the perpetual inventory system

❺ Calculate gross profit and gross margin percentage

❻ Prepare a multistep income statement and classified multistep income statement

❼ Prepare closing entries for a merchandising business under the perpetual inventory system

❽ Identify inventory controls

Appendix

❾ Record journal entries related to inventory purchases under the periodic inventory system

❿ Record journal entries related to inventory sales under the periodic inventory system

⓫ Calculate cost of goods sold under the periodic inventory system

⓬ Prepare closing entries for a merchandising business under the periodic inventory system

AMEENGAGE™ *Access **ameengage.com** for integrated resources including tutorials, practice exercises, the digital textbook and more.*

Merchandising Businesses

A company that sells a product has a number of similarities to a company that sells a service. Both companies will incur expenses to market and sell their product or service. If the businesses have employees, then both will have salaries expenses. Both companies will buy items that are classified as property, plant and equipment, and both companies will likely incur debt and pay it off. Thus, most of the transactions of a service company will be similar to those of a merchandising business. A **merchandising business**, or merchandiser, is any business that buys and sells products for the purpose of making a profit.

The main difference between a merchandising business and a service company is that the merchandising business holds an asset called inventory for sale. **Inventory** is a collection of physical goods that a company has purchased or manufactured to sell to its customers. Inventory is listed on the balance sheet right below accounts receivable because it is a fairly liquid asset. Inventory has a value that can change unpredictably and even decrease over time, but a merchandiser must sell inventory for more than its cost in order to make profit. Senior management and accountants are responsible to ensure controls are in place to accurately track the value of inventory from the point of purchase to the point of sale.

Because merchandisers sell products instead of services, their revenue is called sales revenue. An expense account called **cost of goods sold (COGS)** is used to track the cost of the inventory that was sold during a particular period. For example, if a company purchased a television from a supplier for $200 and sold it for $500, it would have sales revenue of $500 and cost of goods sold of $200. The difference between sales revenue and cost of goods sold is called gross profit.

Gross Profit = Sales Revenue - Cost of Goods Sold

Gross profit is used to pay for all other expenses in the business. The television sale created $300 ($500 – $200) of gross profit which is used to pay for operating expenses such as rent, salaries, and advertising. After operating expenses have been deducted, the remaining amount is net income.

Figure 7.1 illustrates the difference in the configuration of the accounts of a merchandising business and a service company. Notice the new inventory asset, cost of goods sold and gross profit in the merchandising company. Other revenue and other expenses will be covered later in this chapter.

Service Company   **Merchandising Company**

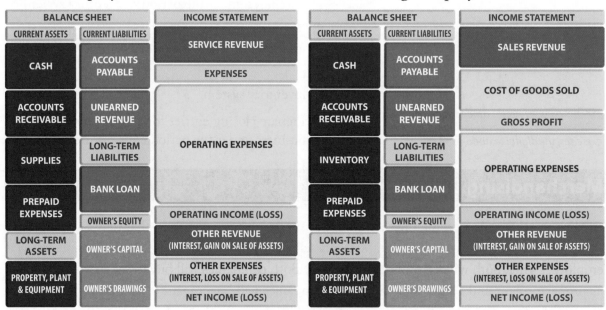

FIGURE 7.1

To see how revenue, cost of goods sold, gross profit and operating expenses interact, consider the following example. A business purchases T-shirts for $5.00 each and plans to sell them for $7.00 each. The business also incurs a variety of operating expenses, totaling $700. Figure 7.2 shows the results of selling 200 T-shirts.

Operating expenses of the business

1. Travel	$100
2. Business cards	100
3. Flyers for advertising	300
4. Temporary rental space	200
Total Operating Expenses	**$700**

Every business has various monthly operating expenses that will occur regardless of services or products sold. The sale of merchandise, less merchandise cost, contributes toward paying these expenses.

Sell 200 T-shirts

Sales Revenue (200 x $7.00)	**$1,400**
Less Cost of Goods Sold	1,000
= Gross Profit	**400**
Less Operating Expenses	700
= Net Income (Loss)	**($300)**

These T-shirts may have been purchased several months earlier. You are now recognizing (matching) the cost of the shirts against the value of the sale. If you only sell 200 T-shirts (COGS = 200 x $5.00), there is not enough gross profit to pay operating expenses, resulting in a net loss of $300.

FIGURE 7.2

The business needs to sell more T-shirts to provide enough gross profit to pay for operating expenses. Figure 7.3 shows the results of selling 350 T-shirts and 500 T-shirts.

Sell 350 T-shirts

Sales Revenue (350 x $7.00)	**$2,450**
Less Cost of Goods Sold	1,750
= Gross Profit	**700**
Less Operating Expenses	700
= Net Income (Loss)	**$0**

By selling 350 T-shirts (COGS = 350 x $5.00), you manage to break even (which means that revenues equal expenses). Therefore, you have not produced net income or suffered a net loss.

Sell 500 T-shirts

Sales Revenue (500 x $7.00)	**$3,500**
Less Cost of Goods Sold	2,500
= Gross Profit	**1,000**
Less Operating Expenses	700
= Net Income (Loss)	**$300**

By selling 500 T-shirts (COGS = 500 x $5.00), you have made sufficient gross profit to cover operating expenses and produce net income.

FIGURE 7.3

Perpetual vs. Periodic Inventory

Imagine you are shopping for a particular item at a department store. You cannot find it on the shelf, so you ask an employee if there are any left. The employee checks the computer, which says there is one left. The employee finds it in the storage room, gives it to you and you go to the cashier. The cashier scans the item, you pay the bill and you leave the store. If another customer asked for that same item after you bought it, the computer would show that there are none in stock.

This example illustrates the perpetual inventory system. The **perpetual inventory system** updates inventory levels after every purchase and sale. Most merchandising companies use technology such as scanners to update their records for inventory, as well as COGS. All the updates happen automatically when the item is scanned.

On the other hand, some small merchandising companies such as a small convenience store may not have scanning technology in place. Without the scanning technology, the business can track its sales, but inventory and COGS will not be updated automatically or regularly. The **periodic inventory system** only updates the inventory and COGS values after physically counting the items on hand. These inventory counts occur periodically, usually at the end of the month or year.

Figure 7.4 highlights the difference between the perpetual and periodic inventory system. It shows sample revenue and COGS amounts for a company under both systems over a period of three months. Notice that the perpetual system updates COGS continuously while the periodic system updates COGS only when a physical inventory count is performed (at the end of March).

Perpetual Inventory System*

Periodic Inventory System**

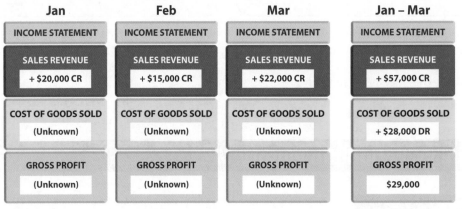

* COGS is updated continuously.
** COGS is only updated when a physical count of inventory is performed.

FIGURE 7.4

Perpetual inventory systems are more commonly used in today's computerized environment. In this textbook, unless otherwise stated, we will always assume the perpetual inventory system is used. We will now examine how to record various transactions regarding the purchase and sale of inventory under the perpetual inventory system.

The Perpetual Inventory System

A perpetual inventory system involves recording all transactions affecting the balance of inventory on hand, as they occur. In reality, most businesses have separate, detailed records for each type of product they sell. For simplicity, our examples will focus on one type of product, where all transactions affect a single inventory account directly.

We will demonstrate various inventory-related transactions using an example of a retail store called Tools 4U, which buys and sells various tools. Tools 4U is a proprietorship owned by Wayne Sanders.

Purchase and Sale of Inventory

When inventory is purchased for resale using a perpetual inventory system, the inventory account is debited and the cash or the accounts payable account is credited. Tools 4U purchased inventory at a cost of $10,000 on January 1, 2016. Assume all purchases and sales are made on account. Figure 7.5 shows how this purchase is journalized.

JOURNAL		Page 1	
Date	**Account Title and Explanation**	**Debit**	**Credit**
2016			
Jan 1	Inventory	10,000	
	Accounts Payable		10,000
	Purchased inventory on account		

FIGURE 7.5

Tools 4U adds this purchase to the inventory it already has on hand that is ready to sell. Suppose inventory worth $7,200 is sold for $15,000 on January 15 on account. The sale of inventory is recorded by using two journal entries

1. Debit accounts receivable and credit sales revenue each for $15,000 to show the sale on account. This records the proceeds from the sale. If the sale was made for cash, then the cash account would be debited instead of accounts receivable.

2. Debit COGS and credit inventory each for $7,200 to show that inventory has been reduced. This entry is necessary because it removes the inventory sold from the balance sheet and records its cost on the income statement as a cost of doing business for the period.

These transactions are shown in Figure 7.6. Note that the gross profit generated by this sale is equal to $7,800 ($15,000 – $7,200).

JOURNAL			Page 1
Date	**Account Title and Explanation**	**Debit**	**Credit**
2016			
Jan 15	Accounts Receivable	15,000	
	Sales Revenue		15,000
	To record product sales on account		
Jan 15	Cost of Goods Sold	7,200	
	Inventory		7,200
	Sold inventory to a customer		

FIGURE 7.6

When inventory is sold by a merchandiser, it can no longer be regarded as an asset by the company because it is now owned by the customer. This is the reason for the second journal entry in Figure 7.6. In a service company, this entry is not recorded because assets are not sold in the ordinary course of business.

Purchase Returns

Goods often need to be returned for reasons such as incorrect product, over-shipments, or inferior product quality.

When the manager of Tools 4U examined the new shipment of inventory from the company's supplier, Roofs and More, he noticed that there were some damaged goods in the shipment. The damaged goods cost $500. The goods were returned and a journal entry for $500 was recorded to reverse part of the original purchase transaction as shown in Figure 7.7.

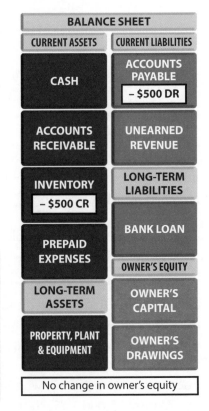

JOURNAL			Page 1
Date	**Account Title and Explanation**	**Debit**	**Credit**
2016			
Jan 2	Accounts Payable	500	
	Inventory		500
	Goods returned to Roofs and More		

FIGURE 7.7

Purchase Allowances

Purchase allowances occur when the buyer agrees to keep the undesirable goods at a reduced cost. Continuing with the above example, assume Tools 4U found another $500 worth of unsatisfactory goods and the supplier offered a 20% allowance for the company to keep the goods, rather than returning them. The journal entry is recorded by debiting accounts payable and crediting inventory as shown in Figure 7.8. The transaction amount is $100 ($500 × 20%).

BALANCE SHEET	
CURRENT ASSETS	CURRENT LIABILITIES
CASH	ACCOUNTS PAYABLE − $100 DR
ACCOUNTS RECEIVABLE	UNEARNED REVENUE
INVENTORY − $100 CR	LONG-TERM LIABILITIES
PREPAID EXPENSES	BANK LOAN
	OWNER'S EQUITY
LONG-TERM ASSETS	OWNER'S CAPITAL
PROPERTY, PLANT & EQUIPMENT	OWNER'S DRAWINGS

No change in owner's equity

JOURNAL			Page 1
Date 2016	Account Title and Explanation	Debit	Credit
Jan 4	Accounts Payable	100	
	Inventory		100
	Allowance from Roofs and More		

FIGURE 7.8

A balance of $4,200 ($4,800 – $500 – $100) is still owing to Roofs and More.

Purchase Discounts

Various types of discounts exist when purchasing products or services. Sellers often give discounts to encourage customers to purchase more and to encourage early payments.

Two types of common discounts given are trade discounts and cash discounts. Only cash discounts will be discussed in detail in this chapter.

Cash discounts are offered to encourage prompt payment from customers in the form of a percentage off the final bill for paying in a short amount of time. For example, a seller may offer a 2% cash discount if the payment is made within 10 days of the date of invoice, otherwise the full amount is payable within 30 days. The term for this arrangement is commonly shown as 2/10, n/30 (read as: "two-ten, net thirty"). This means that a 2% discount is applied if payment is received within 10 days; otherwise the net amount owing is due within 30 days. Another example is 3/15, n/30, which means a 3 percent discount is applied if payment is received within 15 days, otherwise the net amount owing is payable within 30 days. The following example illustrates how to record a purchase discount.

Tools 4U made the original purchase from Roofs and More on January 1, 2016 for $4,800. The amount Tools 4U owes has been reduced by $600 due to returns and allowances, so only $4,200 remains to be paid. The supplier (Roofs and More) allows 2/10, n/30 on all invoices. Since Tools 4U has excess cash at this time, the manager decides to take advantage of the cash discount by paying the invoice within 10 days.

Assume Tools 4U made the payment on January 10, the amount for the bill will be $4,200 less the $84 discount ($4,200 × 2%). Since the business is paying less for the inventory, the value of the inventory needs to decrease by the value of the discount. The entry to record the payment is shown in Figure 7.9.

JOURNAL			Page 1
Date 2016	**Account Title and Explanation**	**Debit**	**Credit**
Jan 10	Accounts Payable	4,200	
	Cash		4,116
	Inventory		84
	Paid invoice and took purchase discount		

FIGURE 7.9

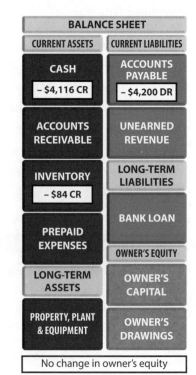

No change in owner's equity

The discount of $84 is credited to inventory because the adjustment is made to reflect the true cost of the goods.

If Tools 4U decides not to pay the amount owing within 10 days, then it is not entitled to take the discount. It must pay the full amount of $4,200 within 30 days of the invoice date. This payment is just like paying any other amount that is owed to a supplier. Cash will decrease and accounts payable will decrease by the amount owed. The entry is shown in Figure 7.10. Notice the date is more than 10 days past the invoice date.

JOURNAL			Page 1
Date 2016	**Account Title and Explanation**	**Debit**	**Credit**
Jan 24	Accounts Payable	4,200	
	Cash		4,200
	Paid amount owing to Roofs and More		

FIGURE 7.10

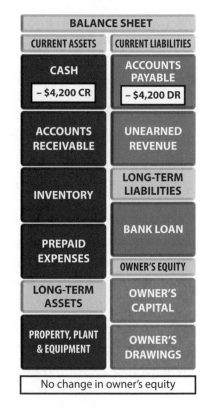

No change in owner's equity

Freight Cost

When one company purchases goods from another, the items purchased must be transported from the seller's place of business to the buyer's place of business. There are a number of ways to transport goods (sea, rail, truck, etc.). The selling company may have its own fleet of vehicles to deliver goods to customers, or it may use a common carrier. A common carrier in this context is a company that provides shipping services to the general public. Examples include railroad or trucking companies.

In addition to arranging transport of the goods, at some point ownership of the goods must be legally transferred from the seller to the buyer. The term used to determine when ownership of the goods changes hands is called the FOB point. FOB stands for Free On Board. There are two possible FOB points: FOB shipping point and FOB destination. Each of these points have implications regarding who pays for shipping, when ownership passes from the buyer to the seller and who bears the risk for the goods during transport.

FOB Shipping Point

FOB shipping point indicates that ownership of the purchased items changes as soon as the goods leave the seller's place of business. In other words, ownership changes at the point when shipping begins. In this case, a common carrier is often used to deliver the items to the buyer. The buyer will pay for shipping and is responsible to insure the items while they are in transport. If anything were to happen to the items while they are being transported, the buyer bears the risk of loss.

The seller records revenue earned and the buyer records an increase to inventory as soon as the goods are loaded on the truck (or other transport). The buyer also includes the shipping cost in the value of inventory. The reason the buyer includes shipping costs in inventory is that the value of the goods must include all costs (such as transportation) that are incurred to get the goods ready to sell. Figure 7.11 illustrates who pays the shipping costs.

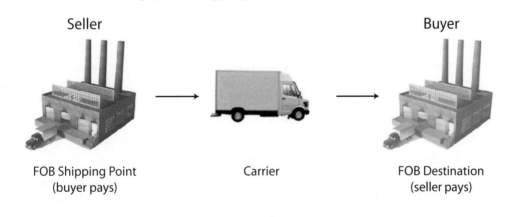

FIGURE 7.11

Assume that Tools 4U had inventory shipped FOB shipping point. This means that Tools 4U must pay the cost of shipping. Suppose the shipping charge totalled $100 and was paid in cash on January 2. This amount must be included in the inventory account. The journal entry is shown in Figure 7.12.

BALANCE SHEET	
CURRENT ASSETS	CURRENT LIABILITIES
CASH −$100 CR	ACCOUNTS PAYABLE
ACCOUNTS RECEIVABLE	UNEARNED REVENUE
INVENTORY +$100 DR	LONG-TERM LIABILITIES
PREPAID EXPENSES	BANK LOAN
	OWNER'S EQUITY
LONG-TERM ASSETS	OWNER'S CAPITAL
PROPERTY, PLANT & EQUIPMENT	OWNER'S DRAWINGS

No change in owner's equity

JOURNAL — Page 1

Date 2016	Account Title and Explanation	Debit	Credit
Jan 2	Inventory	100	
	Cash		100
	Paid for freight costs		

FIGURE 7.12

FOB Destination

FOB destination indicates that ownership of the purchased items changes when the goods arrive at the buyer's place of business. In other words, ownership changes at the point of destination. In this case, the seller may have a fleet of vehicles and uses them to deliver goods to its customers. Thus, the seller pays for the shipping and is responsible for the items while they are in transport. If anything happens to the items while they are being transported, the seller bears the risk of loss.

The seller records revenue earned and the buyer records an increase to inventory once the goods reach their destination (the buyer's place of business). The seller also records the cost of shipping the goods as an expense. This expense is part of the seller's cost of doing business.

Suppose that Tools 4U shipped inventory to a customer FOB destination on January 3. Tools 4U must pay the cost of shipping because it is the selling company. The shipping cost is a delivery expense. Suppose that it cost Tools 4U $120 to ship the order and this amount was paid in cash. The journal entry for this transaction is shown in Figure 7.13.

JOURNAL — Page 1

Date 2016	Account Title and Explanation	Debit	Credit
Jan 3	Delivery Expense	120	
	Cash		120
	To record shipping expenses on a customer order		

FIGURE 7.13

A summary of FOB shipping point and FOB destination is presented in Figure 7.14. Basically, whoever pays for shipping owns the goods while they are being transported and bears the risk of loss.

	FOB Shipping Point	FOB Destination
Ownership Change	When goods leave the seller on a common carrier	When goods arrive at the buyer's place of business
Transportation Costs	Paid by the buyer and recorded in inventory	Paid by the seller and recorded as an expense
Risk of Loss	Buyer bears risk of loss during transport	Seller bears risk of loss during transport

FIGURE 7.14

Sales Returns

A merchandiser may have to deal with numerous returns from customers, and these returns must be tracked over a period of time. High return levels may indicate serious problems with the products being sold. Therefore, instead of reversing the revenue account with a debit when recording returns, a contra-revenue account called **sales returns and allowances** is used to track the amount of returns. Recall that contra means opposite and a contra account holds an opposite normal balance of its related account.

Sales returns and allowances is a contra-revenue account with a normal debit balance. It is generally used to record both sales returns and sales allowances. **Sales returns** occur when undesirable products are returned to the seller. **Sales allowances** occur when the customer decides to keep such undesirable products at a reduced price.

Continuing with our example, suppose that a customer returned $4,000 worth of undesirable goods to Tools 4U (the original cost of the inventory was $3,000). There is nothing wrong with the goods and they can be resold. The journal entries to record this return, using the contra-revenue account, are shown in Figure 7.15. Note that two entries are required: one to record the reduction in sales and accounts receivable (or cash, if applicable) and one to reverse the reduction of inventory.

JOURNAL			Page 1
Date 2016	Account Title and Explanation	Debit	Credit
Jan 18	Sales Returns & Allowances	4,000	
	Accounts Receivable		4,000
	Customer returned items		
Jan 18	Inventory	3,000	
	Cost of Goods Sold		3,000
	Restock returned inventory		

Owner's equity decreases by $1,000 (– $4,000 + $3,000)

FIGURE 7.15

There is a $4,000 increase in the sales returns and allowances account. This amount decreases revenue since the contra-revenue account has the opposite effect than the revenue account.

In the example in Figure 7.15, the inventory that was returned was not what the customer wanted. There was nothing wrong with the product in terms of quality, so it was placed back on the shelf to be sold again. If the items returned by the customer were damaged, then the inventory cannot be sold again. In that case, Tools 4U would not record the second journal entry from Figure 7.15 because the damaged inventory is worthless.

Sales Allowances

There are circumstances where a reduction to the original selling price is given to a customer.

Assume the customer from January 15 discovered that some goods were damaged during shipping. Instead of returning the items, the customer agreed to accept an allowance of 5% on the price of the goods it kept. The customer kept $11,000 ($15,000 original sale – $4,000 return) of goods, so it will get a $550 ($11,000 × 5%) reduction on what it owes Tools 4U.

The journal entry is shown in Figure 7.16. The amount is recorded as a debit to sales returns and allowances and a credit to accounts receivable. The transaction decreases equity by $550.

A balance of $10,450 ($15,000 – $4,000 – $550) is still owed by Tools 4U's customer.

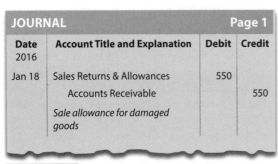

JOURNAL			Page 1
Date 2016	Account Title and Explanation	Debit	Credit
Jan 18	Sales Returns & Allowances	550	
	Accounts Receivable		550
	Sale allowance for damaged goods		

FIGURE 7.16

Sales Discounts

When selling products or services, it is common to offer sales discounts to customers for early payment. The concept works in the same way as the purchase discount. Assume that Tools 4U offered its customer from January 15 terms of 2/10, n/30 in the invoice. If the customer pays by January 25, a 2% discount will be applied on the amount owing of $10,450.

Assume the customer made the payment on January 20; the amount is $10,241 ($10,450 less the 2% discount). The journal entry to record this transaction is shown in Figure 7.17.

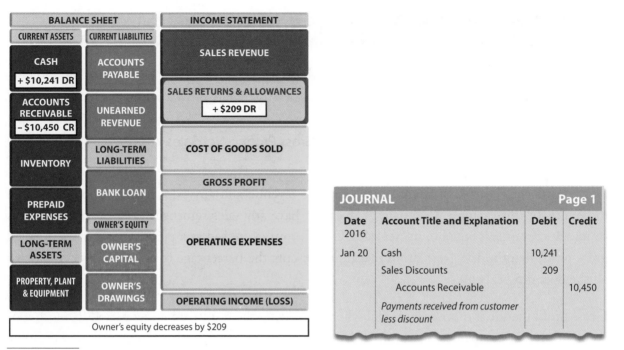

FIGURE 7.17

The $209 discount is recorded as a debit in the **sales discounts** account. Sales discounts is another contra-revenue account which increases with a debit and decreases with a credit.

If the customer decides not to pay the amount owing within the discount period, then it is not entitled to take the discount that Tools 4U offers. Instead, the customer must pay the full amount of $10,450 within 30 days of the sale. The receipt of cash from the customer is just like receiving cash from any customer that owes the company money. Cash increases and accounts receivable decreases. The entry is shown in Figure 7.18. Notice that the date is more than 10 days past the date of the sale.

JOURNAL		Page 1	
Date 2016	Account Title and Explanation	Debit	Credit
Feb 2	Cash	10,450	
	Accounts Receivable		10,450
	Payment received from customer		

FIGURE 7.18

BALANCE SHEET

CURRENT ASSETS	CURRENT LIABILITIES
CASH + $10,450 DR	ACCOUNTS PAYABLE
ACCOUNTS RECEIVABLE − $10,450 CR	UNEARNED REVENUE
INVENTORY	LONG-TERM LIABILITIES
PREPAID EXPENSES	BANK LOAN
	OWNER'S EQUITY
LONG-TERM ASSETS	OWNER'S CAPITAL
PROPERTY, PLANT & EQUIPMENT	OWNER'S DRAWINGS

No change in owner's equity

Gross Profit Margin: A Profitability Ratio

If Company A has sales revenue of $100,000, and its COGS is $60,000, the gross profit is $40,000. When gross profit is expressed as a percentage, it is calculated as shown below.

Gross Profit Margin = Gross Profit ÷ Net Sales x 100%

Net sales is equal to the difference between sales revenue and any sales returns, allowances, and discounts. In this example, Company A does not have any sales returns, allowances, or discounts so its sales revenue is equal to its net sales. Gross profit expressed as a percentage of sales is called gross profit margin. The gross profit margin represents the percentage of sales left over to pay for all the operating expenses.

Gross profit margin is more meaningful when comparing the results from one period to another or among different companies. If Company B has sales of $500,000, with a gross profit of $175,000, which of the two companies is performing better? You may think that Company B is performing better because a gross profit of $175,000 is greater than a gross profit of $40,000. However, to assess the results properly, it is important to compare the two percentages

Company A: $40,000 Gross Profit ÷ $100,000 Sales × 100 = 40%

Company B: $175,000 Gross Profit ÷ $500,000 Sales × 100 = 35%

The results show that Company A is more efficient because it used only 60% of revenue to cover the cost of the product, leaving 40% of every dollar to contribute toward its operating expenses. Company B, on the other hand, used 65% of its revenue to cover the cost of goods sold, leaving only 35% of each dollar to contribute toward its operating expenses.

Keep in mind that ratios should be compared within industry groups, taking industry norms into account. Suppose Company A and Company B are both hardware stores and other hardware stores have a gross profit margin of 38%. In this situation, Company A is doing better than the industry average and Company B is doing worse than the industry average.

Multistep Income Statement

The income statement of a merchandising business follows the same principles as those of a service business. Until now, we have been grouping revenue accounts together and listing all expenses together, without further categorizing. A merchandising business must include the contra-revenue accounts on the income statement. Sales returns and allowances and sales discounts are subtracted from sales revenue. This is shown in Figure 7.19. This format of the income statement classifies expenses by their **nature**. This simply means that expenses are presented together, without further categorizing them by function.

Tools 4U Income Statement For the Year Ended December 31, 2016		
Revenue		
Sales Revenue		$200,000
Less: Sales Returns and Allowances	$4,000	
Sales Discounts	2,000	(6,000)
Interest Revenue		8,000
Total Revenue		202,000
Expenses		
Cost of Goods Sold	100,000	
Depreciation Expense	5,000	
Interest Expense	4,000	
Rent Expense	10,000	
Salaries Expense	40,000	
Supplies Expense	7,000	
Utilities Expense	6,000	
Total Operating Expenses		172,000
Net Income		$30,000

FIGURE 7.19

A **multistep income statement** is an income statement that further divides specific revenues and expenses to show subtotals like gross profit, operating expenses, and operating income. This format classifies expenses by **function**, which means that related expenses are grouped together. Also, important measures such as gross profit and operating income are clearly shown. A multistep income statement is illustrated in Figure 7.20.

	Tools 4U		
	Income Statement		
	For the Year Ended December 31, 2016		
1. Calculate Net Sales and Gross Profit	Sales Revenue		$200,000
	Less: Sales Returns and Allowances	$4,000	
	Sales Discounts	2,000	(6,000)
	Net Sales		194,000
	Cost of Goods Sold		100,000
	Gross Profit		94,000
2. Calculate Operating Income	**Operating Expenses**		
	Depreciation Expense	5,000	
	Rent Expense	10,000	
	Salaries Expense	40,000	
	Supplies Expense	7,000	
	Utilities Expense	6,000	
	Total Operating Expenses		68,000
	Operating Income		26,000
3. Calculate non-operating activities and Net Income	**Other Revenue and Expenses**		
	Interest Revenue	8,000	
	Interest Expense	(4,000)	4,000
	Net Income		$30,000

FIGURE 7.20

The multistep income statement further groups the revenues and expenses that are not part of the main operations of the business, such as interest expense, interest revenue or loss from a lawsuit, under a separate category called Other Revenue and Expenses.

Operating expenses can be further divided by function into selling and administrative expenses. Selling expenses are those related to actually selling inventory. Examples include sales salaries, rent for the retail space and advertising. Administrative expenses are those related to running the business, which are not directly tied to selling inventory. Examples include office salaries, office supplies and depreciation of office equipment.

Using the above example, suppose depreciation is solely on display equipment for inventory and supplies are just office supplies. Salaries, rent and utilities are allocated 80% to selling and 20% to administrative. With this new information, the income statement can be presented as shown in

Figure 7.21, in a **classified multistep income statement**. Classified multistep income statements further divide expenses into selling and administrative categories.

	Tools 4U Income Statement For the Year Ended December 31, 2016			
1. Calculate Net Sales and Gross Profit	**Sales Revenue**			$200,000
	Less: Sales Returns and Allowances		$4,000	
	Sales Discounts		2,000	(6,000)
	Net Sales			194,000
	Cost of Goods Sold			100,000
	Gross Profit			94,000
	Operating Expenses			
2. Calculate Selling Expenses	**Selling Expenses**			
	Depreciation Expense	$5,000		
	Rent Expense	8,000		
	Salaries Expense	32,000		
	Utilities Expense	4,800		
	Total Selling Expenses		49,800	
3. Calculate Administrative Expenses and Operating Income	**Administrative Expenses**			
	Rent Expense	2,000		
	Salaries Expense	8,000		
	Supplies Expense	7,000		
	Utilities Expense	1,200		
	Total Administrative Expenses		18,200	
	Total Operating Expenses			68,000
	Operating Income			26,000
4. Calculate non-operating activities and Net Income	**Other Revenue and Expenses**			
	Interest Revenue		8,000	
	Interest Expense		(4,000)	4,000
	Net Income			$30,000

FIGURE 7.21

The classified multistep income statement is particularly useful for the company's internal analysis. It allows managers and executives to clearly see a detailed breakdown of costs by department and compare performance in different areas against competitors and its own financial history.

ASPE vs IFRS

ASPE allows a company to choose to present its expenses on an income statement by nature, by function, or even by using a mixture of nature and function.

Under IFRS, expenses can be classified either by nature or by function on an income statement. Using a mixture of nature and function is prohibited.

IN THE REAL WORLD

An actual company's balance sheet and income statement will usually look similar to what we have seen up to this point. However, most companies' financial statements will also have an additional column to show amounts from the previous fiscal year. For instance, a company reporting for fiscal year 2016 will have a column with the header "2016" in each of the balance sheet and income statement to report financial information for the most recent fiscal year. There may also be an additional column with the header "2015" to show amounts from the previous fiscal year. This form of financial reports is referred to as comparative financial statements. This allows users to easily compare the financial performance and position of a company to that of the previous year.

Some companies go beyond the two-year comparison. This allows users, such as investors, to identify both short-term and long-term trends in the financial data. The investors can then assess whether or not the business is growing at a rate they anticipated.

Closing Entries

When using a perpetual inventory system, inventory is immediately updated after each purchase and sale transaction. However, the value of inventory on the balance sheet may not accurately represent the value of inventory actually on hand. To verify the accuracy of the accounting records, a physical inventory count should be performed at the end of the reporting period. If the count does not match the records, an adjustment must be made to bring the inventory to its correct balance. This difference is often referred to as "inventory shrinkage," resulting either from an error in recording transactions, theft or breakage. If the amount is considered immaterial, the following entry would be made where the balance in the inventory account was more than the physical count. Assuming that the amount of shrinkage is $200, the journal entry for this transaction is shown in Figure 7.22.

BALANCE SHEET		INCOME STATEMENT
CURRENT ASSETS	CURRENT LIABILITIES	SALES REVENUE
CASH	ACCOUNTS PAYABLE	SALES RETURNS & ALLOWANCES
ACCOUNTS RECEIVABLE	UNEARNED REVENUE	COST OF GOODS SOLD + $200 DR
INVENTORY – $200 CR	LONG-TERM LIABILITIES	GROSS PROFIT
	BANK LOAN	OPERATING EXPENSES

JOURNAL			Page 1
Date	Account Title and Explanation	Debit	Credit
2016			
Dec 31	Cost of Goods Sold	200	
	Inventory		200
	Adjust inventory to physical count		

FIGURE 7.22

After this adjustment and all other adjustments have been made, assume Tools 4U has the adjusted trial balance shown in Figure 7.23.

Tools 4U Adjusted Trial Balance December 31, 2016		
Account Titles	**DR**	**CR**
Cash	$25,000	
Accounts Receivable	18,000	
Inventory	45,000	
Prepaid Expenses	12,000	
Equipment	180,000	
Accumulated Depreciation		$60,000
Accounts Payable		34,000
Unearned Revenue		8,000
Bank Loan		100,000
Sanders, Capital		48,000
Sales Revenue		200,000
Interest Revenue		8,000
Sales Returns & Allowances	4,000	
Sales Discounts	2,000	
Cost of Goods Sold	100,000	
Depreciation Expense	5,000	
Interest Expense	4,000	
Rent Expense	10,000	
Salaries Expense	40,000	
Supplies Expense	7,000	
Utilities Expense	6,000	
Total	**$458,000**	**$458,000**

FIGURE 7.23

The steps to close the books of a merchandising company are similar to closing a service company. Step 1 is to close the revenue account, as shown in Figure 7.24.

JOURNAL			Page 1
Date 2016	**Account Title and Explanation**	**Debit**	**Credit**
Jan 31	Sales Revenue	200,000	
	Interest Revenue	8,000	
	Income Summary		208,000
	Close revenue accounts		

FIGURE 7.24

Step 2 is to close expenses. In this step, we will also close the two contra-revenue accounts (sales returns and allowances and sales discounts) because they have debit balances like the rest of the expense accounts.

JOURNAL			Page 1
Date 2016	**Account Title and Explanation**	**Debit**	**Credit**
Jan 31	Income Summary	178,000	
	Sales Returns & Allowances		4,000
	Sales Discounts		2,000
	Cost of Goods Sold		100,000
	Depreciation Expense		5,000
	Interest Expense		4,000
	Rent Expense		10,000
	Salaries Expense		40,000
	Supplies Expense		7,000
	Utilities Expense		6,000
	Close expense and contra-revenue accounts		

FIGURE 7.25

Step 3 closes the income summary account. Recall from a previous chapter that the income summary account is closed to owner's capital, as shown in Figure 7.26.

JOURNAL			Page 1
Date 2016	**Account Title and Explanation**	**Debit**	**Credit**
Jan 31	Income Summary	30,000	
	Sanders, Capital		30,000
	Close income summary		

FIGURE 7.26

The end result, just as in a service company, is that the equity in the business is updated with the net income as shown in Figure 7.27.

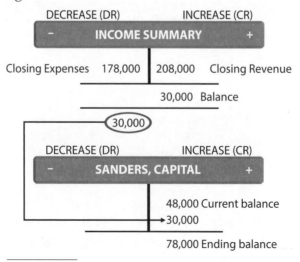

FIGURE 7.27

Controls Related to Inventory

The way a company handles its inventory can have a major impact on the state of the business. After all, basic economic theory is about supply and demand. If customers demand goods or services, the goal of a business is to meet that demand. In essence, this is what inventory management is about: to manage supply in order to meet demand.

A company with too much inventory on hand risks tying up resources that could be used productively in other areas. A company with too little inventory on hand risks not having enough supply to meet customer demand. There is a delicate balance that must be maintained by a company. Perpetual inventory systems help companies to maintain such a balance.

Keeping track of a company's inventory can be a challenge, but computer software can help mitigate this challenge. However, every accountant should have an understanding of how inventory is tracked and recorded manually.

First, even with the use of technology, errors can be made. It is the responsibility of the accounting department and management to ensure that inventory information is accurate and reliable.

Keeping track of inventory is one of the primary challenges of doing business. This is why transactions need to be recorded properly and relevant information presented in a way that helps company decision makers.

Second, a thorough knowledge of manual accounting procedures helps the accountant to develop the kinds of controls necessary to ensure that this type of asset is managed responsibly and with integrity.

We will provide examples to show how an accountant can develop a personal method of controlling inventory manually. We will then take a closer look at the kinds of controls needed when dealing with the inventory section of the balance sheet.

Compliance with Plans, Policies, Procedures, Regulations and Laws

All aspects of doing business should be governed by the appropriate plans, policies, procedures, laws and regulations. This is certainly true regarding a company's handling and control of inventory.

All businesses should have plans that are formalized through general policies that lead to specific procedures. These should all comply with the regulations and laws in place within the jurisdiction of the business.

For example, a company can have a plan to train all inventory personnel. This plan can include detection controls that single out instances of procedures not being followed. An example of such a procedure could be to have all items tagged and scanned

Maintaining the integrity of information is an obligation that companies have when implementing inventory controls.

at checkout. If this procedure is not followed, then a backup measure could be implemented, with alarms going off upon exit.

All these plans, policies and procedures must adhere to relevant laws and regulations, as illustrated in Figure 7.28. For example, customers cannot be strip-searched because the alarm goes off as they are leaving the store because this would be a violation of their rights.

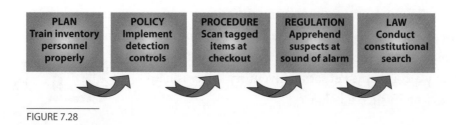

FIGURE 7.28

All employees should be trained in the inventory procedures in place. For example, the receiver should count all goods that enter the premises and match the count with the one initially written on the purchase order. The supervisor should ensure that this procedure is followed. Internal auditors can conduct field visits to ensure that both the supervisor and the receiver are implementing procedures according to plans and policies in place.

Safeguarding Inventory

All company assets must be physically protected. Cash is generally deposited in a bank; securities can be kept with the brokerage house. Inventory, on the other hand, is often located on company premises in a warehouse or onsite storage facility. The location needs to be easily accessible for receiving or shipping, but it also needs to be protected from the possibility of theft. That is why inventory facilities are usually locked up after closing. The more valuable the inventory, the more elaborate the security measures needed to protect it. These measures can include anything from fences and guard dogs to alarm systems, security guards or even hiring an inventory custodian who is charged specifically with protecting the inventory.

The Economical and Efficient Use of Resources

The concept that resources should be used economically and efficiently is especially applicable to inventory. First, financial ratios—which will be examined later in this textbook—can be used to determine if there is too much or too little inventory on hand. If there is too much inventory, then money is tied up that could be used more efficiently elsewhere. If there is too little inventory, then customer demand will not be met.

Second, the physical condition of the inventory should be checked regularly. This can be done visually or through inventory reports. Any inventory items that are old or in disrepair, and therefore difficult to sell at market value, can be sold at reduced prices or disposed of so that valuable storage space can be maximized.

Inventory Objectives

All aspects of a business should be guided by the objectives set by management. This not only allows for the accomplishment of specific objectives, but allows all organizational objectives to be properly coordinated. For example, sales objectives can be tied to inventory objectives; and profit objectives can be tied to those set by the marketing department.

All employees should be aware of stated objectives. For example, if a company wishes to keep items in inventory for only a short period of time before being shipped out, then both the receiver and shipper should be aware of this. This objective would guide much of their short-term and long-term activities.

Meeting inventory objectives must be a total team effort. If inventory levels are not maintained close to management's objective, then initiatives should be implemented to ensure that objectives are reassessed or changed. For example, if inventory levels are higher than expected, the sales department can view it as a challenge to get items moving out faster. The more sales increase, the less inventory builds up in the warehouse.

 *Access **ameengage.com** for integrated resources including tutorials, practice exercises, the digital textbook and more.*

In Summary

Define a merchandising business

⇨ A merchandising business, or merchandiser, is any business that buys and sells products for the purpose of making a profit.

Differentiate between the perpetual and the periodic inventory systems

⇨ The perpetual inventory system constantly updates inventory whenever a purchase or sale is made.

⇨ The periodic inventory system only updates inventory when a physical count of the inventory is taken, usually at the end of a period.

Record journal entries related to inventory purchases under the perpetual inventory system

⇨ Purchase returns and allowances cause accounts payable and inventory to decrease.

⇨ Purchase discounts allow the buyer to save money by paying early. Inventory value is reduced by the amount of the discount to reflect the actual cost of the inventory.

⇨ Goods shipped FOB shipping point are owned by the buyer as soon as they are loaded onto the carrier. The buyer pays for shipping costs and records them in inventory.

⇨ Goods shipped FOB destination are owned by seller until they arrive at the buyer's destination. The seller pays for shipping costs and records them as a delivery expense.

Record journal entries related to inventory sales under the perpetual inventory system

⇨ Inventory sales require two journal entries: one to record the sale and one to remove the inventory from the balance sheet.

⇨ Sales returns and allowances cause an increase to a contra-revenue account called sales returns and allowances. If returned merchandise can be resold, an additional entry must be recorded to increase inventory and decrease COGS.

⇨ Sales discounts allow customers to save money by paying early. Another contra-revenue account called sales discounts is used to track the amount of discounts taken by customers.

Calculate gross profit and gross profit margin

⇨ Gross profit is the amount of profit remaining after the cost of goods sold is deducted from revenue. Gross profit is used to cover operating expenses.

⇨ Gross profit margin is the gross profit as a percentage of sales. The formula is: Gross Profit ÷ Sales Revenue × 100%.

Prepare a multistep income statement and classified multistep income statement

↪ A multistep income statement further categorizes revenue and expenses to show subtotals such as gross profit and operating income. It also separately shows other revenue and expenses that are not part of regular operations.

↪ A classified multistep income statement categorizes expenses as selling expenses and administrative expenses.

Prepare closing entries for a merchandising business under the perpetual inventory system

↪ All revenue accounts are closed to the income summary account.

↪ All expense accounts and contra-revenue accounts are closed to the income summary account.

↪ The income summary account is closed to the owner's capital account.

↪ If there are owner's drawings, they are closed directly to the owner's capital account.

Identify inventory controls

↪ All aspects of doing business should be governed by the appropriate plans, policies, procedures, laws and regulations.

↪ All businesses should have plans that are formalized through general policies that lead to specific procedures.

↪ All company assets must be physically protected.

↪ The concept that resources should be used economically and efficiently is especially applicable to inventory.

Review Exercise

Part 1

The following transactions occurred between George's Gardening Supplies and Michael's Distributing during the month of December 2016.

Dec 3   George's Gardening Supplies purchased $50,000 of inventory on account from Michael's Distributing. The purchase terms were 2/10 n/30. The cost of the goods to Michael's Distributing was $35,000.

Dec 6   Freight charges of $200 were paid in cash by the company which incurred them.

Dec 8   George's Gardening Supplies returned $2,000 of incorrect merchandise from the purchase on December 3. Michael's Distributing put the merchandise back into inventory. The cost of the goods to Michael's Distributing was originally $700.

Dec 11 George's Gardening Supplies paid the balance owing to Michael's Distributing.

Assuming that both companies use the perpetual inventory system, complete the following exercise.

Required

a)   Journalize the December transactions for George's Gardening Supplies. Assume the goods from December 3 were shipped FOB shipping point.

b)   Journalize the December transactions for Michael's Distributing. Assume the goods from December 3 were shipped FOB destination.

See Appendix I for solutions.

a) Journalize the December transactions. Assume the goods were shipped FOB shipping point.

JOURNAL			Page 1
Date	Account Titles and Explanation	Debit	Credit

b) Journalize the December transactions. Assume the goods were shipped FOB destination.

JOURNAL			Page 1
Date	**Account Titles and Explanation**	**Debit**	**Credit**

Part 2

Below is the adjusted trial balance for George's Gardening Supplies at the end of the year.

George's Gardening Supplies Adjusted Trial Balance December 31, 2016		
Account Titles	DR	CR
Cash	$54,830	
Accounts Receivable	33,500	
Inventory	33,440	
Prepaid Insurance	3,600	
Equipment	45,000	
Accumulated Depreciation		$5,000
Accounts Payable		10,000
Bank Loan		30,000
Gregg, Capital		90,000
Gregg, Drawings	5,000	
Sales Revenue		113,500
Interest Revenue		6,500
Sales Returns & Allowances	1,000	
Sales Discounts	1,580	
Cost of Goods Sold	44,700	
Depreciation Expense	5,000	
Insurance Expense	2,500	
Interest Expense	2,600	
Rent Expense	6,000	
Salaries Expense	11,000	
Supplies Expense	4,500	
Utilities Expense	750	
Total	$255,000	$255,000

Note: $10,000 of the bank loan will be paid by December 31, 2017.

Required

a) Prepare a single-step income statement for George's Gardening Supplies for the year ended December 31, 2016.

b) Prepare a multistep income statement for George's Gardening Supplies for the year ended December 31, 2016. Calculate the gross margin percentage.

c) Prepare a classified multistep income statement for George's Gardening Supplies for the year ended December 31, 2016 using the following information

- The equipment is used solely for selling purposes.

- Supplies are used for administrative purposes only.

- Insurance, salaries, rent, and utilities are allocated 85% to selling and 15% to administration.

d) Prepare the statement of owner's equity for George's Gardening Supplies for the year ended December 31, 2016. George invested an additional $10,000 during the year.

e) Prepare the classified balance sheet for George's Gardening Supplies at December 31, 2016.

f) Journalize the closing entries for George's Gardening Supplies for 2016 using the income summary method.

See Appendix I for solutions.

a) Prepare a single-step income statement

b) Prepare a multistep income statement

Gross Profit Margin = _____

c) Prepare a classified multistep income statement

d) Statement of owner's equity

e)   Prepare a classified balance sheet

f) Journalize the closing entries using the income summary method

JOURNAL			Page 1
Date	**Account Titles and Explanation**	**Debit**	**Credit**

Appendix 7A: The Periodic Inventory System

As mentioned, the periodic inventory system determines the quantity of inventory on hand only periodically. A physical count is taken at the end of the period to determine the value of the ending inventory and cost of goods sold.

Thus, a periodic inventory system does not update the inventory account on a regular basis, only when a physical count is taken. On a regular basis, the periodic inventory system updates a new list of income statement accounts which are used to calculate cost of goods sold.

Consider the differences between the perpetual and the periodic inventory system. Figure 7A.1 illustrates the perpetual inventory system. A business that has the technology to properly implement the perpetual inventory system will record purchases, discounts, allowances and other adjustments into the inventory asset account. Inventory is then transferred to cost of goods sold when a sale is made. Cost of goods sold is immediately matched to sales and gross profit is reported every month, although gross profit may be slightly incorrect if an inventory count is not performed.

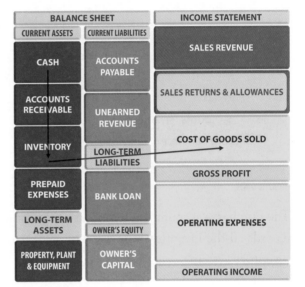

FIGURE 7A.1

A business that does not have the technology to constantly update inventory like in the perpetual inventory system must instead use the periodic inventory system. Figure 7A.2 illustrates the periodic inventory system. Inventory shows an opening value at the beginning of the period, but is only adjusted up or down at the end of the period when an inventory count is performed. All purchases, discounts, allowances and other adjustments are recorded directly into the income statement as part of cost of goods sold.

If purchases were recorded in the inventory account on the balance sheet, they would always remain in inventory since inventory is not transferred to cost of goods sold when a sale is made. This would leave a large amount of inventory remaining on the balance sheet and no cost of goods sold on the income statement. It is more practical to record purchases directly on the income statement, and adjust the inventory account only at year end.

Keep the concept of the periodic inventory system in mind as the journal entries are presented. The transactions are very similar to the perpetual

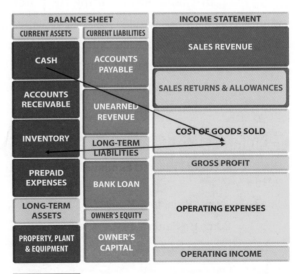

FIGURE 7A.2

inventory system, except that income statement accounts are affected instead of inventory.

Purchases

When inventory is purchased for resale using a periodic inventory system the inventory account is not debited. Instead, we debit an account called purchases on the income statement, which is part of cost of goods sold. If the inventory was paid for on credit, then accounts payable is credited.

If the inventory was paid for with cash, then the cash account is credited. In this example, Tools 4U purchased inventory of $10,000 on January 1, 2016. Assume all purchases and sales are made on account.

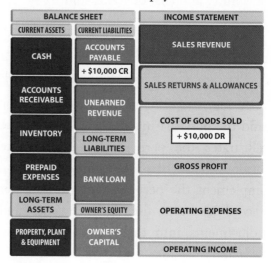

FIGURE 7A.3

The purchases account is a temporary account located on the income statement as part of COGS. It records all the inventory purchased by a company during a specific period of time under the periodic inventory system.

The values of inventory and cost of goods sold are not adjusted until the end of the period when the physical inventory count is taken. As a result, we need to track the costs related to inventory in separate accounts.

Purchase Returns

Continuing with the example of Tools 4U, assume the company returned $300 worth of inventory to its supplier. Instead of just crediting the purchases account, businesses that use a periodic inventory system track these returns by using a temporary contra account to purchases called **purchase returns and allowances**. This new account is also part of cost of goods sold. The journal entry to record the above return is shown in Figure 7A.4.

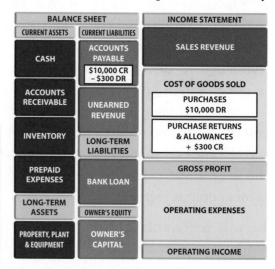

FIGURE 7A.4

Purchase Allowances

Continuing with the above example, assume Tools 4U found another $300 worth of unsatisfactory inventory. Suppose the supplier offers a 20% allowance to Tools 4U to keep the goods, rather than return them. This results in an allowance of $60 ($300 x 20%). When a periodic inventory system is used, the credit will also be recorded in the purchase returns and allowances account as shown in Figure 7A.5.

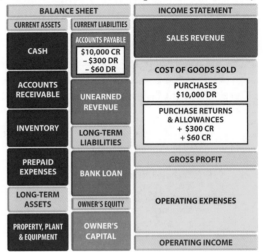

JOURNAL			Page 1
Date 2016	Account Title and Explanation	Debit	Credit
Jan 5	Accounts Payable	60	
	Purchase Returns and Allowances		60
	Record purchase allowance for a supplier		

FIGURE 7A.5

Purchase Discounts

The supplier may offer credit terms and a discount period to encourage early payments. In a periodic inventory system, the amount of the discount is credited to another contra expense to purchases called **purchase discounts**. This is another account that is part of cost of goods sold. By crediting this account, instead of simply crediting the inventory account as in the perpetual inventory system, management is able to track the amount it is saving by paying suppliers within the discount period. We will now show the journal entries for both the purchase and payment from Tools 4U who bought goods from Roofs and More in the amount of $4,200 on January 10. The supplier allows 2/10, n/30 on all invoices. Since Tools 4U had excess cash at this time, the manager chose to take advantage of the cash discount by paying the invoice within 10 days.

The original entry for the purchase is shown in Figure 7A.6.

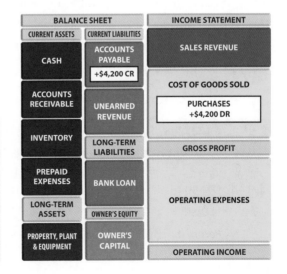

JOURNAL			Page 1
Date 2016	Account Title and Explanation	Debit	Credit
Jan 10	Purchases	4,200	
	Account Payable		4,200
	Purchase of goods from Roofs and More		

FIGURE 7A.6

The payment amount for the bill would be $4,200 less the $84 discount ($4,200 × 2%). Since the business is paying less for the purchases of inventory, the value of the purchase must decrease by the discount amount. The entry to record the discount when the payment was made to Roofs and More on January 12 is shown in Figure 7A.7.

JOURNAL			Page 1
Date 2016	Account Title and Explanation	Debit	Credit
Jan 12	Accounts Payable	4,200	
	Cash		4,116
	Purchase Discounts		84
	Paid invoice owing to Roofs and More less discount for early payment		

FIGURE 7A.7

Both purchase returns and allowances and purchase discounts are known as contra accounts as they have the opposite balance to the account they are related to. They reduce the balance of purchases when reported on the financial statements.

From the above journal entries, the amount of net purchases is determined in Figure 7A.8.

Purchases		$14,200
Less: Purchase Returns and Allowances	$360	
Purchase Discounts	84	444
Net Purchases		$13,756

FIGURE 7A.8

Freight-In and Freight-Out

In a periodic inventory system, shipping charges on inventory shipped FOB shipping point is recorded by the purchaser debiting the **freight-in** account which is an income statement account that is part of cost of goods sold. Similarly, the shipping charges on inventory that is shipped FOB destination are recorded by the seller by debiting the **freight-out** account. Assume Tools 4U paid $100 freight cost for the inventory on January 10, the journal entry is shown in Figure 7A.9.

JOURNAL			Page 1
Date 2016	Account Title and Explanation	Debit	Credit
Jan 10	Freight-In	100	
	Cash		100
	Record the payment of freight cost		

FIGURE 7A.9

Sales

The major difference between the periodic and perpetual system occurs at the point of sale. Unlike the perpetual system which immediately records cost of goods sold when revenue from the sale of inventory is recognized, the periodic system calculates cost of goods sold at the end of the period when ending inventory is determined with a physical count. Assuming inventory is sold on account, the entry should be recorded by debiting accounts receivable and crediting revenue.

Assume Tools 4U sold $13,000 of goods for $20,000 on January 15. In a periodic system, this transaction would be recorded as in Figure 7A.10.

The entry is recorded by debiting accounts receivable and crediting sales. The cost of goods sold and inventory accounts are not updated immediately. Instead, they will be updated at the end of the period when the physical count is taken.

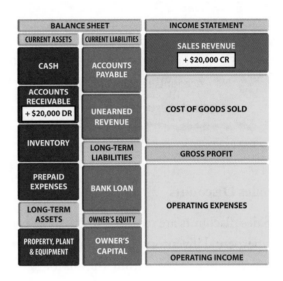

JOURNAL			Page 1
Date 2016	Account Title and Explanation	Debit	Credit
Jan 15	Accounts Receivable	20,000	
	Sales		20,000
	Record sales on account		

FIGURE 7A.10

Sales Returns

If a customer returns goods, in a periodic inventory system, only one journal entry is required to record the sales return and credit the amount owing from the customer (assuming the goods were sold on account). The journal entry for a return of $4,000 worth of goods by a customer on January 16 is shown in Figure 7A.11.

The entry is recorded by debiting sales returns and allowances and crediting accounts receivable. Unlike the perpetual inventory system, the cost of goods sold and inventory are not updated immediately.

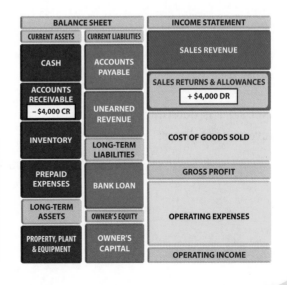

JOURNAL			Page 1
Date 2016	Account Title and Explanation	Debit	Credit
Jan 16	Sales Returns and Allowances	4,000	
	Accounts Receivable		4,000
	Record sales return		

FIGURE 7A.11

Sales Allowances

Sales allowances are recorded in the same way as when a perpetual inventory system is used. Referring to the sales allowances example from the previous section, recall that Tools 4U granted a $300 sales allowance on January 18. The journal entry is recorded as shown in Figure 7A.12 in a periodic inventory system.

JOURNAL			Page 1
Date 2016	**Account Title and Explanation**	**Debit**	**Credit**
Jan 18	Sales Returns & Allowances	300	
	Accounts Receivable		300
	Record sales allowance		

FIGURE 7A.12

Sales Discounts

Sales discounts are recorded in the same way as when a perpetual inventory system is used. In our example, the customer paid within the discount period and received a $250 discount as shown in Figure 7A.13.

JOURNAL			Page 1
Date 2016	**Account Title and Explanation**	**Debit**	**Credit**
Jan 20	Cash	4,750	
	Sales Discounts	250	
	Accounts Receivable		5,000
	Record collection less discount		

FIGURE 7A.13

Net sales is determined by deducting sales returns and allowances and sales discounts from sales revenue as follows:

$$\$20,000 - \$4,000 - \$300 - \$250 = \$15,450$$

Reporting the Cost of Goods Sold

In a periodic system, the cost of goods sold is not known until the end of the period, when the ending inventory is known. This is because, unlike the perpetual system where all costs flowed through the inventory account, the costs that make up the cost of goods available for sale are kept in separate accounts (beginning inventory, purchases, and freight-in). Once ending inventory is determined, it is subtracted from the cost of goods available for sale to determine the cost of goods sold.

Cost of Goods Sold = Beginning Inventory + Net Purchases + Freight-In – Ending Inventory

Assuming the beginning inventory in our example is $20,000 and the ending inventory is $22,856, the cost of goods sold is determined on the income statement as shown in Figure 7A.14.

Cost of Goods Sold = Beginning Inventory + Net Purchases + Freight-In – Ending Inventory		
Beginning Inventory		$20,000
Net Purchases	$13,756	
Freight-In	100	13,856
Cost of Goods Available for Sale		$33,856
Less: Ending Inventory		22,856
Cost of Goods Sold		$11,000

FIGURE 7A.14

The freight-in is added to net purchases to determine cost of goods available for sale. The value of ending inventory is determined by a physical count and subtracted from cost of goods available for sale to determine cost of goods sold. The amounts included in the inventory and cost of goods sold is no different from the example under the perpetual inventory system. It is mainly a timing difference regarding when these amounts are updated.

FOB and Inventory Counts

The terms of shipping items will have an impact on period end inventory counts. An inventory count is supposed to include all inventory that is owned by the company, and this can include items that are not physically at the place of business. All companies must pay careful attention to items in the process of being shipped when counting inventory.

For example, suppose Company A purchases items with a cost of $10,000 with terms of FOB shipping point. This means that Company A takes ownership of the goods as soon as they are loaded onto the carrier, and should include these as part of its inventory. While these goods are in transit, Company A performs an inventory count and does not include the inventory that they just purchased. This means that the value of ending inventory on the balance sheet will be too low, or understated by $10,000. If Company A uses the periodic inventory system, an understated ending inventory will cause COGS to be overstated and net income to be understated. This is shown in Figure 7A.15.

	Correct		Incorrect	
Sales		$160,000		$160,000
Cost of Goods Sold				
Beginning Inventory	50,000		50,000	
Net Purchases	65,000		65,000	
Cost of Goods Available for Sale	115,000		115,000	
Less: Ending Inventory	45,000		35,000	
Cost of Goods Sold		70,000		80,000
Gross Profit		90,000		80,000
Operating Expense		50,000		50,000
Net Income		$40,000		$30,000

FIGURE 7A.15

Similar problems would occur if a company sells inventory with terms of FOB destination. Although the items are not in the seller's warehouse, the seller still owns the items while they are in transit and must include them as part of its inventory.

To summarize the differences between the perpetual and periodic journal entries, the following table in Figure 7A.16 indicates which accounts are affected by the types of transactions we have learned.

Transaction	Perpetual*		Periodic*	
	Debit	Credit	Debit	Credit
Purchase	Inventory (B/S)	Cash or Accounts Payable	Purchases (I/S)	Cash or Accounts Payable
Purchase Return	Cash or Accounts Payable	Inventory (B/S)	Cash or Accounts Payable	Purchase Returns & Allowances (I/S)
Purchase Allowance	Cash or Accounts Payable	Inventory (B/S)	Cash or Accounts Payable	Purchase Returns & Allowances (I/S)
Payment with Discount	Accounts Payable	Cash Inventory (B/S)	Accounts Payable	Cash Purchase Discounts (I/S)
Freight	Inventory (B/S)	Cash or Accounts Payable	Freight-In (I/S)	Cash or Accounts Payable
Sales	Cash or Accounts Receivable Cost of Goods Sold (I/S)	Sales Revenue (I/S) Inventory (B/S)	Cash or Accounts Receivable	Sales Revenue (I/S)

Transaction	Perpetual*		Periodic*	
	Debit	**Credit**	**Debit**	**Credit**
Sales Returns	Sales Returns & Allowances (I/S) Inventory (B/S)	Cash or Accounts Receivable Cost of Goods Sold (I/S)	Sales Returns & Allowances (I/S)	Cash or Accounts Receivable
Sales Allowance	Sales Returns & Allowances (I/S)	Cash or Accounts Receivable	Sales Returns & Allowances (I/S)	Cash or Accounts Receivable
Receipt with Discount	Cash Sales Discounts (I/S)	Accounts Receivable	Cash Sales Discounts (I/S)	Accounts Receivable

*B/S = Balance Sheet and I/S = Income Statement

FIGURE 7A.16

In essence, the mechanisms behind recording these transactions under both inventory tracking methods are the same. They only differ in the way that no "inventory" and "cost of goods sold" accounts are present under the periodic inventory transactions.

A CLOSER LOOK

The accurate financial performance of a company that uses the periodic system can only be calculated when an inventory count is performed and the cost of goods sold is calculated. If a business wanted to see how it was performing between inventory counts, it may have to make some adjustments to the reports before the numbers are useful for decision making.

For example, a nursery selling flowers and other plants may operate from May to October. After closing in October, it performs a physical count of inventory and prepares formal financial statements.

Before it opens in May, it has to purchase soil and seeds and start growing plants in the greenhouses in preparation for spring. These purchases are made before any sales are made. Recall that under a periodic inventory system, cost of goods sold = beginning inventory + purchases – ending inventory. If the company uses the periodic inventory system and wanted to see its performance after one month of operations (May), without counting inventory, only the beginning inventory and purchases amount would be available for the purposes of calculating cost of goods sold. That is, ending inventory would be missing. By not deducting ending inventory, the information presented would be distorted and it would appear the company is operating at a loss.

To prevent the distortion of the financial statements, management can instead estimate what cost of goods sold was using the gross profit method which will be discussed in a later chapter.

For example, if the nursery typically operates at 40% gross profit during the sales season, the following figure illustrates how the income statement could be estimated without doing a physical inventory count.

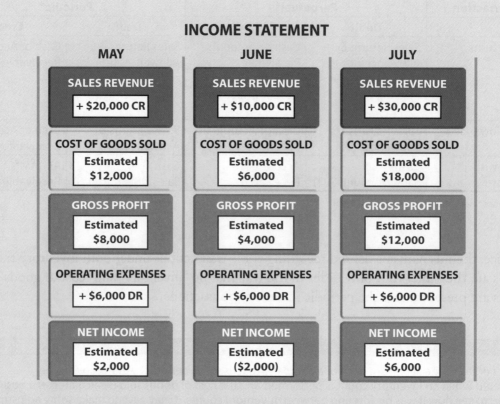

INCOME STATEMENT

MAY	JUNE	JULY
SALES REVENUE	**SALES REVENUE**	**SALES REVENUE**
+ $20,000 CR	+ $10,000 CR	+ $30,000 CR
COST OF GOODS SOLD	**COST OF GOODS SOLD**	**COST OF GOODS SOLD**
Estimated $12,000	Estimated $6,000	Estimated $18,000
GROSS PROFIT	**GROSS PROFIT**	**GROSS PROFIT**
Estimated $8,000	Estimated $4,000	Estimated $12,000
OPERATING EXPENSES	**OPERATING EXPENSES**	**OPERATING EXPENSES**
+ $6,000 DR	+ $6,000 DR	+ $6,000 DR
NET INCOME	**NET INCOME**	**NET INCOME**
Estimated $2,000	Estimated ($2,000)	Estimated $6,000

This estimation can only be used for management purposes and interim statements. Formal financial statements can only be prepared after a physical count has been performed.

Multistep Income Statement

The multistep income under a periodic inventory system is much like that of a perpetual inventory system, except when it comes to COGS. Recall that there is a single line for COGS on the income statement for a perpetual inventory system. However, this line is replaced with a COGS section for a periodic inventory system. The section is taken from the schedule of COGS introduced earlier.

Note that the periodic and perpetual inventory systems both produce the same values for COGS, gross profit, and net income. The only difference is the way in which COGS is calculated. The multistep income statement for Tools 4U is shown in Figure 7A.17 using the same values from the perpetual inventory system.

	Tools 4U Income Statement For the Year Ended December 31, 2016				
1. Calculate Net Sales	**Sales Revenue**				$200,000
	Less: Sales Returns and Allowances			$4,000	
	Sales Discounts			2,000	(6,000)
	Net Sales				194,000
2. Calculate Cost of Goods Sold and Gross Profit	**Cost of Goods Sold**				
	Inventory, January 1, 2016			20,000	
	Purchases		$140,000		
	Less: Purchase Returns and Allowances	$9,000			
	Purchase Discounts	13,000	(22,000)		
	Net Purchases		118,000		
	Freight-In		6,000	124,000	
	Cost of Goods Available for Sale			144,000	
	Inventory, December 31, 2016			44,000	
	Cost of Goods Sold				100,000
	Gross Profit				94,000
3. Calculate Operating Income	**Operating Expenses**				
	Depreciation Expense			5,000	
	Rent Expense			10,000	
	Salaries Expense			40,000	
	Supplies Expense			7,000	
	Utilities Expense			6,000	
	Total Operating Expenses				68,000
	Operating Income				26,000
4. Calculate non-operating activities and Net Income	**Other Revenue and Expenses**				
	Interest Revenue			8,000	
	Interest Expense			(4,000)	4,000
	Net Income				$30,000

FIGURE 7A.17

Closing Entries

Closing Entries and Inventory in a Periodic System

Although there are a few variations of how inventory is adjusted through the closing entries when a periodic system is used, the main objective is the same—to remove the beginning inventory balance and add the new ending inventory balance.

One approach that is frequently used is shown in Figure 7A.18.

JOURNAL			Page 1
Date	**Account Title and Explanation**	**Debit**	**Credit**
2016			
Dec 31	Sales Revenue	20,000	
	Inventory	22,856	
	Purchase Returns & Allowances	360	
	Purchase Discounts	84	
	Income Summary		43,300
	Close revenue and credit balances and update inventory		

FIGURE 7A.18

When closing the accounts with a credit balance on the income statement, the new ending inventory balance of $22,856 is debited to the inventory account. To understand the logic of this entry, refer to the detailed cost of goods sold section previously discussed. The ending inventory is deducted from the cost of goods available for sale to determine the amount of cost of goods sold because ending inventory represents the amount a company still has on hand at the end of the accounting period. It is available for sale at the beginning of the next accounting period.

In closing the expense accounts, notice that the beginning inventory balance

JOURNAL			Page 1
Date	**Account Title and Explanation**	**Debit**	**Credit**
2016			
Dec 31	Income Summary	40,360	
	Inventory		20,000
	Sales Returns & Allowances		4,300
	Sales Discounts		250
	Purchases		14,200
	Freight-in		100
	Operating Expenses		1,510
	Close expenses and debit balances and update inventory		

FIGURE 7A.19

of $20,000 is credited. Refer to Figure 7A.14, the detailed cost of goods sold section is shown. What effect does the beginning inventory have on the cost of goods available for sale? It is added together with purchases and therefore represents an expense of the period. The logic is: expenses are credited through the closing entries; therefore, the beginning inventory balance of $20,000 must be credited.

After the closing entries are posted to the accounts, the inventory account will be updated to reflect the actual amount of inventory on hand, $22,856.

The final step of the closing entry process is to close the income summary account to the owners' capital account. The journal entry on January 31 is shown in Figure 7A.20.

JOURNAL			Page 1
Date	**Account Title and Explanation**	**Debit**	**Credit**
2016			
Dec 31	Income Summary	2,940	
	Sanders, Capital		2,940
	To close income summary account		

FIGURE 7A.20

The T-accounts in Figure 7A.21 below summarize the closing entries under the periodic inventory system. Note how the inventory account is updated following the physical inventory count. Each item that is closed to the income summary account is shown separately so the opening and ending inventory amounts can be highlighted.

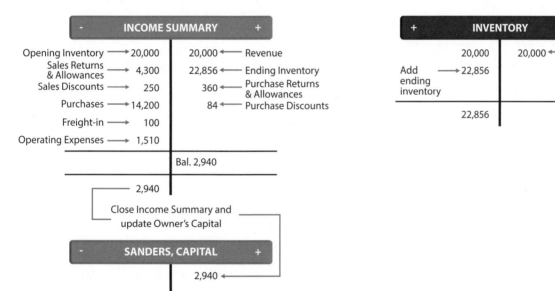

FIGURE 7A.21

In Summary

Record journal entries related to inventory purchases under the periodic inventory system

- ➪ When buying inventory, the purchases account is debited.

- ➪ When returning inventory or taking an allowance on purchased goods, the contra-expense account called purchase returns and allowances is credited.

- ➪ When discounts are taken advantage of on inventory purchases, the contra-expense account called purchase discounts is credited for the amount of the discount.

- ➪ Shipping costs paid on goods purchased FOB shipping point are recorded in the freight-in account.

Record journal entries related to inventory sales under the periodic inventory system

- ➪ When selling inventory, only the sales transaction is recorded. The inventory is not removed from the balance sheet at the time of sale.

- ➪ When customers return goods or take allowances on their purchases, the contra-revenue account called sales returns and allowances is debited.

- ➪ Sales discounts allow customers to save money by paying early. This causes a debit to the contra-revenue account called sales discounts.

- ➪ Shipping costs paid on goods sold FOB destination are recorded in the freight-out account.

Calculate cost of goods sold under the periodic inventory system

- ➪ Cost of goods sold appears as a separate section below net sales on the multistep income statement. The beginning inventory balance is listed first in this section.

- ➪ Net purchases are calculated next by deducting purchase returns and allowances and purchase discounts from the purchases account.

- ➪ Beginning inventory plus net purchases is called cost of goods available for sale.

- ➪ The ending inventory balance (determined by an inventory count) is deducted from the cost of goods available for sale to calculate the cost of goods sold for the period.

Prepare closing entries for a merchandising business under the periodic inventory system

- ➪ All revenue and contra-expense accounts are closed to the income summary account. The balance of ending inventory is also added to the income summary account in this entry.

- ➪ All expense and contra-revenue accounts are closed to the income summary account. The balance of beginning inventory is also removed from the income summary account in this entry.

- ➪ The income summary is closed to the owner's capital account.

- ➪ If there are owner's drawings, they are closed directly to the owner's capital account.

Review Exercise

Part 1

The following transactions occurred between George's Gardening Supplies and Michael's Distributing during the month of December 2016.

Dec 3   George's Gardening Supplies purchased $50,000 worth of inventory on account from Michael's Distributing. The purchase terms were 2/10 n/30. The cost of the goods to Michael's Distributing was $35,000.

Dec 6   Freight charges of $200 were paid in cash by the company which incurred them.

Dec 8   George's Gardening Supplies returned $2,000 of incorrect inventory from the purchase on December 3. Michael's Distributing put the merchandise back into inventory. The cost of the goods to Michael's Distributing was originally $700.

Dec 11   George's Gardening Supplies paid the balance owing to Michael's Distributing.

Assuming that both companies use the perpetual inventory system, complete the following exercise.

a) Journalize the December transactions for George's Gardening Supplies. Assume the goods from December 3 were shipped FOB shipping point.

b) Journalize the December transactions for Michael's Distributing. Assume the goods from December 3 were shipped FOB destination.

See Appendix I for solutions.

a) December transactions for George's Gardening Supplies

JOURNAL			Page 1
Date	Account Titles and Explanation	Debit	Credit

b) December transactions for Michael's Distributing

JOURNAL			Page 1
Date	Account Titles and Explanation	Debit	Credit

Part 2

Below is the adjusted trial balance for George's Gardening Supplies at the end of the year.

George's Gardening Supplies Adjusted Trial Balance December 31, 2016		
Account Titles	**DR**	**CR**
Cash	$54,830	
Accounts Receivable	33,500	
Inventory	16,140	
Prepaid Insurance	36,000	
Equipment	45,000	
Accumulated Depreciation		$5,000
Accounts Payable		10,000
Bank Loan		30,000
Gregg, Capital		90,000
Gregg, Drawings	5,000	
Sales Revenue		113,500
Interest Revenue		6,500
Sales Returns & Allowances	1,000	
Sales Discounts	1,580	
Purchases	70,000	
Purchase Returns and Allowances		5,800
Purchase Discounts		3,200
Freight-In	1,000	
Depreciation Expense	5,000	
Insurance Expense	2,500	
Interest Expense	2,600	
Rent Expense	6,000	
Salaries Expense	11,000	
Supplies Expense	4,500	
Utilities Expense	750	
Total	**$264,000**	**$264,000**

Note:

- The balance in the inventory account is the value at January 1, 2016. An inventory count revealed that $33,440 of inventory is on hand at December 31, 2016.

- $10,000 of the bank loan will be paid by December 31, 2017.

a) Prepare a multistep income statement for George's Gardening Supplies for the year ended December 31, 2016. Calculate the gross profit margin.

b) Prepare the statement of owner's equity for George's Gardening Supplies for the year ended December 31, 2016. George invested an additional $10,000 during the year.

c) Prepare the classified balance sheet for George's Gardening Supplies at December 31, 2016.

d) Journalize the closing entries for George's Gardening Supplies for 2016 using the income summary method.

See Appendix I for solutions.

a) Prepare multistep income statement

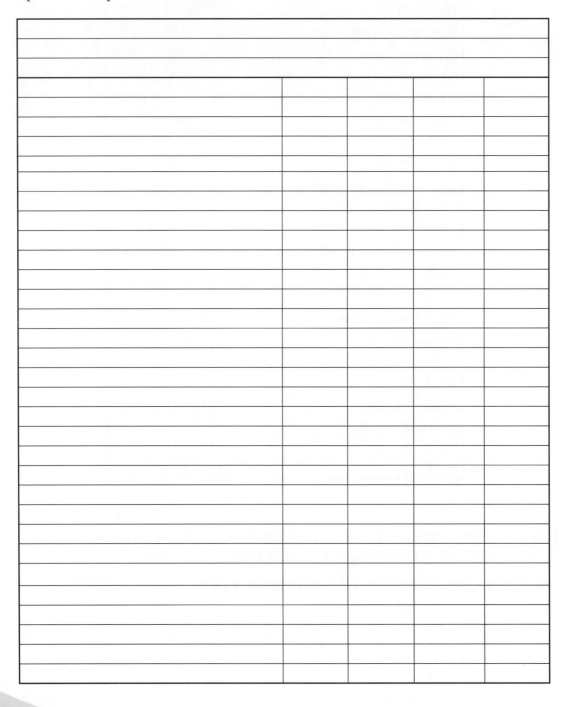

b) Prepare statement of owner's equity

c) Prepare the classified balance sheet

d) Journalize the closing entries using the income summary method

JOURNAL			Page 1
Date	**Account Titles and Explanation**	**Debit**	**Credit**

Chapter 8
INVENTORY VALUATION

AMEENGAGE™ *Access **ameengage.com** for integrated resources including tutorials, practice exercises, the digital textbook and more.*

Inventory Valuation Methods

In the previous chapter, we saw how merchandising businesses account for various transactions involving inventory. A perpetual inventory system updates the inventory and cost of goods sold accounts after every sales transaction. This is straightforward when identical inventory was purchased for the same price, but prices for identical goods often fluctuate. This can make it difficult to calculate the COGS for a particular sale.

For example, suppose that Tools 4U purchased 10 steel hammers for $20 each as inventory in March. When one of these hammers is sold to a customer, inventory must be credited for $20 and COGS must be debited for $20. Due to an increase in the price of steel, Tools 4U must pay $25 per hammer in April. Now it has a mix of identical hammers, some of which cost $20 and some of which cost $25. When a hammer is sold during April, which cost should be used to update inventory and COGS? Ideally, it would be possible to tell which hammers came from which shipment, but the costs and effort of tracking such information often outweigh the benefits.

There are three methods that companies can use, based on the nature of the goods, to determine how inventory costs are handled. These are called **inventory valuation methods** because they will determine the value of inventory on hand at any given time. The three methods used in Canada are specific identification, first-in, first-out, and weighted-average cost.

- The **specific identification** method is used when a business sells goods which are not identical or are customized in some way. This method accurately tracks the costs and value of inventory, but it can be costly to apply. Highly valuable items such as cars, houses, and diamonds are often valued under this method.

- The **first-in, first-out (FIFO)** method is used when a business assumes that the first items received in inventory are also the first items moved out of inventory. Perishable items that expire within a relatively short period of time, such as fruit and vegetables, are often valued under this method.

- The **weighted-average cost** method is used when a business simply applies an average cost to all of the units of a particular inventory item. Homogenous (standardized) materials, such as plastic used in the making of garbage bags, or oil used in making gasoline, are often valued under this method.

The method chosen does not need to perfectly match the actual physical movement of goods. For example, if a business chooses the FIFO method to value its lawn chairs, it is still acceptable to sell newer lawn chairs before older ones in the course of business. Once a valuation is chosen however, accounting standards dictate that the business must use it consistently unless a change can be properly justified. This is done to stop businesses from arbitrarily changing inventory valuation methods for the purpose of manipulating the values of COGS and ending inventory.

WORTH REPEATING

The principle of consistency prevents businesses from changing accounting methods for the sole purpose of manipulating figures on the financial statements.

Applying Valuation Methods

Cool Ink Company sells a number of different high quality pens, pencils, markers and highlighters. Let us examine one item from its inventory to illustrate the three different inventory valuation methods. Assume that Cool Ink uses a perpetual inventory system to account for purchases and sales.

Cool Ink Company currently has ten collector pens in inventory with a cost of $10 each. During the month of March, the following transactions took place with respect to collector pens which is shown in Figure 8.1.

Date	Transaction	Quantity	Unit Cost
March 5	Purchase from Pen Distributers	50	$12
March 7	Sale	15	
March 15	Purchase from Promotional Pens	40	$14
March 19	Purchase from Promotional Pens	20	$16
March 27	Sale	50	

FIGURE 8.1

During the month, the cost of the pen increased as shown from the Unit Cost column. This means that the cost of goods sold applied to each sale will likely be different, based on which pens are actually sold. We can apply the three methods of valuing inventory to the transactions to arrive at different values for inventory and cost of goods sold. This will demonstrate that the choice of inventory valuation method can make a difference on the financial statements of a company.

Specific Identification Method

The specific identification method is used when a company sells goods that are unique in some way and can be distinguished from each other. For example, a jewellery retailer may use this method to value its gold products because its costs can fluctuate significantly.

When using specific identification, it is helpful to list the purchases separately from each other to easily identify the costs associated with each batch of inventory. This is done by using a table as shown in Figure 8.2. The opening balance and the transactions from Figure 8.1 are listed in the table. Purchases cause the balance of inventory to increase and sales cause it to decrease. At the bottom of the figure is the value of ending inventory.

	Date	Purchases			Sales			Balance		
		Quantity	Unit Cost	Value	Quantity	Unit Cost	Value	Quantity	Unit Cost	Value
❶	March 1							10	$10	$100
❷	March 5	50	$12	$600				10	$10	$100
								50	$12	$600
❸	March 7				8	$10	$80	2	$10	$20
					7	$12	$84	43	$12	$516
❹	March 15	40	$14	$560				2	$10	$20
								43	$12	$516
								40	$14	$560
❺	March 19	20	$16	$320				2	$10	$20
								43	$12	$516
								40	$14	$560
								20	$16	$320
❻	March 27				2	$10	$20			
					33	$12	$396	10	$12	$120
					15	$14	$210	25	$14	$350
								20	$16	$320
❼	Ending Inventory									$790

FIGURE 8.2

❶ Record the opening balance of inventory of 10 pens at $10 each.

❷ The purchase of 50 pens on March 5 is added to the value of inventory. These are listed on a separate line from the 10 opening units because they were purchased at a different unit cost.

❸ The sale of 15 pens on March 7 can be specifically identified. Eight of the pens came from opening inventory and seven of the pens came from the purchase on March 5. As a result, the opening balance of 10 pens is reduced to two and the batch of 50 pens is reduced to 43. The value of cost of goods sold for this sale is $164 ($80 + $84).

❹ The purchase of 40 pens on March 15 is added to the value of inventory. Again, a new row is used because the unit cost is different from the current inventory.

❺ The purchase of 20 pens on March 19 is added to the value of inventory. Again, a new row is used because the unit cost is different from the current inventory.

❻ The sale of 50 pens on March 27 can be specifically identified. Two came from opening inventory, 33 from the purchase on March 5 and 15 from the purchase on March 15. The value of the cost of goods sold for this sale is $626 ($20 + $396 + $210).

❼ The value of ending inventory is made up of 10 pens remaining from the March 5 purchase, 25 pens remaining from the March 15 purchase and 20 pens remaining from the March 19 purchase. Total value of ending inventory is $790 ($120 + $350 + $320).

First-In, First-Out (FIFO) Method

The FIFO method is used when the inventory items which are purchased first (first-in) are generally sold first (first-out). For example, a supermarket will try to sell its oldest dairy products first so that they do not expire.

When using the FIFO method, it is helpful to list the purchases in the order they were received. This will clearly show which items were the first ones purchased, which will also be assumed the first ones sold. This is done by using a table as shown in Figure 8.3. The opening balance and the transactions from Figure 8.1 are listed in the table. This is similar to the specific identification method. At the bottom of the figure is the value of ending inventory.

Date	Purchases			Sales			Balance		
	Quantity	Unit Cost	Value	Quantity	Unit Cost	Value	Quantity	Unit Cost	Value
❶ March 1							10	$10	$100
❷ March 5	50	$12	$600				10	$10	$100
							50	$12	$600
❸ March 7				10	$10	$100			
				5	$12	$60	45	$12	$540
❹ March 15	40	$14	$560				45	$12	$540
							40	$14	$560
❺ March 19	20	$16	$320				45	$12	$540
							40	$14	$560
							20	$16	$320
❻ March 27				45	$12	$540			
				5	$14	$70	35	$14	$490
							20	$16	$320
❼ Ending Inventory									$810

FIGURE 8.3

❶ Record the opening balance of inventory of 10 pens at $10 each.

❷ The purchase of 50 pens on March 5 is added to the value of inventory. These are listed on a separate line from the 10 opening units because they were purchased on a different date.

❸ The sale of 15 pens on March 7 must first use the costs from the opening balance. Since there were only 10 pens in the opening balance, another five are taken from the purchase on March 5. This means that the entire opening balance inventory has been sold and only 45 units remain from the purchase on March 5. The value of cost of goods sold for this sale is $160 ($100 + $60).

❹ The purchase of 40 pens on March 15 is added to the value of inventory. Again, a new row is used because they were purchased on a different date.

❺ The purchase of 20 pens on March 19 is added to the value of inventory. Again, a new row is used because they were purchased on a different date.

❻ The sale of the 50 pens on March 27 must first use the costs from the purchase on March 5. Since there are only 45 pens left from that purchase, another five are taken from the purchase on March 15. The value of cost of goods sold for this sale is $610 ($540 + $70).

❼ The value of ending inventory is made up of 35 pens remaining from the March 15 purchase and 20 pens from the March 19 purchase. Total value of inventory is $810 ($490 + $320).

Weighted-Average Cost Method

The weighted-average cost method is used when inventory items are identical and the order they are sold in is irrelevant. For example, a gas station has its gasoline tank filled, and the new product is mixed with the old product.

When using the weighted-average cost method, the total inventory value is divided by the total quantity on hand to arrive at an average cost for each unit. This is done by using a table as shown in Figure 8.4.

Average Unit Cost = Total Value ÷ Total Quantity

The opening balance and the transactions from Figure 8.1 are listed in the table. The average unit cost changes after every purchase, but not after a sale. At the bottom of the figure is the value of ending inventory.

	Date	Purchases			Sales			Balance		
		Quantity	Unit Cost	Value	Quantity	Unit Cost	Value	Quantity	Unit Cost	Value
❶	March 1							10	$10.00	$100.00
❷	March 5	50	$12	$600				60	$11.67	$700.00
❸	March 7				15	$11.67	$175.05	45	$11.67	$524.95
❹	March 15	40	$14	$560				85	$12.76	$1,084.95
❺	March 19	20	$16	$320				105	$13.38	$1,404.95
❻	March 27				50	$13.38	$669.00	55	$13.38	$735.95
❼	**Ending Inventory**									$735.95

FIGURE 8.4

❶ Record the opening balance of inventory of 10 pens at $10 each.

❷ The purchase of 50 pens on March 5 is added to the quantity on hand. The value of the 50 pens is first added to the value of the opening inventory. The average unit cost is approximately $11.67 ($700 ÷ 60 units).

❸ The sale of 15 pens on March 7 is taken from inventory. The most recent unit cost of approximately $11.67 per unit is used to calculate the cost of goods sold of $175.05 ($11.67 x 15). Both the quantity and value of inventory decrease, and the unit cost is still approximately $11.67 ($524.95 ÷ 45 units). The unit cost of inventory will never change after a sale; it can only change after a purchase.

❹ The purchase of 40 pens on March 15 is added to the quantity on hand. The value of the 40 pens is added to current value of inventory. The unit cost is now approximately $12.76 ($1,084.95 ÷ 85 units).

❺ The purchase of 20 pens on March 19 is added to the quantity on hand. The value of the 20 pens is added to current value of inventory. The unit cost is now approximately $13.38 ($1,404.95 ÷ 105 units).

❻ The sale of the 50 pens on March 27 is taken from inventory. The most recent cost of approximately $13.38 per unit is used to calculate the cost of goods sold of $669.00 ($13.38 × 50).

❼ The value of ending inventory is 55 pens at the average unit cost of approximately $13.38. Total value of inventory is $735.95.

The Effect of Different Valuation Methods

As the previous example with Cool Ink Company demonstrates, different ending inventory figures are produced using different valuation methods. The chart in Figure 8.5 summarizes these differences for the Cool Ink example.

	Specific Identification	FIFO	Weighted-Average Cost
Inventory Available for Sale (beginning inventory + purchases)	$1,580	$1,580	$1,580
Ending Inventory	790	810	735.95
Value of COGS	790	770	844.05

FIGURE 8.5

The above example illustrates an important point. In cases where the unit cost of inventory increases over a period of time, the FIFO method results in the highest value of ending inventory and the lowest value of COGS. This also results in the highest profit for the period. Similarly, in cases where the unit cost of inventory decreases over a period of time, the FIFO method results in the lowest value of ending inventory and the highest value of COGS. Therefore, two identical companies using different inventory valuation methods will show different financial results.

> **A CLOSER LOOK**
>
> Accounting software will usually allow you to select which inventory method you wish to use. In addition to using specific identification, FIFO or weighted average, software may also allow for the last-in, first-out (LIFO) valuation method. This method is not allowed under ASPE or IFRS, but is allowed in the United States.

Determining the Actual Quantity of Inventory

Goods are moved in and out of inventory all the time, which is why recording the amount and quantities bought and sold is so important. This is done when the goods enter the premises at purchase and when they leave the premises at sale. The reliability of the information recorded at these points must be assured.

For example, the items must be counted when they are received, and these amounts should be compared to the amounts listed on the original purchase order. Any discrepancies must be noted and followed up. Once the inventory count is complete, the company's records should be updated immediately.

Before goods can leave the premises, a release order, such as a packing slip, must be written up and authorized. Just as goods coming in have to be recorded, goods moving out must also be recorded. The shipper should note which goods are leaving and forward the documents to the accounting department to ensure the information is entered into the system.

Some of this paperwork can take time using a manual system. Computer scanning software can eliminate much of the paperwork and time involved in recording the movement of goods in inventory. Whether items are coming in or moving out, a swipe of the scanner can immediately track their location and status while in inventory.

The Physical Inventory Count

A company must take a physical count of its inventory accounts at least once a year. Companies using the periodic inventory system must take a physical count as it is the only way to determine the amount on hand at the end of a period. Companies using the perpetual inventory system count inventory to ensure the accuracy of their records. While a business may have its own policies and procedures for the process of taking a physical inventory count, the following steps are generally included.

1. Designate an area to a specific person.
2. Count and record each item on pre-numbered sheets that are distributed and controlled by the accounting department.
3. Completed sheets are returned to the accounting department where items are valued and summarized.
4. Where a perpetual system is used, the inventory record (ledger account) is compared to the physical count. Differences are noted and adjustments are recorded accordingly.
5. Where major differences occur between the inventory record and the physical count, further investigation is required.

Effect of Inventory Errors

Inventory is a type of asset that differs somewhat from other assets we have discussed in previous chapters. Unlike cash, the value of which is quite definitive (except when it comes to exchange rates between currencies), or accounts receivable which is also quite definitive, the value of inventory can be subjective to a certain extent.

Attaching a value to inventory involves a different kind of challenge. A warehouse can be full of various products which were bought at a certain price and will be sold at another price, with no clarity as to which items moved when. As we have demonstrated, the choice of valuation system often settles the matter. However, even a valuation system only creates a snapshot in time, one which management can influence by choosing one valuation system over another.

In other words, matching physical items in inventory to specific dollar values using any valuation method can be complicated. This is why the process is prone to errors, and errors can have an impact on the way a company presents its financial figures—both internally and externally. Next, examine the impact that an inventory error can have on gross margin percentage and other aspects of financial reporting.

The Impact of Cost of Goods Sold on Gross Profit

Although inventory is a balance sheet account, it can have an immediate impact on the income statement because the cost of goods sold is used to calculate gross profit. Gross profit in turn is used to calculate the gross margin percentage. The gross margin percentage represents the percentage of sales left to pay the remaining operating expenses of the company.

This relationship between inventory and gross profit is demonstrated in Figure 8.6.

It should become clear that the cost of goods sold is a focal point when dealing with inventory on a company's financial statements.

In a periodic inventory system, COGS is calculated by adding total inventory purchases to the value of inventory on hand at the beginning of the period, then deducting the closing value of inventory at the end of the period. The closing value of inventory is determined by a physical count. An example of the calculation is shown in Figure 8.7.

In other words, a company's COGS represents the amount of inventory that is used/sold in a period.

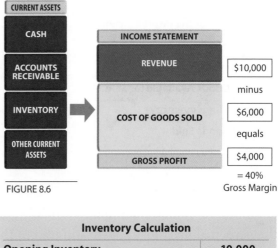

FIGURE 8.6

Inventory Calculation	
Opening Inventory	10,000
Plus: Purchases	60,000
Cost of Goods Available for Sale	70,000
Less: Closing Inventory	20,000
Cost of Goods Sold	50,000

FIGURE 8.7

Errors in valuing closing inventory can affect COGS and, as a result, gross profit. Beyond affecting COGS and gross profit, an incorrect inventory value affects opening inventory for the next period. We will examine the impact on gross profit while ignoring the effects on net income for the year.

The Effect of Overstating Inventory

We will use two examples. One set of charts will include the correct amount for closing inventory; the other set of charts will include an incorrect amount for closing inventory.

We will then look at how this error affects the other important figures on the company's financial statements. Figure 8.8 shows the correct numbers.

Inventory Calculation	
Opening Inventory	5,000
Plus: Purchases	75,000
Cost of Goods Available for Sale	80,000
Less: Closing Inventory	9,000
Cost of Goods Sold	71,000

Income Statement Year 1	
Sales	$100,000
Less: Cost of Goods Sold	71,000
Gross Profit	$29,000

FIGURE 8.8

When closing inventory is correctly valued at $9,000, a COGS value of $71,000 is produced. As a result, the gross profit for the year is $29,000. The gross margin for the reporting period is 29,000 ÷ 100,000 = 29%

What happens if we overstate closing inventory by $1,000? This is shown in Figure 8.9.

Gross profit for the year is $30,000. Gross margin is then 30,000 ÷ 100,000 = 30%

Inventory Calculation	
Opening Inventory	5,000
Plus: Purchases	75,000
Cost of Goods Available for Sale	80,000
Less: Closing Inventory	10,000
Cost of Goods Sold	70,000

Income Statement Year 1	
Sales	$100,000
Less: Cost of Goods Sold	70,000
Gross Profit	$30,000

FIGURE 8.9

As a result, COGS is understated by $1,000, gross profit is overstated by $1,000, and gross margin is overstated by 1%. The same error while performing a physical account for a company that uses the perpetual inventory system will lead to the same problem.

If this error is found and corrected before the end of the period, then a journal entry must be recorded to correct the balances of inventory and COGS. In this example, the correct journal entry is shown in Figure 8.10. If inventory was instead understated by $1,000, the journal entry would debit inventory and credit cost of goods sold.

JOURNAL			Page 1
Date 2016	Account Title and Explanation	Debit	Credit
Dec 31	Cost of Goods Sold	1,000	
	Inventory		1,000
	Corrected overstated inventory		

FIGURE 8.10

If the error is made after the financial reporting period is over, then an assessment of the materiality of the error must be made.

If the error is considered material, then the company's financial statements must be reissued with the amended figures. It is obviously a scenario that companies want to avoid. Such a high profile mistake can only cast doubt on how the company is being run. Nevertheless, if such material errors are found, they must be reported—regardless of any negative impact they may have on the company's reputation.

This is just a snapshot of what errors in valuing inventory can do to a company's financial statements. Both internal and external stakeholders are affected by inventory errors. Such errors can affect business decision-making, tax reporting and adherence to accounting procedures.

The Impact of Inventory Errors

A company that requires debt financing may try to make its financial statements appear better by overstating inventory, which understates COGS and causes gross profit to be overstated. If inventory is overstated unintentionally, it can give management a false sense of confidence in the company. This could lead to bad decisions about pricing, discounts, target market share, or other aspects of business performance. The reverse would be true for understated numbers, which could create unnecessary panic and desperation.

An inaccurate gross profit figure can also have consequences when it comes to paying taxes. A higher gross profit leads to higher net income, which means that a company is paying more tax than it should. On the other hand, understating inventory would overstate COGS, which causes gross profit and net income to be understated. This means that the government would get less in taxes from the company than it should.

Finally, a company could use its inflated financial figures to create a false impression of its performance for external stakeholders, or on banks when trying to secure loans. This can represent an ethical breach in violation of the accounting principle of disclosure.

The Lower of Cost and Net Realizable Value

Market conditions can fluctuate. With respect to inventory, this means that sometimes a company sells its inventory for a lower price than what it was purchased for in the first place (the selling price is lower than cost). This could be due to an advancement in technology or a change in industry trends, rendering older products obsolete or outdated.

The accounting principle of conservatism asserts that, given a choice, the accounting alternative that produces a lower value for assets must always be used. This prevents companies from providing an overly optimistic statement of their finances. This is a trade-off with the accounting principle of measurement which states that inventory should be recorded at the cost identified by the inventory value method used.

When a company determines that inventory must be sold at a price below cost, this asset must be recorded at its **net realizable value (NRV)**. Net realizable value is the price that a company can realistically expect to sell the item for, less any costs incurred to make the item ready for sale, such as repair costs. This method is known as the **lower of cost and net realizable value (LCNRV)**.

For example suppose that Elan's Camera Shop sells point-and-shoot cameras, more expensive DSLR cameras and camera bags. Cost and net realizable value are shown in Figure 8.11.

			LCRNV	
	Cost	NRV	Individual	Category
Point-and-Shoot				
Camera 1	40,000	12,000	12,000	
Camera 2	35,000	45,000	35,000	
Total Point-and-Shoot	75,000	57,000		57,000
DSLR				
Camera A	80,000	110,000	80,000	
Camera B	90,000	130,000	90,000	
Total DSLR	170,000	240,000		170,000
Camera Bags	15,000	20,000	15,000	
Total	$260,000	$317,000		

FIGURE 8.11

The total cost of $260,000 is the current balance of the inventory account and is broken down between the various inventory items carried by the store. NRV is the net realizable value of the different inventory items. Notice that the point-and-shoot camera 1 has an NRV significantly less than the cost. This model may be outdated and thus difficult to sell.

Usually, LCNRV is applied to individual inventory items. In our example, only camera 1 shows an NRV less than cost. The difference between its cost and its NRV is $28,000 ($40,000 – $12,000). Therefore inventory must be written down by $28,000. The write-down decreases inventory and increases cost of goods sold. The journal entry is shown in Figure 8.12.

JOURNAL			Page 1
Date 2016	Account Title and Explanation	Debit	Credit
Dec 31	Cost of Goods Sold	28,000	
	Inventory		28,000
	Adjust inventory to LCNRV		

FIGURE 8.12

LCRNV is generally applied to individual inventory items, but in certain circumstances can be applied to categories of inventory. In our example, if all point-and-shoot cameras are becoming obsolete and will no longer be sold by the store, it may be easier to write-down the entire category. The difference between cost and NRV for the point-and-shoot category is $18,000 ($75,000 – $57,000). If LCNRV were applied to inventory categories, the value used in the journal entry would have been $18,000.

If the NRV of an inventory item increases after it has already been written down, a company may reverse the write-down. However, the reversal cannot exceed the amount of the original write-down. In other words, the value recorded for any inventory item cannot exceed its historical cost.

Methods of Estimating Inventory

In a perpetual inventory system, a company maintains a continuous record of the changes to inventory. This means that, at any given point in time, a company can take an instant snapshot of its inventory value, including the amounts for cost of goods sold and ending inventory. Modern scanning and computer technology can help a company update its financial situation quickly and accurately.

Alternatively, a periodic inventory system poses greater challenges in obtaining up-to-date inventory information, since the value of the inventory cannot be tracked from start to finish. Taking a physical count of inventory can be very costly, therefore a physical count may be done only for year-end reports. If inventory values are required at other times for internal reporting, they will have to be estimated.

We will examine two methods of estimating inventory under a periodic inventory system: the gross profit method and the retail method.

The Gross Profit Method

The **gross profit method** uses a company's gross profit figure to estimate the value of inventory. More specifically, a company analyzes the gross profit numbers of prior years to come up with a current gross profit number to apply to estimation figures.

IN THE REAL WORLD

Every now and then, you might see the term: *pro forma* financial statements. Simply stated, these are statements prepared by a company that do not necessarily adhere to ASPE nor IFRS.

There are various reasons why companies prepare such reports. They can be used in an informal way to temporarily guide managerial decision-making. They can also be used to present financial figures in a way that at times might be distorted by accounting principles. For example, costs associated with a previous accounting scandal must be included in formal reports, yet such numbers may inaccurately reflect how the company is currently performing.

Pro forma statements can provide the public with a clearer snapshot of current organizational performance. In fact, *pro forma* financial figures were reported publicly and often during the dot.com boom of the late 1990s. However, regulators began to crack down on such practices, since even *pro forma* statements have their limitations and are not a substitute for documents that adhere to ASPE or IFRS. For example, critics of *pro forma* statements argue that financial stresses from previous periods happen often and are part of the capitalist economic system. Leaving them out can itself be a distortion of a company's status and not fully reflect its performance.

Nevertheless, *pro forma* financial statements serve as a tool for company management when it wants a financial snapshot of the company that isn't as formal, or potentially cumbersome, as accounting principles require.

Other figures a company needs to complete the gross profit method that can be taken from the general ledger are: sales, opening inventory and purchases. Once an accountant has these numbers, then the rest of the numbers needed to estimate inventory can be determined.

For example, suppose that Van Der Linden must prepare financial statements for the quarter and needs to value its inventory. It will use the gross profit method and is shown in Figure 8.13.

Sales Revenue		$100,000
Cost of Goods Sold		
Opening Inventory	3,000	
Purchases	70,000	
Cost of Goods Available for Sale	73,000	
Closing Inventory	?	
Cost of Goods Sold		?
Gross Profit (Gross Margin = 50%)		?

FIGURE 8.13

Based on an analysis of gross margin in previous years, a figure of 50% is used for current calculations.

Additionally, the following financial numbers were taken from the accountant's general ledger

Sales Revenue: $100,000
Opening Inventory: $3,000
Purchases: $70,000

Van Der Linden's accountant will use these numbers to estimate the value of inventory.

Sales Revenue		100,000
Cost of Goods Sold		
Opening Inventory	3,000	
Purchases	70,000	
Cost of Goods Available for Sale	73,000	
Closing Inventory	?	
Cost of Goods Sold		?
Gross Profit (Gross Margin = 50%)		$50,000

FIGURE 8.14

The cells with a question mark are those that must be calculated step-by-step to complete the estimation process.

If the gross margin is 50% (marked in red) then it is applied to the sales figure (marked in blue) to calculate the estimated gross profit, shown in Figure 8.14 ($100,000 × 50% = $50,000).

Next, the cost of goods sold figure is estimated by subtracting the estimated gross profit from sales revenue, as shown below.

Sales – Gross Profit = COGS
$100,000 – $50,000 = $50,000

The $50,000 COGS is placed into the chart and marked in grey in Figure 8.15.

Sales Revenue		100,000
Cost of Goods Sold		
Opening Inventory	3,000	
Purchases	70,000	
Cost of Goods Available for Sale	73,000	
Closing Inventory	?	
Cost of Goods Sold		50,000
Gross Profit (Gross Margin = 50%)		50,000

FIGURE 8.15

The final step is to estimate the balance of closing inventory. This is done by subtracting COGS from the cost of goods available for sale as shown below.

> Cost of Goods Available for Sale – Cost of Goods Sold = Closing Inventory

$$\$73,000 - \$50,000 = \$23,000$$

Therefore, the gross profit method yields a closing inventory estimate of $23,000, which is marked in grey in Figure 8.16. This figure will be used on the quarterly balance sheet for Van Der Linden.

To summarize: The gross profit method starts with historical analysis that yields a gross profit margin. This is applied to sales revenue, which yields a gross profit figure. Each subsequent step calculates an additional piece of information until a figure for closing inventory is obtained. This is the estimation that is used for the quarterly financial statements.

Sales Revenue		100,000
Cost of Goods Sold		
Opening Inventory	3,000	
Purchases	70,000	
Cost of Goods Available for Sale	73,000	
Closing Inventory	23,000	
Cost of Goods Sold		50,000
Gross Profit (Gross Margin = 50%)		50,000

FIGURE 8.16

The Retail Method

The **retail method** of estimating inventory requires less information and fewer steps than the gross profit method. Specifically, it requires two things: 1) the value of sales at retail prices (which is why it is called the retail method); and 2) the company's cost of goods sold section on the income statement.

For example, refer to Leung Retail Company's information in Figure 8.17. The cost of goods sold section is shown in brown, and the sales figure at retail is shown in red. The section shown in green, which is the cost of goods available for sale, is calculated by adding opening inventory and purchases together. This section is important because the cost and retail figures for cost of goods available for sale will be used in ratio format as shown below.

> Cost of Goods Available for Sale at Cost
> ――――――――――――――――――――――――――
> Cost of Goods Available for Sale at Retail

$$\frac{\$73,000}{\$140,000} = 52.1\%$$

This ratio must be applied to the closing inventory at retail figure, which is marked in blue.

$$\$70,000 \times 52.1\% = \$36,500$$

	At Cost	At Retail
Cost of Goods Sold		
Opening Inventory	3,000	6,000
Purchases	70,000	134,000
Cost of Goods Available for Sale	73,000	140,000
Less: Sales at Retail		70,000
Closing Inventory at Retail		70,000

FIGURE 8.17

Figure 8.18 shows the closing inventory at cost, using the retail method of inventory estimation, which is added to the bottom of the Leung Retail Company chart.

	At Cost	At Retail
Cost of Goods Sold		
Opening Inventory	3,000	6,000
Purchase	70,000	134,000
Cost of Goods Available for Sale	73,000	140,000
Less Sales at Retail		70,000
Closing Inventory at Retail		70,000
Closing Inventory at Cost	$36,500	

FIGURE 8.18

Measuring Inventory Using Financial Ratios

Generally speaking, a business wants to be as precise as possible in buying inventory for resale. Ideally, inventory should be sold as soon as it is bought. In other words, the less time that an item spends in inventory, while still meeting customer demand, the better.

A company can measure the extent to which it is moving inventory through the use of two ratios: inventory turnover and days inventory on hand.

Inventory Turnover Ratio

The extent to which an organization can quickly sell inventory on hand is known as inventory turnover. Specifically, the **inventory turnover ratio** estimates how many times a year a company is buying inventory. The more often a company buys inventory, the less likely it is that the inventory sits for extended periods of time, and the more likely it is that the turnover is high.

The inventory turnover ratio is calculated by taking the cost of goods sold for a year and dividing it by average inventory.

$$\text{Inventory Turnover Ratio} = \frac{\text{Cost of Goods Sold}}{\text{Average Inventory}}$$

Average inventory is calculated by adding the opening and closing inventory numbers and dividing the total by 2.

New Tech Mobile makes mobile devices. Its inventory and cost of goods sold are shown in Figure 8.19. For 2016, it had an inventory turnover of 6.2. This means the company bought and sold its entire inventory just over six times during the year.

Inventory turnover is useful when it is compared to another company within the same industry. Suppose a competitor has an inventory turnover of 9.0. This is higher than that of New Tech Mobile and is more desirable. The higher turnover

Inventory—December 31, 2015	$501.3
Inventory—December 31, 2016	$428.1
Cost of Goods Sold	$2,882.8
Average Inventory (501.3 + 428.1) ÷ 2 = 464.7	
Turnover	2,882.8 ÷ 464. 7 = 6.2

FIGURE 8.19

indicates that inventory is moving faster at the competitor than at New Tech Mobile. Inventory that moves fast is less likely to become outdated.

Inventory Days on Hand

There is another way of looking at inventory turnover. Instead of estimating how often a company sells and replaces inventory over a period of time (which is indicated by the inventory turnover ratio), turnover can be calculated by estimating how many days it takes to move items out of inventory. Expressed another way: **inventory days on hand** is a calculation of how many days inventory will last given the current rate of sales.

The number of days in a year (365) is divided by the inventory turnover ratio, resulting in the inventory days on hand.

$$\text{Inventory Days on Hand} = \frac{365}{\text{Inventory Turnover Ratio}}$$

The inventory days on hand carves up the calendar year into equal-sized chunks. The number of chunks equals the inventory turnover ratio. The size of the chunks translates into the inventory days on hand.

For example, if a company's inventory turnover ratio is 10, then inventory is completely purchased and sold 10 times throughout the year. Since there are 365 days in the year, each chunk is 36.5 days long.

$$\frac{365}{10} = 36.5$$

Therefore, the inventory days on hand is 36.5 days. This means that on average, it takes 36.5 days to "turn over" inventory. This is shown in Figure 8.20.

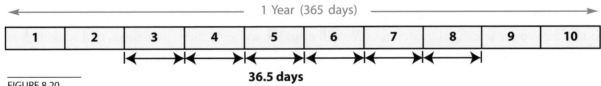

FIGURE 8.20

Returning to the example, New Tech Mobile calculates its inventory days on hand to be 58.9 days (365 ÷ 6.2). Since its competitor had an inventory turnover of 9.0, the competitor's inventory days on hand is 40.6 days (365 ÷ 9.0).

Another way of calculating inventory days on hand is shown below.

$$\text{Inventory Days on Hand} = \frac{\text{Average Inventory}}{\text{Cost of Goods Sold}} \times 365$$

The relationship (ratio) is between: 1) how much inventory is in stock; and 2) the amount of inventory used for the year (which is the Cost of Goods Sold). Dividing the average inventory by how much was used and multiplying this number by 365 (number of days in the year) will convert the ratio to the number of days on hand based on how much was used.

As in the initial way inventory days on hand was calculated, New Tech Mobile keeps inventory for 58.9 days and its competitor keeps inventory for 40.6 days. A lower number for this ratio means that it takes less time for a company to move its inventory. This is another way of saying that its inventory turnover is better.

Management should not make decisions regarding inventory based on ratios alone. There could be many factors that affect such numbers. For example, some industries might require companies to wait longer periods of time to have goods shipped to them. High turnover in these instances may lead to empty warehouses and customer demands not being met.

As an example, a grocery store will have higher inventory turnover than an appliance store. Alternatively, car engines will move out of an auto plant warehouse much slower than light bulbs in a hardware store.

It is the responsibility of accountants and management to know what inventory levels are best for business. Ratios can help but they are only one of many tools that can be used.

An Ethical Approach to Inventory Estimation and Valuation

As mentioned earlier, management is able to choose the method used to value inventory. Thus, inventory may be open to manipulation. A company can purchase, store and sell many items throughout the course of a business year, and how all these items are valued can have a significant impact on a company's bottom line.

For example, inventory can sometimes be used as collateral when taking out a bank loan; or employees may steal from the company's inventory. That is why the inventory asset on a company's balance sheet should be subject to ethical guidelines. We will examine some of these guidelines and suggest how organizations should approach estimating and valuing inventory in an ethical manner.

Impact on Financial Statements

The impact of inflating closing inventory is significant. It reduces the cost of goods sold and increases net income for the year. It also inflates the cost of goods sold and reduces net income for the following year. Therefore, any manipulation of inventory value has negative consequences that extend beyond the current fiscal year. The ethical responsibility of management is to ensure this does not happen by detecting errors and the causes behind them.

Who Commits Fraud and Why?

Companies need to know the kinds of inventory fraud that can be perpetrated and understand who would be most likely to commit fraud.

Inventory fraud from the top down

Various methods are used to pad a company's inventory value. One method is to overstate the value of items deemed obsolete, shop-worn or generally unsaleable. This would overstate the overall value of inventory. Similarly, various overhead costs can be attributed to inventory. These figures can also be manipulated in a way that affects the company's bottom line. In addition, a manufacturer might be tempted to overstate the completion of work-in-process inventories and, again, pad the value of its inventory.

Generally speaking, these kinds of attempts to pad inventory numbers tend to come from the top. Unlike determining fixed costs such as rent, determining inventory costs is a more subjective exercise. Accountants and executives can abuse the subjectivity involved in some of these decisions and errors can be rationalized as a matter of opinion.

Abuses can be avoided by establishing specific policies and guidelines for handling and valuing inventory. Controls should be in place to ensure that these policies are being followed. Companies can also have both internal and external auditors review the design and effectiveness of inventory controls and detect any possible ethical breaches.

In the end, management is responsible for any errors arising from the way its financial situation is reported. There is no excuse for manipulating the value of inventory. Any wrongful reporting should be dealt with at the earliest opportunity.

Inventory fraud from the bottom up

Lower-level employees and thieves can also create havoc with inventory. Their motivation is often associated with greed.

Inventory items are goods that have value and that people want to buy. That is why companies purchase these items and eventually sell them. People who have routine access to such items, such as employees, might be tempted to take them without paying for them. Alternatively, an employee might take funds from the company, buy the inventory, then resell it and pocket the profits. Even borrowing an item without permission, such as a car on a sales lot, is theft, and needs to be prevented.

Some forms of inventory fraud originate from the executive level. Ethical guidelines are needed that detect wrongdoing at any level of the company.

There are red flags that help a company monitor and prevent inventory shrinkage. One such red flag occurs when sales lag inventory levels. In other words, the company is buying more than it is selling. Some of that inventory is obviously not going to the customer. Another potential inventory red flag occurs when shipping costs lag inventory. This indicates that the company is not shipping out as many items as it is receiving in inventory. The missing items might have been taken by thieves.

All companies should be in the practice of noting these red flags and ensuring measures are in place to prevent or detect theft. Furthermore, all businesses should implement security measures that properly safeguard inventory on their premises.

IN THE REAL WORLD

 Perhaps no business philosophy captures the spirit of high inventory turnover more than Just In Time, also known as JIT.

The Japanese first started developing JIT in their manufacturing industries after Word War II. The goal was to gain a competitive advantage by reducing the amount of inventory a company had in storage at any given time, since inventory is often a larger but less liquid asset than other assets on the balance sheet. JIT made its way to North America and has been used to improve manufacturing efficiency in many different industries.

At the heart of JIT is a comprehensive approach not just to reducing inventory, but to managing a business. Under JIT, it is the customer that drives the manufacturing process. That is why JIT systems are often implemented in conjunction with what is known as Total Quality Management, or TQM. Under such philosophies, everything is done to ensure that the customer gets quality goods and services on time, every time.

To that end, JIT systems mobilize efforts to coordinate manufacturing processes and reduce waste. The goal is to have virtually no excess inventory on hand at any time. This can only be achieved if a company thoroughly understands what the customer wants and when they want it. Receiving and shipping schedules, assembly parts, and labour flexibility are all adapted to ensure that customer demand is met while enhancing organizational efficiency and profitability.

JIT stresses the importance of reducing a company's inventory while enhancing customer service. It is a comprehensive approach that has achieved success on a global scale.

In Summary

Determine the value of inventory using the specific identification method under the perpetual inventory system

- ⇨ The specific identification method tracks the cost of each item in inventory separately and is used for unique or custom products such as vehicles and houses.

- ⇨ A schedule is used to track the different costs of purchased inventory and the costs of specific items sold. The value of inventory is made up of the costs of the actual physical items remaining in inventory.

Determine the value of inventory using the first-in, first-out (FIFO) method under the perpetual inventory system

- ⇨ The FIFO method assumes that the first items purchased are also the first items sold, even if this is not the actual flow of inventory. This method is used for many types of inventory, especially perishable goods.

- ⇨ A schedule is used to track the different costs of purchased inventory. The cost of goods sold is calculated using the costs of the earliest purchased inventory. The value of inventory is made up of the costs of the most recently purchased inventory.

Determine the value of inventory using the weighted-average cost method under the perpetual inventory system

- ⇨ The weighted-average cost uses an average unit cost to calculate the value of inventory and the cost of goods sold. It is used when inventory items are identical and when the order in which they are sold is irrelevant.

- ⇨ A schedule is used to track the weighted-average cost of purchased inventory. The unit cost is updated after every purchase and is calculated by dividing the total value of the inventory by the total number of units on hand. The value of inventory is calculated using the unit cost at the end of the period.

Explain the impact of inventory errors

- ⇨ An overstatement of ending inventory results in an understatement of COGS and an overstatement of net income.

- ⇨ An understatement of ending inventory results in an overstatement of COGS and an understatement of net income.

Apply the lower of cost and net realizable value (LCNRV) rule to value inventory

- ➪ Inventory must be recorded at the lower of its cost and its net realizable value. That is, if the value of inventory is calculated to be higher than the amount that could be recovered by selling it, then it must be written down.

- ➪ LCNRV may be applied to either individual inventory items or categories of inventory.

Estimate the value of inventory using the gross profit method under the periodic inventory system

- ➪ The gross profit method is applied by using the estimated gross profit margin for the period to calculate the value of ending inventory.

- ➪ First, multiply the gross profit margin by sales revenue to estimate gross profit. Second, subtract gross profit from sales revenue to estimate COGS. Third, subtract the cost of goods available for sale from COGS to estimate ending inventory.

Estimate the value of inventory using the retail method under the periodic inventory system

- ➪ The retail method is applied by first calculating the ratio of cost to retail for the cost of goods available for sale. Next, this ratio is multiplied by the retail price of ending inventory to estimate the cost of ending inventory.

Measure a company's management of inventory using inventory ratios

- ➪ The inventory turnover ratio is calculated by dividing COGS by the average value of inventory over the period. This ratio is equal to the number of times inventory was completely purchased and sold (turned over) during the period.

- ➪ A higher inventory turnover ratio means that inventory is less likely to become obsolete because it is sold more quickly.

- ➪ The inventory days on hand is calculated by dividing 365 by the inventory turnover ratio. This figure is equal to the number of days on average it takes to sell inventory.

- ➪ A lower inventory days on hand means that inventory is less likely to become obsolete because it is sold in fewer days.

Describe ethics relating to inventory

- ➪ Management has the ability to manipulate inventory values reported on financial statements. Inventory values that deliberately manipulated to deceive readers of the financial statements is unethical and could be considered fraud.

Review Exercise

The following transactions took place at Mike's Tikes Toys during the month of June 2016. The company uses a perpetual inventory system. There are 100 items in opening inventory that cost $12 each.

Jun 3   Purchased 500 items at a cost of $15 each on credit (on account).

Jun 10   Sold 200 items at $45 each on credit.

Jun 12   Purchased 300 items at $18 each on credit.

Jun 20   Sold 300 items at $50 each for cash.

Required

a) Using the FIFO method, prepare the inventory record to demonstrate the closing inventory balance after the above transactions.

b) Prepare the top portion of the multistep income statement showing sales revenue, cost of goods sold, and gross profit for the month ended June 30, 2016. Use the information from part a).

c) Using the weighted-average cost method, prepare the inventory record to demonstrate the closing inventory balance after the above transactions.

d) Prepare the top portion of the multistep income statement showing sales revenue, cost of goods sold, and gross profit for the month ended June 30, 2016. Use the information from part c).

See Appendix I for solutions.

a) Using FIFO, prepare the inventory record to show the closing inventory balance

Date	Purchases			Sales			Balance		
	Quantity	Unit Cost	Value	Quantity	Unit Cost	Value	Quantity	Unit Cost	Value
Ending Inventory									

b) Multistep income statement showing sales revenue, cost of goods sold, and gross profit—using information from part a)

c) Using the weighted-average cost method, prepare the inventory record to show the closing inventory balance

Date	Purchases			Sales			Balance		
	Quantity	Unit Cost	Value	Quantity	Unit Cost	Value	Quantity	Unit Cost	Value
Ending Inventory									

d) Multistep income statement showing sales revenue, cost of goods sold, and gross profit—using information from part c)

Appendix 8A: Periodic Inventory Valuation

Cool Ink Company sells a number of different pens, pencils, markers and highlighters. Examine one item from its inventory to illustrate the three different inventory valuation methods. Assume that Cool Ink uses a periodic inventory system to account for purchases and sales.

Cool Ink Company currently has 10 pens in inventory with a cost of $10 each. During the month of March, the following transactions in Figure 8A.1 took place with respect to collector pens.

Date	Transaction	Quantity	Unit Cost
March 5	Purchase from Pen Distributers	50	$12
March 7	Sale	15	
March 15	Purchase from Promotional Pens	40	$14
March 19	Purchase from Promotional Pens	20	$16
March 27	Sale	50	

FIGURE 8A.1

During the month, the cost of the pen increased. This means that the cost of goods sold applied to the sales will likely be different, based on which pens are actually sold. We can apply the three methods of valuing inventory to the transactions to arrive at different values for inventory and cost of goods sold. This will demonstrate that the choice of inventory valuation method can make a difference on the financial statements of a company.

The main difference between the perpetual and the periodic inventory system is when costs are assigned to the sales. The perpetual system assigns costs to the sales as the sales are made. The periodic system only assigns costs at the end of the period, when a physical count of the inventory is made.

Using Specific Identification

When using specific identification, first list the purchases separately from each other to easily identify the costs associated with each batch of inventory. Then list the sales for the period underneath since inventory costs are not recorded until the end of the period. This is done by using a table as shown in Figure 8A.2. The opening balance and the transactions from Figure 8A.1 are listed in the table. Purchases cause the balance of inventory to increase and sales cause it to decrease. At the bottom of the figure is the value of ending inventory.

Date	Purchases			Sales			Balance		
	Quantity	Unit Cost	Value	Quantity	Unit Cost	Value	Quantity	Unit Cost	Value
❶ March 1							10	$10	$100
❷ March 5	50	$12	$600				10	$10	$100
							50	$12	$600
❸ March 15	40	$14	$560				10	$10	$100
							50	$12	$600
							40	$14	$560
❹ March 19	20	$16	$320				10	$10	$100
							50	$12	$600
							40	$14	$560
							20	$16	$320
❺ Sales for the Month				10	$10	$100			
				40	$12	$480	10	$12	$120
				15	$14	$210	25	$14	$350
							20	$16	$320
Ending Inventory									$790

FIGURE 8A.2

❶ The purchase of 50 pens on March 5 is added to the value of inventory.

❷ The purchase of 40 pens on March 15 is added to the value of inventory.

❸ The purchase of 20 pens on March 19 is added to the value of inventory.

❹ The sales are tallied at the end of the month and are identified based on which batch of inventory they came from. In this example, the entire amount of opening inventory was sold, 40 items from the March 5 purchase were sold and 15 items from the March 15 purchase were sold. Total cost of goods sold is $790 ($100 + $480 + $210).

❺ The value of ending inventory is made up of 10 pens remaining from the March 5 purchase, the 25 pens remaining from the March 15 purchase and the 20 pens remaining from the March 19 purchase. Total value of inventory is $790 ($120 + $350 + $320).

Using First-In, First-Out

When using the FIFO method, list the purchases in the order they were received. This will clearly show which items were the first ones purchased and assumed the first ones to be sold. Then list the sales for the period underneath since inventory costs are not recorded until the end of the period. This is done by using a table as shown in Figure 8A.3. The opening balance and the transactions from Figure 8A.1 are listed in the table. This is similar to the specific identification method. At the bottom of the figure is the value of ending inventory.

Date	Purchases			Sales			Balance		
	Quantity	Unit Cost	Value	Quantity	Unit Cost	Value	Quantity	Unit Cost	Value
❶ March 1							10	$10	$100
❷ March 5	50	$12	$600				10	$10	$100
							50	$12	$600
❸ March 15	40	$14	$560				10	$10	$100
							50	$12	$600
							40	$14	$560
❹ March 19	20	$16	$320				10	$10	$100
							50	$12	$600
							40	$14	$560
							20	$16	$320
❺ Sales for the Month				10	$10	$100			
				50	$12	$600			
				5	$14	$70	35	$14	$490
							20	$16	$320
Ending Inventory									$810

FIGURE 8A.3

❶ The purchase of 50 pens on March 5 is added to the value of inventory.

❷ The purchase of 40 pens on March 15 is added to the value of inventory.

❸ The purchase of 20 pens on March 19 is added to the value of inventory.

❹ There was a total of 65 items sold (15 units + 40 units). Costs are taken from the balance of inventory, starting with the first item at the top of the list. The entire amount of opening inventory, the entire amount of the March 5 purchase, and five items from the March 15 purchase are considered sold. Total cost of goods sold is $770 ($100 + $600 + $70).

❺ The value of ending inventory is made up of 35 pens remaining from the March 15 purchase and the 20 pens remaining from the March 19 purchase. Total value of inventory is $810 ($490 + $320).

Using Weighted-Average Cost

When using the weighted-average cost method, the average cost per unit is only calculated once, at the end of the period. This is done by using a table as shown in Figure 8A.4. Recall that

Average Unit Cost = Total Quantity ÷ Total Value

The opening balance and the transactions from Figure 8A.1 are listed in the table. At the bottom of the figure is the value of ending inventory.

	Date	Purchases			Sales			Balance		
		Quantity	Unit Cost	Value	Quantity	Unit Cost	Value	Quantity	Unit Cost	Value
❶	March 1							10		$100
❷	March 5	50	$12	$600				60		$700
❸	March 15	40	$14	$560				100		$1,260
❹	March 19	20	$16	$320				120		$1,580
❺	Average Inventory for the Month							120	$13.17	$1,580
❻	Sales for the Month				65	$13.17	$856	55	$13.17	$724
	Ending Inventory									$724

FIGURE 8A.4

❶ The purchase of 50 pens on March 5 is added to the quantity on hand. The value of the 50 pens is added to the value of the opening inventory.

❷ The purchase of 40 pens on March 15 is added to the quantity on hand. The value of the 40 pens is added to current value of inventory.

❸ The purchase of 20 pens on March 19 is added to the quantity on hand. The value of the 20 pens is added to current value of inventory.

❹ At the end of the month, there are 120 pens available for sale with a total cost of $1,580. The average cost per pen is approximately $13.17 ($1,580 ÷ 120 units). This average cost is applied to the total sales of 65 pens for the month. Total cost of goods sold is $856 (65 units × $13.17).

❺ The value of ending inventory is 55 pens at the average unit cost of approximately $13.17. Total value of inventory is $724.

The Effect of Different Valuation Methods: Periodic

As the previous example with Cool Ink Company demonstrates, different ending inventory figures are produced by using different valuation methods. The chart in Figure 8A.5 summarizes these differences for the Cool Ink example.

Periodic Inventory System	Specific Identification	FIFO	Weighted-Average Cost
Inventory Available for Sale (beginning inventory + purchases)	$1,580	$1,580	$1,580
Ending Inventory	790	810	724
Value of COGS	790	770	856

FIGURE 8A.5

Note that the FIFO method resulted in the highest value of ending inventory and the lowest value of COGS during a period in which prices were rising. This is the same result as the perpetual inventory system.

Figure 8A.6 shows the results from the perpetual inventory system using the same example. Compare the values in Figures 8A.5 and 8A.6. Specific identification will always provide the same values under both systems since the company is able to specifically identify which items are being sold, regardless of the inventory system being used. FIFO will also provide the same values under both systems because the most recent purchases are always in ending inventory.

Perpetual Inventory System	Specific Identification	FIFO	Weighted-Average Cost
Inventory Available for Sale (beginning inventory + purchases)	$1,580	$1,580	$1,580
Ending Inventory	790	810	736
Value of COGS	790	770	844

FIGURE 8A.6

The weighted-average cost method shows different values for ending inventory and COGS. This is because the perpetual inventory system assigns costs as the items are sold, whereas the periodic inventory system only assigns costs at the end of the period.

In Summary

Determine the value of inventory using the specific identification method under the periodic inventory system

↪ This method is similar to the perpetual inventory system except that sales are grouped at the bottom of the schedule because COGS is not known until the end of the period.

Determine the value of inventory using the first-in, first-out (FIFO) method under the periodic inventory system

↪ This method is similar to the perpetual inventory system except that sales are grouped at the bottom of the schedule because COGS is not known until the end of the period.

Determine the value of inventory using the weighted-average cost method under the periodic inventory system

↪ The average unit cost is only calculated once at the end of the period.

↪ Sales are grouped at the bottom of the schedule because COGS is not known until the end of the period.

Review Exercise

The following transactions took place at Mike's Tikes Toys during the month of March 2016. The company uses a periodic inventory system. There are 100 items in opening inventory that cost $12 each.

Mar 3   Purchased 500 items at a cost of $15 each on credit (on account).

Mar 10   Sold 200 items at $45 each on credit.

Mar 12   Purchased 300 items at $18 each on credit.

Mar 20   Sold 300 items at $50 each for cash.

Required

a) Using the specific identification method, prepare the inventory record to demonstrate the closing inventory balance after the above transactions. Assume that 50 items were sold from opening inventory, 350 items were sold from the purchase on March 3, and 100 items were sold from the purchase on March 12.

b) Using the FIFO method, prepare the inventory record to demonstrate the closing inventory balance after the above transactions.

c) Using the weighted-average cost method, prepare the inventory record to demonstrate the closing inventory balance after the above transactions.

See Appendix I for solutions.

a) Specific Identification

Date	Purchases			Sales			Balance		
	Quantity	Unit Cost	Value	Quantity	Unit Cost	Value	Quantity	Unit Cost	Value
Sales for the Month									
Ending Inventory									

b) FIFO

Date	Purchases			Sales			Balance		
	Quantity	Unit Cost	Value	Quantity	Unit Cost	Value	Quantity	Unit Cost	Value
Sales for the Month									
Ending Inventory									

c) Weighted-Average Cost

Date	Purchases			Sales			Balance		
	Quantity	Unit Cost	Value	Quantity	Unit Cost	Value	Quantity	Unit Cost	Value
Average Inventory for the Month									
Sales for the Month									
Ending Inventory									

Note: numbers may vary due to rounding

Chapter 9

ACCOUNTING INFORMATION SYSTEMS

LEARNING OUTCOMES

❶ Explain the flow of accounting information through the accounting paper trail

❷ Describe and record transactions in special journals

❸ Describe and record transactions in subsidiary ledgers

❹ Identify features of a computerized accounting system

Appendix

❺ Prepare special journals under a periodic inventory system

AMEENGAGE™ *Access **ameengage.com** for integrated resources including tutorials, practice exercises, the digital textbook and more.*

The Accounting Paper Trail

At this point we have learned how the accounting cycle behaves. We have followed the values from source documents to journals and ledgers, then to trial balances and financial statements. This is the paper trail accountants create to ensure all values are stated correctly.

Source documents, which provide evidence that a business transaction has occurred, come in many different forms. The most common examples of source documentation are usually associated with accounts payable and accounts receivable. Source documentation includes purchase orders, sales invoices, cash receipts and contracts.

Accountants use source documentation (in addition to other sources of information) to update the accounting records of an organization. For example, when the accounting department issues a sales invoice, the corresponding journal entry regarding the sale should be made. The procedures surrounding this entry will differ slightly between manual and computerized accounting systems (e.g. in a computerized accounting system, the revenue and accounts receivable accounts are automatically updated while the sales invoice is generated). Our focus in this section, however, will be on manual accounting systems.

Figure 9.1 below outlines the traditional accounting paper trail. Once source documentation is received, the accountant updates the journal. At specified points, this information is transferred to the general ledger. At the end of the accounting period, a trial balance is produced. A trial balance lists all the company's accounts and its corresponding balances. The main purpose of a trial balance is to ensure that all debits equal all credits. The trial balance may need to be adjusted (e.g. to take into account recognition of prepaid expenses, depreciation of assets, etc.) before the financial statements are produced. The financial statements are then organized into a financial report for management to review.

The Traditional Accounting Paper Trail

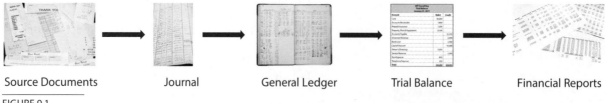

| Source Documents | Journal | General Ledger | Trial Balance | Financial Reports |

FIGURE 9.1

Regardless of whether one is dealing with a manual or a computerized system, an effective accounting system should ensure

- Adequate internal controls to prevent misuse of assets
- Accurate information is provided on a timely basis
- Effective communication across the various components of the system
- Flexibility to allow for changes as the organization grows and evolves
- Maximum benefits at a reasonable cost

In this section, we will focus on two components of the traditional accounting information system: special journals and subsidiary ledgers.

Special Journals

Following the manual accounting paper trail, after the source documentation has been received, the next step for the accountant is to record the transaction in journal format.

In a traditional accounting system, recording all business transactions in one journal could be very time consuming—especially when there are lots of activities concerning specific transactions. For transactions that occur regularly, it is wise to maintain

WORTH REPEATING

All transactions must be recorded in a journal before being posted to the ledgers, regardless of whether special journals are used or not.

a separate book called a **special journal**. Examples of regular transactions include sales, purchases, cash payments, cash receipts and payroll. These journal entries are essentially the same entries already covered, except we will sort them by type and condense the amount of information to be recorded. Maintaining these events in a separate set of books will allow easy access to information pertaining to these activities. For example, if a sales manager wants to see the amount of credit sales generated in May, she could examine the sales journal and add up all the sales for that month. In other words, accounting information is organized into specific categories so that people can look back later and easily extract information. Examples of special journals include

Sales Journal: This journal is used to record all sales made on account.

Purchases Journal: This is similar to the sales journal, but is used to record all purchases (products or services) made on account.

Cash Payments Journal: This journal is used to record all cash payments made by the business (e.g. rent and wages expense) including payments made to suppliers.

Cash Receipts Journal: This journal is used to record all cash deposits (e.g. cash sales) and collections from outstanding accounts receivable.

The **general journal** is the journal that has been used throughout the book up until this point. It is used to record any entry that does not belong in one of the special journals. Typical entries recorded in the general journal include

- purchase and sales returns
- adjustments
- correcting entries

JOURNAL				Page 1
Date	Account Title and Explanation	PR	Debit	Credit

Subsidiary Ledgers

Subsidiary ledgers (also called **subledgers**) are used to provide details that are not kept in the general ledger because too much information will clutter up the general ledger accounts. For example, a company usually deals with many suppliers and customers at the same time and certain information about each supplier and customer is important to the accounting function. This information includes invoice numbers and amounts, dates of purchases or sales and terms of the purchase or sale. Thus, the accounts receivable account in the general ledger has a subledger for each individual customer, and the accounts payable account in the general ledger has a subledger for each individual supplier. This is illustrated in Figure 9.3.

Transactions are initially recorded in one of the five journals listed above and are then posted to the general ledger or the subledgers as needed. The subledgers are usually updated after each transaction, while the general ledger is usually updated at the end of the period, such as the end of the month. Since subledger accounts only contain details about specific customers or suppliers and are not used in preparing financial statements they are not assigned account numbers.

The accounts receivable account in the general ledger is a control account for the individual accounts in the accounts receivable subledger. A **control account** keeps track of the grand total of the amounts in the subledger. For example, suppose a company has the following list of customers who each owe a certain amount

- Customer A owes $400
- Customer B owes $500
- Customer C owes $600

The subsidiary ledger tracks each customer and the amount owing, while the accounts receivable control account simply shows the total amount of $1,500. It is important to note that we do not post amounts from the subledger to the general ledger. Subledgers simply keep a record of detailed information about specific general ledger accounts. All amounts in the general ledger are posted from either the special journal or the general journal.

At the end of a period, the total of the subledger accounts is compared with their respective control account balance. If the sum of the individual ledger accounts is not equal to the control account, an error has occurred and must be corrected.

Just as the accounts receivable subsidiary ledger ensures customer amounts to collect are properly recorded, the accounts payable subsidiary ledger ensures supplier amounts owed are properly recorded. For example, a manager may want to know how much product was purchased from a particular supplier, over which time period, when it was paid for, what discounts were allowed for early payment, etc. To have easy access to this information, an individual ledger is maintained for each supplier. The ledger, which records the activities for each individual supplier, is called the accounts payable subsidiary ledger. The total of all the closing balances for each account in the accounts payable subsidiary ledger must be equal to the accounts payable general ledger balance.

The relationship between the general ledger and the subledger is demonstrated in Figure 9.2 and Figure 9.3.

Subsidiary Ledger

Accounts Payable Subsidiary Ledger

Sellmore Advertising Agency

DATE	PR	DR	CR	BALANCE (DR or CR)	
O/B				4,600	CR
Apr 1		4,600		0	
Apr 12			4,600	4,600	CR

ABC Prize Supply Store

DATE	PR	DR	CR	BALANCE (DR or CR)	
Apr 12			500	500	CR

Sparkies Computer Repairs

DATE	PR	DR	CR	BALANCE (DR or CR)	
Apr 8			400	400	CR
Apr 12		100		300	CR

Control Account

General Ledger

Accounts Payable

DATE	PR	DR	CR	BALANCE
Apr 12			5,400	5,400

Sellmore	$4,600
ABC Prize	$500
Sparkies	$300
Accounts Payable	$5,400

A subsidiary ledger is a group of accounts.

The total of the subsidiary ledger accounts is equal to the control account.

FIGURE 9.2

There are different subsidiary ledgers to control various assets or liabilities (e.g. inventory, long-term assets, accounts receivable). Figure 9.3 illustrates how the accounts payable, accounts receivable and inventory subsidiary ledgers are totalled and reconciled to their corresponding control account in the general ledger.

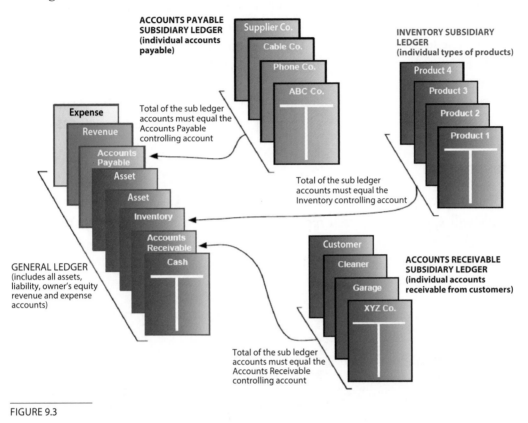

FIGURE 9.3

Once the subledgers have been reconciled to the control accounts in the general ledger, a trial balance can be created with the general ledger accounts and balances. The rest of the accounting cycle continues as previously described.

Using Special Journals and Subsidiary Ledgers

It is important to emphasize that the special journals are used to group similar transactions that would normally appear in the general journal. Transactions are entered into the appropriate journal when they occur. For the most part, the subledgers are immediately updated from the special journals while the general ledger is updated at the end of the accounting period. The details of posting from the special journals to the ledgers will be discussed with each journal.

To help with the posting to the general ledger as we discuss the special journals, we will use the following selected accounts from Jill Hanlon Retailer. You will notice these account numbers being used as we progress through the special journal examples.

Account Description	Account #	Account Description	Account #
Cash	101	Hanlon, Capital	300
Accounts Receivable	110	Hanlon, Drawings	310
Inventory	120	Sales Revenue	400
Accounts Payable	200	Sales Discount	405
Bank Loan	220	Cost of Goods Sold	500
		Maintenance Expense	525

The Sales Journal

The sales journal records all the details of sales on account. Cash sales are not included in this journal. They will appear in the cash receipts journal which records all cash received. The sales journal includes 1) the date of the sale, 2) the name of the customer, 3) the invoice number and 4) the value of the sale and inventory. These items are shown in Figure 9.4.

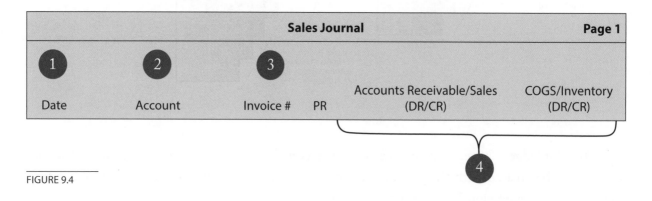

FIGURE 9.4

When a sale is made, as shown on January 5 in Figure 9.5, the customer subledger account must be updated immediately. Updating the subledger account follows these steps.

❶ Transfer the date from the sales journal to the date column in the subledger account.

❷ Make a note of the journal and page number in the PR column of the subledger.

❸ Transfer the amount of the accounts receivable column to the debit column in the subledger.

❹ Indicate the posting is complete by entering a check mark in the PR column in the sales journal.

Companies often offer sales discounts to their customers (i.e. 2/10, n/30). The terms of each sale should be recorded in the sales journal. However, if a company provides the same sales terms to all its customers, there is no need to record the terms in the sales journal.

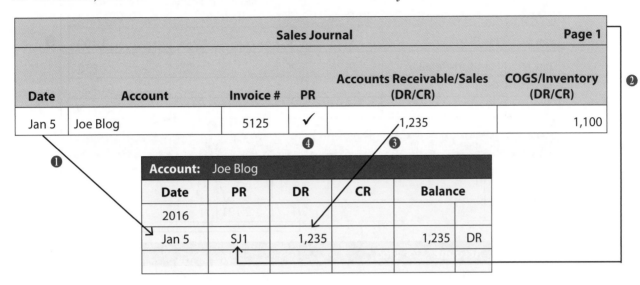

FIGURE 9.5

At the end of the month, the totals of all the columns are posted to the appropriate ledger accounts. The numbers in brackets under the totals represent the ledger numbers of the accounts used. In this example, we are focusing on accounts receivable, account number 110. The posting to the accounts receivable control account in Figure 9.6 follows these steps.

❶ Transfer the date from the sales journal to the date column in the ledger account.

❷ Make a note of the journal and page number in the PR column of the ledger.

❸ Transfer the total of the accounts receivable column to the debit column in the ledger account.

❹ Indicate the posting is complete by writing the general ledger number under the total.

Sales Journal					Page 1
Date	Account	Invoice #	PR	Accounts Receivable/Sales (DR/CR)	COGS/ Inventory (DR/CR)
Jan 5	Joe Blog	5125	✓	1,235	1,100
Jan 16	Furniture Retailers	5126	✓	956	850
Jan 31	Total			$2,191	$1,950
				(110/400)	(500/120)

Account:	Accounts Receivable				GL. No.	110	
Date	Description	PR	DR	CR	Balance		
2016							
Jan 31		SJ1	2,191		2,191	DR	

Account:	Joe Blog				
Date	PR	DR	CR	Balance	
2016					
Jan 5	SJ1	1,235		1,235	DR

Account:	Furniture Retailers				
Date	PR	DR	CR	Balance	
2016					
Jan 16	SJ1	956		956	DR

FIGURE 9.6

The total of $2,191 is posted to the accounts receivable control account and to sales revenue. The total of $1,950 is posted to cost of goods sold and inventory. The total of the two customer accounts ($1,235 and $956) is equal to the balance of the accounts receivable control account.

The Cash Receipts Journal

The cash receipts journal records all receipts of cash. Typical reasons for the receipt of cash are listed in the column headings (Accounts Receivable, Sales and Bank Loan) which vary depending on the company. A column titled Other is used to record cash receipts that do not fall under one of the frequently used categories. Any amount recorded in the Other column is immediately posted to the appropriate general ledger account. The Sales Discount column is used if customers make a payment within the discount period specified by the company.

Cash (DR)	Sales Discount (DR)	Accounts Receivable (CR)	Sales (CR)	Bank Loan (CR)	Other (CR)	COGS/ Inventory (DR/CR)

FIGURE 9.7

Cash sales are recorded in the cash receipts journal, as shown in Figure 9.8. Because accounts receivable is not affected, nothing is posted to the subledger accounts. Because the Other column was not used, no entry is posted to the general ledger at this time. The general ledger is only updated at the end of the month when the columns are totalled.

				Cash Receipts Journal					Page 3
			Cash (DR)	Sales Discount (DR)	Accounts Receivable (CR)	Sales (CR)	Bank Loan (CR)	Other (CR)	COGS/ Inventory (DR/CR)
Date	Account	PR							
Jan 2	Cash Sale		350			350			280

FIGURE 9.8

The transaction on January 4 in Figure 9.9 is an investment into the company by the owner. There is no column with Owner's Capital as a heading, so the amount is recorded in the Other column. The post reference (300) indicates that the amount of the investment shown is immediately updated to owner's capital in the general ledger. At the end of the month, the total of the Other column will not be posted because any amount in this column is posted immediately to the appropriate ledger account.

				Cash Receipts Journal					Page 3
			Cash (DR)	Sales Discount (DR)	Accounts Receivable (CR)	Sales (CR)	Bank Loan (CR)	Other (CR)	COGS/ Inventory (DR/CR)
Date	Account	PR							
Jan 2	Cash Sale		350			350			280
Jan 4	Hanlon, Capital	300	4,000					4,000	

FIGURE 9.9

The partial payment from a customer on January 10 shown in Figure 9.10 will immediately update the subledger account because it affects the accounts receivable account. Since the payment is made within 10 days of the original sale, the customer receives a 2% discount on the amount paid. The discount therefore reduces the amount of cash received, but does not reduce the amount of accounts receivable that is paid off.

Updating the subledger account follows these steps.

❶ Transfer the date from the cash receipts journal to the date column in the subledger account.

❷ Make a note of the journal and page number in the PR column of the subledger.

❸ Transfer the amount of the accounts receivable column to the credit column in the subledger.

❹ Indicate the posting is complete by entering a check mark in the PR column in the cash receipts journal.

				Cash Receipts Journal					Page 3
				Sales	Accounts		Bank		COGS/
			Cash	Discount	Receivable	Sales	Loan	Other	Inventory
Date	Account	PR	(DR)	(DR)	(CR)	(CR)	(CR)	(CR)	(DR/CR)
Jan 2	Cash Sale		350			350			280
Jan 4	Hanlon, Capital	300	4,000					4,000	
Jan 10	Joe Blog	✓	588	12	600				

Account: Joe Blog

Date	PR	DR	CR	Balance	
2016					
Jan 5	SJ1	1,235		1,235	DR
Jan 10	CR3		600	635	DR

FIGURE 9.10

At the end of the month, all columns are totalled and the totals are posted to the appropriate general ledger accounts. In Figure 9.11, this means that $6,938 is posted as a debit to cash, $12 is posted as a debit to sales discounts, $600 is posted as a credit accounts receivable, and so on. The Other column total is not posted, thus an X is used to indicate that no posting is required.

The posting to the accounts receivable control account follows these steps.

❶ Transfer the date from the cash receipts journal to the date column in the ledger account.

❷ Make a note of the journal and page number in the PR column of the ledger.

❸ Transfer the total of the accounts receivable column to the credit column in the ledger account.

❹ Indicate the posting is complete by writing the general ledger number under the total.

				Cash Receipts Journal					Page 3
				Sales	Accounts		Bank		COGS/
			Cash	Discount	Receivable	Sales	Loan	Other	Inventory
Date	Account	PR	(DR)	(DR)	(CR)	(CR)	(CR)	(CR)	(DR/CR)
Jan 2	Cash Sale		350			350			280
Jan 4	Hanlon, Capital	300	4,000					4,000	
Jan 10	Joe Blog	✓	588	12	600				
Jan 22	TD Bank		2,000				2,000		
Jan 31	Total		$6,938	$12	$600	$350	$2,000	$4,000	$280
			(101)	(405)	(110)	(400)	(220)	(X)	(500/120)

Account: Accounts Receivable   **GL. No.** 110

Date	Description	PR	DR	CR	Balance	
2016						
Jan 31		SJ1	2,191		2,191	DR
Jan 31		CR3		600	1,591	DR

Account:	Joe Blog				
Date	PR	DR	CR	Balance	
2016					
Jan 5	SJ1	1,235		1,235	DR
Jan 10	CR3		600	635	DR

Account:	Furniture Retailers				
Date	PR	DR	CR	Balance	
2016					
Jan 16	SJ1	956		956	DR

FIGURE 9.11

The Purchases Journal

The purchases journal records all purchases on account. Several columns are provided to account for common items that the company purchases on account (inventory and office supplies in our example). If anything else is purchased, it is recorded in the Other column.

Inventory (DR)	Office Supplies (DR)	Other (DR)	Accounts Payable (CR)

FIGURE 9.12

When a purchase is made, as shown on January 3 in Figure 9.13, the supplier subledger account must be updated immediately. Notice that the purchases journal has a column for terms. Some suppliers will provide payment terms. Since terms differ from supplier to supplier, the terms column is provided to keep track of them. Updating the subledger account follows these steps.

❶ Transfer the date from the purchases journal to the date column in the subledger account.

❷ Make a note of the journal and page number in the PR column of the subledger.

❸ Transfer the amount of the accounts payable column to the credit column in the subledger.

❹ Indicate the posting is complete by entering a check mark in the PR column in the purchases journal.

Purchases Journal								Page 6
Date	Account	Invoice #	Terms	PR	Inventory (DR)	Office Supplies (DR)	Other (DR)	Accounts Payable (CR)
Jan 3	Antonio's Electric	2089	3/15, n 30	✓ ❹	4,200			4,200

Account:	Antonio's Electric				
Date	PR	DR	CR	Balance	
2016					
Jan 3	PJ6		4,200	4,200	CR

FIGURE 9.13

A purchase of an item that does not have a heading in the journal is placed in the Other column. Suppose the company received an invoice for $80 of maintenance done for the office. The $80 is placed in the Other column and in the Accounts Payable column. Since the amount in the Other column must be posted immediately to the general ledger to the maintenance expense account, the GL number is placed in the PR column. Additionally, since the $80 must also be posted to the accounts payable subledger, a check mark is placed in the PR column.

At the end of the month, the totals of the columns are posted to the general ledger accounts. The posting of the accounts payable is shown in Figure 9.14. The totals of the individual subledger accounts must equal the balance of the accounts payable control account. The posting to the accounts payable control account follows these steps.

❶ Transfer the date from the purchases journal to the date column in the ledger account.

❷ Make a note of the journal and page number in the PR column of the ledger.

❸ Transfer the total of the accounts payable column to the credit column in the ledger account.

❹ Indicate the posting is complete by writing the general ledger number under the total.

	Purchases Journal							Page 6
Date	Account	Invoice #	Terms	PR	Inventory (DR)	Office Supplies (DR)	Other (DR)	Accounts Payable (CR)
Jan 3	Antonio's Electric	2089	3/15, n 30	✓	4,200			4,200
Jan 19	Maintenance Expense/ Doug's Maintenance	6091		525/✓			80	80
Jan 31	Total				$4,200		$80	$4,280
					(120)		(X)	(200)

Account: Accounts Payable — GL. No. 200

Date	Description	PR	DR	CR	Balance
2016					
Jan 31		PJ6		4,280	4,280 CR

Account: Antonio's Electric

Date	PR	DR	CR	Balance
2016				
Jan 3	PJ6		4,200	4,200 CR

Account: Doug's Maintenance

Date	PR	DR	CR	Balance
2016				
Jan 19	PJ6		80	80 CR

FIGURE 9.14

The Cash Payments Journal

The cash payments journal records all cash payments made by the company. There is a column to record the cheque number, since a good control is to have all payments made by a cheque. Various columns are provided for the most common reasons for paying with cash, and an Other column is used to record cash payments for items that do not fall under one of the given columns. Notice that Inventory appears with both a debit and credit column. The debit side is used if inventory is purchased with cash (cheque) and the credit side is used if the company pays a supplier of inventory early and receives a discount.

Chq #	PR	Accounts Payable (DR)	Other (DR)	Inventory (DR)	(CR)	Cash (CR)

FIGURE 9.15

Cash purchases are recorded in the cash payments journal, as shown in Figure 9.16. Accounts payable is not affected, so no entry should be posted to the subledger accounts. The Other column was not used, so no entry should be posted to the general ledger at this time. The general ledger is only updated at the end of the month when the columns are totalled.

	Cash Payments Journal							Page 4
Date	Account	Chq #	PR	Accounts Payable (DR)	Other (DR)	Inventory (DR)	(CR)	Cash (CR)
Jan 6	Electro Parts	748				1,500		1,500

FIGURE 9.16

The transaction on January 15 in Figure 9.17 is a withdrawal from the company by the owner. Since there is no column with Owner's Drawings as a heading, the amount is recorded in the Other column. The post reference (310) indicates that the amount of the withdrawal shown is immediately updated to owner's drawings in the general ledger. At the end of the month, the total of the Other column will not be posted because any amount in this column is posted immediately to the appropriate ledger account.

	Cash Payments Journal							Page 4
Date	Account	Chq #	PR	Accounts Payable (DR)	Other (DR)	Inventory (DR)	(CR)	Cash (CR)
Jan 6	Electro Parts	748				1,500		1,500
Jan 15	Hanlon, Drawings	749	310		500			500

FIGURE 9.17

The payment to a supplier on January 18 immediately updates the subledger account since it affects accounts payable. Similar to the other journals, the posting to the subledger is shown in the cash payments journal with a checkmark. Since the terms of the purchase were 3/15, n/30, the company can take a 3% discount on the payment (the original purchase was on January 3). The discount amount is a credit to inventory and reduces the amount of cash that must be paid to the supplier.

Updating the subledger account in Figure 9.18 follows these steps.

❶ Transfer the date from the cash payments journal to the date column in the subledger account.

❷ Make a note of the journal and page number in the PR column of the subledger.

❸ Transfer the amount of the accounts payable column to the debit column in the subledger.

❹ Indicate the posting is complete by entering a check mark in the PR column in the cash payments journal.

	Cash Payments Journal							Page 4
				Accounts Payable	Other	Inventory		Cash
Date	Account	Chq #	PR	(DR)	(DR)	(DR)	(CR)	(CR)
Jan 6	Electro Parts	748				1,500		1,500
Jan 15	Hanlon, Drawings	749	310		500			500
Jan 18	Antonio's Electric	750	✓	4,200			126	4,074

Account:	Antonio's Electric			
Date	PR	DR	CR	Balance
2016				
Jan 3	PJ6		4,200	4,200 CR
Jan 18	CP4	4,200		0 CR

FIGURE 9.18

A CLOSER LOOK

At times, a transaction recorded in the special journal may require two amounts to be placed in the Other column. When this happens, it is acceptable to use two rows of the special journal to record the transaction. For example, suppose a company makes a $1,050 payment to their bank to pay back a loan which includes $50 interest. If the cash payments journal does not have a column for bank loan or for interest expense, than both amounts must be recorded in the Other column. The journal below shows how this would be recorded.

	Cash Payments Journal							Page 4
				Accounts Payable	Other	Inventory		Cash
Date	Account	Chq #	PR	(DR)	(DR)	(DR)	(CR)	(CR)
Aug 31	Bank Loan	263	210		1,000			1,050
	Interest Expense		530		50			

Notice that cash is credited for the total amount of the payment on the first line. The amount of the bank loan principal and interest are listed on two separate lines and the PR column indicates that both amounts updated the appropriate ledger account.

At the end of the month, all columns are totalled and the amounts are posted to the appropriate general ledger accounts. In Figure 9.19, this means that $4,200 is posted as a debit to accounts payable, $1,500 is posted as a debit to inventory, and so on. The Other column total is not posted, thus an X is used to indicate that no posting is required.

The posting to the accounts payable control account follows these steps.

❶ Transfer the date from the cash payments journal to the date column in the ledger account.

❷ Make a note of the journal and page number in the PR column of the ledger.

❸ Transfer the total of the accounts payable column to the debit column in the ledger account.

❹ Indicate the posting is complete by writing the general ledger number under the total.

Cash Payments Journal									Page 4
Date	Account	Chq #	PR	Accounts Payable (DR)	Other (DR)	Inventory (DR)	(CR)	Cash (CR)	
Jan 6	Electro Parts	748				1,500		1,500	
Jan 15	Hanlon, Drawings	749	310		500			500	
Jan 18	Antonio's Electric	750	✓	4,200			126	4,074	
Jan 31	Total			$4,200	$500	$1,500	$126	$6,074	
				(200)	(X)	(120)	(120)	(101)	

❶ ❹ ❷

Account:	Accounts Payable			GL. No.	200	
Date	Description	PR	DR	CR	Balance	
2016			❸			
Jan 31		PJ6		4,280	4,280	CR
Jan 31		CP4	4,200		80	CR

Account:	Antonio's Electric				
Date	PR	DR	CR	Balance	
2016					
Jan 3	PJ6		4,200	4,200	CR
Jan 18	CP4	4,200		0	CR

Account:	Doug's Maintenance				
Date	PR	DR	CR	Balance	
2016					
Jan 19	PJ6		80	80	CR

FIGURE 9.19

Remember that at the end of the month, when the general ledger is updated by the journals, the total of all the subledger accounts must equal the balance of the appropriate control account (accounts receivable or accounts payable).

To prove that the total of the individual subledger accounts is equal to the respective control account balance in the general ledger, a reconciliation is prepared. From Figure 9.11, the balance of accounts receivable was $1,591. By finding the total of the accounts receivable subledger account, we can prove that the control account and subledger are in balance.

Jill Hanlon Retailer January 31, 2016 General Ledger	
Accounts Receivable	$1,591

Control account in the general ledger

Jill Hanlon Retailer Schedule of Accounts Receivable January 31, 2016	
Joe Blog	$635
Furniture Retailers	956
Total Accounts Receivable	$1,591

The total of all subledger accounts

FIGURE 9.20

A similar listing can be done for the accounts payable subledger. From Figure 9.19, the balance of accounts payable was $80. The total of the accounts payable subledger is shown below.

Jill Hanlon Retailer January 31, 2016 General Ledger	
Accounts Payable	$80

Control account in the general ledger

Jill Hanlon Retailer Schedule of Accounts Payable January 31, 2016	
Antonio's Electric	$0
Doug's Maintenance	80
Total Accounts Payable	$80

The total of all subledger accounts

FIGURE 9.21

If the comparison of the general ledger control account and the total of the subledger accounts shows that they do not balance, the difference must be investigated. The difference must be resolved before the trial balance can be completed.

Returns

The special journals are designed to record specific types of transactions, but some transactions that must be recorded do not fit into these special journals. As mentioned earlier, if a transaction does not belong in one of the special journals, it must be recorded in the general journal. For example, sales and purchase returns do not fit into the special journals and must be recorded in the general journal. The only change to the way these transactions are recorded from what we learned earlier is how the posting is processed for accounts receivable or accounts payable.

Suppose Furniture Retailers, a customer from Figure 9.6, returned some items worth $300 that cost $170 on January 18. The general journal entry is entered as shown in Figure 9.22. The PR for accounts receivable updates the general ledger (shown by the account number 110) and the subsidiary ledger for the customer (shown by the check mark).

JOURNAL				Page 1
Date 2016	**Account Title and Explanation**	**PR**	**Debit**	**Credit**
Jan 18	Sales Returns & Allowances	410	300	
	Accounts Receivable	110/✔		300
	Customer returned items			
	Inventory	120	170	
	Cost of Goods Sold	500		170
	Returned Items to supplier			

FIGURE 9.22

Also, suppose the company returned $500 of the inventory it purchased from Antonio's Electric on January 10 (from Figure 9.14). This purchase return is completed in the general journal, as shown below. The PR for accounts payable updates the general ledger (shown by the account number 200) and the subsidiary ledger for the supplier (shown by the check mark).

JOURNAL				Page 1
Date 2016	**Account Title and Explanation**	**PR**	**Debit**	**Credit**
Jan 10	Accounts Payable	200/✔	500	
	Inventory	120		500
	Returned Items to supplier			

FIGURE 9.23

Computerized Accounting

All journals, ledgers and subledgers have been illustrated in a manual accounting system. For a small business with a small number of transactions, a manual system may be adequate. However, as the number of transactions increases, so does the amount of information that is kept. In a manual accounting system, storing, tracking and finding information can become tedious and difficult.

A computerized system is typically set up in a similar manner to the special journals just described. Sales are entered in one section of the software, while receipts are entered in another. Purchases and payments are also separated into different sections. The general journal is available for any transaction that does not fit into any of the special journals.

Although entries can be recorded in different sections, they will update the appropriate subledgers and the general ledger accounts at the time they are posted. By updating all appropriate ledgers after every posting, reports can be viewed or printed at any time and be up to date.

Details about customers and suppliers are available through the subledgers. Contact information and billing information can be stored. Reports on each customer or supplier can be easily generated to show all transactions and any amounts outstanding.

The computerized system will keep track of the terms of a purchase and indicate to the user when a payment should be made to take advantage of discounts. If no discounts are available, the system will indicate when the bill should be paid so it is not late. For sales, the system can indicate when a customer is overdue for payment so a letter or email can be sent to remind the customer that payments is required.

Access **ameengage.com** *for integrated resources including tutorials, practice exercises, the digital textbook and more.*

In Summary

Explain the flow of accounting information through the accounting paper trail

⇨ Source documents provide evidence for journal entries, which are then posted to the ledger accounts. The values from the ledger accounts are used to create a trial balance and the financial statements.

Describe and record transactions in special journals

⇨ The sales journal is used to record all sales on account.

⇨ The cash receipts journal is used to record all cash received.

⇨ The purchases journal is used to record all purchases on account.

⇨ The cash disbursements journal is used to record all cash paid.

⇨ The general journal is used to record all transactions that do not fit into the other special journals.

Describe and record transactions in subsidiary ledgers

⇨ Subsidiary ledgers are used to track details that would clutter the general ledgers.

⇨ All special journals are totalled at the end of the month and the totals are posted to the general ledger accounts.

⇨ If a transaction in the sales or cash receipts journal affects accounts receivable, the accounts receivable subledger account for that customer will be updated immediately.

⇨ If a transaction in the purchases or cash disbursements journal affects accounts payable, the accounts payable subledger account for that supplier will be updated immediately.

Identify features of a computerized accounting system

⇨ A computerized accounting system will have sections like the special journals to enter transactions. Transactions will automatically update general and subsidiary ledgers.

⇨ Subsidiary ledgers will keep information about suppliers and customers and can be used to generate reports.

Review Exercise

Lin-Z is an owner-operated office furniture retailer. Lin-Z uses the periodic inventory system. The following is a list of transactions for the month of June.

Jun 4   Received $4,000 from a cash sale to Gus Van Sand (sold office furniture costing $2,015).

Jun 5   Lin-Z received a bill (Invoice #4053) for $100 worth of supplies from Stapl-EZ Inc.

Jun 6   Received $480 from Bo Didley regarding outstanding accounts receivable.

Jun 9   Received $2,160 for the cash sale of a lounge suite (costing $1,050) to ReetaPetita.

Jun 9   Lin-Z received a bill from Building Services Inc. (Invoice #124) for $350 for repairs and maintenance of office building.

Jun 10   Received $25 in interest from loan to Kurt Domino.

Jun 12   Paid amount owing (Invoice #4053) to Stapl-EZ Inc. (Cheque #465).

Jun 15   Jo Jo Inc. paid back loan of $2,400.

Jun 18   Sold goods on account (Invoice #10022) to Richard Starkey, for office furniture for $3,000 (and costing $2,000).

Jun 21   Purchased $4,000 worth of inventory from Noel's Inc. using cheque #466.

Jun 22   Paid amount owing (Invoice #124) to Building Services Inc. for repairs (Cheque #467).

Jun 25   Paid $175 to SKG Inc., for general expenses (Cheque #468).

Jun 26   Received bill from Brick & Mortar Inc. (Invoice #404241) for $3,500 worth of inventory.

Jun 28   Sold (Invoice #10023) $5,000 worth of inventory (cost $3,700) on account to Pete Best.

Required

a) Record these transactions in the Cash Receipts, Sales, Purchases and Cash Payments Journal.

b) Post from the special journals to the accounts receivable subledger. At the end of the month, post from the special journals to the general ledger control account the following opening subledger balances.

- Bo Didley: $2,000 (DR)
- Richard Starkey: $1,000 (DR)
- Pete Best: $1,500 (DR)

Note that Lin-Z's accounts receivable records consist of only these three subledgers. Assume no entries were made directly to accounts receivable through the general journal. Reconcile the subledger to the control account at the end of the month.

c) Post from the special journals to the accounts payable subledger and then to the general ledger control account at the end of the month. Assume the following opening subledger balances.

- Stapl-EZ: $500 (CR)
- Building Services Inc: $750 (CR)
- Brick & Mortar Inc: $2,500 (CR)

Note that Lin-Z's accounts payable records consist of only these three subledgers. Assume no entries were made directly to accounts payable through the general journal. Reconcile the subledger to the control account at the end of the month.

See Appendix I for solutions.

a) Record transactions in the Cash Receipts, Sales, Purchases, and Cash Payments journal.

Cash Receipts Journal									Page 1
Date	Account	PR	Cash (DR)	Sales (CR)	Accounts Receivable (CR)	Interest Revenue (CR)	Loans Payable (CR)	Other (CR)	COGS/Inventory (DR/CR)
	TOTAL								

Sales Journal					Page 1
Date	Account	Invoice #	PR	Accounts Receivable/Sales (DR/CR)	COGS/Inventory (DR/CR)
	TOTAL				

Purchases Journal							Page 1
Date	Account	Invoice #	PR	Repairs Expense (DR)	Office Supplies (DR)	Purchases (DR)	Accounts Payable (CR)
	TOTAL						

Cash Payments Journal							Page 1
Date	Account	Chq #	PR	Other (DR)	Purchases (DR)	Accounts Payable (DR)	Cash (CR)
	TOTAL						

b) Post from the special journals to the accounts receivable subledger. At the end of the month, post from the special journals to the general ledger control account.

Accounts Receivable Subsidiary Ledger Bo Didley				
Date	PR	DR	CR	Balance

Accounts Receivable Subsidiary Ledger Richard Starkey				
Date	PR	DR	CR	Balance

Accounts Receivable Subsidiary Ledger Pete Best				
Date	PR	DR	CR	Balance

Post to general ledger.

General Ledger Accounts Receivable				
Date	PR	DR	CR	Balance

Lin-Z June 30, 2016 General Ledger	

Lin-Z Schedule of Accounts Receivable June 30, 2016	

c) Post from the special journals to the accounts payable subledger and then to the general ledger control account at the end of the month.

Accounts Payable Subsidiary Ledger Stapl-EZ Inc.				
Date	PR	DR	CR	Balance

Accounts Payable Subsidiary Ledger Building Services Inc.				
Date	PR	DR	CR	Balance

Accounts Payable Subsidiary Ledger Brick & Mortar Inc.				
Date	PR	DR	CR	Balance

Post to general ledger.

General Ledger Accounts Payable				
Date	PR	DR	CR	Balance

Lin-Z June 30, 2016 General Ledger	

Lin-Z Schedule of Accounts Payable June 30, 2016	

Appendix 9A: Special Journals and Periodic Inventory

Special journals and subledgers can also be used if the company uses the periodic inventory system instead of the perpetual inventory system. Most of the processes covered in chapter 9 still apply. This includes posting totals at the end of the month to the appropriate general ledger accounts, immediately posting amounts in the Other column to the general ledger accounts, and updating the accounts receivable or accounts payable subledger accounts.

The difference lies in the accounts used in the special journals. Remember, the periodic inventory system does not update inventory or cost of goods sold until a physical count is performed at the end of the period. Thus, the sales and cash receipts journals will not update inventory or cost of goods sold when a sale is made. Also, the purchase and cash payments journal will use purchases and purchase discounts instead of inventory.

Figure 9A.1 illustrates the special journals for a periodic inventory system using the same sample transactions used in chapter 9.

Sales Journal				Page 1
Date	Account	Invoice #	PR	Accounts Receivable/Sales (DR/CR)
Jan 5	Joe Blog	5125	✓	1,235
Jan 16	Furniture Retailers	5126	✓	956
Jan 31	Total			$2,191
				(110/400)

Cash Receipts Journal								Page 3
Date	Account	PR	Cash (DR)	Sales Discount (DR)	Accounts Receivable (CR)	Sales (CR)	Bank Loan (CR)	Other (CR)
Jan 2	Cash Sale		350			350		
Jan 4	Owner's Capital	300	4,000					4,000
Jan 10	Joe Blog	✓	588	12	600			
Jan 22	Bank Loan		2,000				2,000	
Jan 31	Total		$6,938	$12	$600	$350	$2,000	$4,000
			(101)	(405)	(110)	(400)	(220)	(X)

Purchases Journal								Page 6
Date	Account	Invoice #	Terms	PR	Purchases (DR)	Office Supplies (DR)	Other (DR)	Accounts Payable (CR)
Jan 3	Antonio's Electric	2089	3/15, n 30	✓	4,200			4,200
Jan 19	Doug's Maintenance	6091		525/✓			80	80
Jan 31	Total				$4,200		$80	$4,280
					(120)		(X)	(200)

Cash Payments Journal								Page 4
Date	Account	Chq #	PR	Accounts Payable (DR)	Other (DR)	Purchases (DR)	Purchase Discounts (CR)	Cash (CR)
Jan 6	Inventory	748				1,500		1,500
Jan 15	Owner's Drawings	749	310		500			500
Jan 18	Antonio's Electric	750	✓	4,200			126	4,074
Jan 31	Total			$4,200	$500	$1,500	$126	$6,074
				(200)	(X)	(120)	(120)	(101)

FIGURE 9A.1

*Access **ameengage.com** for integrated resources including tutorials, practice exercises, the digital textbook and more.*

In Summary

Prepare special journals under a periodic inventory system

↪ Special journals using the periodic inventory system will not update inventory or cost of goods sold. The purchases and cash payments journal will update purchases and purchases discounts.

↪ Posting to the general ledger and subledger accounts is the same as in the perpetual inventory system.

Review Exercise

Lin-Z is an owner-operated office furniture retailer. Lin-Z uses the periodic inventory system. The following is a list of transactions for the month of June.

Jun 4   Received $4,000 from a cash sale to Gus Van Sand (sold office furniture costing $2,015).

Jun 5   Lin-Z received a bill (Invoice #4053) for $100 worth of supplies from Stapl-EZ Inc.

Jun 6   Received $480 from Bo Didley regarding outstanding accounts receivable.

Jun 9   Received $2,160 for the cash sale of a lounge suite (costing $1,050) to ReetaPetita.

Jun 9   Lin-Z received a bill from Building Services Inc. (Invoice #124) for $350 for repairs and maintenance of office building.

Jun 10   Received $25 in interest from loan to Kurt Domino.

Jun 12   Paid amount owing (Invoice #4053) to Stapl-EZ Inc. (Cheque #465).

Jun 15   Jo Jo Inc. paid back loan of $2,400.

Jun 18   Sold goods on account (Invoice #10022) to Richard Starkey, for office furniture for $3,000 (and costing $2,000).

Jun 21   Purchased $4,000 worth of inventory from Noel's Inc. using cheque #466.

Jun 22   Paid amount owing (Invoice #124) to Building Services Inc. for repairs (Cheque #467).

Jun 25   Paid $175 to SKG Inc. for general expenses (Cheque #468).

Jun 26   Received bill from Brick & Mortar Inc. (Invoice #404241) for $3,500 worth of inventory.

Jun 28   Sold (Invoice #10023) $5,000 worth of inventory (cost $3,700) on account to Pete Best.

Required

a) Record these transactions in the Cash Receipts, Sales, Purchases and Cash Payments Journal.

b) Post from the special journals to the accounts receivable subledger. At the end of the month, post from the special journals to the general ledger control account. Assume the following opening subledger balances.

- Bo Didley: $2,000 (DR)
- Richard Starkey: $1,000 (DR)
- Pete Best: $1,500 (DR)

Note that Lin-Z's accounts receivable records consist of only these three subledgers. Assume no entries were made directly to accounts receivable through the general journal. Reconcile the subledger to the control account at the end of the month.

c) Post from the special journals to the accounts payable subledger and then to the general ledger control account at the end of the month. Assume the following opening subledger balances.

- Stapl-EZ: $500 (CR)
- Building Services Inc: $750 (CR)
- Brick & Mortar Inc: $2,500 (CR)

Note that Lin-Z's accounts payable records consist of only these three subledgers. Assume no entries were made directly to accounts payable through the general journal. Reconcile the subledger to the control account at the end of the month.

See Appendix I for solutions.

a) Record transactions in the Cash Receipts, Sales, Purchases, and Cash Payments journals.

Cash Receipts Journal									Page 1
Date	Account	PR	Cash (DR)	Sales (CR)	Accounts Receivable (CR)	Interest Revenue (CR)	Loans Payable (CR)	Other (CR)	
	TOTAL								

Sales Journal				Page 1
Date	Account	Invoice #	PR	Accounts Receivable/Sales (DR/CR)
	TOTAL			

Purchases Journal							Page 1
Date	Account	Invoice #	PR	Repairs Expense (DR)	Office Supplies (DR)	Purchases (DR)	Accounts Payable (CR)
	TOTAL						

	Cash Payments Journal						Page 1
Date	Account	Chq #	PR	Other (DR)	Purchases (DR)	Accounts Payable (DR)	Cash (CR)
	TOTAL						

b) Post from special journals to accounts receivable subledger. At month end, post from special journals to general ledger control account.

Accounts Receivable Subsidiary Ledger Bo Didley				
Date	PR	DR	CR	Balance

Accounts Receivable Subsidiary Ledger Richard Starkey				
Date	PR	DR	CR	Balance

Accounts Receivable Subsidiary Ledger Pete Best				
Date	PR	DR	CR	Balance

Post to general ledger.

General Ledger Accounts Receivable				
Date	PR	DR	CR	Balance

Lin-Z June 30, 2016 General Ledger	

Lin-Z Schedule of Accounts Receivable June 30, 2016	

c) Post from special journals to accounts payable subledger and then to general ledger control account at end of month.

Accounts Payable Subsidiary Ledger Stapl-EZ Inc.				
Date	PR	DR	CR	Balance

Accounts Payable Subsidiary Ledger Building Services Inc.				
Date	PR	DR	CR	Balance

Accounts Payable Subsidiary Ledger Brick & Mortar Inc.				
Date	PR	DR	CR	Balance

Post to general ledger.

General Ledger Accounts Payable				
Date	PR	DR	CR	Balance

Lin-Z June 30, 2016 General Ledger	

Lin-Z Schedule of Accounts Payable June 30, 2016	

Chapter 10
CASH CONTROLS

LEARNING OUTCOMES

❶ Apply cash controls

❷ Prepare journal entries for cash rounding, debit and credit transactions

❸ Prepare a bank reconciliation and related journal entries

❹ Prepare a petty cash fund and record related journal entries

❺ Apply general business controls

AMEENGAGE™ *Access **ameengage.com** for integrated resources including tutorials, practice exercises, the digital textbook and more.*

Cash Controls: An Introduction

FIGURE 10.1

As illustrated in Figure 10.1, the current assets section of the balance sheet starts with cash because it is the most liquid asset. A business receives cash from providing services or selling products to customers and uses that cash to purchase assets and pay for expenses. Without cash, a business will likely fail. Thus, it is important for a business to ensure that controls are in place to protect this valuable asset.

While it is important to have sufficient cash on hand, if a business earns more cash than it currently needs, leaving it in a chequing account will earn little return. Instead of having the cash sitting idle, some companies choose to invest their excess cash into highly liquid investments, known as cash equivalents, expecting to generate a higher return. **Cash equivalents** are considered a short-term investment, usually shorter than three months (or 90 days). They are highly liquid and can be quickly converted into cash when needed. Therefore, they get recorded under cash in the current assets section of the balance sheet. Some examples of cash equivalents are treasury bills, money market funds, commercial paper, and short-term Government bonds. Cash equivalents will not be covered in this textbook.

Alternatively, a business may have less cash than it currently needs. This may cause the cash available in the bank account to be negative. This negative amount is known as **bank overdraft**.

Cash Control Guidelines

Cash is very important to a business and it can be tempting for employees to try and misuse cash. Therefore, it is important to have rules for dealing with cash. The three rules shown below will be discussed in detail.

1. Record cash immediately when it is received.
2. Protect cash when it is on the premises.
3. Remove cash from the premises as soon as possible.

Record Cash Immediately when it is Received

After the receipt of cash is recorded, its movement through an organization should be tracked and its removal detected and noted.

The method of recording cash depends on the size of the business and the systems used. For a small business, a simple book of pre-numbered receipts will suffice. When the customer offers cash for merchandise, a paper receipt is prepared in duplicate (one copy for the customer, and the other copy retained as a permanent record of the receipt of cash). Proper controls include the recording of the receipts. Receipts are issued in a sequential pre-numbered order and are accounted for on a regular basis by a responsible staff member. The amounts shown on the receipts are totalled and compared with the cash on hand on a daily basis.

An improvement to preparing receipts by hand is to use a cash register. The cash register prepares two copies of the receipt, similar to handwritten receipts—one copy maintained in the cash register and the second copy provided to the customer. As with handwritten receipts, individual sales amounts are added and compared to the amount of cash on hand.

For larger companies, the cash register is replaced with a point-of-sale (POS) computer terminal. The terminal connects directly with the company's accounting system, but performs the same functions as a handwritten receipt. Specifically, a receipt is given to the customer and a record is maintained in the system. The sales are totalled and compared with the cash on hand on a regular basis.

All of the above systems require the participation of the customer. When the customer is handed the receipt, he or she is expected to examine the receipt to ensure that it reflects the exact amount of cash paid. If the amount on the receipt is less than the actual amount paid, the customer will complain and a correction will be made, ensuring that the receipt for the correct amount is recorded.

The second feature of these systems is a regular summing-up of the sales amounts and comparison of the total with the cash on hand. Cash shortages and overages are dealt with by management. Cash should be deposited intact into a bank account. The total amount of sales should be the amount deposited into the bank, without any deductions being made.

Protect Cash when it is on the Premises

Having cash on the premises of a business may be a temptation to a dishonest employee. It therefore becomes necessary to protect surplus amounts of cash. When the money reaches a predetermined amount, the overage is placed in a safe area (i.e. a locked office or back room). The business may use a safe to store the cash until it is deposited into a bank account. The combination or key to the safe should only be made available to a limited number of trustworthy employees.

As described previously, cash receipts should be deposited intact. Deposits may be made more than once a day to minimize the amount of cash on the premises. If deposits are to be made after hours, the company can make use of the bank's night deposit box.

For larger companies that have substantial amounts of cash on hand, security guards may be employed to physically protect the premises. Similarly, security firms may be employed when moving large amounts of cash from the company's premises to the bank.

Cheques received, which may be treated like cash, should be stamped "for deposit only" on the back to discourage fraudulent cashing of the cheque.

Remove Cash from the Premises as soon as Possible

Since cash is portable and highly vulnerable to theft, a company should keep minimal cash on site by making regular bank deposits.

In addition, establishing a properly controlled bank account is required to keep cash on the premises to a minimum. Just as all cash receipts are deposited in the bank, all payments are made with cheques, eliminating the need to keep a large amount of cash on the premises. For the few expenses that must be paid in cash, a small amount can be kept as petty cash.

These three rules provide a basis for managing cash in a business. The overall goal is to ensure that cash received is the amount of cash recorded, which in turn is the amount of cash deposited.

The process and controls related to keeping a bank account and maintaining a small amount of cash as petty cash will be discussed in detail.

Cash Transactions

As discussed, any cash that is received must be properly recorded and protected until it is deposited to the business bank account. Cash transactions in Canada are rounded to the nearest nickel since the penny was removed in 2013. It is important to note that only cash transactions are rounded; payments by cheque, debit card or credit card are not rounded. The rounding rules are shown in Figure 10.2.

Round Down		Round Up	
$1.01 or $1.02	$1.00	$1.03 or $1.04	$1.05
$1.06 or $1.07	$1.05	$1.08 or $1.09	$1.10

FIGURE 10.2

All sales should be recorded at the actual amounts calculated and not rounded. Only if cash is received as payment from the customer should the amount received be rounded to the nearest nickel. This rounding means that the amount of cash received will not equal the amount of the sale. To account for this, an account to track the cash over or short should be used. This can be set up as a revenue (cash is over) or expense (cash is short) account on the income statement.

Instead of recording every cash sale separately and accounting for the rounding, a business may decide to make a single transaction at the end of the day for all cash sales. This simplifies the accounting process. In this case, sales amounts would be totalled and only rounded at the very end. Suppose a business recorded cash sales of $1,425.56 for May 25, 2016. The journal entry in Figure 10.3 shows how to account for rounding to the nearest nickel.

JOURNAL			Page 1
Date 2016	**Account Title and Explanation**	**Debit**	**Credit**
May 25	Cash Over and Short	0.01	
	Cash	1,425.55	
	Sales Revenue		1,425.56
	To record cash sales		

FIGURE 10.3

This journal entry shows the Cash Over and Short amount being used as an expense account. It is considered to be short when there is less cash collected than the amount of the sale. This expense account is recorded under the other expenses line item on the income statement. Normally, the balance for this account is small and would be considered immaterial. However, if the balance is larger, this would be investigated because it could be material.

Debit and Credit Card Transactions

In addition to receiving cash from customers for payment, many businesses will also allow customers to pay using debit or credit cards. From the business perspective, these payments are like cash since they will be deposited into the business bank account. The business may have the amounts from debit and credit card sales transferred into the bank account each day or less frequently if it does not have many daily sales.

A debit card sale transfers cash from the customer's bank account to the business bank account. This limits the customer to spending only what they have in their account. A credit card sale gives the customer access to credit which usually available through their bank. This is like a loan from the bank to the customer.

In both cases, a sale paid for by credit card or debit card will result in a small transaction fee the business must pay to the bank or processing company. This fee is to cover the bank's cost of providing the equipment and technology to allow these transactions. In the case of credit card fees, it also covers the risk that the customer may not repay the bank the money they borrowed. From the business' perspective, this fee is a cost of processing the sale and is recorded as an expense.

For example, suppose a business made total credit card sales of $2,000 on May 25, 2016. The bank will charge 2.5% of total sales as the transaction fee to the business. Thus, $50 ($2,000 x 2.5%) will be kept by the bank and only $1,950 will be deposited to the business bank account. The transaction is illustrated in Figure 10.4.

JOURNAL			Page 1
Date 2016	Account Title and Explanation	Debit	Credit
May 25	Debit/Credit Card Expense	50	
	Cash	1,950	
	Sales Revenue		2,000
	To record credit card sales		

FIGURE 10.4

On the other hand, a bank can charge a fixed percentage of all debit transactions, such as 1% or 2%, or charge a per-transaction fee, such as $0.006 per transaction, depending on the terms of the bank account. This debit card expense is recorded in the journal under the Debit/Credit Card Expense account as shown in Figure 10.4.

Bank Reconciliations

A simple internal control is comparing and reconciling the items in the company's cash records with the items shown on the bank statements. This is done by preparing a schedule called a **bank reconciliation.** A bank reconciliation compares, reconciles, and explains the difference between a company's bank statement and their own cash accounting records. This is usually done at the end of a statement period.

The bank statement balance and the cash ledger balance at the end of the month may not be the same. The bank reconciliation is prepared to reconcile these two balances and to ensure no errors have been made by either the bank or the company bookkeeper. If an error has been made, it must be corrected.

In the process of comparing the items in your records with the items shown on the bank statement, you may notice that some items shown correctly on the bank statement may not appear in your records. Similarly, some items shown correctly in your records may not appear on the bank statement.

Typical reasons for the bank making additional deductions from the company's cash account include

- loan interest charges
- repayment of a bank loan
- bank charges
- electronic fund transfers (EFTs): automatic cash payments to other accounts
- non-sufficient funds (NSF) cheques

Typical reasons for the bank making additional deposits to the company's cash account include

- interest deposited directly into the account
- payment from a customer deposited directly into the account
- EFTs: automatic cash receipts from other accounts

A bank reconciliation addresses all of the differences between the bank statement and the cash ledger account. In the following sections, each reason will be analyzed individually for the purpose of illustration. A complete bank reconciliation statement will be presented at the end of the discussion.

Unrecorded Deposits from the Bank Statement

From time to time, the bank may automatically record a deposit in the company's bank account. The company would be unaware of the amount until it receives the bank statement. For example, compare the bank statement for HR Clothing Company to the company's cash ledger entries.

Company's Records

GENERAL LEDGER

Account: Cash				GL. No.	101
Date	Description	DR	CR	Balance	
Jun 1	Opening Balance			5,000	DR
Jun 2	Cheque #1		300	4,700	DR
Jun 3	Cheque #2		500	4,200	DR
Jun 10	Cheque #3		700	3,500	DR

Bank's Records

Bank Statement				June 1–June 30, 2016
Date	Description	Withdrawal	Deposit	Balance
Jun 1	Opening Balance			5,000
Jun 2	Cheque #1	300		4,700
Jun 3	Cheque #2	500		4,200
Jun 10	Cheque #3	700		3,500
Jun 30	Interest		5	3,505

FIGURE 10.5

If the deposit is correct, you will have to record it in the ledger account. For example, in Figure 10.5, the bank has recorded interest of $5 in the account of HR Clothing on June 30. All the other cheques have been recorded by the bank as well as by the company. Since the interest earned is correctly shown on the bank statement, it should also be recorded in the general ledger by debiting (increasing) cash and crediting (increasing) interest revenue.

Assume that HR Clothing's ledger balance is $3,500, and the bank statement for the month shows a balance of $3,505. The bank reconciliation for this is shown in Figure 10.6.

HR Clothing Bank Reconciliation June 30, 2016		
	Ledger	Bank
Balance as per records	$3,500	$3,505
Add: Unrecorded deposits		
Interest June 30	5	
Reconciled balance	$3,505	$3,505

FIGURE 10.6

Notice that the adjusting amount is in the ledger column. This means that you must correct the general ledger balance with an adjusting journal entry. The entry is shown in Figure 10.7. Notice that the journal entry includes interest revenue. On the Accounting Map, interest revenue is listed under other revenue on the income statement.

JOURNAL			Page 1
Date	Account Title and Explanation	Debit	Credit
2016			
Jun 30	Cash	5	
	Interest Revenue		5
	Bank interest earned		

FIGURE 10.7

BALANCE SHEET

ASSETS	LIABILITIES
CASH +$5 DR	ACCOUNTS PAYABLE
ACCOUNTS RECEIVABLE	UNEARNED REVENUE
INVENTORY	LOANS PAYABLE
	OWNER'S EQUITY

INCOME STATEMENT

OPERATING EXPENSES

OPERATING INCOME (LOSS)

OTHER REVENUE
INTEREST REVENUE +$5 CR

OTHER EXPENSES
(INTEREST, LOSS ON SALE OF ASSETS)

NET INCOME (LOSS)

Unrecorded Charges from the Bank Statement

As with unrecorded deposits, there may be charges shown on the bank statement that are not yet recorded in the general ledger. Typical examples are the monthly bank charges or an annual fee for a safe deposit box. Such charges should be adjusted in the ledger.

Figure 10.8 shows that HR Clothing has a cash ledger balance of $3,500. The bank statement reflects a balance of $3,450. All cheques are recorded in both the bank statement and the general ledger. Upon comparison, the bookkeeper of the company notices that the bank recorded bank charges of $50 on the last day of the month. This change must be updated in the general ledger.

GENERAL LEDGER

Account: Cash				GL. No. 101	
Date	Description	DR	CR	Balance	
Jun 1	Opening Balance			5,000	DR
Jun 2	Cheque #1		300	4,700	DR
Jun 3	Cheque #2		500	4,200	DR
Jun 10	Cheque #3		700	3,500	DR

Bank Statement			June 1–June 30, 2016	
Date	Description	Withdrawal	Deposit	Balance
Jun 1	Opening Balance			5,000
Jun 2	Cheque #1	300		4,700
Jun 3	Cheque #2	500		4,200
Jun 10	Cheque #3	700		3,500
Jun 30	Bank Charges	50		3,450

FIGURE 10.8

The bank reconciliation for this item is shown in Figure 10.9.

HR Clothing Bank Reconciliation June 30, 2016	Ledger	Bank
Balance as per records	$3,500	$3,450
Less: Unrecorded charges		
Bank Charges June 30	**(50)**	
Reconciled balance	$3,450	$3,450

FIGURE 10.9

As with the unrecorded deposit shown previously, the adjustment is shown in the ledger column, so it must be updated with a journal entry as shown in Figure 10.10. Notice that the journal entry includes the account bank charges expense. On the Accounting Map, bank charges are listed under operating expenses on the income statement.

JOURNAL			Page 1
Date	Account Title and Explanation	Debit	Credit
2016			
Jun 30	Bank Charges Expense	50	
	Cash		50
	Bank service charge		

FIGURE 10.10

The journal entry is recorded by debiting (increasing) bank charges expense and crediting (decreasing) cash (an asset).

Another type of bank charge can occur as a result of **non-sufficient funds (NSF)** cheques. NSF cheques are payments made to the company by a customer who does not have sufficient funds in their bank account to cover the amount of the cheque. If the customer does not have enough money in their bank account to cover the cheque, their bank will charge them an NSF fee. The company's bank will also charge the company with an NSF fee. The fee is to cover the bank's administrative costs of dealing with the NSF cheque.

For example, HR Clothing receives a $400 cheque from a customer and deposits the cheque into the company bank account on June 17. However, the bank cannot successfully collect the $400 from the customer's account because the customer does not have enough money in his account to support this withdrawal. The bank would return the cheque to the company and charge an additional service fee. These two transactions are illustrated in Figure 10.11 between the general ledger and the bank statement respectively.

GENERAL LEDGER

Account: Cash				GL. No. 101	
Date	Description	DR	CR	Balance	
Jun 1	Opening Balance			5,000	DR
Jun 2	Cheque #1		300	4,700	DR
Jun 3	Cheque #2		500	4,200	DR
Jun 10	Cheque #3		700	3,500	DR
Jun 17	Deposit	400		3,900	DR

Bank Statement				June 1–June 30, 2016
Date	Description	Withdrawal	Deposit	Balance
Jun 1	Opening Balance			5,000
Jun 2	Cheque #1	300		4,700
Jun 3	Cheque #2	500		4,200
Jun 10	Cheque #3	700		3,500
Jun 17	Deposit		400	3,900
Jun 19	NSF Cheque	400		3,500
Jun 19	NSF Charge	10		3,490

FIGURE 10.11

The bank reconciliation for this item is shown in Figure 10.12.

HR Clothing Bank Reconciliation June 30, 2016		
	Ledger	Bank
Balance as per records	$3,900	$3,490
Less: **NSF Cheque**	(400)	
Charges for NSF Cheque	(10)	
Reconciled balance	$3,490	$3,490

FIGURE 10.12

This adjustment should also be recorded in the journal and updated in the ledger. Since an NSF cheque represents the amount of cash receipts unsuccessfully collected, this amount should be added to the company's accounts receivable account. In addition, the bank charge associated with the NSF cheque should also be recorded. The journal entries are shown in Figure 10.13. To keep the charges separate from the other bank charges, an account called NSF charges expense is used.

JOURNAL			Page 1
Date	**Account Title and Explanation**	**Debit**	**Credit**
2016			
Jun 30	Accounts Receivable	400	
	Cash		400
	NSF cheque returned by bank		
Jun 30	NSF Charges Expense	10	
	Cash		10
	Bank charge for NSF cheque		

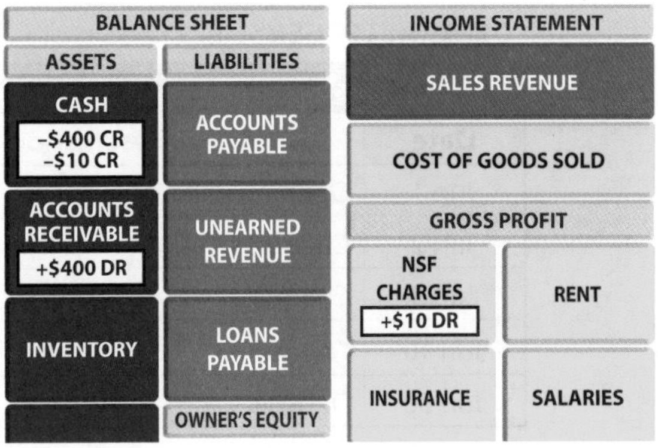

FIGURE 10.13

Notice that HR Clothing received a charge because the customer was unable to honour the cheque. The company will not want to have to pay the extra fee for the customer's error. HR Clothing will create a new invoice to the customer, charging the customer an extra amount to cover the NSF fee. Some companies just charge the customer the NSF fee it was charged, in this case $10. Other companies charge the customer a flat fee greater than the NSF charge of $10 to cover the NSF fee and to cover the administrative process of handling the NSF cheque.

IN THE REAL WORLD

Non-sufficient funds (NSF) cheques are commonly known as bad cheques or bounced cheques. In our example, it is assumed that non-sufficient funds (NSF) cheques occur because the issuer of the cheque does not have enough money in their own bank account to support the cheque. However, NSF cheques can result from a variety of reasons including.

1. The issuer purposely cancels the cheque.
2. The account is frozen.
3. The account does not exist (i.e. the issuing party engaged in a fraudulent act).
4. The account is under investigation.

Outstanding Deposits

An outstanding deposit is one that has been recorded in the company's general ledger but not shown on the bank statement. These are also referred to as *deposits in transit*. This can occur when the company makes a deposit in the bank (perhaps using the night deposit box) on the last day of the month, but the bank does not record the deposit until the following business day—in the next month. The bank statement and the company's ledger account may appear as shown in Figure 10.14.

GENERAL LEDGER

Account: Cash				GL. No.	101
Date	**Description**	**DR**	**CR**	**Balance**	
Jun 1	Opening Balance			5,000	DR
Jun 2	Cheque #1		300	4,700	DR
Jun 3	Cheque #2		500	4,200	DR
Jun 10	Cheque #3		700	3,500	DR
Jun 30	Deposit	1,000		4,500	DR

Bank Statement				June 1–June 30, 2016
Date	**Description**	**Withdrawal**	**Deposit**	**Balance**
Jun 1	Opening Balance			5,000
Jun 2	Cheque #1	300		4,700
Jun 3	Cheque #2	500		4,200
Jun 10	Cheque #3	700		3,500

FIGURE 10.14

The balance on the bank statement is $3,500. The balance in the general ledger is $4,500. There was a deposit of $1,000 on June 30 that was not recorded by the bank. Since the balance is missing from the bank statement, it should be added to the bank balance as shown in Figure 10.15.

HR Clothing Bank Reconciliation June 30, 2016		
	Ledger	**Bank**
Balance as per records	$4,500	$3,500
Add: **Outstanding deposit June 30**		**1,000**
Reconciled balance	$4,500	$4,500

FIGURE 10.15

Notice that the reconciled balances are the same for the bank and the ledger columns. There is no adjustment required in the ledger because the entry is only in the bank account column of the bank reconciliation worksheet. The outstanding deposit is a timing difference; it should appear on the bank statement which includes the following business day (in July). If the deposit does not show up within one or two business days, further investigation should be made to rule out theft or fraud.

Outstanding Cheques

The next reconciling item to consider is *outstanding cheques*. An outstanding cheque (issued by the company) is one that has been recorded in the general ledger, but has not been recorded on the bank statement. This can happen because after the company records the cheque, it is mailed to the supplier. The supplier then records it in its books, prepares the deposit and takes it to the bank. The process can take several days, so the cheque mailed on June 29 may not appear on the bank statement until July 2 or 3.

Consider an example: three cheques have been recorded in the ledger between June 28 and 30, as reflected in Figure 10.16. None of these cheques have been processed by the bank by June 30. The cheques are therefore outstanding.

To reconcile the ledger account with the bank statement, we must treat the cheques as if the transaction had been completed by the bank (i.e. deduct the amounts from the bank record).

GENERAL LEDGER

Account: Cash				GL. No. 101	
Date	Description	DR	CR	Balance	
Jun 1	Opening Balance			5,000	DR
Jun 2	Cheque #1		300	4,700	DR
Jun 3	Cheque #2		500	4,200	DR
Jun 10	Cheque #3		700	3,500	DR
Jun 15	Deposit	1,000		4,500	DR
Jun 28	Cheque #4		400	4,100	DR
Jun 29	Cheque #5		800	3,300	DR
Jun 30	Cheque #6		700	2,600	DR

Bank Statement			June 1–June 30, 2016	
Date	Description	Withdrawal	Deposit	Balance
Jun 1	Opening Balance			5,000
Jun 2	Cheque #1	300		4,700
Jun 3	Cheque #2	500		4,200
Jun 10	Cheque #3	700		3,500
Jun 15	Deposit		1,000	4,500

FIGURE 10.16

The bank reconciliation for outstanding cheques is shown in Figure 10.17.

HR Clothing Bank Reconciliation June 30, 2016	Ledger	Bank
Balance as per records	$2,600	$4,500
Less: **Outstanding cheques**		
Cheque #4 June 28		(400)
Cheque #5 June 29		(800)
Cheque #6 June 30		(700)
Reconciled balance	$2,600	$2,600

FIGURE 10.17

No adjustment is required in the ledger account because the cheques are correctly recorded in the general ledger but have not been cashed by the bank. The bank will eventually include them on the bank statement.

Bank Errors

Although rare, it is possible that banks will make errors, such as charging the company incorrectly with a cheque belonging to another company. In that case, the company's ledger balance is correct and the bank must correct the error.

Consider an example: when the bookkeeper receives the bank statement and compares it with the company records, she notices that the bank processed a cheque for $800 on June 8, but the company has no knowledge of the cheque. This is shown in Figure 10.18.

At that point, the bookkeeper calls the bank and discovers that the cheque belongs to another bank client.

GENERAL LEDGER

Account: Cash				GL. No.	101	
Date	**Description**	**DR**	**CR**	**Balance**		
Jun 1	Opening Balance			5,000	DR	
Jun 2	Cheque #1		300	4,700	DR	
Jun 3	Cheque #2		500	4,200	DR	
Jun 10	Cheque #3		700	3,500	DR	

Bank Statement				June 1–June 30, 2016
Date	Description	Withdrawal	Deposit	Balance
Jun 1	Opening Balance			5,000
Jun 2	Cheque #1	300		4,700
Jun 3	Cheque #2	500		4,200
Jun 8	Cheque #108	800		3,400
Jun 10	Cheque #3	700		2,700

FIGURE 10.18

The bank reconciliation for this item is shown in Figure 10.19.

HR Clothing Bank Reconciliation June 30, 2016		
	Ledger	Bank
Balance as per records	$3,500	$2,700
Add: **Bank Error**, cheque incorrectly charged to account June 8		800
Reconciled balance	$3,500	$3,500

FIGURE 10.19

Since the adjustment is in the bank column, it does not need to be adjusted in the company's books. The amount is an error, not a timing difference, and the bank must correct the error by depositing funds back into the company's account. The company needs to follow up to ensure that the bank corrects the error.

An incorrect deposit may also appear on the bank statement. In that case, the bank reconciliation would reflect a deduction from the bank balance because it is overstated as a result of the deposit. The company would follow up to ensure that the amount was deducted from its bank account.

Ledger Errors

It is possible for bookkeepers to make errors. These errors would appear in the company's records.

Consider an example: upon investigating the difference between the bank statement and the ledger, the bookkeeper discovers that a cheque recorded as $950 in the ledger should have been recorded as $590.

The bank cashed the correct amount of the cheque ($590). The bank reconciliation for this item is shown in Figure 10.20.

GENERAL LEDGER

Account: Cash					GL. No.	101
Date	Description	DR	CR	Balance		
Jun 1	Opening Balance			5,000	DR	
Jun 2	Cheque #1		300	4,700	DR	
Jun 3	Cheque #2		950	3,750	DR	
Jun 10	Cheque #3		700	3,050	DR	

Bank Statement				June 1–June 30, 2016
Date	Description	Withdrawal	Deposit	Balance
Jun 1	Opening Balance			5,000
Jun 2	Cheque #1	300		4,700
Jun 3	Cheque #2	590		4,110
Jun 10	Cheque #3	700		3,410

FIGURE 10.20

In this situation, more was deducted from the general ledger than was on the cheque. To correct this error, the bookkeeper will have to add to the general ledger the difference between what was recorded and the actual amount deducted by the bank. This amounts to $360 ($950 – $590). The bank reconciliation would appear as shown in Figure 10.21.

HR Clothing Bank Reconciliation June 30, 2016		
	Ledger	Bank
Balance as per records	$3,050	$3,410
Recording error		
Add: **Error on cheque #2**	360	
Reconciled balance	$3,410	$3,410

FIGURE 10.21

Because the correcting entry is in the ledger column, an adjusting entry must be recorded in the journal. Assuming the original cheque was written to purchase inventory by using a perpetual method, the journal entry to correct the ledger is shown in Figure 10.22.

JOURNAL			Page 1
Date	**Account Title and Explanation**	**Debit**	**Credit**
2016			
Jun 30	Cash	360	
	Inventory		360
	Correct error in ledger		

FIGURE 10.22

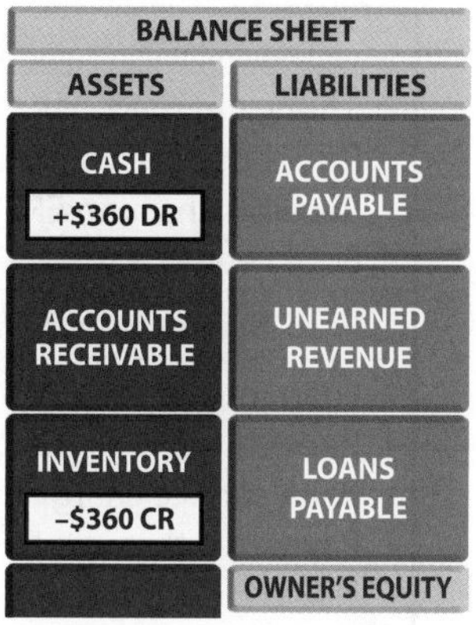

When an error is made by the bookkeeper, the bookkeeper must go back into the records to determine what the original entry was for. This will determine which account will be used to offset the cash account. In our example, the payment was for inventory. If the payment was to pay off an account, use accounts payable; if it was to pay this month's rent, use rent expense; if it was to pay a telephone bill, use telephone expense, etc.

As with the previous examples, any discrepancy between the bank statement and the ledger record should be examined and then corrected with the appropriate entries.

Incorrect amounts in the ledger can be more or less than the amounts shown on the bank statement. Each error must be analyzed carefully for appropriate adjustments.

A CLOSER LOOK

In a computerized accounting system, errors in the ledger, such as the one described in Figure 10.22, are corrected using two entries instead of one. The first entry would be a $950 debit to cash and a $950 credit to inventory. This entry reverses the original incorrect entry. The second entry would be a $590 debit to inventory and a $590 credit to cash to record the correct amount of the June 3 cheque. The net result is the same as the single entry in the amount of $360 shown above. Manual accounting systems may not use this method because it requires more entries and provides more room for error.

Bank Reconciliation Summary

Once all the items on a bank statement and the ledger have been matched up, only a few items should remain that need to be reconciled. Figure 10.23 summarizes how items will be treated on a bank reconciliation. Remember that all items that must be added to or subtracted from the ledger balance must be recorded in a journal entry.

Add to Ledger Balance*	Add to Bank Balance
• Interest earned • Direct deposit from customer • Receipts through EFT • Bookkeeper error	• Outstanding deposits • Bank error
Subtract from Ledger Balance*	**Subtract from Bank Balance**
• Loan interest charges • Repayment of bank loan • Bank service charges • Payments through EFT • NSF cheques • Bookkeeper error	• Outstanding cheques • Bank error

*Must also create a journal entry to update the ledger balance.

FIGURE 10.23

To illustrate, we will complete a bank reconciliation with journal entries for HR Clothing for the month of October 2016. Before comparing the new items, it is always important to consider the outstanding items from the last period. We need to ensure these items have been cleared. The completed bank reconciliation from September is shown in Figure 10.24. There are three items in the bank column that are outstanding as of September 20, 2016: the deposit for $2,200 and cheques #57 and #59. It is likely that these will clear the bank in October and must be compared to the October bank statement. If they appear on the bank statement, we will check the items on the September bank reconciliation and the October bank statement.

HR Clothing Bank Reconciliation September 30, 2016	Ledger	Bank
Balance as per records	$7,360	$4,930
Add: Outstanding Deposit		✓ 2,200
Less: Outstanding Cheques		
Cheque #57		✓ (350)
Cheque #59		✓ (480)
Add: EFT Deposit	250	
Less: EFT Rent	(1,300)	
Service Charge	(10)	
Reconciled Balance	$6,300	$6, 300

FIGURE 10.24

The cash ledger account and the bank statement for October are shown in Figure 10.25.

GENERAL LEDGER

Account: Cash				GL. No.	101
Date	Description	DR	CR	Balance	
Oct 1	Opening Balance			6,300	DR
Oct 2	Cheque #62		✓ 140	6,160	DR
Oct 4	Deposit M. Smith	✓ 200		6,360	DR
Oct 7	Cheque #63		570	5,790	DR
Oct 15	Cheque #64		820	4,970	DR
Oct 17	Deposit	✓ 1,200		6,170	DR
Oct 21	Cheque #65		✓ 540	5,630	DR
Oct 25	Cheque #66		320	5,310	DR
Oct 29	Cheque #67		410	4,900	DR
Oct 31	Deposit	900		5,800	DR

Bank Statement			October 1–October 31, 2016	
Date	Description	Withdrawal	Deposit	Balance
Oct 1	Opening Balance			4,930
Oct 1	EFT Rent	1,300		3,630
Oct 2	Deposit		✓ 2,200	5,830
Oct 4	Cheque #57	✓ 350		5,480
Oct 5	Deposit		✓ 200	5,680
Oct 6	NSF Cheque	200		5,480
Oct 6	NSF Fee	15		5,465
Oct 8	Cheque #62	✓ 140		5,325
Oct 10	Cheque #59	✓ 480		4,845
Oct 15	EFT Deposit		300	5,145
Oct 18	Deposit		✓ 1,200	6,345
Oct 23	Cheque #63	750		5,595
Oct 25	Cheque #65	✓ 540		5,055
Oct 31	Service Cheque	10		5,045

Cheque #63 was for advertising and was cashed for the correct amount by the bank
The NSF cheque was from a customer as payment of their account
The EFT deposit was a customer paying their account

FIGURE 10.25

Compare the items on the October bank statement to the October general ledger and the September bank reconciliation. The green check marks, in Figures 10.24 and 10.25, indicate that the item on the bank statement matches an item from the ledger or September's bank reconciliation. As shown in the Figure 10.26, only the items without a check mark need to be included on the bank reconciliation for October.

HR Clothing Bank Reconciliation October 31, 2016	Ledger	Bank
Balance as per records	$5,800	$5,045
Add: Outstanding Deposit		900
Less: Outstanding Cheques		
Cheque #64		(820)
Cheque #66		(320)
Cheque #67		(410)
Add: EFT Deposit	300	
Less: EFT Rent	(1,300)	
NSF Cheque	(200)	
NSF Fee	(15)	
Service Charge	(10)	
Error on Cheque #63	(180)	
Reconciled balance	$4,395	$4,395

FIGURE 10.26

Once the bank is reconciled to the ledger, all items that increase or decrease the ledger balance must be recorded in the journal. The journal entries are shown in Figure 10.27.

JOURNAL			Page 1
Date 2016	Account Title and Explanation	Debit	Credit
Oct 31	Cash	300	
	Accounts Receivable		300
	Collection from customer		
Oct 31	Rent Expense	1,300	
	Cash		1,300
	Payment for rent		
Oct 31	Accounts Receivable	200	
	Cash		200
	NSF cheque from customer		
Oct 31	NSF Charges Expense	15	
	Cash		15
	Record NSF fee		
Oct 31	Bank Charges Expense	10	
	Cash		10
	Record bank service charge		
Oct 31	Advertising Expense	180	
	Cash		180
	Correct error on cheque		

FIGURE 10.27

An alternate way to record the journal entries is to make compound journal entries to combine similar transactions. For example, all transactions that credit cash could be combined into a single transaction. Each of the debited accounts would still be listed, but there would be a single credit to cash for $1,705.

Petty Cash

At times, a business may require small amounts of cash to pay for petty (small) expenses such as parking, postage stamps and courier fees. Instead of issuing a cheque each time, the business will set up a petty cash fund to pay for these small amounts in cash.

Petty cash is usually operated on what is known as an *imprest system*. An imprest system for petty cash ensures that spending is limited to the amount available in petty cash fund. For example, if a petty cash fund starts with $100, that is the maximum amount that can be spent. When the amount spent approaches the $100 limit, the petty cash fund will be replenished up to $100.

Setting Up a Petty Cash Fund

1. **Designate one individual as the petty cash custodian.** There are many ways in which petty cash can be mishandled. Having one person responsible for the fund increases transparency and accountability. The petty cash custodian ensures that petty cash is properly safeguarded and disbursed for legitimate reasons and that an accurate record is maintained for all activities related to the fund.

2. **Establish the amount of the fund.** The petty cash custodian needs to determine the amount of the fund as well as the frequency with which it is replenished.

3. **Record the initial petty cash transaction.** The establishment of a petty cash fund requires one initial transaction. The journal entry is shown in Figure 10.28.

JOURNAL			Page 1
Date 2016	**Account Title and Explanation**	**Debit**	**Credit**
Dec 10	Petty Cash	100	
	Cash		100
	To set up the petty cash fund		

ASSETS
CASH
–$100 CR
PETTY CASH
+$100 DR

FIGURE 10.28

4. **Require users of petty cash to provide receipts.** Any employee who requires petty cash must provide a receipt from the supplier indicating the amount of money spent. The petty cash custodian will require the person to sign the receipt, indicating that the person has been reimbursed. Figure 10.29 shows a petty cash receipt.

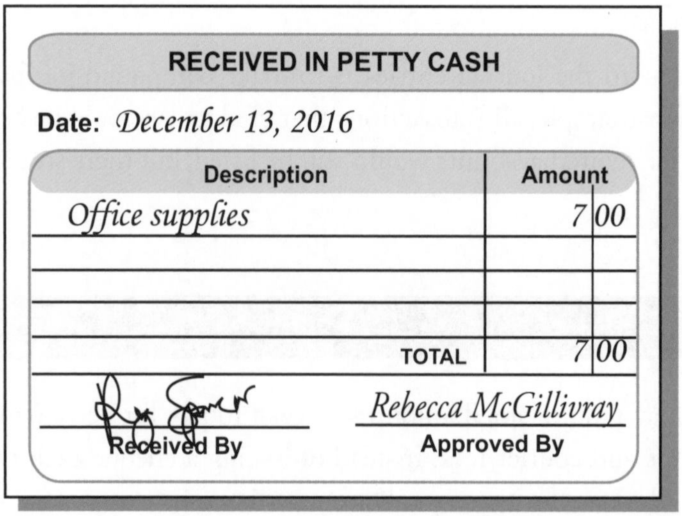

RECEIVED IN PETTY CASH

Date: *December 13, 2016*

Description	Amount	
Office supplies	7	00
TOTAL	7	00

Received By: *(signature)*

Approved By: *Rebecca McGillivray*

FIGURE 10.29

5. **Provide a summary of petty cash.** At the end of the period, which in this example is one week, the petty cash custodian prepares a summary that lists the details of the fund before it is reimbursed. The summary sheet is shown in Figure 10.30.

The petty cash summary should include a list of all the items, in groups, paid with the petty cash fund. Both subtotals and a grand total should be calculated. In this example the grand total comes to

Petty Cash Summary Sheet		
Period: Dec. 10–Dec. 17		
Opening Balance		**$100.00**
Parking		
Dec. 10	$10.00	
Dec. 12	6.00	
Dec. 14	5.00	$21.00
Delivery		
Dec. 10	$18.00	
Dec. 11	6.00	$24.00
Office Supplies		
Dec. 13	$ 7.00	
Dec. 16	13.00	$20.00
Gasoline		
Dec. 14	$18.00	$18.00
Total Disbursements		**$83.00**
Cash over and short	$2.00	
Total to be reimbursed to Petty Cash		**$85.00**

Opening balance less disbursements

FIGURE 10.30

$83. Subtracting $83 from the original balance of $100 gives us an amount of $17. This should be the remaining balance in the petty cash box.

6. **Reconcile any overage or shortage.** The petty cash custodian must take care of any amounts short or over in the petty cash box. This is done by making additions or subtractions to the account called cash over and short. In our current example, there was only $15 in the petty cash box, meaning there was a $2 shortage. Such discrepancies can result from a miscount of coins, an overpayment during the period, or rounding cash transactions to the nearest nickel. The total disbursements recorded, along with any cash short or over, constitute the total amount to be reimbursed to petty cash to restore it to its original value of $100. In this case, the amount is $85.

7. **Present summary slip to a supervisor.** The petty cash custodian presents her supervisor with a summary slip, together with all supporting vouchers. After reviewing these documents, the supervisor provides the petty cash custodian with a cheque to reimburse the petty cash fund. The receipts are stamped "paid" so that they cannot be reused.

8. **Reimburse the petty cash fund.** The petty cash custodian cashes the cheque (in this example the cheque is for $85) and replenishes the fund to its original amount ($100).

Posting Petty Cash to the General Ledger

We have examined the steps that an organization must take when establishing a petty cash fund. Now look at how this process affects the organization's general ledger.

We have already described the transaction that occurs when the petty cash fund is initially established. Cash is credited and petty cash is debited—both for the same amounts, which in our example was $100 as shown in Figure 10.28. Until now, all the activity has been in the physical petty cash box itself, with no transactions

WORTH REPEATING

Transferring assets from one account (e.g. cash) to another account (e.g. petty cash) has no impact on owner's equity.

affecting the ledger. When it is time to replenish the fund, we need to increase the amount of petty cash to $100 and allocate the amounts used to the appropriate expense accounts.

The cheque is recorded with a debit to various expenses (parking, delivery, office supplies, gasoline, cash over and short), and a credit to cash in the amount of $85. Figure 10.31 shows this transaction. Notice that the journal entry includes the numerous expenses. On the Accounting Map, these expenses are listed under operating expenses on the income statement.

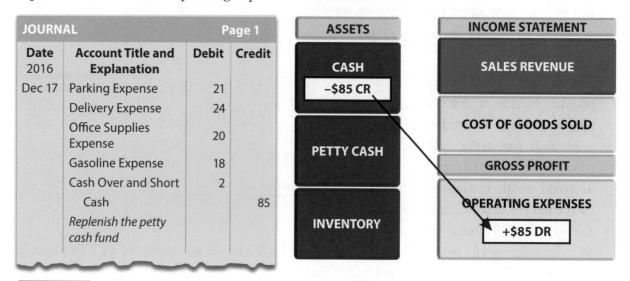

FIGURE 10.31

The cash over and short account behaves like an expense account when there is a shortage. It will be debited in the journal entry. If there is an overage, the cash over and short account behaves like a revenue account. It will be credited in the journal entry.

No change is made in the amount of the petty cash ledger account when the reimbursement cheque is issued, and the reimbursed cash is placed in the petty cash box. You may think that the transaction should be recorded by debiting expenses and crediting petty cash, followed by a debit to petty cash and a credit to cash. However, in practice, when the bookkeeper records the cheque there is no change to the petty cash account.

It is important to note that the *only* time the petty cash account in the ledger is debited or credited is when the account is established or when the amount in the petty cash fund is increased or decreased.

Assume that on December 31, the manager decided to increase the petty cash fund to $150. The journal entry to record the $50 increase is shown in Figure 10.32.

JOURNAL			Page 1
Date 2016	**Account Title and Explanation**	**Debit**	**Credit**
Dec 31	Petty Cash	50	
	Cash		50
	Increase the petty cash fund		

FIGURE 10.32

When the petty cash fund is increased, the petty cash account should be debited (increased) and the cash account should be credited (decreased).

Petty cash can also increase at the same time it is replenished. If on December 17 petty cash was replenished and increased at the same time, Figures 10.31 and 10.32 would be combined, meaning cash would be credited by a total of $135. The combined transaction is shown in Figure 10.33.

JOURNAL			Page 1
Date 2016	**Account Title and Explanation**	**Debit**	**Credit**
Dec 17	Parking Expense	21	
	Delivery Expense	24	
	Office Supplies Expense	20	
	Gasoline Expense	18	
	Cash Over and Short	2	
	Petty Cash	50	
	Cash		135
	Replenish and increase petty cash		

FIGURE 10.33

A spreadsheet may be maintained listing the various expenses so that each month the general ledger can be updated with the correct allocation of expenses. An example is shown in Figure 10.34.

HR Clothing Petty Cash Expenses Paid July 2016						
Description	**Receipt #**	**Amount**	**Office**	**Travel**	**Meals**	**Marketing**
Photo Developing	1	8.07				8.07
Taxis	2	65.00		65.00		
Meals	3	33.00			33.00	
Batteries	4	11.00				11.00
Photocopying—brochures	5	23.32				23.32
Photocopying—general	6	3.05	3.05			
Parking	7	1.87		1.87		
Parking	8	10.26		10.26		
Parking	9	3.00		3.00		
Parking	10	4.00		4.00		
Parking	11	6.50		6.50		
Parking	12	7.00		7.00		
Parking	13	6.00		6.00		
Parking	14	3.94		3.94		
Parking	15	1.00		1.00		
Gas	16	10.00		10.00		
Meals	17	8.10			8.10	
Travel	18	49.01		49.01		
TOTALS		**$254.12**	**$3.05**	**$167.58**	**$41.10**	**$42.39**

Cash will be credited with this amount. (assuming no cash over/short).

= $254.12
Each of these amounts will be debited to the respective GL expense accounts.

FIGURE 10.34

Petty Cash Controls

Using petty cash funds can be a convenient way to purchase small items. However, the funds also provide opportunities for abuse. It is therefore important to regulate the use of the petty cash fund to ensure that it is not mishandled. Here are a few tips to ensure that petty cash is used appropriately.

1. **Establish guidelines.** The first step in ensuring that your petty cash is used properly is to draw up a list of items that can be purchased with petty cash. Determine what purchases may be made with purchase orders, and then make a list of other types of regular purchases. The fund should be reserved strictly for small ("petty") expenses and not for items such as long-term assets or inventory, or for paying accounts payable and independent contractors.

2. **Maintain documentation.** It is difficult to keep accurate records unless you have a uniform documentation system. Establish an easy-to-use system and follow it consistently. The easiest way to do this is by keeping track of all receipts, whether they are register receipts or written invoices. Each receipt should have the date of purchase, the name of the vendor, a list of the items or services purchased, the price of each item and the total cost. Accurate recordkeeping also requires that

    - the person who made the purchase signs the receipt
    - all receipts are filed correctly so they can be checked for discrepancies

3. **Review the rules with employees.** If the regulations are not well known, abuse of the petty cash fund becomes easier. Keep everyone up-to-date and do not allow exceptions to the rules.

4. **One person should be responsible for petty cash—the petty cash custodian.** The appointment of one person to administer and be exclusively responsible for the fund limits the opportunities for mismanagement.

5. **Periodically count the petty cash fund.** Have a person independent from the petty cash custodian, such as a manager, count the fund with the custodian present. This discourages misuse of the funds and can detect shortages early.

This chapter discusses cash equivalents and petty cash as separate functions within a business. At this point, we can look at the impact of these two items and how they affect the balance sheet and its presentation. Figure 10.35 shows a partial balance sheet of Donatello's restaurant.

Donatello's Restaurant Balance Sheet As at December 31, 2016	
ASSETS	
Current Assets	
Cash and cash equivalents	
Bank account—chequing	$13,220
Bank account—savings	4,700
Petty cash fund	300
Cash equivalents	6,500
Total cash and cash equivalents	$24,720

FIGURE 10.35

Figure 10.35 shows the presentation of cash items shown in order of liquidity, with actual cash items listed before cash equivalents. Specifically, petty cash and cash equivalents are shown as separate line items.

Controls in Business

While this chapter looks in depth at cash controls, there are many control aspects that pertain to businesses which are not related to cash. Consider the controls in your personal life. You have a lock on the doors and windows to your house or apartment. You have a PIN on your bank card or credit card. You have access to a bank statement which allows you to monitor all the deposits and withdrawals from your bank account. The lock, PIN and bank statement are all considered controls. Why do you have controls? Although you might believe that most people are honest and trustworthy, you want to protect the things you own and make sure that all payments and transactions are authorized. Businesses also implement controls to protect what they have.

Definition of Controls

Controls are procedures and methods used to protect assets, monitor cash payments, ensure transactions are authorized and generally make sure the accounting records are accurate. These procedures can include cash controls, budgetary controls, credit controls, working procedures, inventory controls, production processes, hiring policies and quality measures.

The purpose of internal controls is to provide reasonable assurance regarding the

*   effectiveness and efficiency of operations
*   reliability of financial reporting
*   compliance with applicable laws and regulations

Internal controls are designed to

*   align objectives of the business
*   safeguard assets
*   prevent and detect fraud and error
*   encourage good management
*   allow action to be taken
*   reduce exposure to risks
*   ensure proper financial reporting
*   ensure accuracy and validity

Implementing Controls

Under an adequate system of internal controls, each business transaction is complete, accurate, authorized, real (i.e. it exists), and valid. In addition, when internal controls are present, errors in the system are automatically identified and corrected, duties are segregated and financial reports are timely.

Generally, internal controls can be classified as preventive (i.e. to stop an incident before it happens), or detective (i.e. to discover an incident after it happens). Obviously, it is better to prevent incidents than to discover them after they occur.

Consider the following situation. Michael purchased a family restaurant, which he managed himself. He bought supplies, paid bills, opened and closed the restaurant himself each day. He was doing so well that he decided to buy another location in another suburb of the city. He promoted an employee, who had worked with him for the past three years, to manage the old location while he focused on setting up the new location.

Michael disliked anything to do with accounting. He operated a simple hands-on business and his bookkeeper updated the books each month to ensure that sales taxes were paid and payroll was disbursed on time. Other than these two functions, the bookkeeper relied on the accountant to complete the financial statements at the end of each year and complete Michael's annual tax return.

Michael's business was performing well, so Michael and his wife decided to take a vacation. Not long after they returned, Michael received a call from one of his suppliers to say that a payment he had issued a few days before was returned by the bank because of insufficient funds in Michael's account. Michael was not only frustrated but also extremely embarrassed. He had to transfer money from his personal savings account to cover the shortfall and immediately started looking into what happened.

Since Michael knew very little about accounting, he contacted his accountant to investigate. An entire year had passed since the accountant had worked with Michael's financial statements, so the investigation was no easy task. The following issues were discovered.

1. Cash was only being deposited every few days, rather than daily and the cash receipts did not match the cash register.

2. Payroll was considerably higher, relative to sales, than it had been in previous years. It appears that the manager was paying ghost employees—he was making payments to contract staff that did not actually exist.

3. His trusted manager was stealing food supplies and selling them for cash. This increased the food costs and decreased profits.

4. Some of the servers were "sweet-hearting" customers—meaning that friends were being served with free meals or extras at no charge.

As a result of a lack of controls, poor bookkeeper oversight and fraudulent behaviour, Michael nearly went bankrupt. He hired a new manager, and with the help of his accountant he implemented the following controls to prevent this from happening again.

1. The new manager does not handle any sales and deposits the cash every day. Any discrepancies between the cash receipts and the register are investigated by the manager immediately.

2. The new manager is responsible for scheduling and keeping payroll costs to a certain percentage of sales.

3. The head chef at the restaurant counts food supplies at the beginning of each day and is responsible for ordering replacement food. The manager compares the daily inventory counts to the inventory used in the daily sales to ensure there are no anomalies.

4. A hiring package was created to collect personal information on new employees (such as name, address, SIN, bank account number). Michael had to approve all new hires and payroll was deposited directly into employees' bank accounts.

5. A computerized system is now used to record sales. All servers have their own pass code to record sales. Discounts or free meals must be approved by the manager entering a special code to allow the discount or free meal.

6. Overall, the bookkeeper still updates the books every month, but also prepares financial statements on a monthly basis for Michael to examine.

As this example shows, there are many types of controls that apply to businesses. When controls are not in place, organizations are vulnerable to activities that will be detrimental to continuing operations. The example above shows a case of theft and **fraud**. Fraud is defined as any illegal intentional act of deception that results in a financial benefit or gain. It may not always be easy to identify because the intention is to hide the fraudulent act within normal business activities.

IN THE REAL WORLD

Lack of proper controls and shady accounting led to the bankruptcy of Enron in 2001. Enron was a large energy company that earned about $100 billion in revenue in the year before it went bankrupt. As a result of the bankruptcy and discovery of misleading accounting practices, the United States introduces the Sarbanes-Oxley Act (SOX) in 2002.

SOX affects all public U.S. corporations by setting higher standards for reporting and ensuring that controls are in place to properly report all aspects of the financial statements. Canadian companies that are traded on a U.S. stock market must also comply with SOX.

In 2003, Canada introduced Bill 198, which applied stricter controls to Canadian public corporations. Management is now required to test internal controls over financial reporting and the chief executive officer (CEO) of the corporation must personally vouch for the accuracy of the financial statements.

In Summary

Apply cash controls

↪ Cash must be recorded immediately when it is received so it can be tracked from receipt to deposit in the business bank account.

↪ Cash should be stored in a secure place until it can be deposited to the business bank account.

↪ Regular bank deposits should be made to ensure a minimal amount of cash is kept on site.

Prepare journal entries for cash rounding, debit and credit transactions

↪ All sales should be recorded at the actual amounts calculated and not rounded.

↪ An account to track the cash over and short should be used. This includes any rounded, over and short amounts.

↪ Many businesses will allow customers to pay using debit or credit cards. A sale paid for by credit card or debit card will result in a small transaction fee the business must pay to the bank or processing company.

Prepare a bank reconciliation and related journal entries

↪ A bank reconciliation compares the bank statement to the cash ledger account to ensure no errors have been made.

↪ Amounts added or deducted by the bank which do not appear in the ledger must be added or deducted from the cash ledger balance. These amounts must also be recorded in the journal to update the cash ledger account.

↪ Amounts added or deducted by the business which do not appear in the bank statement must be added or deducted from the bank balance.

Prepare a petty cash fund and record related journal entries

↪ A petty cash fund is used to pay for small, incidental expenses. A cheque is cashed and the money is kept by a petty cashier in a secure location.

↪ As cash is spent, receipts are placed in the petty cash box to explain why the cash was spent.

↪ A comparison of remaining cash and the total receipts may indicate a cash overage or shortage. The receipts and any over or short is recorded in a journal entry.

Apply general business controls

↪ Controls are procedures and methods used to protect assets, monitor cash payments, ensure transactions are authorized and generally make sure the accounting records are accurate.

↪ Generally, internal controls can be classified as preventive (i.e. to stop an incident before it happens), or detective (i.e. to discover an incident after it happens).

Review Exercise 1

JP has been running his dry cleaning business, called Clean 4U, since he purchased it last year. It is a small business with eight employees. He has run into some difficulty with his business. His cash flow has declined every month, but he is as busy as last year.

Every single order has its own multiple-part receipt: the office gets a copy, the cash drawer gets a copy, and the customer gets a copy when they pay. The customer gets a ticket stub as part of the receipt based on their first and last name only. The garments get tagged and matched to the receipt to get processed and returned to the receipt.

The company has only a cash drawer to accept cash payments. The drawer does not lock, and the cash cannot be locked away when the business is closed. Cash is deposited when large quantities of cash are on hand. The company uses a manual point-of-sale (POS) terminal to accept debit and credit payments and the counter clerk must enter the dollar amount before the customer can complete the transaction.

Recently, JP discovered a small pile of cash-drawer receipts in the garbage while he was cleaning the storefront. He knows that many of the customers are regulars and always pay cash. The counter clerk has been committing fraud and has been stealing cash.

What recommendations should be made with respect to cash controls for a company this size? What is the overall goal for cash controls? What recommendations should be made for Clean 4U in general?

See Appendix I for solutions.

_____

_____

_____

_____

_____

_____

_____

_____

_____

Review Exercise 2

The following is the general ledger and bank statement for Martin Furniture.

GENERAL LEDGER

Account: Cash				GL. No.	101
Date	**Description**	**DR**	**CR**	**Balance**	
Jun 1	*Opening Balance*			3,100.50	DR
Jun 6	Chicago Hardware Traders Inc.		900.50	2,200.00	DR
Jun 9	Reo's Interiors Inc.	1,925.00		4,125.00	DR
Jun 10	Air-conditioning Repair & Co.		1,600.00	2,525.00	DR
Jun 16	Alex Santiago Payroll		400.00	2,125.00	DR
Jun 16	Martin Furnishings Inc.	2,000.00		4,125.00	DR
Jun 19	Line-wire Electric		110.00	4,015.00	DR
Jun 19	Rice Inc.		500.00	3,515.00	DR
Jun 28	Eric Draven Enterprises	1,300.00		4,815.00	DR
Jun 30	*Closing Balance*			4,815.00	DR

Reserve Bank
146 Lineage Avenue, Ottawa

Martin Furniture
234 Lakeview Drive
Ottawa, Ontario

Date	Explanation	Withdrawal	Deposit	Balance
Jun 1	Balance Forward			3,100.50
Jun 8	Cheque #541	900.50		2,200.00
Jun 9	Deposit		1,925.00	4,125.00
Jun 10	Cheque #543	1,600.00		2,525.00
Jun 16	Deposit		2,000.00	4,525.00
Jun 16	Cheque #542	400.00		4,125.00
Jun 18	NSF Cheque #256	2,000.00		2,125.00
Jun 18	NSF Charge	6.00		2,119.00
Jun 21	Cheque #544	110.00		2,009.00
Jun 27	Interest on Bank Account		5.00	2,014.00
Jun 29	Service Charge	14.00		2,000.00
Jun 30	Ending Balance			2,000.00

Required

Reconcile the ledger and bank statement and record the relevant transactions on the general journal.

See Appendix I for solutions.

Martin Furniture Bank Reconciliation June 30, 2016		
Explanation	**Ledger**	**Bank**

JOURNAL			Page 1
Date	**Account Titles and Explanation**	**Debit**	**Credit**

————————————— **Review Exercise 3** —————————————

On April 1, 2016 Clayton Company established a petty cash fund of $200.

During the month, the custodian placed the following receipts in the petty cash box.

Apr 6   Paid $40 for postage.
Apr 8   Paid $20 to FedEx for delivery of a package
Apr 10   Paid $25 for travel expenses of employees on company business.
Apr 14   Paid $8 for coffee and donuts for a client meeting.
Apr 15   Paid $7 for paper for the photocopier.

The custodian counted the fund on April 16 and found $95 in the petty cash box.

Required

a) Prepare the journal entry to record the establishment of the fund.
b) Prepare the journal entry to record the reimbursement of the fund on April 16.

See Appendix I for solutions.

a)

JOURNAL			Page 1
Date	Account Titles and Explanation	Debit	Credit

b)

JOURNAL			Page 1
Date	Account Titles and Explanation	Debit	Credit

Notes

Chapter 11
PAYROLL

LEARNING OUTCOMES

❶ Describe payroll accounting

❷ Calculate gross pay and net pay

❸ Describe payroll liabilities, employer's contributions and payroll payments

❹ Record payroll liabilities, employer's contributions and payroll payments

❺ Prepare payroll registers

❻ Describe payroll controls

Appendix

❼ Calculate statutory deductions

AMEENGAGE™ *Access **ameengage.com** for integrated resources including tutorials, practice exercises, the digital textbook and more.*

Payroll Accounting

Payroll is one of the most important business obligations of any organization. Employees expect to be treated fairly and to receive a timely and accurate paycheque. Employers are required to follow all employment laws relating to payroll.

There is a lot of legislation surrounding how employees are treated and how they are paid. The federal government and each province has a set of employment standards that apply to businesses that operate in their jurisdiction. Employment standards include minimum guidelines for items such as pay rate, vacation time allowed, and how much time must be given or paid out to terminate the employment. These standards outline the minimum requirements however, employers are allowed to offer more (e.g. pay more than minimum wage or give employees more vacation time).

Payroll accounting involves three types of payroll liabilities: 1) the net pay owed to an employee, 2) amounts deducted from employee paycheques and owed to others, and 3) employer payroll expense. Any business that hires people to work on its behalf will incur these liabilities and related expenses.

What an employee earns and what an employee actually takes home on their paycheque are often two different amounts. What an employee earns is called **gross pay**. The amount actually received is called **net pay** and is less than the gross pay amount because several items are deducted. Deductions can include

* Canada Pension Plan
* Employment Insurance
* Federal and Provincial Income Taxes
* Other voluntary deductions

Before discussing how to calculate gross pay and how to determine which deductions must be subtracted from gross pay, it is important to determine the pay frequency when dealing with payroll. The amount of gross pay and deductions on each paycheque are affected by the pay period (pay frequency). Pay period refers to the number of times an employee is paid during one year. The table below shows how many pay periods there are in a year for the most common pay frequencies.

Pay Frequency	Number of Pay Periods in a Year
Weekly	52
Bi-weekly	26
Semi-monthly	24
Monthly	12

FIGURE 11.1

Gross Pay

When an employee is paid, employers generally pay either with a salary or an hourly rate. A salary is a set annual amount that is then divided by the number of pay periods to determine the gross pay for each period. A sales manager who is paid $52,000 per year would earn $1,000 per week. If he was paid on a bi-weekly basis, his gross pay would be $2,000 for each pay period.

An hourly rate is a set dollar amount for each hour worked and is multiplied by the hours worked in a period to determine the gross pay for the period. If a factory worker is paid $17.00 per hour and he works for 65 hours in a two-week period, his gross pay would be $1,105 (65 hours x $17.00 per hour = $1,105).

In addition to regular pay, employers must also pay for statutory holidays and overtime. Overtime pay is owed for any hours worked beyond a certain number of hours per period. Employment standards in each jurisdiction specify what is considered overtime and how much should be paid for each overtime hour. In many cases, overtime hours are paid at 1.5 times the regular hourly rate. Suppose a person works 48 hours in a week, and any hours over 40 must be paid at 1.5 times the regular hourly rate. Assuming the hourly rate is $15 per hour, the overtime rate would be $22.50 per hour ($15 x 1.5). Gross pay would be calculated as shown below.

Regular pay	40 hours × $15/hour =	$600
Overtime pay	8 hours × ($15 x 1.5) =	$180
Gross pay		$780

Employees are also generally paid their regular wages for statutory holidays (such as Christmas day), even though they do not work on those days. If an employee does work on a statutory holiday, they are typically paid their regular wages for the statutory holiday, plus 1.5 times their regular hourly rate for the hours they actually work. Again, this may vary slightly in different jurisdictions.

Vacation pay is also an amount that must be paid to employees. Generally, employers must provide two weeks or 4% of the employee's gross pay as vacation amounts. This can vary from jurisdiction to jurisdiction. The business can accumulate the vacation pay each time payroll is processed, and then pay it out when the employee takes vacation. In this situation, the employee will always receive a paycheque, even when on vacation.

Alternatively, the business can pay the extra vacation amount on every paycheque. In this case, the employee receives a slightly higher pay on every paycheque, but will not be paid any amount when they take vacation. For example, suppose an employee has a gross pay of $780 on their paycheque and assume vacation pay will be paid out at 4%. The employee will receive an extra $31.20 ($780 x 4%) on their paycheque, increasing their gross amount to $811.20 ($780 + $31.20).

The gross pay shown on a pay stub is not the amount that is deposited into an employee's bank account. Gross pay is reduced by statutory and voluntary deductions, leaving a net pay amount. The amounts that are subtracted from a paycheque are referred to as payroll deductions.

Employee Payroll Deductions

Statutory Deductions

Every business is required to subtract (withhold) amounts from an employee's gross pay. Statutory deductions are paid to the appropriate tax authority in the country. In most of Canada, the sole payroll tax authority is the Canada Revenue Agency (CRA). In Quebec, businesses must work with Revenu Quebec (RQ) in addition to the CRA. Statutory deductions in Canada are

- Canada Pension Plan (CPP) or Quebec Pension Plan (QPP) in Quebec
- Employment Insurance (EI)
- Quebec Parental Insurance Plan (QPIP) in Quebec only
- Federal and Provincial income tax

Each of the above statutory deductions is calculated using software or tax tables, which are updated annually. The calculated amounts are then subtracted/withheld from an employee's gross pay. The business is responsible for keeping track of payroll and the associated deductions and must send the amounts deducted to the appropriate tax authority (CRA or Revenu Quebec). For the purposes of this chapter, we will focus on a business that is not located in the province of Quebec. Most of what is discussed regarding CPP, EI and income taxes will apply to businesses operating in Quebec.

The amounts withheld are required under law and failure to withhold the amounts from the employee's pay and remit them to the tax authorities can result in severe penalties.

At the end of the year, the employer provides all its employees with a tax slip indicating their gross pay and all the statutory deductions for the year. This is called a T4 slip. This slip is used by employees to prepare their tax returns to the government. Any difference between the amount already submitted to the government and the amount actually owed results in the employee either getting a refund (they paid too much over the year) or paying extra (they did not pay enough over the year). The system is designed this way to reduce the financial burden on individuals who, if they did not pay tax on every paycheque during the year, would otherwise have to pay huge amounts when they file their tax returns every year.

As a business withholds and remits these statutory deduction amounts to the tax authorities, it assists in paying for government services provided all year. Examples of these services include education, medical care, public safety, roads and bridges. Regardless of the level of government that provides these services, the majority of the funding comes throughout the year from tax remittances.

Canada Pension Plan (CPP)

Every business that is not located in the province of Quebec is required to withhold CPP from an employee's gross pay. The business is also required to pay an amount equal to 100% of the amount withheld from the employee's pay. For example, if the employee were to have $50 deducted from her gross pay for CPP, the business would have to pay an additional $50 toward CPP on her behalf.

Most employees must have CPP deducted from their pay. There are a few exceptions; anyone under the age of 18, over the age of 70, or who is collecting a pension from CPP will not have any amounts deducted from their gross pay for CPP.

Businesses will only withhold CPP from an employee's pay until the employee has reached the specified maximum earnings each year. For 2015, this maximum is $53,600. As an example, this means that an employee who earns $55,000 in 2015 will have CPP deducted from his pay for every pay period starting in January until his gross pay for the year reaches $53,600. Any gross pay received after that will not have any CPP deducted from it. A detailed look at the calculation of CPP is illustrated in the chapter 11 appendix.

Employment Insurance (EI)

Every business is required to withhold EI from an employee's gross pay. The business is also required to pay an amount equal to 140% of the amount withheld from the employee's pay. For example, if the employee were to have $50 deducted from her gross pay for EI, the business would have to pay an additional $70 ($50 x 140%) towards EI on her behalf.

Unlike CPP, there is no age limit restricting employees from paying EI. Thus, anyone who is working and receiving a paycheque will have EI deducted from their gross pay.

Businesses will only withhold EI from an employee's pay until the employee has reached the specified maximum earnings each year. For 2015, this maximum is $49,500. This means that an employee who earns $55,000 in 2015 will have EI deducted from his pay for every pay period starting in January until his gross pay for the year reaches $49,500. Any gross pay received after that will not have any EI deducted from it. A detailed look at the calculation of EI is illustrated in the chapter 11 appendix.

Income Taxes

Every business is required to withhold income tax from an employee's gross pay. There is no age limit for paying taxes and there is no maximum on the total earnings for which taxes must be paid. The more an employee earns, the more tax will be deducted from their pay. The business does not have to make any extra payments regarding the income tax withheld from an employee's pay.

Income tax is deducted in two parts: there is the federal income tax and the provincial income tax component. In Quebec, the federal income tax portion is sent to the CRA and the provincial income tax portion is sent to Revenu Quebec. In the rest of the country, businesses must send both federal and provincial income taxes to the CRA.

The calculation of CPP, EI and income taxes is usually done automatically by accounting software. For a business that does not use accounting software, the CRA provides payroll deduction tables based on gross pay and the pay period frequency. There is also the Payroll Deductions Online Calculator which will calculate all statutory deductions to provide a net pay. More details on calculating income tax are in the chapter 11 appendix.

Voluntary Deductions

A voluntary deduction is a deduction that is not a requirement from the government. This could include items such as union dues, health plan contributions, charitable donations or saving plans. Some, such as charitable donations and savings plans, are usually plans set up by the employer in which the employee has an option to participate. Employees must sign up for these plans; they cannot be taken from an employee's paycheque without permission.

Other deductions, such as union dues or health plans, may be required as part of the employment agreement. Thus, once an employee starts working for the business, these deductions will be taken automatically. By agreeing to work for the business, the employee is agreeing to these deductions.

Employer Payroll Contributions

As already mentioned, both CPP and EI require the employer to pay an additional amount to these programs on behalf of their employees. These employer portions are expenses which are the sole responsibility of the employer. The employer is not allowed to deduct these extra amounts from the employee's pay.

In addition to the CPP and EI contributions, employers must usually contribute to their provincial workers' compensation board. These are private programs that fund income replacement, rehabilitation and re-training for employees injured on the job. The amount paid for workers compensation for each employee depends on the risk of injury in the industry and the company's own safety record. Like the employer portions of CPP and EI, the employer is responsible for these payments and cannot deduct these amounts from the employee's pay. Also, since workers' compensation is a required deduction, failure to make these payments can result in penalties and interest. For the examples in the textbook, we will assume a percentage of gross pay must be paid to the workers' compensation board. More details on calculating workers' compensation is in the chapter 11 appendix.

Employers may also voluntarily contribute towards other plans on behalf of the employee. For example, an employer may provide health benefits or savings plans for their employees. An employer may decide to pay for all of the health benefits, or split the payment with the employees through a voluntary deduction. Or, an employer may make a contribution to an employee's savings if the employee decides to sign up for the savings plan voluntary deduction.

Payroll Example

Let us examine how a basic payroll journal entry would be calculated and recorded. Assume Glen Booth is a salaried employee who earns $54,000 per year and is paid on a monthly basis. This means his monthly gross pay is $4,500 ($54,000 ÷ 12 months).

We will assume the following deductions are taken from his paycheque.

*   Canada Pension Plan deduction is $208.31.
*   Employment Insurance is $84.60.
*   Federal and Provincial income tax is $802.90.
*   He is a member of a union and has $50 deducted per month for his union dues.
*   His employer provides a health insurance plan which costs $30 per month, however the employer pays for half of this amount.

The calculation of Glen's net pay is shown in Figure 11.2.

Gross Pay		$4,500.00
Deductions		
CPP	$208.31	
EI	84.60	
Income taxes	802.90	
Union dues	50.00	
Heath insurance (only half)	15.00	
Total deduction		1,160.81
Net pay		$3,339.19

FIGURE 11.2

For all of the journal entries in this chapter, we will illustrate the impact on the liability accounts using T-accounts. On January 31, 2015, the journal entry to record payroll expense and deductions is shown in Figure 11.3.

For this example, we should consider categorizing based on three levels.

1. the net pay owed to an employee
2. amounts deducted from employee paycheques and owed to others
3. employer payroll expense

JOURNAL			Page 1
Date 2015	Account Title and Explanation	Debit	Credit
Jan 31	Salaries Expense	4,500.00	
	CPP Payable		208.31
	EI Payable		84.60
	Income Tax Payable		802.90
	Union Dues Payable		50.00
	Health Insurance Payable		15.00
	Salaries Payable		3,339.19
	To record employee payroll		

- CPP PAYABLE +	- EI PAYABLE +
208.31	84.60

- INCOME TAXES PAYABLE +	- UNION DUES PAYABLE +
802.90	50.00

- HEALTH INSURANCE PAYABLE +	- SALARIES PAYABLE +
15.00	3,339.19

FIGURE 11.3

The transaction shows the salaries expense broken down into various liability amounts. All the deductions will be recorded in liability accounts until it is time to send these amounts to the institutions to which they are owed. In a perfect world with no liabilities, all the amounts withheld from the employee's paycheque would immediately be paid to the CRA and others with cash. In reality, there is usually a difference in timing from withholding the deductions to actually sending them to the CRA and others. Businesses act as an intermediary taking the money from the employee and sending it to the institutions at a later date. The business effectively has a debt (liability) for a short period of time until it sends the money where it is supposed to go.

The net pay may be recorded as a liability (salaries payable) if the actual cash payment will happen a few days later. If however the employee is paid immediately, cash would be credited for the net pay amount instead of salaries payable.

Vacation pay must also be accounted for. We will assume the business must pay 4% of the gross pay as vacation pay and the business accrues the vacation pay for its employees. This means $180 ($4,500 x 4%) will be accrued for Glen Booth. The journal entry for this accrual is shown in Figure 11.4.

JOURNAL			Page 1
Date 2015	Account Title and Explanation	Debit	Credit
Jan 31	Vacation Pay Expense	180	
	Vacation Pay Payable		180
	To accrue vacation pay		

- VACATION PAY PAYABLE +
180

FIGURE 11.4

The amount recorded as vacation pay will accrue over time. The amount in the liability account will grow until the employee takes time off. At that point, the vacation pay liability will decrease as the amount is paid to the employee during his time off. When the vacation pay is paid out, statutory deductions and any other deductions must be withheld.

The last portion of a payroll journal entry is to record the employer's portion of the statutory deductions, plus any other contributions it makes for its employees. In this example, the employer will pay the following

*   match the employees' CPP deduction of $208.31
*   pay 1.4 times the amount of the employees' EI deduction of $118.44
*   the health insurance plan costs $30 per month, however the employer pays for half of it
*   workers' compensation is assumed to be 0.5% of gross pay

On January 31, 2015, the journal entry to record the employer contributions is shown in Figure 11.5.

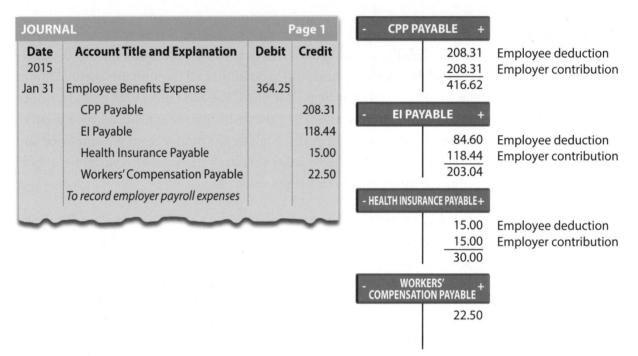

FIGURE 11.5

The employer portions (CPP, EI and the health insurance plan) are added to the existing liability accounts. These liability accounts already have the employee portions recorded in them from Figure 11.3. Workers' compensation is solely the responsibility of the employer. A single expense account called employee benefits expense is used to record the extra employer expenses. Some companies prefer to have separate expense accounts for each of the employer contributions; however, we will only use one expense account in this textbook.

An important point is that the $4,500 of gross payroll actually incurred expenses of $5,044.25 (gross pay, vacation pay and employee benefits expenses). This means that in our example, for every $1 of gross payroll, the actual cost to the business is approximately $1.12. Payroll can be much more expensive to a business than the amount received by employees, depending on the types and amounts of benefits that the business pays.

At this point, payroll for the employee is complete. It is now time for the employer to pay the payroll liabilities that have been created.

Paying the Payroll Liabilities

Amounts deducted from payroll are owed to the government and other institutions. After recording the journal entries for the employee payroll and the employer contributions, the employer has a number of liability accounts that must be paid.

First, the employer must actually pay the employee. Initially the net pay was recorded in salaries payable because the actual pay is going to be paid on a different day. Thus, to pay the employee, decrease cash and decrease the liability, shown in Figure 11.6. Remember, if the employee was paid on the same day as the payroll entry, cash would have been credited in Figure 11.3 instead of salaries payable and this entry on February 1 would not be needed.

JOURNAL			Page 1
Date 2015	**Account Title and Explanation**	**Debit**	**Credit**
Feb 1	Salaries Payable	3,339.19	
	Cash		3,339.19
	To pay employee		

- SALARIES PAYABLE +	
Feb 1 3,339.19	3,339.19 Jan 31

FIGURE 11.6

Next, because our example is not in the province of Quebec, all the statutory deductions must be sent to the CRA. This is called a payroll remittance. This remittance includes the employee and employer portion of CPP,

> **A CLOSER LOOK**
> In Quebec, QPP, QPIP and provincial income tax are sent to Revenu Quebec and the EI and federal income tax is sent to the CRA.

the employee and employer portion of EI and the income tax. The business will have a schedule to follow to make the remittance to the CRA. Most moderate-sized businesses must send the amount by the 15th of the following month. If the employer fails to make the remittance on time, it will pay penalties and interest on the amount owing.

Since the payroll in our example is for January, the remittance must be made by February 15, 2015. The journal entry to make the payment is shown in Figure 11.7. All the liability accounts are debited by their balance to clear them, and the total amount is cash sent to the CRA.

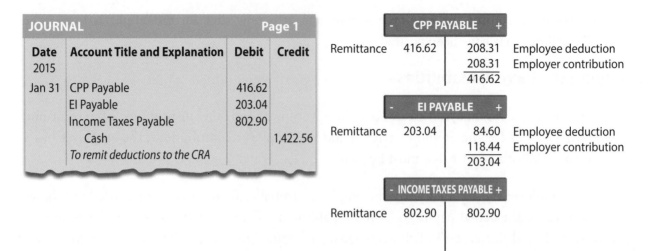

JOURNAL		Page 1	
Date 2015	**Account Title and Explanation**	**Debit**	**Credit**
Jan 31	CPP Payable	416.62	
	EI Payable	203.04	
	Income Taxes Payable	802.90	
	Cash		1,422.56
	To remit deductions to the CRA		

CPP PAYABLE

	-	+	
Remittance	416.62	208.31	Employee deduction
		208.31	Employer contribution
		416.62	

EI PAYABLE

	-	+	
Remittance	203.04	84.60	Employee deduction
		118.44	Employer contribution
		203.04	

INCOME TAXES PAYABLE

	-	+
Remittance	802.90	802.90

FIGURE 11.7

Lastly, any amount owing to other institutions must be paid. The institution will have a schedule for when payments must be sent in. In our example, the employer has a liability to pay union dues, health insurance premiums and workers' compensation premiums. Each of these liabilities will be cleared out and payment will be sent to the union, the health insurance company and the workers' compensation board. These transactions are shown in Figure 11.8.

JOURNAL		Page 1	
Date 2015	**Account Title and Explanation**	**Debit**	**Credit**
Feb 28	Health Insurance Payable	30	
	Cash		30
	To pay health insurance premiums		

HEALTH INSURANCE PAYABLE

	-	+
Remittance	30.00	15.00
		15.00
		30.00

JOURNAL		Page 1	
Date 2015	**Account Title and Explanation**	**Debit**	**Credit**
Feb 28	Union Dues Payable	50	
	Cash		50
	To pay union dues		

UNION DUES PAYABLE

	-	+
Remittance	50.00	50.00

JOURNAL		Page 1	
Date 2015	**Account Title and Explanation**	**Debit**	**Credit**
Feb 28	Workers' Compensation Payable	22.50	
	Cash		22.50
	To pay workers' compensation		

WORKERS' COMPENSATION PAYABLE

	-	+
Remittance	22.50	22.50

FIGURE 11.8

Payroll Register

Since businesses usually have multiple employees, a payroll register is often used rather than preparing individual entries. A payroll register will list every employee along with their gross pay, deductions and net pay. The bottom of the payroll register will calculate totals that can be used to complete the journal entries. Computer software will have a similar tool for creating paycheques for multiple employees at one time.

Figure 11.9 shows a sample payroll register. The first person listed is our example of earning $4,500 gross pay per month as a salary. The rest of the employees are paid various hourly wages and work a different number of hours. We will assume all employees must pay monthly union dues of $50 and monthly health insurance of $15. The monthly health insurance premiums are actually $30 per person, but the business pays half. By completing the rest of the payroll information for all the employees, we can use the totals to create our journal entries.

PAYROLL PERIOD JANUARY 1 TO JANUARY 31, 2015

Name	Hourly Wage	Hours	Gross Earnings
Booth, Glen		160	4,500.00
Dickens, Charlie	$18.00	170	3,060.00
Smith, Adam	$18.56	160	2,969.60
Wood, Amy	$19.23	175	3,365.25
Totals			$13,894.85

PAYROLL REGISTER

Gross Earnings	Deductions					Total Deductions	Net Pay
	CPP	EI	Income Tax	Union Dues	Health Insurance		
4,500.00	208.31	84.60	802.90	50.00	15.00	1,160.81	$3,339.19
3,060.00	137.03	57.53	403.25	50.00	15.00	662.81	$2,397.19
2,969.60	132.56	55.83	387.55	50.00	15.00	640.94	$2,328.66
3,365.25	152.14	63.27	469.90	50.00	15.00	750.31	$2,614.94
$13,894.85	$630.04	$261.23	$2,063.60	$200.00	$60.00	$3,214.81	$10,679.98

FIGURE 11.9

The journal entry to be prepared from the payroll register is shown in Figure 11.10.

JOURNAL			Page 1
Date 2015	Account Title and Explanation	Debit	Credit
Jan 31	Salaries Expense	13,894.85	
	CPP Payable		630.04
	EI Payable		261.23
	Income Taxes Payable		2,063.60
	Union Dues Payable		200.00
	Health Insurance Payable		60.00
	Salaries Payable		10,679.98
	To record employee payroll		

− CPP PAYABLE +	− EI PAYABLE +
630.04	261.23

− INCOME TAXES PAYABLE +	− UNION DUES PAYABLE +
2,063.60	200

− HEALTH INSURANCE PAYABLE +	− SALARIES PAYABLE +
60	10,679.98

FIGURE 11.10

Vacation pay is accrued on the total gross pay for all the employees at 4%. The journal entry is shown in Figure 11.11.

JOURNAL			Page 1
Date 2015	Account Title and Explanation	Debit	Credit
Jan 31	Vacation Pay Expense	555.79	
	Vacation Pay Payable		555.79
	To accrue vacation pay		

− VACATION PAY PAYABLE +
555.79

FIGURE 11.11

The business also must pay its own payroll contributions relating to the employees. Recall that the business will match 100% of the CPP deductions and pay 140% of the EI deductions. The business also pays $15 per employee for health insurance and must pay 0.5% of gross pay for workers' compensation.

JOURNAL			Page 1
Date 2015	**Account Title and Explanation**	**Debit**	**Credit**
Jan 31	Employee Benefits Expense	1,125.23	
	CPP Payable		630.04
	EI Payable		365.72
	Health Insurance Payable		60.00
	Workers' Compensation Payable		69.47
	To record employer payroll expenses		

– CPP PAYABLE +

630.04	Employee deduction
630.04	Employer contribution
1260.08	

– EI PAYABLE +

261.23	Employee deduction
365.72	Employer contribution
626.95	

– HEALTH INSURANCE PAYABLE +

60.00	Employee deduction
60.00	Employer contribution
120.00	

– WORKERS' COMPENSATION PAYABLE +

69.47	

FIGURE 11.12

Payroll Records

The business must keep a record of gross pay, deductions, hours worked, and a variety of other information about every employee. This information is collected at the time the employee is hired and updated every pay or when some other important piece of information relating to payroll changes. A computerized system will update the payroll record automatically after every pay.

Booth, Glen 5234 North Street Sudbury, ON T5R 4R9	Phone: 705-555-5672 Date of Birth: February 16, 1977 SIN: 123 456 789	Employee No.: 35025 Date of Hire: June 20, 2008
Claim Code: 1	**Pay Rate: $4,500 per month**	**Date Employment Terminated:**

Month Ended	Hours	Earnings	Deductions					Total Deductions	Net Pay
			CPP	EI	Income Taxes	Union Dues	Health Insurance		
Jan 31, 2015	160	4,500.00	208.31	84.60	802.90	50.00	15.00	1,160.81	$3,339.19
Feb 28, 2015	160	4,500.00	208.31	84.60	802.90	50.00	15.00	1,160.81	$3,339.19
Mar 31, 2015	160	4,500.00	208.31	84.60	802.90	50.00	15.00	1,160.81	$3,339.19
Apr 30, 2015	160	4,500.00	208.31	84.60	802.90	50.00	15.00	1,160.81	$3,339.19
May 31, 2015	160	4,500.00	208.31	84.60	802.90	50.00	15.00	1,160.81	$3,339.19

FIGURE 11.13

The records for every employee will be used to create a year-end tax form called a T4. The T4 will report total gross earnings by the employee, and total CPP, EI and income tax deducted. These tax forms must be sent to the employees and the government by the last day of February of the following year.

Payroll records will also be used when an employee terminates their employment or has their employment terminated by their employer. Once an employee is no longer employed, the business must issue a Record of Employment (ROE) within five days. The ROE will show earnings and hours that the employee has worked over a specified period.

Payroll Controls

The payroll system must be carefully monitored to prevent abuse. There must be rules established by the business to ensure that an employee actually exists and is getting paid properly.

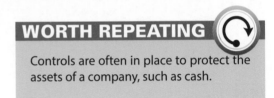

WORTH REPEATING

Controls are often in place to protect the assets of a company, such as cash.

- Ensure the person hiring employees is not the same person paying employees. An employee start package should be created to collect important information about the employee, including the employee's social insurance number (SIN). This package should be passed to the person who prepares payroll cheques. If the person hiring employees also pays them, it is possible to create a phantom employee and collect the phantom's paycheque.
- Monitor the hours worked by employees. Management should be responsible for ensuring that employees work the hours they claim they work. A time clock with punch cards or electronic swipe cards can track exactly how much time employees work. It would be a good idea for managers to physically see the individuals checking in and out to ensure that they are actually starting work after checking in and that one person is not checking in many people.
- There should be proper authorization for pay increases or employee termination.
- If manual cheques are being created, the person creating the cheques should not be the same person who signs the cheques.
- An **imprest bank account** could be set up for payroll. This is a separate bank account from the main bank account of the business. All payroll cheques are cashed against the imprest account, and only enough cash is available in the imprest account to cover the payroll cheques. This will make reconciliation easier and help prevent theft through payroll.

*Access **ameengage.com** for integrated resources including tutorials, practice exercises, the digital textbook and more.*

In Summary

Describe payroll accounting

⇨ Employment standards include minimum guidelines for items such as pay rate, vacation time allowed, and how much time must be given or paid out to terminate the employment.

Calculate gross pay and net pay

⇨ Gross pay is the amount earned by the employee and can be calculated as a salary amount or an hourly amount.

⇨ Deductions are subtracted from the gross pay, which leaves the net pay that the employee actually receives in cash. Net Pay = Gross Pay – Deductions

Describe payroll liabilities, employer's contributions and payroll payments

⇨ Statutory payroll liabilities include the Canada Pension Plan (CPP), Employment Insurance (EI) and income taxes. In Quebec, employers have the Quebec Pension Plan (QPP) instead of the CPP, plus an additional deduction for the Quebec Parental Insurance Plan (QPIP).

⇨ Voluntary deductions can include items such as union dues, health plans, savings plan and charitable donations.

Record payroll liabilities, employer's contributions and payroll payments

⇨ A payroll journal entry includes a debit to increase salaries expense by the gross pay amount. All deductions are recorded as credits to liability accounts to increase the amounts owed.

⇨ The employer must match the employee's deduction for CPP and pay 140% of employees' EI deductions. These are required by the government.

⇨ Employers may also pay for other benefits for the employee, such as all or some of a health plan.

⇨ Payments of payroll deductions to the government must be made on a regular schedule. This includes the employee and employer portions of CPP and EI, as well as the income tax deducted from the employees pay.

⇨ Payments to other institutions, such as unions or insurance companies, must also be made on a regular schedule.

Prepare payroll registers

⇨ A payroll register is used to record gross pay, deductions and net pay when a business has more than one employee. The totals from the register are used to create the payroll entries.

⇨ The business must keep records of gross pay, deductions, hours worked, and a variety of other information about every employee.

⇨ The information is used for hiring, creating tax forms and employment termination.

Describe payroll controls

⇨ Payroll controls can protect the company's payroll from theft. Controls can include start packages, tracking hours worked, authorization for pay increase and terminations or an imprest bank account.

Review Exercise

Michelle's Crafts has three employees. They get paid bi-weekly (every two weeks). The following table lists the employees, the hours they worked over the last two weeks and their pay rate.

Name	Hourly Wage	Hours
Flower, Blossom	$14.00	88
Painter, Rob	$13.50	76
Scrap, Brook	$14.50	82

Any hours over 40 per week (or 80 in two weeks) is overtime and paid at 1.5 times the regular rate. Each employee donates $10 to a charity and contributes $25 to a health plan. The company matches the employees' health plan deduction. Deductions for CPP and EI are already provided. Assume income tax is calculated at 18% of their gross pay. Michelle's Crafts also accrues 4% vacation pay for all employees and pays workers' compensation at 0.6% of the gross pay.

Required

a) Complete a payroll register for the bi-weekly pay.

b) Prepare a journal entry to pay the employees.

c) Prepare a journal entry to accrue vacation pay.

d) Prepare a journal entry to record the additional employer expense.

e) Prepare a journal entry to make a government remittance on July 15, 2015 using just the numbers from this pay period.

See Appendix I for solutions.

a) Payroll register

Payroll Period June 8 to June 19, 2015		Payroll Register						
		Deductions						
Name	Gross Earnings	CPP	EI	Income Tax	Charitable Donations	Health Plan	Total Deductions	Net Pay

b) Pay employees

Date	Account Titles and Explanation	Debit	Credit
JOURNAL			Page 1

c) Accrue vacation pay

Date	Account Titles and Explanation	Debit	Credit
JOURNAL			Page 1

d) Employer expenses

JOURNAL			Page 1
Date	Account Titles and Explanation	Debit	Credit

e) Government remittance

JOURNAL			Page 1
Date	Account Titles and Explanation	Debit	Credit

Appendix 11A: Payroll Deduction Calculations

CPP Calculation

Canadian Pension Plan deduction amounts can be easily calculated manually if software or tax tables provided by the CRA are not used. There are three basic values that must be known.

1. Maximum pensionable earnings is $53,600
2. Basic personal income tax exemption is $3,500
3. CPP rate is 4.95%

The amounts given are for 2015. They can change every year. In Quebec, employees have the Quebec Pension Plan (QPP) which is calculated identically to the CPP.

The maximum pensionable earnings means the employer must deduct CPP on gross pay up to the maximum for the year. Any gross pay received above the maximum is exempt from CPP.

The basic exemption amount of $3,500 per year means that any employee earning less than $3,500 per year will not have any CPP deducted from their pay. Those who earn more than $3,500 per year will not have CPP deducted on the first $3,500 they earn, although the exempt amount is spread evenly throughout the year. This is done by dividing $3,500 by the number of pay periods in a year. For example, if an employee is paid monthly he will be paid 12 times a year. The exemption amount for each pay period will be

Exemption Amount ÷ Number of Pay Periods in a Year = Pay Period Exemption

$3,500 ÷ 12 = $291.66 Monthly Exemption
(Note that there is no rounding on the exemption amount.)

This means the first $291.66 of gross pay in the month will not have CPP deducted from it.

The CPP rate of 4.95% is applied to the gross pay of the employee. Thus the most any employee should have deducted from their pay for 2015 is

(Maximum Pensionable Earnings – Exemption Amount) x CPP Rate = Maximum CPP Deductions

($53,600 – $3,500) x 4.95% = $2,479.95 Maximum CPP Deductions

The above example shows how CPP works on a yearly amount, however employees are paid much more frequently. As mentioned earlier, the exemption of $3,500 must be spread evenly throughout the year.

For example, if an employee earned $4,500 gross pay each month this is how to calculate how much CPP to deduct from the employee's pay in January.

> (Gross Pay – Pay Period Exemption) x CPP Rate = CPP Deduction

($4,500 – $291.66) x 4.95% = $208.31 CPP Deduction

By the end of November, the employee would have earned $49,500 ($4,500 x 11 months) and have had $2,291.41 ($208.31 x 11 months) deducted for CPP. December's pay will bring the total gross earnings to $54,000 which is more than the maximum earnings for deducting CPP. The employee's CPP deductions for December will be slightly less than they were for every other month. We simply find the difference between the maximum that should be deducted this year and what has already been deducted from the employee.

$2,479.95 – $2,291.41 = $188.54 CPP deduction for December

Since there is less of a deduction in December, the employee will have a higher net pay in that month.

EI Calculations

Employment Insurance deduction amounts can be easily calculated manually if software or tax tables provided by the CRA are not used. There are two basic values that must be known.

IN THE REAL WORLD

If an employee works for multiple employers during the year, each employer is responsible for CPP and EI deductions. This may lead to an overpayment for the employee at year end. Any extra deduction will be refunded when completing their personal tax return.

1. Maximum insurable earnings is $49,500
2. EI rate is 1.88%

The amounts given are for 2015. They can change every year. In Quebec, employees also have the Quebec Parental Insurance Plan (QPIP) in addition to EI, thus the EI rate in Quebec is less than the rate used in the rest of the country.

The maximum insurable earnings means the employer must deduct EI on gross pay up to the maximum for the year. Any gross pay received above the maximum is exempt from EI. Employment Insurance does not have a basic exemption like CPP does, which means EI will be calculated on the entire amount of gross pay, up to the maximum.

The EI rate of 1.88% is applied to the gross pay of the employee. Thus the most any employee should have deducted from their pay for 2015 is

> Maximum Insurable Earnings x EI Rate = Maximum EI Deductions

$49,500 x 1.88% = $930.60 Maximum EI Deductions

For example, if an employee earned $4,500 gross pay each month this is how to calculate how much EI to deduct from the employee's pay in January.

$$Gross\ Pay \times Current\ EI\ Rate = EI\ Deduction$$

$$\$4,500 \times 1.88\% = \$84.60\ EI\ Deduction$$

By the end of November, the employee would have earned $49,500 ($4,500 x 11 months) and have had $930.60 ($84.60 x 11 months) deducted for EI. Since this is the maximum amount of EI that can be deducted for the year, the next pay at the end of December will have no deduction for EI. This means the net pay for December will be higher than in the previous months.

Income Tax Calculations

The calculation of income tax is a little more involved than the calculation of CPP or EI. Every employee receives tax credits. Tax credits allow an employee to earn a certain amount of money and not have to pay any income tax on that amount. Tax credits are dependent upon the personal situation of the employee and increase with factors such as young children, disabilities, a non-working spouse, etc. The total tax credits claimed by an employee are related to claim codes (numbered 0 to 10), which assist in determining how much income tax to deduct from the employee's pay.

IN THE REAL WORLD

To calculate total tax credits and determine an employee's claim code, employers should issue a TD1 form to new employees when they are hired, and ideally at the beginning of each year in case an employee's personal circumstances change. Employees complete the form based on their personal circumstances and total the tax credits they will receive. If an employer neglects or forgets to provide a TD1 form to employees, by default the employee will only receive a basic tax credit and will be given a claim code 1.

If an employee does not take advantage of the tax credits on the TD1 form, it does not mean they will miss out on the tax credits they are entitled to. At the end of the year when the employee completes their tax return, they can claim all the tax credits they are entitled to and receive a tax refund from the government.

If a business is going to manually prepare its payroll, it will need to use the income tax tables available from the CRA website. A sample federal monthly tax table taken from the CRA website is shown Figure 11A.1. The income tax tables are divided into the main pay periods (monthly, semi-monthly, bi-weekly and weekly) for both the federal and provincial income tax amounts. Once the correct pay period is selected, it is just a matter of using the employee's gross pay (listed down the left side of the table) and tax credit claim code (CC 0 to CC 10 across the top of the table) to determine the amount of income tax to deduct. For example, a person paid $1,700 per month and a claim code of 1 will have $84.40 deducted for federal income tax.

Federal tax deductions
Effective January 1, 2015
Monthly (12 pay periods a year)
Also look up the tax deductions in the provincial table

Pay From	Less than	CC0	CC1	CC2	CC3	CC4	CC5	CC6	CC7	CC8	CC9	CC10
1533	1551	203.35	61.75	48.25	21.20							
1551	1569	205.85	64.25	50.75	23.70							
1569	1587	208.35	66.80	53.25	26.20							
1587	1605	210.90	69.30	55.80	28.75	1.70						
1605	1623	213.40	71.80	58.30	31.25	4.20						
1623	1641	215.90	74.35	60.80	33.75	6.70						
1641	1659	218.45	76.85	63.30	36.25	9.20						
1659	1677	220.95	79.35	65.85	38.80	11.75						
1677	1695	223.45	81.90	68.35	41.30	14.25						
1695	1713	226.00	84.40	70.85	43.80	16.75						
1713	1731	228.50	86.90	73.40	46.35	19.30						

FIGURE 11A.1

Workers' Compensation

Workers' compensation is calculated on gross pay for most employees in a business. There are two items that must be known to calculate the workers' compensation premium

1. Maximum insurable earnings ceiling
2. Rate assigned

Each provincial workers' compensation board will determine the maximum insurable earnings ceiling and assign rates for each broad industry category. The maximum insurable earnings ceiling indicates that the employer must pay workers' compensation on gross pay up to the maximum specified. In Ontario, the maximum insurable earnings ceiling is $85,200 for 2015.

The rates are assigned as a dollar amount per $100 of gross payroll. The rates are different for each broad industry category the workers' compensation board has defined and can change each year. In Ontario for 2015, the lowest rate is for businesses classified as legal and financial services. They pay $0.21 per $100 of gross payroll. The highest rate is for businesses classified as form work and demolition. They pay $18.31 per $100 of gross payroll. Each individual business can lower its rate if it meets certain criteria, such as having a very safe work record. Conversely, having many work-related injuries can cause the rate to increase.

The calculation for the workers' compensation payment is shown below.

$$\text{Gross Pay} \times \frac{\text{Rate}}{100} = \text{Workers' Compensation Payment}$$

Suppose an employee earns $4,500 per month, and the business is assigned the lowest rate of $0.21 per $100 of gross pay. The amount the business must pay to workers' compensation is

$$\$4,500 \times \frac{\$0.21}{100} = \$9.45$$

If instead the business must pay the highest rate of $18.31 per $100 of gross payroll, the amount of workers' compensation to pay is

$$\$4,500 \times \frac{\$18.31}{100} = \$823.95$$

This amount must be accumulated by the business every pay period and remitted to the provincial workers' compensation board. If at any time during the year the employee reaches the maximum insurable earnings ceiling, workers' compensation will no longer be paid for the remainder of the year.

Notes

Chapter 12

USING ACCOUNTING INFORMATION

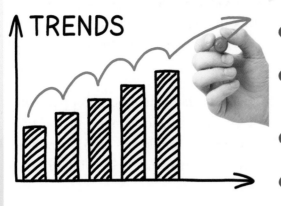

AMEENGAGE Access **ameengage.com** for integrated resources including tutorials, practice exercises, the digital textbook and more.

LEARNING OUTCOMES

❶ Explain the shareholders' equity section of a corporation's balance sheet

❷ Explain the key items in a corporation's income statement that are different from those in a sole proprietorship's income statement

❸ Conduct horizontal and vertical analysis of financial statements

❹ Assess a company's liquidity, profitability, operations management and leverage using financial ratios

❺ Analyze the cash flow statement by interpreting the three sources and uses of cash

Reading the Balance Sheet

In this course, you learned that the fundamental objective of accounting is to provide complete and accurate financial information to users for decision-making purposes. But what types of decisions do users need to make and how can they use financial information to make them? This chapter will provide details on how the financial statements discussed thus far can be used to make decisions.

In your daily life, you can use your personal financial information to make informed financial decisions. You regularly make personal financial decisions such as how to save or invest money, how much you can afford to spend in your next shopping trip or even when you can retire. Your personal financial statements can be used to help with these decisions by showing you, among other things, how much cash you have and how much your net worth has changed over time. When you apply for a mortgage or for a credit card, the bank uses your financial information to determine how much to lend you. The government uses your financial information to determine how much tax you owe each year. Therefore, your personal financial information is useful not only for you, but also for other people that need your financial information to make their decisions.

In the business setting, business financial statements are similarly useful for both internal and external users. Internal users such as managers and executives analyze financial information to correct negative results and take advantage of positive results. External users, such as investors and suppliers, analyze financial information to determine whether to invest money or extend credit terms. Regardless of the decisions financial statement users are trying to make, all users must first learn how to properly read and understand financial statements. We will begin with the balance sheet.

The balance sheet is a snapshot of a company's financial position at a single point in time. For instance, a company's balance sheet for the year 2015 may show a large increase in assets and liabilities compared to its 2014 balance sheet due to its purchase of a large piece of equipment with a large bank loan during 2015. A user of the company's financial statements may see the big increases in the company's loans and equipment in the 2015 balance sheet, and wonder whether the company will be able to make the loan payments or whether the company is using the equipment effectively. There are several analysis tools that can be used to help answer these questions. We will examine these tools later in this chapter.

Up to this point, we have prepared financial statements for sole proprietorships. Sole proprietorships are generally smaller in terms of financing, number of employees, and number of locations. Corporations can be large in size with multiple locations and many employees in different cities. Because corporations are a very common form of organization in Canada, it is important to understand how to read the financial statements of a corporation.

For example, the Proctor & Gamble Company (P&G) has operating branches on four continents that are responsible for selling its approximately 100 brands of consumer products globally. Obviously, this means the company is financially larger than a sole proprietorship. It also means that managers of P&G have a lot to track and oversee. Financial statement analysis helps the internal users (management) evaluate their company's operations and explain changes to external users (shareholders/investors).

The presentation of the corporate balance sheet is similar to that of a sole proprietorship's but usually has more details and more accounts. The Proctor & Gamble Company Consolidated Balance Sheet from 2014 is provided in Figure 12.1. It should be pointed out that the equity section in Figure 12.1 looks different from the equity section in a sole proprietorship's balance sheet that you have seen before. We will look at the highlighted differences in detail.

The Procter & Gamble Company
Consolidated Balance Sheet
Amounts in millions; June 28, 2014

	2014
ASSETS	
CURRENT ASSETS	
Cash and cash equivalents	$8,558
Available-for-sale investment securities	2,128
Accounts receivable	6,386
INVENTORIES	
Materials and supplies	1,742
Work in process	684
Finished goods	4,333
Total inventories	6,759
Deferred income taxes	1,092
Prepaid expenses and other current assets	3,845
Assets held for sale	2,849
TOTAL CURRENT ASSETS	31,617
NET PROPERTY, PLANT AND EQUIPMENT	22,304
GOODWILL	53,704
TRADEMARKS AND OTHER INTANGIBLE ASSETS, NET	30,843
OTHER NONCURRENT ASSETS	5,798
TOTAL ASSETS	**$144,266**
LIABILITIES AND SHAREHOLDERS' EQUITY	
CURRENT LIABILITIES	
Accounts payable	$8,461
Accrued and other liabilities	8,999
Liabilities held for sale	660
Debt due within one year	15,606
TOTAL CURRENT LIABILITIES	33,726
LONG-TERM DEBT	19,811
DEFERRED INCOME TAXES	10,218
OTHER NONCURRENT LIABILITIES	10,535
TOTAL LIABILITIES	74,290
SHAREHOLDERS' EQUITY	
Convertible Class A preferred stock, stated value $1 per share (600 shares authorized)	1,111
Non-Voting Class B preferred stock, stated value $1 per share (200 shares authorized)	–
Common stock, stated value $1 per share (10,000 shares authorized; shares issued 2014—4009.2, 2013—4,009.2	4,009
Additional paid-in capital	63,911
Reserve for ESOP debt retirement	(1,340)
Accumulated other comprehensive income (loss)	(7,662)
Treasury stock, at cost (shares held: 2014—1,298.4, 2013—1,266.9)	(75,805)
Retained earnings	84,990
Non-controlling interest	762
TOTAL SHAREHOLDERS' EQUITY	69,976
TOTAL LIABILITIES AND SHAREHOLDERS' EQUITY	**$144,266**

FIGURE 12.1

Shareholders' Equity

Owners of a corporation are referred to as shareholders. This is because a corporation can sell a fraction of its ownership to the general public in the form of shares. Corporations use the term "shareholders' equity" instead of "owner's equity" to present the equity section of the balance sheet. The shareholders' equity category includes two sub categories, which are share capital, and retained earnings.

Share Capital

Share capital is a subsection on the balance sheet that includes accounts for a company's equity raised through different types of shares. Corporate shares can be divided into two major types, "common shares" and "preferred shares."

Common shares are sold to investors, known as shareholders, in exchange for an investment (e.g. cash) in the company. Shares that have been sold are called outstanding shares. Common shares also represent a portion of ownership of the company. This means that common shareholders have the right to vote for the directors and executives of the corporation. Basically, the shareholders vote on who is in charge of running the company. The common shares section for the Proctor & Gamble Company is highlighted in Figure 12.1.

Preferred shares may also be sold to shareholders in exchange for an investment in the company. However, preferred shareholders do not have any voting rights so they cannot decide on who is in charge of running the company. Instead, preferred shares offer a higher claim on the assets of the business. This means that in the event of bankruptcy, preferred shareholders are paid before common shareholders. Accordingly, the preferred shares always appear before the common shares in the shareholders' equity section of a corporation's balance sheet. The preferred shares section for the Proctor & Gamble Company is highlighted in Figure 12.1. P&G's outstanding preferred shares are "convertible," meaning that the preferred shareholders have an option to convert their preferred shares into common shares. Unlike common shares, preferred shares may have different features attached to them. Convertibility is only one example of preferred share's features.

The common shares and preferred shares accounts separately track the total investments received by the corporation through the sale of those share types. This is in contrast to sole proprietorships, in which additional investments made by the owner are recorded directly in the owner's capital account. Sole proprietorships' net income (loss) and cash withdrawal by the owner are also transferred to the owner's capital account. Corporations, on the other hand, have a separate account for recording their net income (loss) and dividends, called "retained earnings," which will be discussed next.

Retained Earnings

A corporation's net income (or loss) for each period is transferred neither to the owner's capital account nor common/preferred shares account, but to the retained earnings account. When the corporation pays dividends to shareholders, the dividends are also deducted from the retained earnings account. In other words, the **retained earnings** account represents the cumulative net income of a corporation, net of dividends. It is important not to confuse retained earnings with cash or other assets within the business. The retained earnings account is presented in the equity section of the balance sheet. The retained earnings section for the Proctor & Gamble Company is highlighted in Figure 12.1.

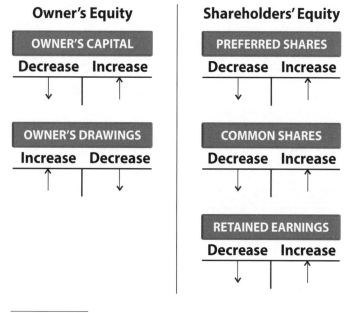

FIGURE 12.2

Figure 12.2 illustrates the primary differences between the equity sections for a sole proprietorship and a corporation. Notice the separation of the share types for a corporation.

We have identified some key differences between a corporation's and sole proprietorship's respective balance sheets. In addition to share capital and retained earnings on the balance sheet, there are terms that corporations commonly use on the income statement that are not usually seen in a sole proprietorship's income statement. These are discussed in the following section.

Reading the Income Statement

The income statement is a summary of how profits or losses were generated during an accounting period. Once again, the presentation of corporations' income statements is similar to that of sole proprietorships', but there are some new terms that will be explained in this section. The income statement is also called "statement of income," "statement of earnings," or "statement of operations."

Consider P&G's 2014 Consolidated Statement of Earnings shown in Figure 12.3. This is similar to the multistep income statement you have already encountered. Recall that in a sole proprietorship's multistep income statement, the earnings are subdivided into gross profit, operating income and net income. A corporation's multistep income statement follows the same basic idea. However, due to the more complicated nature of the corporation's operations, its income statement is more complicated and lists more items. For example, a corporation that has multiple operating segments may decide to discontinue an unprofitable segment. The earnings from this discontinued segment have to be reported as a separate item from the earnings from the continuing segments.

The Procter & Gamble Company
Consolidated Statement of Earnings
Amounts in millions except per share amounts; Year ended June 29, 2014

	2014
NET SALES	$83,062
Cost of products sold	42,460
Selling, general and administrative expense	25,314
Goodwill and indefinite lived intangibles impairment charges	–
OPERATING INCOME	15,288
Interest expense	709
Interest Income	100
Other non-operating income/(expense), net	206
EARNINGS FROM CONTINUING OPERATIONS BEFORE INCOME TAXES	14,885
Income taxes on continuing operations	3,178
NET EARNINGS FROM CONTINUING OPERATIONS	11,707
NET EARNINGS FROM DISCONTINUED OPERATIONS	78
NET EARNINGS	11,785
Less: Net earnings attributable to noncontrolling interests	142
NET EARNINGS ATTRIBUTABLE TO PROCTER & GAMBLE	**$11,643**
BASIC NET EARNINGS PER COMMON SHARE:	
Earnings from continuing operations	$4.16
Earnings from discontinued operations	0.03
BASIC NET EARNINGS PER COMMON SHARE	**4.19**
DILUTED NET EARNINGS PER COMMON SHARE	
Earnings from continuing operations	$3.98
Earnings from discontinued operations	0.03
DILUTED NET EARNINGS PER COMMON SHARE	4.01
DIVIDENDS PER COMMON SHARE	**$2.45**

(1) Basic net earnings per common share and diluted net earnings per
common share are calculated on net earnings attributable to Procter & Gamble

FIGURE 12.3

Discontinued Operation

A **discontinued operation** is a segment of a business that is no longer part of regular operating activities. However, other business segments are still operational. There are a variety of reasons that a corporation may want to discontinue a business segment. For example, the segment may no longer be profitable, so the corporation is shutting it down or selling it. Or management has shifted the corporate mission and the segment no longer fits the company's focus.

Normally, sole proprietorships have a single business segment, meaning the business only has one type of operation (e.g. providing a service or operating as a retailer). Because corporations are usually larger in nature, they tend to be divided into more than one business segment. These segments may operate independently and contribute to the revenues and expenses of the corporation as a whole.

Discontinued operations are accounted for and presented in the financial statements in the following manner. The corporation liquidates the net assets of the discontinued business segment. The revenues and expenses generated by discontinued operations, as well as any gains or losses associated with the disposal of net assets, are presented in a separate section called discontinued operations. P&G's net earnings from discontinued operations are highlighted in Figure 12.3.

Other Comprehensive Income

A corporation's income statement, unlike that of a sole proprietorship's, may contain "other comprehensive income." Other comprehensive income can either be shown as a separate section in the income statement, or separated into a stand-alone statement. P&G chose to report its other comprehensive income in a stand-alone statement, called "Consolidated Statement of Comprehensive Income," which is shown in Figure 12.4. This statement tracks the value of activities that are not part of the main operations. Other comprehensive income can arise from changes in the value of assets such as investments, property, plant and equipment, and other items not in the scope of this textbook. The increases or decreases in the value of assets result in gains or losses for a corporation. Such gains and losses are discussed in more details below.

The Procter & Gamble Company Consolidated Statement of Comprehensive Income Amounts in millions; Year ended June 29, 2014	
	2014
NET EARNINGS	**$11,785**
OTHER COMPREHENSIVE INCOME (LOSS), NET OF TAX	
Financial statement translation	1,044
Unrealized gains/(losses) on hedges (net of $209, $92 and $441 tax, repectively)	(347)
Unrealized gains/(losses) on investment securities (net of $4 $5 and $3 tax, respectively)	9
Defined benefit retirement plans (net of $356, $637 and $993 tax, respectively)	(869)
TOTAL OTHER COMPREHENSIVE INCOME (LOSS), NET OF TAX	(163)
TOTAL COMPREHENSIVE INCOME	11,622
LESS TOTAL COMPREHENSIVE INCOME ATTRIBUTABLE TO NONCONTROLLING INTERESTS	150
TOTAL COMPREHENSIVE INCOME ATTRIBUTABLE TO PROCTOR & GAMBLE	**$11,472**

FIGURE 12.4

Gains and Losses

Sometimes a corporation may incur gains or losses through transactions or events that are not part of its daily operating activities. In most cases, a **gain** is an increase in the value of long-term assets that gives the assets a higher worth than their net book value. A gain increases the value of shareholders' equity. On the other hand, a **loss** is a decrease in the value of long-term assets that gives the assets a lower worth than their net book value. A loss decreases the value of shareholders' equity. Gains and losses may result from selling assets such as equipment or recording the changes in value of investments. In other cases, gains or losses happen with activities irrelevant from long-term assets. For example, the proceeds from winning a lawsuit settlement are considered a gain, while expenditures from losing a lawsuit settlement are considered a loss.

In the case of P&G, the company experienced both gains and losses in 2014. As highlighted in Figure 12.4, the company reported an unrealized gain on investment securities in 2014. The gains and losses are reported on the statement of comprehensive income as being "unrealized" because the investment securities have yet to be sold. The gains and losses are estimated based on available fair market value information. The estimation allows users of the financial statements to have a clearer idea of how the company's financial situation would be affected if the assets were sold at the end of the accounting period. While such gains and losses are not part of the daily operating activities, they still affect the company's comprehensive income. This means they must be presented on the statement of comprehensive income.

We have reviewed the balance sheet and income statement from the perspectives of both a sole proprietorship and a corporation. Now, the financial statements can be analyzed and we can learn more about how accounting information can be used for decision making.

Horizontal and Vertical Analysis

We will inspect the balance sheet of Star Hotel, a Canadian hotel corporation. Suppose this company is planning to renovate to offer more rooms and services. It has contacted the bank to secure a bank loan, but the bank must determine whether the company is profitable and will be able to afford the loan and interest payments. The bank has asked for Star Hotel's financial statements for the last three years. Star Hotel's comparative balance sheet is presented in Figure 12.5. A **comparative balance sheet** is simply a balance sheet that shows the balances for multiple years for easy comparison. For readability, a single column is used for each year.

Star Hotel Balance Sheet As at December 31, 2014 - 2016			
	2016	**2015**	**2014**
Assets			
Current Assets			
Cash	$8,000	$20,000	$32,000
Accounts Receivable	100,000	70,000	40,000
Food Inventory	40,000	28,000	16,000
Prepaid Expenses	12,000	12,000	12,000
Total Current Assets	160,000	130,000	100,000
Property, Plant & Equipment			
Building, Net	390,000	400,000	410,000
Equipment, Net	50,000	55,000	60,000
Total Property, Plant & Equipment	440,000	455,000	470,000
Total Assets	$600,000	$585,000	$570,000
Liabilities			
Current Liabilities			
Accounts Payable	$50,000	$60,000	$80,000
Unearned Revenue	30,000	25,000	20,000
Total Current Liabilities	80,000	85,000	100,000
Total Liabilities	80,000	85,000	100,000
Shareholders' Equity			
Share Capital			
Common Shares—10,000 outstanding	100,000	100,000	100,000
Preferred Shares—5,000 outstanding	20,000	10,000	10,000
Retained Earnings	400,000	390,000	360,000
Total Shareholders' Equity	520,000	500,000	470,000
Total Liabilities and Shareholders' Equity	$600,000	$585,000	$570,000

FIGURE 12.5

The comparative balance sheet is a tool used to perform **horizontal analysis** because it compares information from one accounting period to another, usually from year to year. This means that you can compare similar line items to see how that item has changed from year to year.

Using the comparative balance sheet, the bank can easily see the increases and decreases in assets and liabilities, and estimate the future trends of the financial information. Specifically, we can quickly see that total assets have increased while total liabilities have decreased, which is a good sign. However, the company's cash balance is dwindling while accounts receivable significantly increased, indicating that there may be some cash or collection issues. To make its decision, the bank needs more in-depth information.

Figure 12.6 summarizes some key financial information for Star Hotel's previous three years. Just examining dollar amounts may not reveal trends in the company. Instead we can present the values as percentages. This will show the value of the item compared to a base-year. A **base-year** is usually the earliest year shown and will be the basis for comparison.

To calculate the percentages, we will use the following formula.

$$\text{Percentage of base-year} \ = \ \frac{\text{New account balance}}{\text{Base-year account balance}}$$

In this example, 2014 will be the base-year. For each line, we will use the 2014 value as the denominator in the calculation. So for cash, we will always divide by $32,000. For 2014, $32,000 divided by $32,000 is 100%. For 2016, the calculation would look like this

$$\frac{\$8,000}{\$32,000} \ = \ 0.25 \ or \ 25\%$$

A way to describe this trend is that cash in 2016 is at 25% of the balance in 2014. Repeat this calculation for each separate line item across the years.

Star Hotel Key Figures As at December 31, 2014 - 2016			
	2016	**2015**	**2014**
Cash	$8,000	$20,000	$32,000
Total Current Assets	160,000	130,000	100,000
Property, Plant & Equipment	440,000	455,000	470,000
Total Assets	600,000	585,000	570,000
Total Current Liabilities	80,000	85,000	100,000
Total Shareholders' Equity	520,000	500,000	470,000

Star Hotel Percentage of 2014 Base-Year As at December 31, 2014 - 2016			
	2016	**2015**	**2014**
Cash	25%*	63%	100%
Total Current Assets	160%	130%	100%
Property, Plant & Equipment	94%	97%	100%
Total Assets	105%	103%	100%
Total Current Liabilities	80%	85%	100%
Total Shareholders' Equity	111%	106%	100%

*$8,000 ÷ $32,000 = 25%

FIGURE 12.6

Using this method, the bank can see trends emerging in the data. Despite cash significantly decreasing over time, total current assets have been steadily increasing. Liabilities have been reduced while shareholders' equity has been increasing since 2014. There are no major concerns with these observations.

Alternatively, there is another calculation method which describes percentage changes between years for line items. The method simply subtracts an old figure from a new figure, and then it divides the result by the old figure of the same line item. The formula is as follows.

$$\text{Percentage changed since base-year} = \frac{\text{New account balance} - \text{Base-year account balance}}{\text{Base-year account balance}}$$

Figure 12.7 summarizes some key financial information for Star Hotel's previous three years. As before, 2014 is selected as the base-year. For cash, we will always subtract $32,000 from the year we are examining and divide the result by $32,000. For example, the balance of cash in 2016 was $8,000.

$$\frac{\$8,000 - \$32,000}{\$32,000} = -0.75 \; or -75\%$$

A way to describe this trend is that the cash balance decreased by 75% between 2014 and 2016. This could be the reason why Star Hotel needs a loan, because the company does not have enough cash to pay for renovations.

Star Hotel Key Figures As at December 31, 2014 - 2016			
	2016	**2015**	**2014**
Cash	$8,000	$20,000	$32,000
Total Current Assets	160,000	130,000	100,000
Property, Plant & Equipment	440,000	455,000	470,000
Total Assets	600,000	585,000	570,000
Total Current Liabilities	80,000	85,000	100,000
Total Shareholders' Equity	520,000	500,000	470,000

Star Hotel Percentage Changed with 2014 Base-Year As at December 31, 2014 - 2016			
	2016	**2015**	**2014**
Cash	-75%*	-38%	0%
Total Current Assets	60%	30%	0%
Property, Plant & Equipment	-6%	-5%	0%
Total Assets	5%	3%	0%
Total Current Liabilities	-20%	-15%	0%
Total Shareholders' Equity	11%	6%	0%

*($8,000 − $32,000) ÷ $32,000 = -75%

FIGURE 12.7

One item to note in Figure 12.6 is that there 0% changes for 2014. There is no percent change from the base-year figure, because they are the same dollar amounts (i.e. $32,000 minus $32,000 equals $0. Next, $0 divided by $32,000 equals $0).

Instead of comparing the dollars to a base year, the bank could use one of the line items as a base-figure. Usually, the **base-figure** is a total dollar amount such as total assets. Figure 12.8 shows the percentage of line items by using total assets as the base. This is called **vertical analysis** because each separate line item is being compared to the base-figure within the specific year.

Star Hotel Key Percentages As at December 31, 2014 - 2016			
	2016	**2015**	**2014**
Cash	1%*	3%	6%
Total Current Assets	27%	22%	18%
Property, Plant & Equipment	73%	78%	82%
Total Assets	100%	100%	100%
Total Current Liabilities	13%	15%	18%
Total Shareholders' Equity	87%	85%	82%

*$8,000 ÷ $600,000 = 1%

FIGURE 12.8

To calculate the percentages, we will use the following formula.

$$\text{Percentage of base-figure} = \frac{\text{Line item account balance}}{\text{Base-figure account balance}}$$

To start, a base-figure must be selected. In 2016, Star Hotel had a total asset balance of $600,000. Next, divide all line items in the 2016 balance sheet by the base-figure selected. For cash, divide the balance of $8,000 by the total assets. The result is 0.01 or 1%.

$$\frac{\$8,000}{\$600,000} = 0.01 \text{ or } 1\%$$

This type of analysis reveals that cash currently only represents 1% of total assets. Star Hotel should consider holding more cash in case of unexpected events. Fortunately, current assets represent 27% of total assets and have grown to more than double that of current liabilities. Using this information, the bank decides that Star Hotel is in an overall healthy financial position.

The next step is to use the same tools to analyze the company's income statement. Horizontal analysis is done in much the same way on the income statement as it is on the balance sheet. Star Hotel's comparative income statement is shown in Figure 12.9 for the past three years.

Star Hotel Income Statement For the Year Ended December 31, 2014 - 2016			
	2016	**2015**	**2014**
Revenue			
Service Revenue	$270,000	$200,000	$180,000
Food Sales Revenue	80,000	50,000	40,000
Total Revenue	350,000	250,000	220,000
Cost of Goods Sold	50,000	30,000	25,000
Gross Profit	300,000	220,000	195,000
Operating Expenses			
Advertising Expense	33,000	15,000	5,000
Depreciation Expense	15,000	15,000	15,000
Insurance Expense	12,000	12,000	12,000
Salaries Expense	200,000	150,000	140,000
Supplies Expense	20,000	18,000	15,500
Total Expenses	280,000	210,000	187,500
Net Income	$20,000	$10,000	$7,500

FIGURE 12.9

The comparative income statement allows the bank to quickly see which revenues and expenses have increased or decreased and whether net income is rising or falling. Star Hotel has seen a large increase in revenue, perhaps attributable to an increased advertising budget. The company's net income has doubled since 2015 which is a good sign of profitability. However, if the bank grants a loan, Star Hotel will be required to incur an interest expense which would reduce the profitability of the company. The bank decides to look at other trends in the company.

Figure 12.10 lists the key figures from the income statement for the previous three years as dollars, percentage of, as well as percentage changed for the base year of 2014.

Star Hotel Key Figures For the Year Ended December 31, 2014 - 2016			
	2016	**2015**	**2014**
Total Revenue	$350,000	$250,000	$220,000
Cost of Goods Sold	50,000	30,000	25,000
Gross Profit	300,000	220,000	195,000
Total Expenses	280,000	210,000	187,500
Net Income	20,000	10,000	7,500

Star Hotel Percentage of 2014 Base-Year For the Year Ended December 31, 2014 - 2016			
	2016	**2015**	**2014**
Total Revenue	160%	114%	100%
Cost of Goods Sold	200%	120%	100%
Gross Profit	154%	113%	100%
Total Expenses	150%	112%	100%
Net Income	267%	133%	100%

Star Hotel Percentage Changed with 2014 Base-Year For the Year Ended December 31, 2014 - 2016			
	2016	**2015**	**2014**
Total Revenue	60%	14%	0%
Cost of Goods Sold	100%	20%	0%
Gross Profit	54%	13%	0%
Total Expenses	50%	12%	0%
Net Income	167%	33%	0%

FIGURE 12.10

Star Hotel's sales have been increasing at a faster rate than its expenses, resulting in higher net income. After seeing these trends, the bank decides that the company is likely to continue operating profitably into the future.

Finally, the bank can also use vertical analysis on Star Hotel's income statement by converting everything to a percentage of total revenue for each year, as shown in Figure 12.11.

Star Hotel Percentage of Base-Figure Total Revenue For the Year Ended December 31, 2014 - 2016			
	2016	**2015**	**2014**
Total Revenue	100%	100%	100%
Cost of Goods Sold	14%	12%	11%
Gross Profit	86%	88%	89%
Total Expenses	80%	84%	85%
Net Income	6%	4%	3%

FIGURE 12.11

This analysis reveals that gross profit has remained quite steady, but operating expenses have been gradually falling in relation to total revenue. This indicates that sales have risen without causing as much of an increase to operating expenses, allowing for more net income per dollar of sales.

Considering all of the conclusions, the bank decides to grant the loan to Star Hotel because it has been growing steadily over the past three years and is in a healthy enough financial position to expand operations without much risk.

The Star Hotel example used horizontal and vertical analysis tools to make a decision. While these tools are helpful in providing insight on a company's financial position, there are limitations to what they can actually show. The tools do not consider errors in the figures. Also, the trends may not continue because businesses change and evolve constantly. Fortunately, there are many other analysis tools available to users. These will be discussed next.

Analyzing the Statements

Now that the balance sheet for a corporation has been introduced, it is time to discuss its analysis in depth. We will use the financial statements of Second Cup Coffee Co. (Second Cup), a Canadian corporation that sells specialty coffee and baked goods. The comparative balance sheet is shown in Figure 12.12. As you have learned, this is an important tool in conducting horizontal and vertical analysis, but it also allows users to easily calculate various financial ratios for the company to even better understand its finances. There are several assets and liabilities listed which you may have never seen before, but we will focus on the analysis of the statement as a whole rather than on individual accounts.

We will dissect sections of the balance sheet to perform our analysis. The analysis will involve the calculation of ratios. Ratios measure different aspects of a company's financial situation, and they are divided into four categories based on what they measure: liquidity, profitability, operations management and leverage.

Second Cup Coffee Co. Statement of Financial Position As at December 27, 2014 and December 28, 2013 (Expressed in thousands of Canadian dollars)		
	2014	**2013**
Assets		
Current Assets		
Cash	$10,918	$6,501
Accounts Receivable	4,026	4,368
Notes and Leases Receivable	81	220
Inventory	221	123
Prepaid Expenses	485	190
Income Tax Recoverable	699	-
Total Current Assets	16,430	11,402
Non-Current Assets		
Notes and Leases Receivable	302	701
Property and Equipment	4,380	3,507
Intangible Assets	32,337	61,730
Total Assets	$53,449	$77,340
Liabilities		
Current Liabilities		
Accounts Payable	$6,011	$4,586
Provisions	1,937	847
Other Liabilities	512	717
Income Tax Payable	-	138
Gift Card Liability	3,727	3,895
Deposits From Franchises	378	878
Current Portion of Long-Term Debt	11,119	-
Total Current Liabilities	23,684	11,061
Non-Current Liabilities		
Provisions	1,133	1,380
Other Liabilities	368	428
Long-Term Debt	-	11,089
Deferred Income Taxes	3,270	7,418
Total Liabilities	28,455	31,376
Shareholders' Equity		
Share Capital—Common Shares	8,652	1,000
Contributed Surplus	61,651	61,557
Retained Earnings (Deficit)	(45,309)	(16,593)
Total Shareholders' Equity	24,994	45,964
Total Liabilities and Shareholders' Equity	$53,449	$77,340

FIGURE 12.12

Liquidity Analysis

Liquidity refers to the ability of a company to convert current assets into cash. This is important because paying off liabilities, purchasing assets, and paying for business expenses are generally done using cash. The more liquid a company is, the easier it is to cover obligations such as accounts payable and loan payments. There are several ways to measure liquidity detailed in this section.

Working Capital

Working capital is a measure of liquidity. It can be quickly calculated and easily understood. The formula for working capital is shown below.

$$\text{Working Capital} = \text{Current Assets} - \text{Current Liabilities}$$

Working capital is a dollar figure, not a ratio, so it is difficult to say how much working capital is enough. A positive working capital indicates that the company has enough liquid assets to pay off its upcoming debts. The working capital of Second Cup is calculated in Figure 12.13 for 2013 and 2014.

	2014	2013
Current Assets	$16,430	$11,402
Current Liabilities	$23,684	$11,061
Working Capital	**$(7,254)**	**$341**

FIGURE 12.13

The working capital has gone from positive to negative which is an indication of poor liquidity. The company may have to sell a long-term asset or raise cash through other means to pay off its current liabilities.

Current Ratio

The current ratio is a useful ratio for determining the company's ability to repay its upcoming debts and obligations. The current ratio is calculated as shown below.

$$\text{Current Ratio} = \frac{\text{Current Assets}}{\text{Current Liabilities}}$$

The current ratio assesses business liquidity by determining the extent to which current assets can cover current debts. This means the business' ability to pay off its debt due within one year. No business wants to find itself in a position of having to sell long-term assets to pay current bills. A current ratio of 1.0 indicates that the business has just enough current assets to pay for its current liabilities.

Depending on the industry, the higher the current ratio, the more assurance that the business has enough of a cushion that it can afford to have some cash tied up in current assets, such as inventory and accounts receivable. However, a very high current ratio could indicate poor management of current assets. For example, if the current ratio of a business is 5.0, it has $5.00 in current assets for every dollar that it owes in the next 12 months. This indicates that the business may have too much cash. Money in a bank account earning 0.1% interest is not an efficient use of assets, especially if the business can earn a better rate of return elsewhere. Cash should either be invested in new long-term assets or perhaps invested in the short term until a better use for the cash can be established.

The chart in Figure 12.14 calculates the current ratio using the numbers provided in Second Cup's financial statements.

	2014	2013
Current Assets	$16,430	$11,402
Current Liabilities	$23,684	$11,061
Current Ratio	0.69	1.03

FIGURE 12.14

In this case, the ratio indicates an unhealthy situation. Not only is the ratio well below 1 in the most recent year, but it has decreased from one year to the next. Second Cup may run into cash flow problems within the next year.

Quick Ratio

The other liquidity ratio that is relevant to the analysis of a business is the quick ratio (also known as the acid test). The ratio is calculated as shown below.

$$\text{Quick Ratio} = \frac{\text{Cash} + \text{Short-Term Investments} + \text{Accounts Receivable}}{\text{Current Liabilities}}$$

The quick ratio is much like the current ratio; the only difference is that the quick ratio excludes some current assets which cannot be quickly converted to cash (such as inventory and prepaid expenses). Short-term investments occur when a company has excess cash and wishes to invest it.

This cash can be invested in shares of other companies. The accounting for short-term investments is beyond the scope of this course.

In essence, the quick ratio assesses the ability of the business to meet its most immediate debt obligations without relying on the liquidation of inventory (which may take some time to sell). A quick ratio of 1 indicates that the business has just enough liquid assets to pay for its current liabilities. Anything below 1 might mean the business has too much of its money tied up in inventory or other less liquid assets and may be unable to pay its short-term bills.

Quick ratios have been calculated using the numbers from Second Cup's balance sheet in Figure 12.15. Note that Second Cup does not have any short-term investments.

	2014	2013
Cash + Short-Term Investments + Accounts Receivable	$14,944	$10,869
Current Liabilities	$23,684	$11,061
Quick Ratio	**0.63**	**0.98**

FIGURE 12.15

Notice that the quick ratio has decreased from 2013 (0.98) to 2014 (0.63). This means that the company has gone from a nearly adequate short-term liquidity position to a dangerous one.

To address any potential problems here, and since the balance sheet provides only a snapshot of business finances, further analyses should be performed over the course of the next few months on the specific assets and liabilities of the business. This is to ensure that bills can be paid on time.

This situation could have worsened due to too much money being invested in inventory or fixed assets. A review should be performed to address the situation and rectify any problems found.

Profitability Analysis

Profitability refers to the ability of a company to generate profits. The greater the profitability, the more valuable the company is to shareholders. A consistently unprofitable company is likely to go bankrupt. There are several ratios available to help analyze the profitability of a company. They are calculated using figures from the income statement as opposed to the balance sheet. The income statement for Second Cup is shown in Figure 12.16. There are several revenues and expenses listed which you may have never seen before, but we will focus on the analysis of the statement as a whole rather than on individual accounts.

Second Cup Coffee Co. Statement of Comprehensive Income For the Periods Ended December 27, 2014 and December 28, 2013 (Expressed in thousands of Canadian dollars, except for per share amounts)		
	2014	**2013**
Revenue		
Royalties	$12,350	$14,117
Sale of Goods	9,287	5,506
Services and Other Revenue	6,535	7,565
Total Revenue	28,172	27,188
Cost of Services	7,679	4,054
Gross Profit	20,493	23,134
Operating Expenses		
Salaries, Benefits, and Incentives	6,496	6,866
Coffee Central Overheads	6,700	5,647
Depreciation Expense	933	749
Amortization Expense	339	502
Lease Expense	2,692	1,775
Loss (Gain) on Disposal of Equipment	34	(197)
Total Expenses	17,194	15,342
Operating Income	3,299	7,792
Other Revenue and Expenses		
Restructuring Charges	2,166	883
Provisions for Café Closures	1,630	479
Impairment Charges	29,708	13,552
Loss on Acquisition of Cafes	692	-
Interest and Financing Expense	478	516
Loss Before Income Taxes	(31,375)	(7,638)
Income Tax Recovery	4,343	269
Net Loss	$(27,032)	$(7,369)
Basic and Diluted Loss Per Share	$(2.66)	$(0.74)

FIGURE 12.16

As you can see from Figure 12.16, Second Cup's income statement is also shown in horizontal form, allowing users to easily compare the financial results of the company over two years. We can instantly see, for example, that Second Cup has not generated a profit for the past two years. We can also see that revenues have remained somewhat level while expenses have significantly increased overall, resulting in a higher net loss for 2014. In addition to these observations, several more ratios can be calculated to assess profitability.

Gross Profit Margin

The gross profit margin is used to demonstrate the impact of cost of goods sold on the income statement. In other words, the gross profit margin subtracts cost of goods sold from sales revenue, the result of which is divided by sales revenue. The formula is shown below.

$$\text{Gross Profit Margin} = \frac{\text{Gross Profit*}}{\text{Sales Revenue}}$$

$$\text{*Gross Profit} = \text{Sales Revenue} - \text{Cost of Goods Sold}$$

Gross profit margin reveals the percentage of revenues left after costs which are directly involved in producing the goods or services of the business are deducted. That is, the amount of profits remaining after deducting the cost of goods sold. The remainder is used to pay for operating and other expenses. Figure 12.17 calculates the gross profit margin using figures from Second Cup's income statement for 2013 and 2014.

	2014	2013
Gross Profit	$20,493	$23,134
Total Revenue	$28,172	$27,188
Gross Profit Margin	**73%**	**85%**

FIGURE 12.17

A higher gross profit margin means that the company has an easier time covering its expenses and is more likely to be profitable. However, gross profit margins should be compared to an industry average to determine whether they are healthy or not. Also, a decline in the gross profit margin, such as with Second Cup, indicates that the company is either not generating enough revenue, has experienced an increase in inventory costs or both.

Net Profit Margin

The **net profit margin** assesses a company's profitability after all expenses have been deducted. This is the amount of net profit or loss per dollar of revenue. The formula is shown below.

$$\text{Net Profit Margin} = \frac{\text{Net Income}}{\text{Sales Revenue}}$$

As with the gross profit margin, a higher net profit margin is generally considered a better sign than a lower one, although it should be always be compared to an industry average and previous results. Figure 12.18 calculates the net profit margin margins for Second Cup for both 2013 and 2014.

	2014	2013
Gross Profit	($27,032)	($7,369)
Total Revenue	$28,172	$27,188
Net Profit Margin	**−96%**	**−27%**

FIGURE 12.18

Although total revenues have increased since 2013, net income has remained negative and significantly worsened. This is a bad sign for the shareholders because their investments have not earned a return in more than two years. To perform a complete analysis of net profit margins, comparisons should be made on a monthly and yearly basis to historical company performance, industry averages and direct competitors. Only then will these net income figures be placed in context so that conclusions can be drawn.

Return on Equity (ROE)

Return on equity (ROE) is a measure of what the owners are getting out of their investment in the company. It is often the most important ratio for investors because it has a large impact on the value of one's investment. This ratio requires information from both the balance sheet and income statement to be calculated. The formula is shown below.

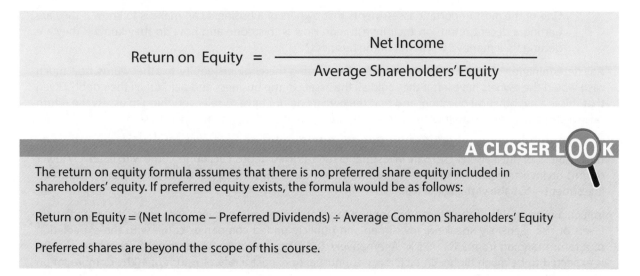

$$\text{Return on Equity} = \frac{\text{Net Income}}{\text{Average Shareholders' Equity}}$$

A CLOSER LOOK

The return on equity formula assumes that there is no preferred share equity included in shareholders' equity. If preferred equity exists, the formula would be as follows:

Return on Equity = (Net Income − Preferred Dividends) ÷ Average Common Shareholders' Equity

Preferred shares are beyond the scope of this course.

Notice that the calculation requires average shareholders' equity. Whenever a ratio is calculated that uses some information from the balance and some from the income statement, the balance sheet information is always averaged. This is because the balance sheet represents a snapshot in time while the income statement represents an entire accounting period. By averaging the balance sheet accounts, we are simulating a figure that covers the same period of time as the income statement. This makes the ratio more comparable and reliable.

Although not shown in Figure 12.14, we need to know the balance of shareholders' equity at December 29, 2012 to calculate the average shareholders' equity for 2013. Assume that the balance on this date was $56,700,000. Then, the calculations of ROE for Second Cup in 2013 and 2014 are shown in Figure 12.19.

	2014	2013
Net Income (Loss)	($27,032)	($7,369)
Average Shareholders' Equity[1]	$35,479	$51,332
Return on Equity	**−76%**	**−14%**
Industry Average	**13%**	**16%**

(1)   Average Shareholders' Equity for 2013: ($56,700 + $45,964) ÷ 2 = $51,332
       Average Shareholders' Equity for 2014: ($45,964 + $24,994) ÷ 2 = $35,479

FIGURE 12.19

A high ROE is desirable because it means that investors made a good decision by investing in the company. Shareholders like to see a return that is as good or better than they could have received by investing elsewhere. A negative ROE indicates that shareholders actually lost money on their investments over the year. It also deters investors from investing more money at the risk of losing it. Second Cup's return on equity has gone from bad to worse recently while other companies in the same industry have been able to generate a positive return for their shareholders.

IN THE REAL WORLD

One of the most important assessments that owners of a business can make is to know if they are getting a decent return on their investment. How is this done and how do they know if they are getting their money's worth out of the business?

Any determination of return on investment revolves around shareholders' equity. In other words, how much cash would the owners have left if they sold all the assets of the business and paid off all their debt? Given that this is a hypothetical question, and that the owners do not have to sell everything to assess the return on investment, there are other ways of assessing the value of the investment in the business.

For example, the owners could ask themselves another theoretical question: Should we keep our money in the business, or put it elsewhere? Safe investments such as fixed deposit accounts come with relatively lower returns on investment. Investing in a friend's new business comes with a potentially much larger return on investment—but also with greater risk.

In fact, a general rule of thumb can be applied to assessing return on investment associated with certain levels of risk. Generally speaking, investments in publicly traded companies come with the expectation of a return ranging from 15% – 25%. Alternatively, the rate of return associated with private companies is expected to be much higher. In fact, it is not unusual to expect a rate of return of 100% or more for an investment in a small private company.

As with most things in life, everything comes at a price. With return on investment, the price can be a matter of risk. If owners want a better return, they must have a greater tolerance for risk.

Operations Management Analysis

Operations management refers to the ability of a company to manage its assets such as inventory and accounts receivable. Accounts receivable may be a large source of cash for a company, but it is not worth anything if it cannot be collected. As well, inventory is converted into cash by selling it, but it must be managed properly to ensure that it can actually be sold in a timely manner. To determine whether inventory is being managed properly, there are two ratios that can be calculated.

Inventory Turnover Ratio

Management is often concerned with the company's ability to sell, or "turn over," inventory. In industries that deal with food and beverage sales, it is especially important because of the short product life of the inventory. Throwing away expired products is just like throwing away cash. The inventory turnover ratio is calculated as shown below.

$$\text{Inventory Turnover Ratio} = \frac{\text{Cost of Goods Sold}}{\text{Average Inventory}}$$

The inventory turnover ratio represents the number of times that the company sold its entire inventory. The industry the company is in determines the desirable value for this ratio. For example, hardware stores may only turn over their inventory once or twice per year because the goods do not expire or become obsolete very quickly. The fashion industry may turn over inventory four times per year because fashion trends tend to change quickly and with the seasons. Second Cup's inventory turnover ratio is calculated in Figure 12.20. Assume that the inventory balance at December 29, 2012 was $137,000.

	2014	2013
Cost of Gods Sold	$7,679	$4,054
Average Inventory[(1)]	$172	$130
Inventory Turnover	**44.6**	**31.2**
Industry Average	**25.8**	**23.1**

(1)   Average Inventory for 2013: ($123 + $137) ÷ 2 = $130
      Average Inventory for 2014: ($221 + $123) ÷ 2 = $172

FIGURE 12.20

Second Cup's high inventory turnover ratio indicates that it has very little wastage, which is important in the food and beverage industry. This is a sign of good inventory management. To get a better understanding of what this ratio means, we can also calculate the inventory days on hand.

Inventory Days on Hand

This ratio states the same thing as the inventory turnover ratio but in a different way. **Inventory days on hand** is equal to the average number of days that it took to turn over inventory during the year. Some users prefer to use this ratio because they are familiar with working in units such as days and months. The formula is shown below.

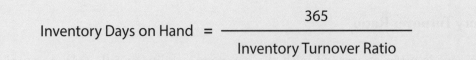

$$\text{Inventory Days on Hand} = \frac{365}{\text{Inventory Turnover Ratio}}$$

This ratio converts the number of times inventory is turned over into the average number of days it took to turn over inventory. For example, a company that sells its entire inventory twice a year would have an inventory turnover ratio of 2 and an inventory days on hand of 182.5 days. The ratio is calculated for Second Cup in Figure 12.21.

	2014	2013
Days in a Year	365 days	365 days
Inventory Turnover Ratio	44.6	31.2
Days Inventory on Hand	**8.2**	**11.7**
Industry Average	**14.1**	**15.8**

FIGURE 12.21

The lower the result, the faster inventory is sold on average. This means that on average it took just over a week for Second Cup to sell the inventory on hand in 2014. It likely purchased new inventory once a week to keep its products fresh. This is a sign of good inventory management.

Leverage Analysis

There are two ways to finance a business: debt and equity. Debts are the liabilities of the business, such as bank loans and accounts payable. Equity is generated by selling shares and generating profits. **Leverage** relates to the amount of debt and risk the company has. Companies often take on debt to finance the purchase of large assets. It then uses these assets to expand operations and generate sales. However, there is usually a high cost of debt in the form of interest expense, which is where the risk comes in. The company must be able to increase profits by more than the interest expense to benefit the shareholders. One measure of leverage is the debt-to-equity ratio.

Debt-to-Equity Ratio

The **debt-to-equity ratio** is used to assess the balance of debt and equity in a business. The debt-to-equity ratio is calculated as shown below.

$$\text{Debt-to-Equity Ratio} = \frac{\text{Total Liabilities}}{\text{Total Shareholders' Equity}}$$

It is not healthy for a business to borrow too much relative to what it is worth. This is because there is a cost of debt in the form of interest. The industry the business is in usually influences how much should be borrowed. For example, capital-intensive industries such as auto manufacturers have higher debt-to-equity ratios than software developers. The

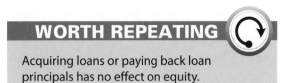

WORTH REPEATING

Acquiring loans or paying back loan principals has no effect on equity.

past two debt-to-equity ratios for Second Cup are calculated in Figure 12.22. The industry averages are also shown for comparison purposes.

	2014	2013
Total Liabilities	$28,455	$31,376
Shareholders' Equity	$24,994	$45,964
Debt-to-Equity Ratio	1.14	0.68
Industry Average	2.08	2.24

FIGURE 12.22

As you can see, the debt-to-equity ratio has increased from 2013 to 2014 and has risen above 1. This is not a good sign, especially considering the significant decrease in shareholders' equity. It implies that Second Cup has suffered a loss and was unable to pay off much debt during the year. However, Second Cup's debt-to-equity ratio is still much lower than the industry average.

There are a few ways a business can improve the debt-to-equity ratio. First, making more profit might do the trick (although it is easier said than done), since it directly results in an increase to shareholders' equity. Second, the business might think about issuing more shares in exchange for cash.

The Cash Flow Statement

Accountants are required to prepare balance sheets and income statements for the business. These important documents represent the state of company finances and adhere to accounting principles. As such, balance sheets and income statements are filled with promises of an exchange of money that must be recorded in one period, but may take place in another period. Company bills may not get paid for several months. Prepaid expenses can be left unadjusted for a number of periods. A borrower may default on a loan. Depreciation is recorded in the books, but there is no exchange of cash. Because of the way these transactions are accounted for on the balance sheet and income statement, it can be difficult to know where the cash is actually going within the business. As a result, the accounting profession created another financial statement whose purpose is to specifically indicate both the sources of cash and the uses of cash within an organization. This document is known as the cash flow statement.

The **cash flow statement** shows how net income is converted to cash, basically where the cash came from and how cash was used during the financial period. Remember, net income does not necessarily translate into cash in the bank. The way a business is structured—in terms of financing, debt collection, etc.—can have a significant impact on the way net income is turned into cash. It is this aspect of a business that the cash flow statement reveals to users or readers, who may include management, accountants, potential lenders and investment analysts. Although cash flow statements can be of significant help to these financial players, their preparation is also required under ASPE and IFRS. In other words, cash flow statements are not only useful but also necessary. Knowing what they are and understanding what they present are essential tasks for an accountant. The cash flow statement for Second Cup is presented in Figure 12.23. Cash inflows are shown as positive numbers and cash outflows are shown in parentheses. Rather than showing how to prepare this statement, this section will explain the three sources and uses of cash in a business in order to further analyze a company's financial information.

	2014	**2013**
Second Cup Coffee Co.		
Statement of Cash Flows		
For the Periods Ended December 27, 2014 and December 28, 2013		
(Expressed in thousands of Canadian dollars)		
CASH PROVIDED BY (USED IN)		
Operating Activities		
Net Loss	$(27,032)	$(7,369)
Items Not Involving Cash		
Depreciation Expense	933	749
Amortization Expense	339	502
Loss (Gain) on Disposal of Equipment	186	(197)
Impairment Charges	29,708	13,552
Other	(3,902)	393
Changes in Non-Cash Working Capital		
Accounts Receivable	177	248
Notes and Leases Receivable	(150)	191
Inventory	(31)	14
Prepaid Expenses	(295)	505
Accounts Payable	1,426	1,463
Provisions	899	1,212
Other Liabilities	(301)	(65)
Gift Card Liability	(168)	(665)
Deposits From Franchisees	(500)	(602)
Income Taxes	(837)	(180)
Cash Provided by Operating Activities	452	7,621
Investing Activities		
Cash from Disposal of Equipment	234	1,240
Cash from Disposal of Intangible Assets	84	-
Cash Payment for Equipment	(1,575)	(2,117)
Cash Payment for Intangible Assets	(750)	(787)
Investment in Notes Receivable	-	(10)
Other	147	70
Cash Provided by Investing Activities	(1,860)	(1,604)
Financing Activities		
Dividends Paid to Shareholders	(1,684)	(3,367)
Issuance of Common Shares	7,509	-
Deferred Financing Charges	-	(29)
Cash Provided by Financing Activities	5,825	(3,396)
Increase in Cash During the Period	4,417	2,621
Cash and Cash Equivalents—Beginning	6,501	3,880
Cash and Cash Equivalents—Ending	$10,918	$6,501

FIGURE 12.23

Three Sources and Uses of Cash

A business generates and consumes cash in three ways

- Operating Activities
- Investing Activities
- Financing Activities

As you can see in Figure 12.23, the cash flow statement is broken into these three sections. At this point, we are not concerned with the individual line items, only the purposes of each section.

Cash Flows from Operating Activities

Operating activities are those necessary to run the daily operations of the business. This section of the cash flow statement tracks the movement of cash within a business on the basis of day-to-day activities. It is the most important section of the cash flow statement because the future of a business largely depends on the activities reported in this section. This section includes items such as the cash regularly received from revenues and collections of receivables throughout the year. It also includes items such as regular payments of cash for expenses, inventory, and accounts payable.

Second Cup has been able to generate positive cash flows from operating activities in both 2013 and 2014. This is a good sign because it means that the business does not rely on selling capital assets or shares to fund its daily operations.

Cash Flows from Investing Activities

Investing activities includes any exchange of cash related to the long-term financial investments or capital assets of the business. Capital assets are long-term assets such as vehicles, equipment, and land. The purchase of these assets can be thought of as the business investing in itself because they usually result in increased operations. For example, if a truck is purchased during the year, cash flows from investing activities decrease. Alternatively, if the business sells land, cash flows increase because the business receives cash in exchange for the land.

It is not necessarily a bad thing to have negative cash flows from investing activities. In fact, positive cash flows from investing activities can be a red flag, especially when cash flows from operations are negative. As shown in the investing activities section of the cash flow statement, Second Cup used a lot of cash to purchase new equipment over the past two years. This is a good sign because it shows that the company is investing in its future by upgrading its capital assets and/or expanding into new markets.

Cash Flows from Financing Activities

Recall that both debt and equity are used to finance businesses. **Financing activities** are any payments or receipts of cash that relate to changes in either long-term debt or shareholders' equity. This section of the cash flow statement tracks the movement of cash within a business based on the way a company receives money from those providing financing and pays it back. Companies pay back loans with interest to banks and they pay out cash dividends to shareholders. They also receive cash by selling shares and taking out bank loans.

A business that is focused on growth and expansion is likely to be raising money through financing activities such as selling shares or acquiring bank loans. In this case, it would have positive cash flows from financing activities. On the other hand, a well-established business may be attempting to pay back its banks loans and reward shareholders with dividend payments. Therefore it would have negative cash flows from financing activities. For example, Second Cup has been paying dividends to shareholders, but it made a large sale of common shares in the past year. This, combined with the purchase of new equipment, indicates that it may have recently developed new expansion plans.

As you can see, there are no hard and fast rules to analyze cash flows. However, it is never a good sign to have consistently overall negative cash flows or to have a dangerously low balance of cash at any point in time. Companies can be quite profitable and have excellent financial ratios, but if they don't have any cash to pay their bills with, they will soon be in big trouble. Companies can avoid certain financial issues by always remaining aware of their financial situation.

In Summary

Explain the shareholders' equity section of a corporation's balance sheet

↪ Corporations use the term "shareholders' equity" instead of "owner's equity" to present the equity section of the balance sheet.

↪ The shareholders' equity category includes two sub categories, share capital and retained earnings.

↪ The two types of share capital, which are preferred shares and common shares, are reported separately in the shareholders' equity section.

Explain the key items in a corporation's income statement that are different from those in a sole proprietorship's income statement

↪ Unlike sole proprietorships, corporations tend to have multiple operating segments. When some segments are discontinued, the income (or loss) from discontinued operations is reported as a separate line item from the income (or loss) from continuing operations in corporations' income statement.

↪ Other comprehensive income is reported either as a separate section in a corporation's income statement or in a standalone statement.

↪ Gains or losses from the change in value of such assets as investments or property, plant and equipment are not considered to be a part of operating income, but are instead reported as other comprehensive income.

Conduct horizontal and vertical analysis of financial statements

↪ The comparative balance sheet is used to perform horizontal analysis because it compares information from one accounting period to another.

↪ One way of conducting horizontal analysis is by calculating succeeding year's balance sheet items as a percentage of the base-year's number.

↪ Another way of conducting horizontal analysis is by calculating the percentage change from a base-year to show percentage increase or decrease of each balance sheet item over time.

↪ Vertical analysis is conducted by converting each separate line item in a financial statement into percentage of the base figure within the specific year.

Assess a company's liquidity, profitability, operations management, and leverage using financial ratios

↪ Ratios measure different aspects of a company's financial situation. They are divided into four categories based on what they measure: liquidity, profitability, operations management and leverage.

↪ A company's liquidity can be assessed using working capital, current ratio, and quick ratio.

22

- A company's profitability can be assessed using gross profit margin, net profit margin, and return on equity (ROE).
- A company's operations management can be assessed using inventory turnover and inventory days on hand.
- A company's leverage can be assessed using debt-to-equity ratio.

Analyze the cash flow statement by interpreting the three sources and uses of cash

- The cash flow statement reports sources and uses of cash within an organization.
- Cash is generated and consumed by a business through three types of activities, including operating activities, investing activities and financing activities.
- Operating activities are those necessary to run the daily operations of the business.
- Investing activities include any exchange of cash related to the long-term financial investments or capital assets of the business.
- Financing activities are any payments or receipts of cash that relate to changes in either long-term debt or shareholders' equity.

Review Exercise 1

Use the financial statements for Basil's Bakery to perform a horizontal and vertical analysis and calculate the following financial ratios and figures for 2016.

- Working capital
- Current ratio
- Quick ratio
- Gross profit margin
- Net profit margin
- Return on equity
- Inventory turnover ratio
- Inventory days on hand
- Debt-to-equity ratio

After calculating the ratios, comment on the result for each ratio. In your explanation, ensure you state whether or not the result is good along with the possible reasoning behind that determination.

	Basil's Bakery **Balance Sheet** **As at December 31, 2016 and 2015**	
	2016	**2015**
ASSETS		
Current Assets		
Cash	$1,605	$987
Accounts receivable	1,175	573
Inventory	396	256
Other current assets	301	103
Total Current Assets	3,477	1,919
Property, plant & equipment	2,034	1,170
TOTAL ASSETS	$5,511	$3,089
LIABILITIES AND EQUITY		
LIABILITIES		
Current liabilities	$1,474	$547
Non-current liabilities	104	58
TOTAL LIABILITIES	1,578	605
SHAREHOLDERS' EQUITY	3,933	2,484
TOTAL LIABILITIES AND EQUITY	$5,511	$3,089

*Note: the numbers in this financial statement is expressed in thousands of Canadian dollars.

Basil's Bakery
Income Statement
For the Year Ended December 31, 2016

Sales Revenue	$6,009
Cost of goods sold	2,928
Gross Profit	3,081
Operating Expenses	
Depreciation	108
Interest	518
Other operating expenses	723
Total Operating Expenses	1,349
Income from Operations	1,732
Investment income	79
Operating Income Before Tax	1,811
Income tax	516
Net Income	$1,295

*Note: the numbers in this financial statement is expressed in thousands of Canadian dollars.

In addition to the financial statements above, the following data is known. The bakery industry average for gross profit margin is 49.47% for 2016, and the industry average for net profit margin is 20.36% of the same time period.

In 2015, Basil's Bakery had a gross profit margin of 52.13% and a net profit margin of 21.95%.

See Appendix I for solutions.

Basil's Bakery				
Balance Sheet				
As at December 31, 2016				
	2016	**2015**	**% Change**	**% of Base-Figure 2016**
Cash	$1,650	$987		
Accounts Receivable	1,175	573		
Inventory	396	256		
Other current assets	301	103		
Total Current Assets	3,522	1,919		
Property, plant & equipment	2,034	1,170		
TOTAL ASSETS	$5,556	$3,089		
Current Liabilities	$1,474	$547		
Non-current liabilities	104	58		
TOTAL LIABILITIES	1,578	605		
SHAREHOLDERS' EQUITY	3,978	2,484		
TOTAL LIABILITIES AND EQUITY	$5,556	$3,089		

_____

_____

_____

_____

_____

_____

_____

_____

_____

_____

Financial Ratio or Figure	Calculation	Result
Working Capital		
Current Ratio		
Quick Ratio		
Gross Profit Margin		
Net Profit Margin		
Return on Equity		
Inventory Turnover Ratio		
Inventory days on hand		
Debt-to-Equity Ratio		

Review Exercise 2

Using one or two sentences each, name and describe the three sources and uses of cash based on the cash flow statement.

See Appendix I for solutions.

_____

_____

_____

_____

_____

_____

_____

_____

_____

_____

_____

_____

_____

_____

_____

_____

_____

_____

_____

_____

Appendix I

REVIEW EXERCISE SOLUTIONS

Chapter 1 Review Exercise—Solutions

T-account Worksheet

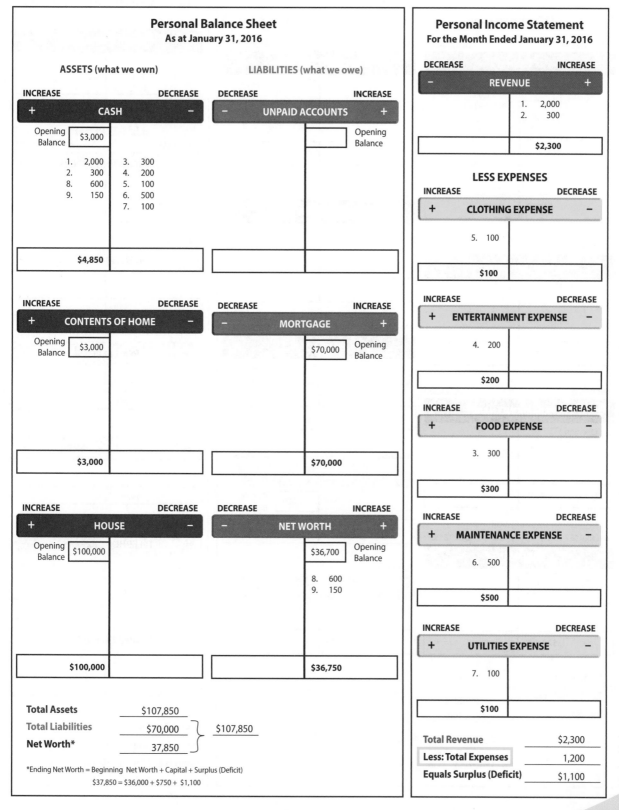

Personal Balance Sheet
As at January 31, 2016

ASSETS (what we own)

INCREASE / DECREASE
CASH + / −

Opening Balance	$3,000		
1.	2,000	3.	300
2.	300	4.	200
8.	600	5.	100
9.	150	6.	500
		7.	100

$4,850

INCREASE / DECREASE
CONTENTS OF HOME + / −

| Opening Balance | $3,000 |

$3,000

INCREASE / DECREASE
HOUSE + / −

| Opening Balance | $100,000 |

$100,000

LIABILITIES (what we owe)

DECREASE / INCREASE
UNPAID ACCOUNTS − / +

Opening Balance

DECREASE / INCREASE
MORTGAGE − / +

| | $70,000 | Opening Balance |

$70,000

DECREASE / INCREASE
NET WORTH − / +

	$36,700	Opening Balance
8.	600	
9.	150	

$36,750

Total Assets	$107,850	
Total Liabilities	$70,000	} $107,850
Net Worth*	37,850	

*Ending Net Worth = Beginning Net Worth + Capital + Surplus (Deficit)
$37,850 = $36,000 + $750 + $1,100

Personal Income Statement
For the Month Ended January 31, 2016

DECREASE / INCREASE
REVENUE − / +

| | | 1. | 2,000 |
| | | 2. | 300 |

$2,300

LESS EXPENSES

INCREASE / DECREASE
CLOTHING EXPENSE + / −

| 5. | 100 |

$100

INCREASE / DECREASE
ENTERTAINMENT EXPENSE + / −

| 4. | 200 |

$200

INCREASE / DECREASE
FOOD EXPENSE + / −

| 3. | 300 |

$300

INCREASE / DECREASE
MAINTENANCE EXPENSE + / −

| 6. | 500 |

$500

INCREASE / DECREASE
UTILITIES EXPENSE + / −

| 7. | 100 |

$100

Total Revenue	$2,300
Less: Total Expenses	1,200
Equals Surplus (Deficit)	$1,100

Chapter 2 Review Exercise—Solutions

T-account Worksheet

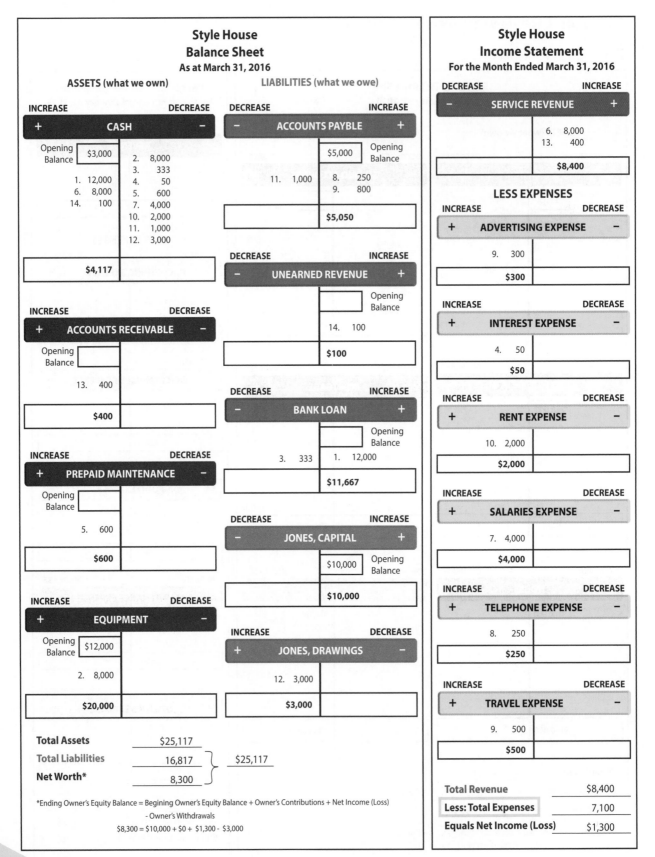

Style House
Balance Sheet
As at March 31, 2016

ASSETS (what we own) | **LIABILITIES (what we owe)**

CASH (INCREASE + / DECREASE −)

Opening Balance	$3,000	2.	8,000
		3.	333
1.	12,000	4.	50
6.	8,000	5.	600
14.	100	7.	4,000
		10.	2,000
		11.	1,000
		12.	3,000

$4,117

ACCOUNTS RECEIVABLE (INCREASE + / DECREASE −)

Opening Balance	
13.	400

$400

PREPAID MAINTENANCE (INCREASE + / DECREASE −)

Opening Balance	
5.	600

$600

EQUIPMENT (INCREASE + / DECREASE −)

Opening Balance	$12,000
2.	8,000

$20,000

ACCOUNTS PAYBLE (DECREASE − / INCREASE +)

		$5,000	Opening Balance
11.	1,000	8.	250
		9.	800

$5,050

UNEARNED REVENUE (DECREASE − / INCREASE +)

	Opening Balance
	14. 100

$100

BANK LOAN (DECREASE − / INCREASE +)

			Opening Balance
3.	333	1.	12,000

$11,667

JONES, CAPITAL (DECREASE − / INCREASE +)

	$10,000 Opening Balance

$10,000

JONES, DRAWINGS (INCREASE + / DECREASE −)

12.	3,000

$3,000

Total Assets	$25,117	
Total Liabilities	16,817	$25,117
Net Worth*	8,300	

*Ending Owner's Equity Balance = Begining Owner's Equity Balance + Owner's Contributions + Net Income (Loss) - Owner's Withdrawals

$8,300 = $10,000 + $0 + $1,300 - $3,000

Style House
Income Statement
For the Month Ended March 31, 2016

SERVICE REVENUE (DECREASE − / INCREASE +)

6.	8,000
13.	400

$8,400

LESS EXPENSES

ADVERTISING EXPENSE (INCREASE + / DECREASE −)

9.	300

$300

INTEREST EXPENSE (INCREASE + / DECREASE −)

4.	50

$50

RENT EXPENSE (INCREASE + / DECREASE −)

10.	2,000

$2,000

SALARIES EXPENSE (INCREASE + / DECREASE −)

7.	4,000

$4,000

TELEPHONE EXPENSE (INCREASE + / DECREASE −)

8.	250

$250

TRAVEL EXPENSE (INCREASE + / DECREASE −)

9.	500

$500

Total Revenue	$8,400
Less: Total Expenses	7,100
Equals Net Income (Loss)	$1,300

Complete the income statement, statement of owner's equity and balance sheet for this exercise.

Style House Income Statement For the Month Ended March 31, 2016		
Revenue		
Service Revenue		$8,400
Expenses		
Advertising Expense	$300	
Interest Expense	50	
Rent Expense	2,000	
Salaries Expense	4,000	
Telephone Expense	250	
Travel Expense	500	
Total Expenses		7,100
Net Income		$1,300

Style House Statement of Owner's Equity For the Month Ended March 31, 2016	
Jones, Capital, March 1, 2016	$10,000
Add: Net Income	1,300
Less: Jones, Drawings	3,000
Jones, Capital, March 31, 2016	$8,300

Style House Balance Sheet As at March 31, 2016			
Assets		**Liabilities**	
Cash	$4,117	Accounts Payable	$5,050
Accounts Receivable	400	Unearned Revenue	100
Prepaid Maintenance	600	Bank Loan	11,667
Equipment	20,000	**Total Liabilities**	16,817
		Owner's Equity	
		Jones, Capital	8,300
Total Assets	$25,117	**Total Liabilities and Owner's Equity**	$25,117

Chapter 3 Review Exercise—Solutions

Part 1

Prepare the assets portion of the balance sheet assuming it was prepared under IFRS. Do not adjust the account balances.

Hollinger Runners Inc.
Balance Sheet
As at April 30, 2016

	2016	2015
ASSETS		
	(in thousands)	
Non-Current Assets		
Property, plant and equipment	1,210	2,120
Goodwill	40	50
Available-for-sale investments	60	65
Total Non-Current Assets	1,310	2,235
Current Assets		
Inventory	5	120
Accounts receivable	10	140
Other current assets	60	70
Cash	10	500
Total Current Assets	85	830
TOTAL ASSETS	1,395	3,065

Part 2

Which of the four fundamental characteristics of financial information has HRI failed to apply? Explain.

Relevance

- A particular piece of information is relevant if its omission means that the user's decision may change. In the financial statements, the company did not disclose that two different currencies were used in the comparative balance sheet (one for 2016 and another for 2015). This omission can potentially affect users' (investors') decisions.

- A component of relevance is timeliness. HRI only prepares financial statements on an annual basis. However, the company's hundreds of shareholders would benefit from more timely financial statements (e.g. quarterly or monthly).

Reliability

- A component of reliability is verifiability. Since several invoices did not match the cost amounts listed in HRI's accounting records, the reported costs are not verifiable. Therefore, total expenses is not a reliable number in the company's income statement.

Comparability

- Even though the company provided balance sheet amounts from the previous year, two different currencies are used from one year to the next. One currency has consistently been stronger than the other. Therefore, it is not straightforward to compare the financial information of HRI through time.

Part 3

Which of the basic accounting principles and/or assumptions has HRI violated? Explain.

The Business Entity Assumption

- The HRI cash account includes the personal savings of some of the shareholders. This indicates that the accounting for the business was not kept separate from the personal affairs of the owners.

The Monetary Unit Assumption

- HRI has included values in two different currencies on its financial statements.

The Objectivity Principle

- The objectivity principle is closely linked to the reliability characteristic. Many invoices did not match the cost amounts listed in HRI's accounting records. Therefore, the accounting for expenses was not done objectively.

Measurement

- Assets must be recorded at their historical cost. However, HRI has valued its purchases at fair market value.

Consistency

- The method of depreciation is inconsistent from 2015 to 2016. Sometimes, an inconsistency can be fully justified. However, HRI did not explain the reason or provide backup for changing this particular accounting method.

Disclosure

- HRI did not disclose the justification for changing the depreciation method.

- HRI did not disclose the information related to changing the location of the headquarters and the inconsistent measures of currency.

The Going Concern Assumption *(requires critical thinking)*

- There is evidence that the company may not exist and operate in the foreseeable future

    o HRI has experienced a significant net loss for each of the past three years (even before adjusting for the unverified expense amounts).

    o The cash balance and inventory balances are extremely low in 2016.

    o The company's property, plant and equipment balance declined significantly from 2015 and 2016 (even after adjusting for exchange rates). It is possible some of these assets were sold during 2016.

    o The above examples of HRI's poor financial performance occurred during a time when the economy was booming. HRI's performance is normally aligned with the state of economy. This discrepancy should cause shareholders to question the going concern assumption with respect to HRI.

Chapter 4 Review Exercise—Solutions

a)   Journal Entries

JOURNAL				Page 1
Date	**Account Titles and Explanation**	**PR**	**Debit**	**Credit**
2016				
Jun 1	Rent Expense	540	900	
	Cash	101		900
	Paid cash for month's rent			
Jun 3	Prepaid Insurance	110	1,200	
	Cash	101		1,200
	Prepaid a one-year insurance policy			
Jun 6	Cash	101	2,100	
	Service Revenue	400		2,100
	Received cash for services			
Jun 11	Advertising Expense	500	450	
	Accounts Payable	200		450
	Received invoice for advertising			
Jun 13	Cash	101	3,000	
	Gordon, Capital	300		3,000
	Owner invested cash in business			
Jun 16	Cash	101	300	
	Unearned Revenue	210		300
	Received deposit from customer			
Jun 18	Accounts Receivable	105	1,500	
	Service Revenue	400		1,500
	Provided services on account			
Jun 23	Bank Loan	215	950	
	Cash	101		950
	Paid bank loan principal			
Jun 30	Gordon, Drawings	310	1,000	
	Cash	101		1,000
	Owner drawing for personal use			

b) General Ledger

GENERAL LEDGER

Account: Cash					GL. No.	101
Date	**Description**	**PR**	**DR**	**CR**	**Balance**	
2016						
Jun 1	Opening Balance				4,200	DR
Jun 1		J1		900	3,300	DR
Jun 3		J1		1,200	2,100	DR
Jun 6		J1	2,100		4,200	DR
Jun 13		J1	3,000		7,200	DR
Jun 16		J1	300		7,500	DR
Jun 23		J1		950	6,550	DR
Jun 30		J1		1,000	5,550	DR

Account: Accounts Receivable					GL. No.	105
Date	**Description**	**PR**	**DR**	**CR**	**Balance**	
2016						
Jun 1	Opening Balance				3,100	DR
Jun 18		J1	1,500		4,600	DR

Account: Prepaid Insurance					GL. No.	110
Date	**Description**	**PR**	**DR**	**CR**	**Balance**	
2016						
Jun 1	Opening Balance				0	DR
Jun 3		J1	1,200		1,200	DR

Account: Equipment					GL. No.	120
Date	**Description**	**PR**	**DR**	**CR**	**Balance**	
2016						
Jun 1	Opening Balance				6,000	DR

Account: Accounts Payable					GL. No.	200
Date	**Description**	**PR**	**DR**	**CR**	**Balance**	
2016						
Jun 1	Opening Balance				2,300	CR
Jun 11		J1		450	2,750	CR

Account: Unearned Revenue					GL. No.	210
Date	**Description**	**PR**	**DR**	**CR**	**Balance**	
2016						
Jun 1	Opening Balance				600	CR
Jun 16		J1		300	900	CR

Account: Bank Loan — GL. No. 215

Date	Description	PR	DR	CR	Balance	
2016						
Jun 1	Opening Balance				4,000	CR
Jun 23		J1	950		3,050	CR

Account: Gordon, Capital — GL. No. 300

Date	Description	PR	DR	CR	Balance	
2016						
Jun 1	Opening Balance				6,400	CR
Jun 13		J1		3,000	9,400	CR

Account: Gordon, Drawings — GL. No. 310

Date	Description	PR	DR	CR	Balance	
2016						
Jun 30		J1	1,000		1,000	DR

Account: Service Revenue — GL. No. 400

Date	Description	PR	DR	CR	Balance	
2016						
Jun 6		J1		2,100	2,100	CR
Jun 18		J1		1,500	3,600	CR

Account: Advertising Expense — GL. No. 500

Date	Description	PR	DR	CR	Balance	
2016						
Jun 11		J1	450		450	DR

Account: Rent Expense — GL. No. 540

Date	Description	PR	DR	CR	Balance	
2016						
Jun 1		J1	900		900	DR

c) Trial Balance

CG Accounting Trial Balance June 30, 2016		
Account Titles	DR	CR
Cash	$5,550	
Accounts Receivable	4,600	
Prepaid Insurance	1,200	
Equipment	6,000	
Accounts Payable		$2,750
Unearned Revenue		900
Bank Loan		3,050
Gordon, Capital		9,400
Gordon, Drawings	1,000	
Service Revenue		3,600
Advertising Expense	450	
Rent Expense	900	
Total	$19,700	$19,700

Chapter 5 Review Exercise—Solutions

a) Complete the worksheet.

	CG Accounting Worksheet June 30, 2016					
	Unadjusted Trial Balance		Adjustments		Adjusted Trial Balance	
Account Titles	DR	CR	DR	CR	DR	CR
Cash	$5,550				$5,550	
Accounts Receivable	4,600		$900		5,500	
Prepaid Insurance	1,200			$100	1,100	
Equipment	6,000				6,000	
Accumulated Depreciation		$0		100		$100
Accounts Payable		2,750				2,750
Interest Payable		0		25		25
Unearned Revenue		900	450			450
Bank Loan		3,050				3,050
Gordon, Capital		9,400				9,400
Gordon, Drawings	1,000				1,000	
Service Revenue		3,600		1,350		4,950
Advertising Expense	450				450	
Depreciation Expense	0		100		100	
Insurance Expense	0		100		100	
Interest Expense	0		25		25	
Rent Expense	900				900	
Total	$19,700	$19,700	$1,575	$1,575	$20,725	$20,725

b) Prepare the adjusting journal entries.

JOURNAL				Page 2	
Date	Account Title and Explanation	PR	Debit	Credit	
2016					
Jun 30	Insurance Expense	515	100		
	Prepaid Insurance	110		100	
	Recognized one month of insurance used				
Jun 30	Unearned Revenue	210	450		
	Service Revenue	400		450	
	Recognized revenue previously unearned				
Jun 30	Interest Expense	520	25		
	Interest Payable	205		25	
	Accrued interest on bank loan				
Jun 30	Depreciation Expense	510	100		
	Accumulated Depreciation	125		100	
	Recorded depreciation of equipment				
Jun 30	Accounts Receivable	105	900		
	Service Revenue	400		900	
	Record accrued revenue				

GENERAL LEDGER

Account: Cash					GL. No. 101	
Date	Description	PR	DR	CR	Balance	
2016						
Jun 1	Opening Balance				4,200	DR
Jun 1		J1		900	3,300	DR
Jun 3		J1		1,200	2,100	DR
Jun 6		J1	2,100		4,200	DR
Jun 13		J1	3,000		7,200	DR
Jun 16		J1	300		7,500	DR
Jun 23		J1		950	6,550	DR
Jun 30		J1		1,000	5,550	DR

Account: Accounts Receivable   **GL. No. 105**

Date	Description	PR	DR	CR	Balance	
2016						
Jun 1	Opening Balance				3,100	DR
Jun 18		J1	1,500		4,600	DR
Jun 30	Adjusting Entry	J2	900		5,500	DR

Account: Prepaid Insurance   **GL. No. 110**

Date	Description	PR	DR	CR	Balance	
2016						
Jun 1	Opening Balance				0	DR
Jun 3		J1	1,200		1,200	DR
Jun 30	Adjusting Entry	J2		100	1,100	DR

Account: Equipment   **GL. No. 120**

Date	Description	PR	DR	CR	Balance	
2016						
Jun 1	Opening Balance				6,000	DR

Account: Accumulated Depreciation   **GL. No. 125**

Date	Description	PR	DR	CR	Balance	
2016						
Jun 30	Adjusting Entry	J2		100	100	CR

Account: Accounts Payable   **GL. No. 200**

Date	Description	PR	DR	CR	Balance	
2016						
Jun 1	Opening Balance				2,300	CR
Jun 11		J1		450	2,750	CR

Account: Interest Payable   **GL. No. 205**

Date	Description	PR	DR	CR	Balance	
2016						
Jun 30	Adjusting Entry	J2		25	25	CR

Account: Unearned Revenue   **GL. No. 210**

Date	Description	PR	DR	CR	Balance	
2016						
Jun 1	Opening Balance				600	CR
Jun 16		J1		300	900	CR
Jun 30	Adjusting Entry	J2	450		450	CR

Account: Bank Loan · GL. No. 215

Date	Description	PR	DR	CR	Balance	
2016						
Jun 1	Opening Balance				4,000	CR
Jun 23		J1	950		3,050	CR

Account: Gordon, Capital · GL. No. 300

Date	Description	PR	DR	CR	Balance	
2016						
Jun 1	Opening Balance				6,400	CR
Jun 13		J1		3,000	9,400	CR

Account: Gordon, Drawings · GL. No. 310

Date	Description	PR	DR	CR	Balance	
2016						
Jun 30		J1	1,000		1,000	DR

Account: Service Revenue · GL. No. 400

Date	Description	PR	DR	CR	Balance	
2016						
Jun 6		J1		2,100	2,100	CR
Jun 18		J1		1,500	3,600	CR
Jun 30	Adjusting Entry	J2		450	4,050	CR
Jun 30	Adjusting Enry	J2		900	4,950	CR

Account: Advertising Expense · GL. No. 500

Date	Description	PR	DR	CR	Balance	
2016						
Jun 11		J1	450		450	DR

Account: Depreciation Expense · GL. No. 510

Date	Description	PR	DR	CR	Balance	
2016						
Jun 30	Adjusting Entry	J2	100		100	DR

Account: Insurance Expense · GL. No. 515

Date	Description	PR	DR	CR	Balance	
2016						
Jun 30	Adjusting Entry	J2	100		100	DR

Account: Interest Expense					GL. No.	520
Date	Description	PR	DR	CR	Balance	
2016						
Jun 30	Adjusting Entry	J2	25		25	DR

Account: Rent Expense					GL. No.	540
Date	Description	PR	DR	CR	Balance	
2016						
Jun 1		J1	900		900	DR

Chapter 5 Appendix Review Exercise—Solutions

JOURNAL				Page 2
Date	Account Title and Explanation	PR	Debit	Credit
2016				
Jun 28	Cash		400	
	Automobile			400
	To reverse incorrect entry			
Jun 28	Maintenance Expense		400	
	Cash			400
	To correctly pay for automobile maintenance			
Jun 28	Cash		200	
	Equipment			200
	To reverse incorrect entry			
Jun 28	Office Supplies		200	
	Cash			200
	To correctly pay for office supplies			

Chapter 6 Review Exercise—Solutions

a) Prepare the income statement, statement of owner's equity and the classified balance sheet.

CG Accounting Income Statement For the Month Ended June 30, 2016		
Service Revenue		$4,950
Expenses		
Advertising Expense	$450	
Depreciation Expense	100	
Insurance Expense	100	
Interest Expense	25	
Rent Expense	900	
Total Expenses		1,575
Net Income (Loss)		$3,375

CG Accounting Statement of Owner's Equity For the Month Ended June 30, 2016		
Gordon, Capital at June 1		$6,400
Add:		
Additional Investment	$3,000	
Net Income	3,375	6,375
Subtotal		12,775
Less:		
Gordon, Drawings		1,000
Gordon, Capital at June 30		$11,775

CG Accounting Classified Balance Sheet As at June 30, 2016		
Assets		
Current Assets		
Cash	$5,550	
Accounts Receivable	5,500	
Prepaid Insurance	1,100	
Total Current Assets		$12,150
Property, Plant & Equipment		
Equipment	6,000	
Less: Accumulated Depreciation	(100)	
Total Property, Plant & Equipment		5,900
Total Assets		$18,050
Liabilities		
Current Liabilities		
Accounts Payable	$2,750	
Interest Payable	25	
Unearned Revenue	450	
Current Portion of Bank Loan	800	
Total Current Liabilities		$4,025
Long-Term Liabilities		
Long-Term Portion of Bank Loan	2,250	
Total Long-Term Liabilities		2,250
Total Liabilities		6,275
Owner's Equity		
Gordon, Capital		11,775
Total Owner's Equity		11,775
Total Liabilities and Owner's Equity		$18,050

b) Complete the closing entries using the income summary method and post them to the general ledger.

JOURNAL					Page 3
Date	**Account Title and Explanation**	**PR**	**Debit**		**Credit**
2016					
Jun 30	Service Revenue	400	4,950		
	Income Summary	315			4,950
	Close revenue to income summary				
Jun 30	Income Summary	315	1,575		
	Advertising Expense	500			450
	Depreciation Expense	510			100
	Insurance Expense	515			100
	Interest Expense	520			25
	Rent Expense	540			900
	Close expenses to income summary				
Jun 30	Income Summary	315	3,375		
	Gordon, Capital	300			3,375
	Close income summary to capital				
Jun 30	Gordon, Capital	300	1,000		
	Gordon, Drawings	310			1,000
	Close drawings to capital				

GENERAL LEDGER

Account: Cash					GL. No. 101	
Date	**Description**	**PR**	**DR**	**CR**	**Balance**	
2016						
Jun 1	Opening Balance				4,200	DR
Jun 1		J1		900	3,300	DR
Jun 3		J1		1,200	2,100	DR
Jun 6		J1	2,100		4,200	DR
Jun 13		J1	3,000		7,200	DR
Jun 16		J1	300		7,500	DR
Jun 23		J1		950	6,550	DR
Jun 30		J1		1,000	5,550	DR

Account: Accounts Receivable — GL. No. 105

Date	Description	PR	DR	CR	Balance	
2016						
Jun 1	Opening Balance				3,100	DR
Jun 18		J1	1,500		4,600	DR
Jun 30	Adjusting Entry	J2	900		5,500	DR

Account: Prepaid Insurance — GL. No. 110

Date	Description	PR	DR	CR	Balance	
2016						
Jun 1	Opening Balance				0	DR
Jun 3		J1	1,200		1,200	DR
Jun 30	Adjusting Entry	J2		100	1,100	DR

Account: Equipment — GL. No. 120

Date	Description	PR	DR	CR	Balance	
2016						
Jun 1	Opening Balance				6,000	DR

Account: Accumulated Depreciation — GL. No. 125

Date	Description	PR	DR	CR	Balance	
2016						
Jun 30	Adjusting Entry	J2		100	100	CR

Account: Accounts Payable — GL. No. 200

Date	Description	PR	DR	CR	Balance	
2016						
Jun 1	Opening Balance				2,300	CR
Jun 11		J1		450	2,750	CR

Account: Interest Payable — GL. No. 205

Date	Description	PR	DR	CR	Balance	
2016						
Jun 30	Adjusting Entry	J2		25	25	CR

Account: Unearned Revenue — GL. No. 210

Date	Description	PR	DR	CR	Balance	
2016						
Jun 1	Opening Balance				600	CR
Jun 16		J1		300	900	CR
Jun 30	Adjusting Entry	J2	450		450	CR

Account: Bank Loan GL. No. 215

Date	Description	PR	DR	CR	Balance	
2016						
Jun 1	Opening Balance				4,000	CR
Jun 23		J1	950		3,050	CR

Account: Gordon, Capital GL. No. 300

Date	Description	PR	DR	CR	Balance	
2016						
Jun 1	Opening Balance				6,400	CR
Jun 13		J1		3,000	9,400	CR
Jun 30	Closing Entry	J3		3,375	12,775	CR
Jun 30	Closing Entry	J3	1,000		11,775	CR

Account: Gordon, Drawings GL. No. 310

Date	Description	PR	DR	CR	Balance	
2016						
Jun 30		J1	1,000		1,000	DR
Jun 30	Closing Entry	J3		1,000	0	DR

Account: Income Summary GL. No. 315

Date	Description	PR	DR	CR	Balance	
2016						
Jun 30	Closing Entry	J3		4,950	4,950	CR
Jun 30	Closing Entry	J3	1,575		3,375	CR
Jun 30	Closing Entry	J3	3,375		0	CR

Account: Service Revenue GL. No. 400

Date	Description	PR	DR	CR	Balance	
2016						
Jun 6		J1		2,100	2,100	CR
Jun 18		J1		1,500	3,600	CR
Jun 30	Adjusting Entry	J2		450	4,050	CR
Jun 30	Adjusting Entry	J2		900	4,950	CR
Jun 30	Closing Entry	J3	4,950		0	CR

Account: Advertising Expense GL. No. 500

Date	Description	PR	DR	CR	Balance	
2016						
Jun 11		J1	450		450	DR
Jun 30	Closing Entry	J3		450	0	DR

Account: Depreciation Expense					GL. No.	510
Date	Description	PR	DR	CR	Balance	
2016						
Jun 30	Adjusting Entry	J2	100		100	DR
Jun 30	Closing Entry	J3		100	0	DR

Account: Insurance Expense					GL. No.	515
Date	Description	PR	DR	CR	Balance	
2016						
Jun 30	Adjusting Entry	J2	100		100	DR
Jun 30	Closing Entry	J3		100	0	DR

Account: Interest Expense					GL. No.	520
Date	Description	PR	DR	CR	Balance	
2016						
Jun 30	Adjusting Entry	J2	25		25	DR
Jun 30	Closing Entry	J3		25	0	DR

Account: Rent Expense					GL. No.	540
Date	Description	PR	DR	CR	Balance	
2016						
Jun 1		J1	900		900	DR
Jun 30	Closing Entry	J3		900	0	DR

c) Prepare the post-closing trial balance.

CG Accounting Post-Closing Trial Balance June 30, 2016		
Account Titles	DR	CR
Cash	$5,550	
Accounts Receivable	5,500	
Prepaid Insurance	1,100	
Equipment	6,000	
Accumulated Depreciation		$100
Accounts Payable		2,750
Interest Payable		25
Unearned Revenue		450
Bank Loan		3,050
Gordon, Capital		11,775
Total	$18,150	$18,150

Chapter 6 Appendix Review Exercise—Solutions

CG Accounting
Worksheet
June 30, 2016

Account Titles	Unadjusted Trial Balance		Adjustments		Adjusted Trial Balance		Income Statement		Balance Sheet & Equity	
	DR	CR	DR	CR	DR	CR	DR	CR	DR	CR
Cash	$5,550				$5,550				$5,550	
Accounts Receivable	4,600		$900		5,500				5,500	
Prepaid Insurance	1,200			$100	1,100				1,100	
Equipment	6,000				6,000				6,000	
Accumulated Depreciation		$0		100		$100				$100
Accounts Payable		2,750				2,750				2,750
Interest Payable		0		25		25				25
Unearned Revenue		900	450			450				450
Bank Loan		3,050				3,050				3,050
Gordon, Capital		9,400				9,400				9,400
Gordon, Drawings	1,000				1,000				1,000	
Service Revenue		3,600		1,350		4,950		$4,950		
Advertising Expense	450				450		$450			
Depreciation Expense	0		100		100		100			
Insurance Expense	0		100		100		100			
Interest Expense	0		25		25		25			
Rent Expense	900				900		900			
Total	$19,700	$19,700	$1,575	$1,575	$20,725	$20,725	1,575	4,950	19,150	15,775
Net Income (Loss)							3,375			3,375
Total							$4,950	$4,950	$19,150	$19,150

Chapter 7 Review Exercise—Solutions

Part 1

a) Journalize the December transactions. Assume the goods were shipped FOB shipping point.

JOURNAL			Page 1
Date 2016	**Account Title and Explanation**	**Debit**	**Credit**
Dec 3	Inventory	50,000	
	Accounts Payable		50,000
	Purchased inventory on account		
Dec 6	Inventory	200	
	Cash		200
	Paid freight charges		
Dec 8	Accounts Payable	2,000	
	Inventory		2,000
	Purchase return		
Dec 11	Accounts Payable	48,000	
	Inventory		960
	Cash		47,040
	Paid supplier and took discount		

b) Journalize the December transactions. Assume the goods were shipped FOB destination.

JOURNAL			Page 1
Date 2016	**Account Title and Explanation**	**Debit**	**Credit**
Dec 3	Accounts Receivable	50,000	
	Sales Revenue		50,000
	Sold inventory on account		
Dec 3	Cost of Goods Sold	35,000	
	Inventory		35,000
	Cost of goods sold for above sale		
Dec 6	Delivery Expense	200	
	Cash		200
	Paid freight charges		
Dec 8	Sales Returns and Allowances	2,000	
	Accounts Receivable		2,000
	Customer returned incorrect merchandise		
Dec 8	Inventory	700	
	Cost of Goods Sold		700
	Inventory returned to stock		
Dec 11	Cash	48,000	
	Sales Discounts	960	
	Accounts Receivable		47,040
	Received payment from customer		

Part 2

a) Prepare a single-step income statement

George's Gardening Supplies Income Statement For the Year Ended December 31, 2016		
Revenue		
Sales Revenue		$113,500
Less: Sales Returns and Allowances	$1,000	
Sales Discounts	1,580	(2,580)
Interest Revenue		6,500
Total Revenue		117,420
Expenses		
Cost of Goods Sold	44,700	
Depreciation Expense	5,000	
Insurance Expense	2,500	
Interest Expense	2,600	
Rent Expense	6,000	
Salaries Expense	11,000	
Supplies Expense	4,500	
Utilities Expense	750	
Total Operating Expenses		77,050
Net Income		$40,370

b) Prepare a multistep income statement

George's Gardening Supplies Income Statement For the Year Ended December 31, 2016		
Sales Revenue		$113,500
Less: Sales Returns and Allowances	$1,000	
Sales Discounts	1,580	(2,580)
Net Sales		110,920
Cost of Goods Sold		44,700
Gross Profit		66,220
Operating Expenses		
Depreciation Expense	5,000	
Insurance Expense	2,500	
Rent Expense	6,000	
Salaries Expense	11,000	
Supplies Expense	4,500	
Utilities Expense	750	
Total Operating Expenses		29,750
Operating Income		36,470
Other Revenue and Expenses		
Interest Revenue	6,500	
Interest Expense	(2,600)	3,900
Net Income		$40,370

Gross Profit Margin = 66,220 ÷ 110,920 = 60%

c) Prepare a classified multistep income statement

George's Gardening Supplies Income Statement For the Year Ended December 31, 2016			
Sales Revenue			$113,500
Less: Sales Returns and Allowances		$1,000	
Sales Discounts		1,580	(2,580)
Net Sales			110,920
Cost of Goods Sold			44,700
Gross Profit			66,220
Operating Expenses			
Selling Expenses			
Depreciation Expense	$5,000		
Insurance Expense	1,750		
Rent Expense	4,200		
Salaries Expense	7,700		
Utilities Expense	525		
Total Selling Expenses		19,175	
Administrative Expenses			
Insurance Expense	750		
Rent Expense	1,800		
Salaries Expense	3,300		
Supplies Expense	4,500		
Utilities Expense	225		
Total Administrative Expenses		10,575	
Total Operating Expenses			29,750
Operating Income			36,470
Other Revenue and Expenses			
Interest Revenue		6,500	
Interest Expense		(2,600)	3,900
Net Income			$40,370

d) Statement of owner's equity

George's Gardening Supplies Statement of Owner's Equity For the Year Ended December 31, 2016		
Gregg, Capital at January 1, 2016		$80,000
Add		
Additional Investment	$10,000	
Net Income	40,370	50,370
Subtotal		130,370
Less		
Gregg, Drawings		5,000
Gregg, Capital at December 31, 2016		$125,370

411

e) Prepare a classified balance sheet

George's Gardening Supplies Classified Balance Sheet As at December 31, 2016		
Assets		
Current Assets		
Cash	$54,830	
Accounts Receivable	33,500	
Inventory	33,440	
Prepaid Insurance	3,600	
Total Current Assets		$125,370
Property, Plant & Equipment		
Equipment	45,000	
Less Accumulated Depreciation	(5,000)	
Total Property, Plant, & Equipment		40,000
Total Assets		$165,370
Liabilities		
Current Liabilities		
Accounts Payable	$10,000	
Current Portion of Bank Loan	10,000	
Total Current Liabilities		$20,000
Long-Term Liabilities		
Long-Term Portion of Bank Loan	20,000	
Total Long-Term Liabilities		20,000
Total Liabilities		40,000
Owner's Equity		
Gregg, Capital		125,370
Total Owner's Equity		125,370
Total Liabilities and Owner's Equity		$165,370

f) Journalize the closing entries using the income summary method

JOURNAL			Page 1
Date 2016	**Account Title and Explanation**	**Debit**	**Credit**
Dec 31	Sales Revenue	113,500	
	Interest Revenue	6,500	
	Income Summary		120,000
	Close revenue accounts		
Dec 31	Income Summary	79,630	
	Sales Returns & Allowances		1,000
	Sales Discounts		1,580
	Cost of Goods Sold		44,700
	Depreciation Expense		5,000
	Insurance Expense		2,500
	Interest Expense		2,600
	Rent Expense		6,000
	Salaries Expense		11,000
	Supplies Expense		4,500
	Utilities Expense		750
	Close expense and debit accounts		
Dec 31	Income Summary	40,370	
	Gregg, Capital		40,370
	Close income summary		
Dec 31	Gregg, Capital	5,000	
	Gregg, Drawings		5,000
	Close drawings account		

Chapter 7 Appendix Review Exercise—Solutions

Part 1

a) December transactions for George's Gardening Supplies

JOURNAL			Page 1
Date 2016	**Account Title and Explanation**	**Debit**	**Credit**
Dec 3	Inventory	50,000	
	Accounts Payable		50,000
	Purchased inventory on account		
Dec 6	Freight-In	200	
	Cash		200
	Paid freight charges		
Dec 8	Accounts Payable	2,000	
	Purchase Returns and Allowances		2,000
	Purchase return		
Dec 11	Accounts Payable	48,000	
	Purchase Discounts		960
	Cash		47,040
	Paid supplier and took discount		

b) December transactions for Michael's Distributing

JOURNAL			Page 1
Date 2016	**Account Title and Explanation**	**Debit**	**Credit**
Dec 3	Accounts Receivable	50,000	
	Sales Revenue		50,000
	Sold inventory on account		
Dec 6	Freight Out	200	
	Cash		200
	Paid freight charges		
Dec 8	Sales Returns and Allowances	2,000	
	Accounts Receivable		2,000
	Customer returned incorrect merchandise		
Dec 11	Cash	47,040	
	Sales Discounts	960	
	Accounts Receivable		48,000
	Received payment from customer		

Part 2

a) Prepare multistep income statement

George's Gardening Supplies Income Statement For the Year Ended December 31, 2016				
Sales Revenue				$113,500
Less: Sales Returns and Allowances			$1,000	
Sales Discounts			1,580	(2,580)
Net Sales				110,920
Cost of Goods Sold				
Inventory, January 1, 2016			16,140	
Purchases		$70,000		
Less: Purchase Returns and Allowances	$5,800			
Purchase Discounts	3,200	(9,000)		
Net Purchases		61,000		
Freight-In		1,000	62,000	
Cost of Goods Available For Sale			78,140	
Inventory, December 31, 2016			33,440	
Cost of Goods Sold				44,700
Gross Profit				66,220
Operating Expenses				
Depreciation Expense			5,000	
Insurance Expense			2,500	
Rent Expense			6,000	
Salaries Expense			11,000	
Supplies Expense			4,500	
Utilities Expense			750	
Total Operating Expenses				29,750
Operating Income				36,470
Other Revenue and Expenses				
Interest Revenue			6,500	
Interest Expense			(2,600)	3,900
Net Income				$40,370

b) Prepare statement of owner's equity

George's Gardening Supplies Statement of Owner's Equity For the Year Ended December 31, 2016		
Gregg, Capital at January 1, 2016		$80,000
Add		
Additional Investment	$10,000	
Net Income	40,370	50,370
Subtotal		130,370
Less		
Gregg, Drawings		5,000
Gregg, Capital at December 31, 2016		$125,370

c) Prepare the classified balance sheet

George's Gardening Supplies Classified Balance Sheet As at December 31, 2016		
Assets		
Current Assets		
Cash	$54,830	
Accounts Receivable	33,500	
Inventory	33,440	
Prepaid Insurance	3,600	
Total Current Assets		$125,370
Property, Plant & Equipment		
Equipment	45,000	
Less: Accumulated Depreciation	(5,000)	
Total Property, Plant, & Equipment		40,000
Total Assets		$165,370
Liabilities		
Current Liabilities		
Accounts Payable	$10,000	
Current Portion of Bank Loan	10,000	
Total Current Liabilities		$20,000
Long-Term Liabilities		
Long-Term Portion of Bank Loan	20,000	
Total Long-Term Liabilities		20,000
Total Liabilities		40,000
Owner's Equity		
Gregg, Capital		125,370
Total Owner's Equity		125,370
Total Liabilities and Owner's Equity		$165,370

d) Journalize the closing entries using the income summary method

JOURNAL		Page 1	
Date 2016	**Account Title and Explanation**	**Debit**	**Credit**
Dec 31	Sales Revenue	113,500	
	Interest Revenue	6,500	
	Inventory	33,440	
	Purchase Returns & Allowances	5,800	
	Purchase Discounts	3,200	
	Income Summary		162,440
	Close revenue and credit accounts and update inventory balance		
Dec 31	Income Summary	122,070	
	Inventory		16,140
	Sales Returns & Allowances		1,000
	Sales Discounts		1,580
	Purchases		70,000
	Freight-In		1,000
	Depreciation Expense		5,000
	Insurance Expense		2,500
	Interest Expense		2,600
	Rent Expense		6,000
	Salaries Expense		11,000
	Supplies Expense		4,500
	Utilities Expense		750
	Close expense and debit accounts and update inventory balance		
Dec 31	Income Summary	40,370	
	Gregg, Capital		40,370
	Close income summary		
Dec 31	Gregg, Capital	5,000	
	Gregg, Drawings		5,000
	Close drawings account		

Chapter 8 Review Exercise—Solutions

a) Using FIFO, prepare the inventory record to show the closing inventory balance

Date	Purchases			Sales			Balance		
	Quantity	Unit Cost	Value	Quantity	Unit Cost	Value	Quantity	Unit Cost	Value
June 1							100	$12	$1,200
June 3	500	$15	$7,500				100	$12	$1,200
							500	$15	$7,500
June 10				100	$12	$1,200			
				100	$15	$1,500	400	$15	$6,000
June 12	300	$18	$5,400				400	$15	$6,000
							300	$18	$5,400
June 20				300	$15	$4,500	100	$15	$1,500
							300	$18	$5,400
Ending Inventory									$6,900

b) Multistep income statement showing sales revenue, cost of goods sold, and gross profit—using information from part a)

Mike's Tikes Toys
Income Statement (Excerpt)
For the Month Ended June 30, 2016

Sales Revenue*	$24,000
Cost of Goods Sold**	7,200
Gross Profit	16,800

*$24,000 = (200 × $45) + (300 × $50)

**$7,200 = $1,200 + $1,500 + $4,500

c) Using the weighted-average cost method, prepare the inventory record to show the closing inventory balance

Date	Purchases			Sales			Balance		
	Quantity	Unit Cost	Value	Quantity	Unit Cost	Value	Quantity	Unit Cost	Value
June 1							100	$12.00	$1,200
June 3	500	$15	$7,500				600	$14.50	$8,700
June 10				200	$14.50	$2,900	400	$14.50	$5,800
June 12	300	$18	$5,400				700	$16.00	$11,200
June 20				300	$16.00	$4,800	400	$16.00	$6,400
Ending Inventory									$6,400

d) Multistep income statement showing sales revenue, cost of goods sold, and gross profit—using information from part c)

Mike's Tikes Toys
Income Statement (Excerpt)
For the Month Ended June 30, 2016

Sales Revenue	$24,000
Cost of Goods Sold*	7,700
Gross Profit	16,300

* $7,700 = $2,900 + $4,800

Chapter 8 Appendix Review Exercise—Solutions

a) Specific Identification

Date	Purchases			Sales			Balance		
	Quantity	Unit Cost	Value	Quantity	Unit Cost	Value	Quantity	Unit Cost	Value
Mar 1							100	$12	$1,200
Mar 3	500	$15	$7,500				100	$12	$1,200
							500	$15	$7,500
Mar 12	300	$18	$5,400				100	$12	$1,200
							500	$15	$7,500
							300	$18	$5,400
Sales for the Month				50	$12	$600	50	$12	$600
				350	$15	$5,250	150	$15	$2,250
				100	$18	$1,800	200	$18	$3,600
Ending Inventory									$6,450

b) FIFO

Date	Purchases			Sales			Balance		
	Quantity	Unit Cost	Value	Quantity	Unit Cost	Value	Quantity	Unit Cost	Value
Mar 1							100	$12	$1,200
Mar 3	500	$15	$7,500				100	$12	$1,200
							500	$15	$7,500
Mar 12	300	$18	$5,400				100	$12	$1,200
							500	$15	$7,500
							300	$18	$5,400
Sales for the Month				100	$12	$1,200			
				400	$15	$6,000	100	$15	$1,500
							300	$18	$5,400
Ending Inventory									$6,900

c) Weighted-Average Cost

Date	Purchases			Sales			Balance		
	Quantity	Unit Cost	Value	Quantity	Unit Cost	Value	Quantity	Unit Cost	Value
Mar 1							100		$1,200
Mar 3	500	$15	$7,500				600		$8,700
Mar 12	300	$18	$5,400				900		$14,100
Average Inventory for the Month							900	$15.67	$14,100
Sales for the Month				500	$15.67	$7,835	400	$15.67	$6,265
Ending Inventory									$6,265

Note: numbers may vary due to rounding

Chapter 9 Review Exercise—Solutions

a) Record transactions in the Cash Receipts, Sales, Purchases, and Cash Payments journal.

	Cash Receipts Journal									Page 1
Date	Account	PR	Cash (DR)	Sales (CR)	Accounts Receivable (CR)	Interest Revenue (CR)	Loans Payable (CR)	Other (CR)	COGS/Inventory (DR/CR)
Jun 4	Cash Sale		4,000	4,000					4,000
Jun 6	B. Didley	✓	480		480				
Jun 9	Cash Sale		2,160	2,160					2,160
Jun 10	K. Domino		25			25			
Jun 15	Jo Jo Inc.		2,400				2,400		
	TOTAL		9,065	6,160	480	25	2,400		6,160

	Sales Journal					Page 1
Date	Account	Invoice #	PR	Accounts Receivable/Sales (DR/CR)	COGS/Inventory (DR/CR)
Jun 18	Richard Starkey	10022	✓	3,000	2,000
Jun 28	Pete Best	10023	✓	5,000	3,700
	TOTAL			8,000	5,700

	Purchases Journal						Page 1
Date	Account	Invoice #	PR	Repairs Expense (DR)	Office Supplies (DR)	Purchases (DR)	Accounts Payable (CR)
Jun 5	Stapl-EZ	4053	✓		100		100
Jun 9	Building Services Inc.	124	✓	350			350
Jun 26	Brick & Mortar	404241	✓			3,500	3,500
	TOTAL			350	100	3,500	3,950

	Cash Payments Journal						Page 1
Date	Account	Chq #	PR	Other (DR)	Purchases (DR)	Accounts Payable (DR)	Cash (CR)
Jun 12	Stapl-EZ Inc.	465	✓			100	100
Jun 21	Noel's Inc.	466			4,000		4,000
Jun 22	Building Services Inc.	467	✓			350	350
Jun 25	SKG Inc.	468		175			175
	TOTAL			175	4,000	450	4,625

b) Post from the special journals to the accounts receivable subledger. At the end of the month, post from the special journals to the general ledger control account.

Accounts Receivable Subsidiary Ledger Bo Didley				
Date	PR	DR	CR	Balance
Opening Bal				2,000 DR
Jun 6	CR1		480	1,520 DR

Accounts Receivable Subsidiary Ledger Richard Starkey				
Date	PR	DR	CR	Balance
Opening Bal				1,000 DR
Jun 18	SJ1	3,000		4,000 DR

Accounts Receivable Subsidiary Ledger Pete Best				
Date	PR	DR	CR	Balance
Opening Bal				1,500 DR
Jun 28	SJ1	5,000		6,500 DR

Post to general ledger.

General Ledger Accounts Receivable				
Date	PR	DR	CR	Balance
Opening Bal.				4,500 DR
Jun 30	CRI		480	4,020 DR
Jun 30	SJ1	8,000		12,020 DR

Lin-Z June 30, 2016 General Ledger	
Accounts Receivable	$12,020

Lin-Z Schedule of Accounts Receivable June 30, 2016	
Bo Didley	$1,520
Richard Starkey	4,000
Pete Best	6,500
Total Accounts Receivable	$12,020

c) Post from the special journals to the accounts payable subledger and then to the general ledger control account at the end of the month.

Accounts Payable Subsidiary Ledger Stapl-EZ Inc.				
Date	PR	DR	CR	Balance
Opening Bal.				500 CR
Jun 5	PJ1		100	600 CR
Jun 12	CP1	100		500 CR

Accounts Payable Subsidiary Ledger Building Services Inc.				
Date	PR	DR	CR	Balance
Opening Bal.				750 CR
Jun 9	PJ1		350	1,100 CR
Jun 22	CP1	350		750 CR

Accounts Payable Subsidiary Ledger Brick & Mortar Inc.				
Date	PR	DR	CR	Balance
Opening Bal.				2,500 CR
Jun 26	PJ1		3,500	6,000 CR

Post to general ledger.

General Ledger Accounts Payable				
Date	PR	DR	CR	Balance
Opening Bal.				3,750 CR
Jun 30	PJ1		3,950	7,700 CR
Jun 30	CP1	450		7,250 CR

Lin-Z June 30, 2016 General Ledger	
Accounts Receivable	$7,250

Lin-Z Schedule of Accounts Payable June 30, 2016	
Stapl-EZ Inc.	$500
Building Services Inc.	750
Brick & Mortar Inc.	6,000
Total Accounts Payable	$7,250

Chapter 9 Appendix Review Exercise—Solutions

a) Record transactions in the Cash Receipts, Sales, Purchases, and Cash Payments journals.

Cash Receipts Journal							**Page 1**
Date	Account	PR	Cash (DR)	Sales (CR)	Accounts Receivable (CR)	Interest Revenue (CR)	Loans Payable (CR)	Other (CR)

Date	Account	PR	Cash (DR)	Sales (CR)	Accounts Receivable (CR)	Interest Revenue (CR)	Loans Payable (CR)	Other (CR)
Jun 4	Cash Sale		4,000	4,000				
Jun 6	B. Didley	✓	480		480			
Jun 9	Cash Sale		2,160	2,160				
Jun 10	K. Domino		25			25		
Jun 15	Jo Jo Inc.		2,400				2,400	
	TOTAL		9,065	6,160	480	25	2,400	

Sales Journal				**Page 1**
Date	Account	Invoice #	PR	Accounts Receivable/Sales (DR/CR)
Jun 18	Richard Starkey	10022	✓	3,000
Jun 28	Pete Best	10023	✓	5,000
	TOTAL			8,000

Purchases Journal							**Page 1**
Date	Account	Invoice #	PR	Repairs Expense (DR)	Office Supplies (DR)	Purchases (DR)	Accounts Payable (CR)
Jun 5	Stapl-EZ	4053	✓		100		100
Jun 9	Building Services Inc	124	✓	350			350
Jun 26	Brick & Mortar	404241	✓			3,500	3,500
	TOTAL			350	100	3,500	3,950

Cash Payments Journal							**Page 1**
Date	Account	Chq #	PR	Other (DR)	Purchases (DR)	Accounts Payable (DR)	Cash (CR)
Jun 12	Stapl-EZ Inc.	465	✓			100	100
Jun 21	Noel's Inc.	466			4,000		4,000
Jun 22	Building Services Inc.	467	✓			350	350
Jun 25	SKG Inc.	468		175			175
	TOTAL			175	4,000	450	4,625

b) Post from special journals to accounts receivable subledger. At month end, post from special journals to general ledger control account.

Accounts Receivable Subsidiary Ledger Bo Didley				
Date	PR	DR	CR	Balance
Opening Bal				2,000 DR
Jun 6	CR1		480	1,520 DR

Accounts Receivable Subsidiary Ledger Richard Starkey				
Date	PR	DR	CR	Balance
Opening Bal				1,000 DR
Jun 18	SJ1	3,000		4,000 DR

Accounts Receivable Subsidiary Ledger Pete Best				
Date	PR	DR	CR	Balance
Opening Bal				1,500 DR
Jun 28	SJ1	5,000		6,500 DR

Post to general ledger.

General Ledger Accounts Receivable				
Date	PR	DR	CR	Balance
Opening Bal.				4,500 DR
Jun 30	CRI		480	4,020 DR
Jun 30	SJ1	8,000		12,020 DR

Lin-Z June 30, 2016 General Ledger	
Accounts Receivable	$12,020

Lin-Z Schedule of Accounts Receivable June 30, 2016	
Bo Didley	$1,520
Richard Starkey	4,000
Pete Best	6,500
Total Accounts Receivable	$12,020

c) Post from special journals to accounts payable subledger and then to general ledger control account at end of month.

Accounts Payable Subsidiary Ledger Stapl-EZ Inc.				
Date	PR	DR	CR	Balance
Opening Bal.				500 CR
Jun 5	PJ1		100	600 CR
Jun 12	CP1	100		500 CR

Accounts Payable Subsidiary Ledger Building Services Inc.				
Date	PR	DR	CR	Balance
Opening Bal.				750 CR
Jun 9	PJ1		350	1,100 CR
Jun 22	CP1	350		750 CR

Accounts Payable Subsidiary Ledger Brick & Mortar Inc.				
Date	PR	DR	CR	Balance
Opening Bal.				2,500 CR
Jun 26	PJ1		3,500	6,000 CR

Post to general ledger.

General Ledger Accounts Payable				
Date	PR	DR	CR	Balance
Opening Bal.				3,750 CR
Jun 30	PJ1		3,950	7,700 CR
Jun 30	CP1	450		7,250 CR

Lin-Z June 30, 2016 General Ledger	
Accounts Receivable	$7,250

Lin-Z Schedule of Accounts Payable June 30, 2016	
Stapl-EZ Inc.	$500
Building Services Inc.	750
Brick & Mortar Inc.	6,000
Total Accounts Payable	$7,250

Chapter 10 Review Exercise—Solutions

Review Exercise 1

Recommendations for Cash Controls

Record cash immediately when received

- Use sequential pre-numbered receipts.
- Purchase and use a cash register.
- Compare and reconcile the sum of sales amounts (office copy) to the cash on hand (cash drawer or cash register copy).

Protect cash when it is on the premises

- Lock the cash drawer or cash register when not in use.
- Remove the cash from the cash drawer or cash register at night. Lock it in a safe, or the office.
- Create a customer policy of free cleaning if no receipt is given by the counter clerk. This ensures the customer is always given a receipt when they pay cash.

Remove cash from the premises as soon as possible

- Deposit cash into the bank daily, multiple times if necessary.

Overall Goal for Cash Controls

- The overall goal for cash controls is to ensure that the amount of cash received is the amount of cash recorded, which is the amount of cash deposited.

Recommendations for Clean 4U

- Contact authorities to report the counter clerk for fraudulent activities and theft, and provide information for their investigation.
- Terminate the employment of the counter clerk.
- JP can step in as the counter clerk until another employee is found.

Review Exercise 2

Martin Furniture Bank Reconciliation June 30, 2016		
Explanation	Ledger	Bank
Opening Balance	4,815	2,000
Add: Interest on bank account	5	
Add: Outstanding deposit—June 29		1,300
Less: NSF cheque	(2,000)	
Less: NSF Charge	(6)	
Less: service charge	(14)	
Less: outstanding cheque		(500)
Reconciled Balance	2,800	2,800

JOURNAL				Page 1
Date	Account Title and Explanation		Debit	Credit
2016				
Jun 30	Cash		5	
	Interest Revenue			5
	To record deposit of interest earned			
Jun 30	Accounts Receivable		2,000	
	Cash			2,000
	Reinstate accounts receivable for NSF cheque			
Jun 30	NSF Charges Expense		6	
	Cash			6
	To record NSF charges			
Jun 30	Bank Charges Expense		14	
	Cash			14
	To record payment of bank service charges			

Review Exercise 3

a)

JOURNAL			Page 1
Date	**Account Title and Explanation**	**Debit**	**Credit**
2016			
Apr 1	Petty Cash	200	
	Cash		200
	To establish petty cash fund		

b)

JOURNAL			Page 1
Date	**Account Title and Explanation**	**Debit**	**Credit**
2016			
Apr 16	Postage Expense	40	
	Delivery Expense	20	
	Travel Expense	25	
	Entertainment Expense	8	
	Office Expenses	7	
	Cash Over and Short	5	
	Cash		105
	To reimburse petty cash fund		

Chapter 11 Review Exercise—Solutions

a) Payroll register

Payroll Period June 8 to June 19, 2015		Payroll Register							
		Deductions							
Name	Gross Earnings	CPP	EI	Income Tax	Charitable Donations	Health Plan	Total Deductions	Net Pay
Flower, Blossom	1,288.00	57.09	24.21	231.84	10.00	25.00	348.14	$939.86
Painter, Rob	1,026.00	44.12	19.29	184.68	10.00	25.00	283.09	$742.91
Scrap, Brook	1,203.50	52.91	22.63	216.63	10.00	25.00	327.17	$876.33
Totals	$3,517.50	$154.12	$66.13	$633.15	$30.00	$75.00	$958.40	$2,559.10

b) Pay employees

JOURNAL			Page 1
Date 2015	Account Title and Explanation	Debit	Credit
Jun 19	Salaries Expense	3,517.50	
	CPP Payable		154.12
	EI Payable		66.13
	Income Tax Payable		633.15
	Charitable Donations Payable		30.00
	Health Plan Payable		75.00
	Cash		2,559.10
	Record salaries and deductions		

c) Accrue vacation pay

JOURNAL			Page 1
Date 2015	Account Title and Explanation	Debit	Credit
Jun 19	Vacation Pay Expense	140.70	
	Vacation Pay Payable		140.70
	To accrue vacation play		

Vacation pay = $3,517.50 \times 4\%$

d) Employer expenses

JOURNAL			Page 1
Date 2015	**Account Title and Explanation**	**Debit**	**Credit**
Jun 19	Employee Benefits Expense	342.81	
	CPP Payable		154.12
	EI Payable		92.58
	Health Plan Payable		75.00
	Workers' Compensation Payable		21.11
	Record business expense		

Employer portion of EI = 66.13×1.4

Workers' compensation = $3,517.50 \times 0.6\%$

e) Government remittance

JOURNAL			Page 1
Date 2015	**Account Title and Explanation**	**Debit**	**Credit**
Jul 15	CPP Payable	308.24	
	EI Payable	158.71	
	Income Tax Payable	633.15	
	Cash		1,100.10
	Payment to the government		

CPP Payable = $154.12 + $154.12

EI Payable = $66.13 + $92.58

Chapter 12 Review Exercise—Solutions

Review Exercise 1

				% of Base-
Basil's Bakery **Percentage Change and Vertical Analysis** **As at December 31**				
	2016	**2015**	**% Change**	**Figure 2016**
Cash	$1,650	$987	67.17%	29.70%
Accounts Receivable	1,175	573	105.06%	21.15%
Inventory	396	256	54.69%	7.13%
Other current assets	301	103	192.23%	5.42%
Total Current Assets	3,522	1,919	83.53%	63.39%
Property, plant & equipment	2,034	1,170	73.85%	36.61%
TOTAL ASSETS	$5,556	$3,089	79.86%	100.00%
Current Liabilities	$1,474	$547	169.47%	26.53%
Non-current liabilities	104	58	79.31%	1.87%
TOTAL LIABILITIES	1,578	605	160.83%	28.40%
SHAREHOLDERS' EQUITY	3,978	2,484	60.14%	71.60%
TOTAL LIABILITIES AND EQUITY	$5,556	$3,089	79.86%	100.00%

Basil's Bakery has grown considerably in 2016 compared to 2015, as witnessed by the positive percentage changes in all categories. While shareholders' equity increased 60.14% from 2015, total liabilities increased even more at 160.83%. This larger percentage increase in liabilities is not necessarily a bad thing, considering that the total liabilities balance is still much lower than shareholders' equity balance. As shown in the vertical analysis, total liabilities are only 28.40% of total assets, compared to shareholders' equity which is 71.60% of total assets. Additionally, liquidity does not appear to be a problem, considering that Basil's Bakery has far more current assets (63.39% of total assets) than current liabilities (26.53% of total assets). Therefore, the company is in a good position to take advantage of higher leverage provided it can cover the interest expense that comes with more debt. Another important thing to note from the annual percentage change is the 105.06% increase in accounts receivable, which is higher than the percentage increases of cash and inventory. This means that Basil's Bakery has been growing its business partly by increasing credit sales. The company may need to put more focus on management and control of accounts receivable, as the company's success will increasingly depend on its ability to collect its accounts receivable.

Financial Ratio or Figure	Calculation	Result
Working Capital	$3,477 – $1,474	$2,003
Current Ratio	$\dfrac{\$3,477}{\$1,474}$	2.36
Quick Ratio	$\dfrac{\$1,605 + \$1,175}{\$1,474}$	1.89
Gross Profit Margin	$\dfrac{\$3,081}{\$6,009}$	0.5127 or 51.27%
Net Profit Margin	$\dfrac{\$1,295}{\$6,009}$	0.2155 or 21.55%
Return on Equity	$\$1,295 \div \dfrac{(\$3,933 + \$2,484)}{2}$	0.4036 or 40.36%
Inventory Turnover Ratio	$\$2,928 \div \dfrac{(\$396 + \$256)}{2}$	8.98
Inventory Days on Hand	$\dfrac{365}{8.98}$	40.65 days
Debt-to-Equity Ratio	$\dfrac{\$1,578}{\$3,933}$	0.4012 or 40.12%

Basil's Bakery has a positive **working capital** of $2,003 which indicates that the company has enough liquid assets to pay off its upcoming short-term debts.

The company has a **current ratio** of 2.36 which indicates that the business has double and a bit of current assets to pay for its current liabilities. It could be argued that the Bakery has enough of a cushion that it could afford to have more cash tied up in current assets, such as inventory and accounts receivable. It could also invest a small portion to earn more investment income.

The Bakery has a **quick ratio** of 1.89 which indicates that the business can meet its most immediate debt obligations without relying on the liquidation of inventory. In terms of liquidity as a whole, Basil's Bakery is highly liquid based on the above three financial ratios and figures, indicating a strong financial position in its short-term goals.

The organization has a **gross profit margin** of 51.27% which means that the company has an easier time covering its expenses and is more likely to be profitable. Compared to 2015, the gross profit margin declined, indicating that the company is either not generating enough revenue, has experienced an increase in inventory costs or both. This should be a point of concern, indicating a downward trend. Comparing 2016's gross profit margin to the industry average of 49.47% shows that the bakery is doing better than the average company in the same industry. It must work to ensure that it remains above this amount by managing costs and expenses.

The business has a **net profit margin** of 21.55% which means that the company is earning 21 cents of net income for every one dollar of revenue earned. Compared to 2015, the net profit margin declined, indicating that the company's costs have increased. This should be a point of concern, indicating a downward trend. Comparing 2016's net profit margin to the industry average of 20.36% shows that the bakery is doing better than the average company in the same industry. It must work to ensure that it remains above this amount by managing costs and expenses.

It has a positive 40.36% **return on equity** which is a good for investors, and as always, shareholders could look elsewhere for a better return. Shareholders like to see a return that is as good or better than they could have received by investing elsewhere. In terms of profitability, the company is doing well.

Basil's Bakery has an **inventory turnover ratio** of 8.98 which represents the number of times that the company sold its entire inventory within the year. Bakeries should have a higher turnover ratio because some of the input products they use can expire, such as milk and eggs. Once items are baked, they have a short shelf life as well.

The company has an **inventory days on hand ratio** of 40.65 days. This indicates that the inventory is sold rather slowly. This paired with the inventory turnover ratio, shows that the Bakery could be selling inventory faster. This is a point of concern. In terms of operations management, inventory must be addressed immediately. Inventory should be turning over more quickly to ensure that the bakery is not throwing out expired products. A turnaround in operations management could mean more success in profitability and liquidity.

The bakery has a **debt-to-equity ratio** of 40.12% indicating that the total debt is significantly comparable to equity. Recall that it is not healthy for a business to borrow too much relative to what it is worth. This is because there is a cost of debt in the form of interest. The bakery could improve the debt-to-equity ratio by trying to make more profit by increasing revenues and decreasing costs. This would ultimately lead to increased equity for the business. As a form of leverage, the business could improve.

Review Exercise 2

Operating activities are those necessary to run the daily operations of the business. This section of the cash flow statement tracks the movement of cash within a business on the basis of day-to-day activities.

Investing activities include any exchange of cash related to the long-term financial investments or capital assets of the business. The purchase of these assets can be thought of as the business investing in itself because the assets usually result in increased operations.

Financing activities are any payments or receipts of cash that relate to changes in either long-term debt or shareholders' equity. This section of the cash flow statement tracks the movement of cash within a business based on the way a company receives money from those providing financing and pays it back.

Appendix II
SUMMARY OF FINANCIAL RATIOS

The following is a guide to some common ratios used to measure the financial performance of a business. Different industries have different benchmarks for each ratio. It is important to understand the trends in a company's performance from period-to-period and the relative performance of a company within its industry for each ratio.

Working Capital

Corrent Assets - Liabilities	Represents the excess dollar amount of current assets available after paying current liabilities.

Gross Profit Margin

$$\frac{\text{Gross Profit}}{\text{Sales Revenue}}$$	Measures the percentage of revenue remaining to contribute towards operating expenses, after deducting product costs per dollar of revenue. The higher the percentage, the higher the contribution per dollar of revenue.

Net Profit Margin

$$\frac{\text{Net Income}}{\text{Sales Revenue}}$$	Represents the profitability and efficiency of the business. Generally, the higher the percentage, the better because it indicates efficient management and expense control.

Return on Equity (ROE)

$$\frac{\text{Net Income}}{\text{Average Shareholders' Equity}}$$	Tests the financial return the owners of a business are earning, relative to their investment. Generally, the higher the percentage, the better. Use this ratio to assess risk and reward.

Current Ratio

$$\frac{\text{Current Assets}}{\text{Current Liabilities}}$$

Measures the ability of the company to pay current debt over the next 12 months (specifically, the number of times current assets can cover current debts). Generally, the higher the number the better. If the ratio is too high, it indicates inefficient use of capital as current assets generally have the lowest returns.

Quick Ratio (or Acid Test)

$$\frac{\text{Cash + Short-Term Investments + Accounts Receivable}}{\text{Current Liabilities}}$$

The number of times the most liquid assets (e.g. cash, short-term investments, and accounts receivable) can cover immediate debts (usually 90 days). Generally, the higher the number the better. If the ratio is too high, it indicates inefficient use of capital (see current ratio).

Debt-to-Equity Ratio

$$\frac{\text{Total Liabilities (Debt)}}{\text{Total Shareholders' Equity}}$$

Used by lenders to examine their risk relative to the owners' risk. Some debt is good, but too much can cause financial distress.

Inventory Turnover

$$\frac{\text{Cost of Goods Sold}}{\text{Average Inventory}}$$

Calculates the number of times inventory is replenished within one year. Generally, the lower the inventory turnover, the less times per year inventory is being replenished which results in elevated holding costs. Inventory turnover should be compared to similar periods in a cyclical business.

Inventory Days on Hand

$$\frac{365}{\text{Inventory Turnover Ratio}}$$

Calculates the average number of days the current inventory will last, and how well the inventory is being managed. Generally, the lower the inventory days on hand, the less the holding costs (e.g. shrinkage, interest, etc.). Inventory days on hand should be compared to similar periods in a cyclical business.

Note

The purpose of ratio analysis is to help the reader of financial statements ask the appropriate questions and understand which issues need to be addressed. Keep in mind that no single ratio will be able to provide the complete story. Much like a puzzle, you need all the pieces to see the whole picture.

Appendix III

ASPE VS IFRS

Chapter	Topic	Accounting Standards for Private Enterprises (ASPE)	International Financial Reporting Standards (IFRS)
3	When to use	• Private organization (sole proprietorship, partnership, private corporations) • No plans to become public in the near future • ASPE also used by most competitors	• Public corporation or owned by a public company • Private organization intending to become public in the near future • IFRS already adopted by most competitors • Private enterprises adopting IFRS by choice for other reasons, such as, in anticipation of a bank's requirement for IFRS-based financial statements in loan application
	Cost	Less costly and simpler to implement	Can be costly to implement
	Number of disclosure requirements	Fewer disclosures are required	More disclosures are required
	Comparability	Less comparable on a global scale	More relevant, reliable and comparable on a global scale
	Development status	ASPE may eventually evolve into IFRS in the future	IFRS is positioned to be the global accounting standards for the foreseeable future
	Level of judgments required	More specific rules; fewer judgments required	Fewer hard-and-fast rules; more judgments required
5	Frequency of financial statement issuance	Companies are required to prepare financial statements at least once a year. This implies that the end-of-period adjustments process must also be completed at least once a year.	Companies are required to prepare financial statements at least once per quarter. This implies that the end-of-period adjustments process must be completed at least four times a year.
6	Balance Sheet or Statement of Financial Position terminology	The term "Balance Sheet" is more often used, although the term "Statement of Financial Position" is also allowed.	The term "Statement of Financial Position" is more often used, although the term "Balance Sheet" is also allowed.
	Order of items listed on the balance sheet or statement of financial position	The listing order of items on a balance sheet is not specified, although ordering items from most liquid to least liquid on the balance sheet is a common practice among the companies adopting ASPE.	IFRS also does not prescribe the listing order of items on a statement of financial position. However, a common practice among the companies adopting IFRS, particularly European companies, is ordering assets from least liquid to most liquid. Additionally, equity is commonly presented before long-term liabilities, followed by current liabilities.
7	Expense classification on income statement	A company can choose to present its expenses on an income statement by nature, or by function, or even by using a mixture of nature and function.	Expenses can be classified either by nature or by function on an income statement. Using a mixture of nature and function is prohibited.

GLOSSARY

A

Account — A record that allows detailed information to be tracked about the values of individual items.

Accountants — Individuals who prepare financial information to ensure that internal and external users have the information they need to make informed decisions.

Accounting — A system to identify, measure and communicate all the financial activities of an individual or a business.

Accounting Cycle — The steps required to complete the financial statements.

Accounting Equation — Double entry accounting is based on this equation: Assets = Liabilities + Owner's Equity.

Accounting Ethics — The standards by which the actions are judged as being honest versus dishonest, right or wrong, fair or unfair.

Accounting Period — The time frame in which the financial statements are prepared.

Accounting Standards for Private Enterprises (ASPE) — Accounting standards developed by the AcSB followed by private enterprises.

Accounts Payable — When a company owes a supplier for a product or service, the money owed is recorded as a liability called accounts payable.

Accounts Receivable — The money owed to the company when the company provides payment terms to sell its products or services to its customers.

Accrual - Based Accounting — Revenue and expenses are recorded in the period in which they occur, regardless of when cash payment is received or paid.

Accruals — An accrual can add or subtract to net worth or equity for an accounting period and helps in recognizing how much you are worth at a point in time.

Accrued Expenses — Accrued expenses are expenses that have been incurred but have not yet been recorded.

Accrued Revenue — Accrued revenue is revenue that has been earned but not yet recorded.

Accumulated Depreciation — In the case of property, plant and equipment (PPE), the contra asset account is called accumulated depreciation.

Accumulated Surplus (deficit) — Some government institutions refer to net worth or equity as accumulated surplus (deficit).

Adjusted Trial Balance — The trial balance after the adjustments are made.

Adjusting Entries — Journal entries made at the end of the accounting period to record assets, liabilities, equity, revenue and expenses according to revenue and expense recognition.

Asset — An asset is something you own that will benefit you now and in the future.

B

Balance Sheet — A permanent document that is used to record what you own (assets), what you owe (liabilities) and what you are worth (net worth/equity) on a specific date.

Bank Overdraft — The cash available in the bank account is negative.

Bank Reconciliation — A schedule that compares, reconciles, and explains the difference between a company's bank statement and its own cash accounting records.

Base-Figure — A dollar amount that is used for comparison when performing a vertical analysis. It is usually total assets on the balance sheet or revenue on the income statement.

Base-Year — A year that is used for comparison when performing a horizontal analysis.

Business Entity Assumption — The business entity assumption states that accounting for a business must be kept separate from the personal affairs of its owner or any other business.

C

Capital — Any non-revenue transaction that increases net worth. This is used in calculating ending net worth.

Cash Discounts — Discounts offered to encourage prompt payment from customers by offering a percentage off the final bill for paying early.

Cash Equivalents — A short-term investment, usually shorter than three months (or 90 days). They are highly liquid and can be quickly converted into cash when needed.

Cash Flow — Cash flowing into and out of the bank account, which is not necessarily directly connected to net worth.

Cash Flow Statement — A statement prepared to show how cash was generated and how was used within the business.

Cash Payments Journal — This journal is used to record all cash payments made by the business (e.g. rent and wages expense) including payments made to suppliers.

Cash Receipts Journal — This journal is used to record all cash deposits (e.g. cash sales) and collections from outstanding accounts receivable.

Cash-Based Accounting — Revenue and expenses are recorded only when the cash is received or paid.

Chart of Accounts — The list of all the accounts in the general ledger.

Classified Multistep Income Statement — Classified multistep income statements are a variation of the multistep income statements where expenses are divided into categories such as administrative and selling expenses.

Closing Entries — Journal entries made to close revenues, expenses and drawings to owner's capital at the end of an accounting period.

Closing the Books — The process to update owner's capital and starts a new income statement for the next accounting period.

Common Shares — Shares of a corporation that give ownership and the right to vote for directors executives.

Comparability — Comparability means that the financial statements of a company must be prepared in a similar way year after year, or between accounting periods.

Comparative Balance Sheet — A balance sheet showing financial results for multiple years for easy comparison.

Compound Journal Entries — Journal entries affect three or more accounts.

Conceptual Framework — The basis to determine how business transactions should be measured and reported.

Conservatism — Selection of the least optimistic option whenever an accountant needs to exercise their own interpretation or judgment in applying an accounting standard.

Consistency — Preparing reports following the same standards and guidance from period to period.

Contra Account — Contra means opposite. A contra account is linked to another account and records decreases in the value of that account. It behaves in a manner opposite to the way a regular asset account behaves.

Control Account — A control account keeps track of the grand total of the amounts in the subledger.

Corporation — A business that is registered with the provincial or federal government as a separate legal entity from its owners, the shareholders.

Cost Constraint — The value of reported information compared to the costs to produce the financial statements. If the value of the information does not outweigh the costs, the company should not prepare it.

Cost of Goods Sold (COGS) — Cost of goods sold is the value of all the goods sold and is subtracted from sales revenue to determine gross profit.

Credit — A credit means an entry on the right side of the account, and it may cause the account to increase or decrease, depending on the type of account.

Current Assets — Current assets are those that are likely to be converted into cash or used up within the next 12 months through the day-to-day operations of the business.

Current Liabilities — Current liabilities are amounts due to be paid within the next 12 months.

Current Ratio — The current ratio measures a company's ability to pay off short-term debt. The formula is: Current Ratio = Current Assets ÷ Current Liabilities.

Customer Deposit — A customer that pays a business for services before they are performed.

D

Days Inventory on Hand Ratio — Calculates how many days that inventory will last given the current rate of sales.

Debit — A debit means an entry on the left side of the account and it may cause the account to increase or decrease, depending on the type of account.

Debt-to-Equity Ratio — Assess the balance of debt and equity in a business.

Depreciation — Allocating the cost of a long-term asset over its useful life.

Disclosure — Disclosure states that any and all information that affects the full understanding of a company's financial statements must be included with the financial statements.

Discontinued Operations — A segment of a business that is no longer part of regular operations.

E

Equity — The net worth of a business, after all assets have been sold and all liabilities have been paid.

Event — An occurrence in business where nothing of value is traded and no transaction is recorded.

Expense Recognition — Expense recognition requires that expenses must be recorded in the same period in which they were used to generate revenue.

Expenses — Expenses are costs and a decrease to equity caused by day-to-day activities.

External Users — People or organizations outside the business, such as suppliers, banks and external accountants that use the financial information of the business.

F

Financial Accounting — The process of recordkeeping for the business and preparing the financial statements.

Financing Activities — A section on the cash flow statement that shows cash movement within a business based on changes to long-term debt or equity.

First-In, First-Out (FIFO) Method — The first-in, first-out (FIFO) method is used when a business assumes that the first items received in inventory are also the first items moved out of inventory.

Fiscal Year — A one year time frame for preparing financial statements. The fiscal year is not necessarily the same as the calendar year.

Fraud — Any illegal intentional act of deception that results in a financial benefit or gain. It may not always be easy to identify because the intention is to hide the fraudulent act within normal business activities.

Freight-In — Shipping costs paid on goods purchased FOB shipping point are recorded in the freight-in account.

Freight-Out — Shipping costs paid on goods sold FOB destination are recorded in the freight-out account.

Function — A classification method used to prepare the income statement based on the relatability of particular revenues and expenses.

G

Gain — An increase in the value of long-term assets.

General Journal — A book of original entry used to record transactions. The journal lists all the transactions of the business in one place and in chronological order. It is used to record any entry that does not belong in one of the special journals.

General Ledger — A book used to record and organize all the accounts and balances of the business.

General Partnership — A partnership in which all partners are subject to unlimited liability. All partners are considered to be general partners.

Generally Accepted Accounting Principles (GAAP) — Standards created by the accounting profession, which provide guidance on how financial information should be reported.

Going Concern Assumption — The going concern assumption assumes that a business will continue to operate into the foreseeablefuture.

Gross Pay — The amount of wages or pay that an employee earns.

Gross Profit — The difference between service revenue and cost of sales is called gross profit.

Gross Profit Margin — The ratio of gross profit to sales revenue.

Gross Profit Method — The gross profit method uses a company's gross profit figure to estimate the value of inventory. More specifically, a company analyzes the gross profit numbers of prior years to come up with a current gross profit number to apply to estimation figures.

H

Horizontal Analysis — Analysing financial information from year to year.

I

Imprest Bank Account — This is a separate bank account from the main account of the business. It is used specifically for one function such as payroll.

Income Statement — Atemporary record to record transactions relating to revenue and expenses. It is made to determine the change in net worth or equity over a specific period of time.

Income Summary — A temporary holding account to close the revenue and expense accounts.

Internal Users — People who own the business and/or work in the business.

International Financial Reporting Standards (IFRS) — Standards created by International Accounting Standards Board (IASB), which provide guidance on how financial information should be reported.

Inventory — It is a collection of physical goods that a company has purchased or manufactured to sell to its customers.

Inventory Days on Hand — A calculation of how many days inventory will last given the current rate of sales.

Inventory Turnover Ratio — The inventory turnover ratio estimates how many times a year a company is buying inventory.

Inventory Valuation Methods — There are three methods that companies can use, based on the nature of the goods, to determine how inventory costs are handled. These are called inventory valuation methods because they will determine the value of inventory on hand at any given time.

Investing Activities — A section on the cash flow statement that shows cash movement within a business based on investing in long-term assets.

Invoice — The invoice includes the details of the items sold or services rendered, the agreed-upon price, and the due date.

J

Journal — Once analysis is done on a transaction, it will be recorded in a journal, which is referred to as a book of original entry.

Journalizing — The act of recording in the journal.

L

Leverage — The amounts of risk and debt the company has.

Liabilities — Liabilities are what you owe, your obligations.

Limited Liability Partnership (LLP) — Partners to have limited liability regarding the misconduct or negligence of the other partners.

Limited Partnership — One general partner who accepts unlimited liability and one or more limited partners with liability limited to the amount they invested.

Liquid Asset — Cash is the most liquid asset and is therefore listed first on the balance sheet, followed by accounts receivable, inventory, and so on.

Liquidity — Liquidity is the ease with which the asset can be converted to cash. The assets of a business are listed in sequence according to their liquidity.

Long-Term Assets — Long-term assets are used to operate a business and are not expected to turn into cash or be used up within the next 12 months unless they are sold for reasons other than the day-to-day operations of the business.

Long-Term Liabilities — Long-term liabilities are amounts due to be paid after 12 months.

Loss — A decrease in the value of long-term assets.

Lower of Cost and Net Realizable Value (LCNRV) — The method of estimating inventory valuation being recorded at the lower of its cost and its net realizable value.

M

Managerial Accounting — Preparing specialized reports to assist in decision making inside the business.

Materiality — The significance of information to users. A piece of information is considered material if it could influence or change a user's decision.

Measurement — The process of determining the amount at which an item is recorded in the financial statements.

Merchandising Business — Any company that buys products to resell to customers.

Monetary Unit Assumption — Accounting records are expressed in terms of money.

Multistep Income Statement — An income statement that further breaks down specific revenues and expenses to show subtotals like gross profit, operating expenses, and operating income.

Mutual Agency — Each partner is able to speak for the other partners and bind them to business contracts. In other words, each partner is bound by the business actions of the other partners.

N

Nature — A classification method by grouping similar items based on broad categories like combining all revenues together.

Net Book Value — Original value of the asset less the total depreciation that has been recognized.

Net Income — Net income occurs when revenue exceeds expenses for the period and will increase equity.

Net Loss — A net loss occurs when expenses exceed revenue for the period and will decrease equity.

Net Pay — The amount of pay actually received by the employee. This is less than gross pay because of several payroll deductions.

Net Profit Margin — The profitability of a company after all expenses have been paid. Net profit margin is expressed as a percentage of sales.

Net Realizable Value (NRV) — Net realizable value is the price that a company can realistically expect to sell the item for, less any costs incurred to make the item ready for sale, such as repair costs.

Net Worth — Net worth is what is left if you cash out (i.e. successfully sell all your assets and get the value equivalent to the recorded amount) and pay everything you owe.

Neutrality — This states that financial information must be free from bias.

Non-Sufficient Funds (NSF) — A payment cheque made to the company by a customer who does not have sufficient funds in their bank account to cover the amount of the cheque.

Normal Balance — Indicates a positive balance for the account.

Not-For-Profit Organization — Organizations aim to improve society in some way with no intention of making a profit.

O

Operating Activities — A section on the cash flow statement that shows cash movement within a business based on day-to-day activities.

Operations Management — This is the ability of the company to manage its assets, such as inventory.

Owner's Capital Account — The owner's capital account is used to record the amount of the owner's equity including owner's contributions.

Owner's Contribution — The amount of cash or assets invested in the business by the owner.

Owner's Drawings — The owner's drawings account is used to record the amount of the owner's cash withdrawn by the owner from the business to pay for personal items.

Owner's Equity — Equity is the net worth of a business, after all assets have been sold and all liabilities have been paid. In a proprietary business (owned by a single person), it is referred to as owner's equity.

Owner's Withdrawals — The amount of cash or assets taken by the business owner for personal use.

P

Partners' Equity — Equity is the net worth of a business, after all assets have been sold and all liabilities have been paid. In a partnership, it is referred to as partners' equity.

Partnership — A partnership is a business owned by two or more people called partners.

Periodic Inventory System — A periodic inventory system determines the quantity of inventory on hand only periodically, usually at the end of the month or year.

Perpetual Inventory System — A perpetual inventory system involves recording all transactions affecting the balance of inventory on hand, as they occur. This means that the system updates after every purchase and sale.

Post-Closing Trial Balance — The post-closing trial balance only lists accounts that have a balance.

Preferred Shares — Shares of a corporation that have priority over common shares, but do not provide voting rights to elect directors of the corporation.

Prepaid Expense — A prepaid expense occurs when you pay cash for an expense before you use it.

Principles-Based Accounting — The principles under the conceptual framework allow accountants to make appropriate decisions under different circumstances.

Private Enterprise — Any business or organization in which ownership is restricted to a select group of people.

Profitability — The ability of a company to generate profits.

Property, Plant and Equipment — Equipment, buildings, land and other similar assets that provide the business with benefits for a long period of time are called property, plant and equipment or long-term assets. These items are not intended to be sold to customers.

Purchase Discounts — The discounts given by the sellers to encourage customers to make early payments.

Purchase Returns and Allowances — Instead of just crediting the purchases account, businesses that use a periodic inventory system track these returns by using a temporary contra account to purchases called purchase returns and allowances.

Purchases Journal — The purchases journal records all purchases on account.

Q

Quick Ratio — The quick ratio is similar to the current ratio, but only counts assets that can easily be turned into cash.

R

Recognizing — Recognizing an expense or revenue simply means recording the expense or revenue on the income statement.

Relevance — All information useful for decision making is present in the financial statements.

Reliability — Reliability means that information is free from significant error and bias.

Representational Faithfulness — A piece of reliability which means that transactions must be presented as their true economic substance rather than their legal form.

Residual Value — Residual value is the estimated value of the asset at the end of its useful life.

Retail Method — An inventory estimation method that requires two things: the value of sales at retail prices and the company's cost of goods sold section on the income statement.

Retained Earnings — The cumulative net income of a corporation, less any amounts paid out as dividends.

Return on Equity (ROE) — A measure of the return owners are receiving based on their investment in the business.

Revenue — Revenue is an increase to net worth caused by providing goods or services in exchange for an asset, usually cash.

Revenue Recognition — Revenue recognition states that revenue can only be recorded (recognized) when goods are sold or when services are performed.

Rules-Based Accounting — The accounting standards are stated as a list of specific, detailed rules that must be followed when preparing financial information.

S

Sales Allowances — Sales allowances occur when the customer decides to keep such undesirable products at a reduced price.

Sales Discounts — When selling products or services, it is common to offer sales discounts to customers for early payment.

Sales Journal — A sales journal is used to record all sales on account.

Sales Returns — Sales returns occur when undesirable products are returned to the seller.

Sales Returns and Allowances — A contra-revenue account used to track sales allowances and returns so as to not adjust sales revenue.

Sales Revenue — A business that sells products to its customers.

Service Revenue — A business that provides services to its customers.

Share Capital — A section of a corporation's balance sheet showing equity raised by selling shares.

Shareholder — An owner of a corporation through ownership of shares.

Shareholders' Equity — Equity is the net worth of a business, after all assets have been sold and all liabilities have been paid. In a corporation, it is referred to as shareholders' equity.

Shares — Each share provides partial ownership of a corporation.

Sole Proprietorship — A business owned and generally operated by one owner.

Source Documents — Provide evidence of a transactions that get recorded in journal entries, which are then posted to the ledger accounts.

Special Journal — A separate book used to maintain transactions that occur regularly.

Specific Identification Method — The specific identification method is used when a business sells goods which are not identical or are customized in some way. This method accurately tracks the costs and value of inventory, but it can be costly to apply.

Statement of Owner's Equity — The Statement of Owner's Equity is the formal statement to show how owner's equity changed during the accounting period.

Straight-Line Depreciation — Straight-line depreciation is a method to allocate the cost of the asset evenly over the life of the asset.

Subsidiary Ledger (Subledger) — A subsidiary ledger is used to provide details that are not kept in the general ledger because too much information will clutter up the general ledger accounts.

T

T-Account — T-accounts are used to track the increases and decreases in the value of assets, liabilities, net worth or equity, revenue and expenses.

Temporary Accounts — Revenue and expenses are considered to be temporary accounts because they are brought back to a zero balance at the end of each period. This is done so that a new income statement can be prepared for the next period with a fresh start.

Time Period Concept — Accounting takes place over specific time periods known as fiscal periods. These fiscal periods are of equal length, and are used when measuring the financial progress of a business.

Timeliness — Information is timely if there is no delay in reporting crucial information.

Transaction — A transaction is a trade or exchange with someone else in order to receive something of value.

Trial Balance — A list of all accounts in the general ledger and their balances at a specific date.

U

Unadjusted Trial Balance — The original trial balance is called the unadjusted trial balance because these values represent account balances before adjustments are made.

Understandability — The financial information can be reasonably understood by its users if the users have knowledge of the business and a basic knowledge of accounting.

Unearned Revenue — Unearned revenue is an obligation the business has to provide products or service to a customer. It is used when a customer prepays the business for services or products.

Unlimited Liability — If the business is unable to pay its debts, creditors of the business can force the owner to sell his or her personal assets to pay the business debts.

Useful Life — The length of time the asset can be used is called the useful life.

V

Verifiability — Verifiability is a component of reliability. The proof of a transaction would be some form of paperwork that relates to the transaction. This proof verifies the transaction.

Vertical Analysis — Analysing financial information on a statement compared to a base-figure.

W

Weighted-Average Cost Method — The weighted-average cost method is used when a business simply applies an average cost to all of the units of a particular inventory item.

Working Capital — Working capital is the difference between current assets and current liabilities.

Worksheet — The worksheet can be used to display the trial balance before and after adjustments are made. They can also include before and after closing entries are made. Worksheets come in two sizes, six-column and ten-column. The worksheet is only a working paper for accountants, it is not meant to be read by external users of financial information.

Notes

INDEX